# Concise Dictionary of the Occult and New Age

# Concise Dictionary of the Occult and New Age

## DEBRA LARDIE

### DAN LIOY & PAUL INGRAM
**Contributing Editors**

kregel
PUBLICATIONS

Grand Rapids, MI 49501

*Concise Dictionary of the Occult and New Age*

© 2000 by Debra Lardie

Published by Kregel Publications, a division of Kregel, Inc., P.O. Box 2607, Grand Rapids, MI 49501. Kregel Publications provides trusted, biblical publications for Christian growth and service. For more information about Kregel Publications, visit our web site: www.kregel.com

Book and cover design: Nicholas G. Richardson

**Library of Congress Cataloging-in-Publication Data**
Lardie, Debra.
    Concise dictionary of the occult and New Age / Debra Lardie.
        p.      cm.
    Includes bibliographical references.
    1. Occultism—Encyclopedias. 2. New Age Movement—Encyclopedias. I. Title.
BF1407.L37        1999        299'.93—dc20        96-30481
                                                                        CIP

ISBN 0-8254-3090-9

Printed in the United States of America

1  2  3  4  5 / 04  03  02  01  00

*In loving memory of my father, G. Melvin Lardie,
my mother, E. Carlay Lardie, and my brother, Mark E. Lardie,
I dedicate this book to the kingdom of God.*

*To Dennis P. Lardie and Mary E. Parmerlee,
who continue to bless me with their laughter and love.*

*And to all the other wonderful family members and friends
who were there in support when I needed them most.*

# CONTENTS

# PREFACE

This dictionary opens the door to the vast world of cults and the occult. It is constructed around the New Age ties that bind many cultic groups and all of the occult world together. We tend to think of the New Age as a "new" phenomenon. Its view of reality is ancient, though it puts on fresh dress from time to time. Most New Age thought would have raised few eyebrows in the Athens society that Paul called "religious." That marketplace of ideas also was littered with idols (see Acts 17).

In this marketplace, those we dismiss as "unbelievers" have definite beliefs and a strong worldview, even those who cannot express as "doctrines" their religious tenets. New Age and occult beliefs are so diverse. Wiccans hardly seem to belong in the same category as the suicidal UFO followers of Heaven's Gate and the Rastafarians in Ethiopia. However, commonalities lurk below the surface. The idea that most unites this philosophical kaleidoscope is hostility, and at times even hatred, for the values and faith understandings expressed within historic Christianity.

Any religious organization is, broadly speaking, a "cult." The term "occult" describes those who are convinced that they have access to "mysteries" or "hidden knowledge." Those in occult belief systems are certain that they know secrets of the natural or supernatural world. Most try to use this mysterious knowledge to shape the reality around them or at least see into future realities. To answer those who would also categorize Christianity with extremist cults, articles are included that compare historic Christian doctrines with New Age teachings.

"New Age" encompasses a storehouse of concepts in which people mix and match a do-it-yourself religious experience. The New Age umbrella mixes revived Gnosticism and Eastern mysticism with exercise regimens. New Agers are so named because most adhere to an eschatology or view of future world history wherein humankind will enter the Aquarian Age, a utopia in which humanity will move up the evolutionary ladder toward godhood. Most practice a strong social justice ethic that borrows on socialist and even communist economic theory. Most hold a strong regard for protecting the natural environment. Their environmental motivation is pantheism, rather than a divine stewardship mandate to care for the earth, as understood in orthodox Christianity.

New Age and occult lines truly blur when New Age adherents credulously accept astrology, spiritualist mediums, and channelers. The New Age person usually wants desperately to believe in something transcendent, so long as it isn't the God who exists.

It would be impossible for any one belief system to encompass all beliefs comprising New Age thought. Christians err badly when they make blanket descriptions of the New Age Movement or its occult cousins. We must accurately understand these opponents for at least three reasons:

First, we want to bear witness to Christ before a world that is immersed in anti-Christian values and prejudices, a society that screams for tolerance, while working intolerantly to suppress Christianity. The New Age coalition unites in communicating the doctrine that Christians are narrow-minded bigots who must be enlightened or removed. Even once-orthodox churches teach that there is no lie so monstrous as the one that there is an absolute truth and that Jesus Christ is the only way to peace with God.

Second, this generation needs to be aware of both the content and expressions of New Age thought. New Age ideals have so successfully shaped culture that it is difficult to find a movie or television comedy or radio talk show that doesn't honor the New Age agenda. The cultural fascination with UFOs, angels, rainbows, and whimsical unicorns all have strong New Age overtones that we can take into our lives and place on our walls without a thought. Christians wear the occult ankh symbol on jewelry because it has an interesting cross-like shape. Christians see and use symbols intended to represent occult or Eastern mystical philosophy. This dictionary includes some of the common symbols to acquaint readers with their religious significance.

Third, Christianity is in direct competition with an utterly incompatible view of the world, and that worldview is being preached passionately and with reasoned apologetics on thousands of websites that are as close as a few mouse clicks. Christians can buy filters to protect their children from most pornographic sites. But no filter could protect children or their parents from the gurus and Internet "churches" whose messages are mysterious and different. In the 1990s the Internet became the pulpit of choice for every conceivable (and many seemingly inconceivable) ideas. It is impossible to even keep up with the new religions that spring up along the cyberspace roadside each day. We can only sample from among these new organizations.

Should we stoop to think about ideas that are perverse? Unfortunately, yes, for the same reasons the writers of New Testament epistles had to learn all about the philosophies that were infecting the early church. In those dangerous times, people were being led astray if they lacked informed discernment. Those times are much like our own.

This volume attempts to present the claims of individuals, groups, and religions as accurately and objectively as possible. We have noted some changes in teaching within fringe Christian groups. Some individuals and groups are mentioned that are not part of the New Age movement because their ideas have been taken over and twisted to serve an agenda.

It is worth noting that thousands of solid Christian organizations also use the Internet to advance the kingdom. This volume could not have been nearly so thorough if not for access to secular and Christian research available on the Internet. Of enormous assistance in this volume was the Religious Movements Project, an ongoing research project of the University of Virginia. Some excellent Christian sites are dedicated to combatting the errors of one group or examining the claims of many. Excellent sites include the American Family Federation, Apologetics Index, Christian Apologetics and Research Ministry, Christian Research Institute, and Watchman Fellowship. These and other organizations are vital watchmen on the wall for the kingdom of God.

—PAUL INGRAM

# A

## ABORTION

The termination of pregnancy, resulting in the death of the unborn child. In Christian ethics, which recognizes the image of the Creator in every human being, human life is regarded as innately sacred. The deliberate abortion of a fetus is viewed as the taking of a human life. The biblical concept is that all human life has intrinsic value or worth and is viewed as precious in the sight of God (Gen. 1:26–28; 5:1; 9:6; Exod. 20:13; James 3:9). The biblical view holds that every person has divinely ordained, inviolable rights and is responsible to maintain and preserve human life.

Some Christians hold that abortion is only acceptable as an act of self-defense by the mother when the pregnancy presents life-threatening complications.

New Age philosophy views humanity from a dualistic, Eastern perspective, in which matter is regarded as evil or in which the spiritual is deemed to be more valuable than the material. This results in a pro-abortion inclination, which minimizes the importance of human existence. New Age adherents may justify the taking of life through abortion by asserting that the unborn child is not yet a person and has no status nor rights in society.

In practice, the New Age ethical system meshes with that of secular humanism in stressing the woman's "right" to control what goes on in her own body. In this system of reasoning, they maintain that, because the individual is the measure of all things, pregnant women have a "right" to abortion. They also hold that the needs of the individual surpass the concept of good and evil. Therefore moral absolutes and the concept of an indwelling sin nature simply do not exist.

New Age adherents may also add a metaphysical logic to the justification of abortion.

An avid New Age woman may attribute an abortion to the fulfillment of the laws of karma. She may maintain that the fetus, in its divine nature, chose not to proceed with its life plan and communicated these wishes to its birth mother through psychic means. In this way, the mother is considered virtuous for having freed the fetal soul to reincarnate at will. The abortion experience then becomes a necessary step in the balance of karmic law for misdeeds done in some past life.

Abortion is presented as an acceptable form of birth control—a reasonable solution to untimely pregnancies. In humanistically-oriented educational programs, parental influence usually is deemed less important than the ideal of personal choice. This emphasis upon individual autonomy directly opposes the moral values of biblical Christianity, and elevates abortion as a symbol of personal freedom that demands social acceptance.

*See also:* BLOOD SACRIFICE, KARMA

## ACUPRESSURE

A method of treatment based on ancient metaphysical and occult beliefs. Acupressure operates on the premise that ill-health is the result of an obstruction or imbalance in the flow of cosmic energy. Adherents believe that this life force travels through the human body by way of twelve invisible channels called *meridians.* Practitioners contend that when direct pressure is applied to specific acupoints along a meridian, the flow of energy will be corrected and healing will occur. In a Japanese healing technique known as Shiatsu, when extended pressure is applied to any given point, connecting nerves supposedly become fatigued and relax, allowing energy to rebalance.

*See also:* ACUPUNCTURE, BALANCING, MERIDIANS, POLARITY THERAPY

# ACUPUNCTURE

Traditional Chinese therapy used to alleviate pain or treat the pathology through the insertion of needles at strategic points in the body. About 880 specific points are designated. Acupuncture operates on the premise that ill-health is the result of an imbalance in the energy force that flows within the human body. By inserting needles at the appropriate points, an unbalanced energy flow is set back into balance. Once the energy flow is set right, pain is relieved, the white blood count returned to normal, and physical and mental diseases cured. Practitioners say acupuncture can alleviate stress, straighten teeth, and even smoothe wrinkles.

Acupuncture originated in China over three thousand years ago. It is an extension of Taoism, the chief philosophy and system of religion of China. Taoism teaches that a universal energy force (ch'i) flows through all living things, instilling life and health when unimpeded. Opposite but complementary forces called yin and yang exist throughout the universe. Yin is the passive, negative, female cosmic element, whereas yang is an active, positive, masculine cosmic element. The opposition of yin/yang forces within the ch'i creates a balance that translates into good health and well-being. When this life force becomes unbalanced or obstructed while traveling through meridians or channels within the body, disease results. Practitioners say that by inserting and twisting needles into the meridians, the flow of balanced cosmic energy can be restored.

Needles made from bone, stone, and bamboo have given way in modern times to needles made of gold and silver.

Although Western medicine has grudgingly accepted acupuncture in some cases, a number of questions remain. For example, how can the same acupoint be a healing point for ailments that afflict the body in opposite ways? Scientific explanations for the apparent success of acupuncture vary as well. Some medical researchers theorize that the meridian exists, and the acupoints simply influence organ function. Others suggest that the needles interrupt messages of pain being sent to the brain. Still others think that acupuncture causes the release of endorphins, the body's own pain relievers. Despite these uncertainties, acupuncturists usually adhere to an Eastern or New Age philosophy. Acupuncture therapy often accompanies efforts to induce an altered state of consciousness, leaving patients open to hypnotic suggestion, hallucinogenic manifestations, and occult influence.

*See also:* BALANCING, CH'I, ENDORPHINS, HOLISM, MERIDIANS

# ADAM KADMON

In Jewish Kabbalism, a mystical representation of Adam as the supreme man, as well as the highest conception of God of which human beings are capable. The idea is quite similar to that of the ascended masters and the Cosmic Christ. Kabbalists sometimes illogically identify this figure with Satan, the Messiah, and revered teachers of the past.

*See also:* ASCENDED MASTER, COSMIC CHRIST

# ADIDAM, THE WAY OF THE HEART

Founded in 1970, a religion based in the worship of its founder and in the concept of "free daism," a belief that human beings must conquer their obsession with the self or ego in order to be liberated to divine enlightenment. There are about three thousand members of Adidam, most living in the United States, Canada, and the Fiji Islands. Adidam maintains a resident retreat center in the Fiji Islands. The central belief is that Adi Da (Franklin Albert Jones, the founder) is the divine incarnation in bodily form. No one needs to search for God, truth, and reality any longer because he is here, and he personally approaches man. Adi Da has made it possible to have a living relationship with the divine being, and this can bring absolute freedom from a meaningless life and from the pain of a self-obsessed existence.

In addition to Adi Da, Jones goes by the

names Bubba Free John, Da Free John, Dau Loloma, Da Love-Ananda, Da Avadhoota, Da Kalki, Santosha Da, Da Avabhasa, and Ruchira Avatar Adi Da Samraj. Jones experimented with drugs, religions, and spiritual paths to find truth. He studied at Columbia and Stanford universities and claimed to have attended three Christian seminaries. He also became a disciple of Swami Rudrananda in the practice of Siddha Yoga, which emphasizes that the key to God-realization is to awaken energy at the base of the spine. By drawing this energy up the spine into a crown above the head, one may become spiritually enlightened. Adi Da teaches a way to transcend the ego. Through Adi Da's divine influence, the practitioner who is devoted to the guru can be released from the ego, which keeps human beings from realizing their true divinity. With release comes awareness of divinity and ultimately freedom from suffering.

*See also:* YOGA

# AETHERIUS SOCIETY

An international UFO organization dedicated to world peace and enlightenment. The society's religious beliefs encompass the root teachings of world religions, relying heavily on the Theosophical tradition, scientific findings and developments, and a cosmic concept of humanity that they claim to have received from the extraterrestrials. George King (1919–1977) was a researcher in radionics and a yoga practitioner when he received a message during a meditative trance from Cosmic Master Aetherius. King claims that he was appointed to become Earth's representative to the Interplanetary Parliament, with headquarters on Saturn.

After receiving the command to become a channel for the cosmic masters, King mastered the power to communicate with beings from other spiritual energy spheres. In this state of consciousness, King was able to receive many teachings from the cosmic masters that the Aetherius Society believes will guide humanity to spiritual enlightenment. George King founded the Aetherius Society in 1955 and started to publish *The Cosmic Voice*, transcripts of his communications. He also published *Spiritual Healing Bulletin* and lectured around England telling about his spiritual experiences. A 1959 trance was broadcast over the British Broadcasting Company radio network. In 1960 the first North American center was established in Hollywood, California. Centers exist around the world, according to the organization.

Among cosmic master writings that are intended to bring humanity to enlightenment are "The Twelve Blessings" received in 1958 from Master Jesus on Venus. The last transmission was in 1961 from the Lord of Karma on Mars. Aetherius Society writings explain the major steps one must take in the journey towards Cosmic Consciousness.

According to King, space masters have come to earth to forewarn humankind of impending doom, to offer the universal wisdom of salvation, and to escort the earth into a new age. King invented the "Spiritual Energy Battery." This device stores prayer energy that can be retrieved to prevent earthquakes, epidemics, famines, droughts, and wars.

According to Master Aetherius, humankind is witnessing the transition of this world from one age to the next. In order for this to occur successfully, a critical mass of people must voluntarily enter altered states of consciousness. Proponents claim that in the near future, a UFO will bring Lord Maitreya to earth to personally guide the human race into the New Age. Supposedly under his leadership, all life forms emitting negative vibrations will be transported to other dimensions of space and time, leaving the enlightened to populate the earth in peace, harmony, and joy.

*See also:* ASCENDED MASTER, EXTRATERRESTRIAL INTELLIGENCE, TRANCE CHANNELING

# AFFIRMATIONS

The repetition of mystical syllables or sacred formulas that are believed to evoke psychic powers. Affirmations also include New Age initiates agreeing with statements made by fellow disciples. For example, such assertions as "I Am" or "I Am God" reflect the belief that each person is a divine entity. Proponents claim that the repeated affirmation of positive statements will penetrate the mind and transform thought into reality. Negative affirmations are avoided, as they prevent people from making full use of the cosmic life force. Positive declarations supposedly focus the mind and spirit on a higher plane of consciousness, thus allowing initiates to alter reality and reach new spiritual dimensions. Affirmations of godhood are promoted as the best way to align physical, mental, and spiritual energies because this allows people to exercise the full benefits of the god-force.

Those who practice affirmations for extended periods are seeking to transcend the world of illusion and come into contact with entities from the ethereal dimension. Consequently, avid disciples often display a seeming detachment from reality. Adherents suggest that repeated affirmations are an effective tool in thought transformation. There are frequent reports of public education proposals and test programs in which elementary schools have adopted affirmation exercises to focus group energy on a particular target. These exercises go by many names, including "seed planting," where one child is encircled by classmates. The class projects repeated affirmations upon the individual in an attempt to evoke peace, love, joy, and unity.

*See also:* LOGOS, MANTRA

## AGAPE

The English transliteration of a Greek word for "love." New Testament writers used *agape* to indicate the selfless, unconditional love of God. Scripture reveals that such love is prompted by volition and purpose rather than emotion. God's love seeks to reach out to humankind, even though sinful man is unworthy of being loved (John 3:16; Rom. 5:8). Scholars point out that *agape* differs from *eros,* a Greek term that denotes love of a sensual nature.

*Eros* is characterized by strong physical attraction and the desire to obtain sexual satisfaction. Despite the overwhelming contrary evidence from the New Testament and ancient history, some New Age adherents claim that *agape feasts* (the gathering of the early church for communion worship) were primitive Christian rituals adapted from pagan feasts that involved sexual perversion.

New Age adherents allege that the ritual was suppressed by church leaders before the seventh century, but believers revived it to enable their fellowships to obtain ultimate unity through the sexual exchange of body fluids.

*See also:* SOPHIA MOVEMENT

## AGENT

One who attempts to send messages telepathically to a receptive medium through the emanation of extra-dimensional psychic energy. Proponents claim that an agent translates thoughts into images. The medium then converts the images into organized, understandable patterns.

Occultists allege that telepathic communication through an agent originates from cosmic energies in alternate dimensions of space and time. Some mediums contend that when they enter a trancelike state, they can receive communication from beings in other realms of existence apart from verbal exchange or other physical means of interaction. Others assert that by transcending the many levels of consciousness, they can remove psychic barriers, paving the way for the development of a wide range of telepathic powers. This leads to enlightenment and union with the cosmic life force.

New Age adherents claim that, as more people learn about telepathy, evolutionary advancement of humankind will make a quantum leap—a prerequisite to the dawn of the Aquarian Age.

*See also:* COSMIC ENERGY, PSYCHIC, TELEPATHY, THOUGHT ADJUSTERS

## AIWAZ

*See:* CROWLEY, ALEISTER

# AKASHIC RECORDS

The sacred text that reputedly holds all of humankind's accumulated unconscious thoughts. The *akasha* is the Hindu belief that a cosmic consciousness permeates all of reality. Supposedly the Universal Mind holds the thoughts, words, and events of all human life. Proponents assert that this Mind is an energy source that created humanity, exists everywhere, and is responsible for humanity's spiritual evolution. Channeled spirits and inner guides claim to have access to the Universal Mind. Therefore they possess the ability to reveal past incarnations, to interpret dreams, and to answer all of life's questions. Occult leaders maintain that, through altered states of consciousness, humans can tap into this vast reservoir of knowledge and achieve enlightenment, unlimited powers of the mind, and the ability to manipulate reality.

Akashic void— empty reality filled with a universal mind

*See also:* ALTERED STATE, COLLECTIVE UNCONSCIOUS, UNIVERSAL MIND

# ALCHEMY

An ancient blend of pseudoscience, mystical philosophy, and magic. Alchemy was originally practiced in China and Egypt as early as the third century B.C. Arabs in Alexandria, Egypt, revived the practice in the eighth century A.D. Crusaders returning from the Holy Land between the eleventh and thirteenth centuries took alchemy to medieval Europe.

Alchemists believed that all matter was made up of a single substance that, when influenced by temperature or moisture, could be reduced into the four basic elements of earth, air, fire, and water. They believed an alteration in the balance of these elements would change a substance from one form, appearance, or nature to a different and usually higher one. Alchemists contended that through manipulation of the basic elements of nature they could fathom the mysteries of life and secrets of creation, gaining access to the cosmic mind and immortality.

One goal was to find a way to change base metals into gold, which they considered the perfect metal. Another was to discover the magical elixir that would enable people to live forever. The idea was to transmute people from a lesser state of existence to a divine one. Alchemy cults in Eastern religions combined their search for magical liquids with various meditation and breathing techniques. In their quest for immortality, devotees would sometimes ingest metallic poison. The resulting death was viewed as a necessary step in attaining eternal life. Later cults searched for elixirs to cure disease and lengthen life.

When alchemists failed to achieve their goals, the practice fell into disrepute. Nevertheless the legacy left by alchemy is extensive. As pioneers of scientific experimentation, alchemists paved the way for chemistry, metallurgy, pharmaceuticals, and medicine. They also paved the way for astrology, occultism, symbology, and other pseudosciences. Alchemists believed that minerals were the physical embodiment of spiritual qualities, the vital bones of Mother Earth through which people could discover the secrets of the cosmos. They believed that celestial bodies represented and controlled specific metals. Thus the position of planets, moons, and stars influenced the outcome of experimentation.

Similar ideas have been adopted by a variety of modern cults. For example, the alchemists' attempts to change lesser metals into gold is a paradigm of the transformational journey from a human state to the divine nature of existence. The alchemists' search for a "philosopher's stone" that would make transmigration easier is reflected in the multimillion-dollar crystal industry. The occult has also embraced many symbols used in alchemy texts. These symbols include the wingless dragon to represent the earth; the dove to represent the divine spirit trapped in matter; Helios, or the Solar Logos, to represent Sunday; the alchemical rose to represent the Mother Goddess; and the alchemical tree of life to represent immortality.

*See also:* ASTROLOGY; SCIENCE, NEW AGE; SYMBOLISM; TRANSMIGRATION

## ALLOPATHY

A holistic therapy devised by Samuel Hahnemann (1755–1843) in the eighteenth century. Allopathy operates on the premise that if too much of a substance causes a particular symptom, then minute amounts of it will alleviate the same. Practitioners work with an elaborate collection of plant, animal, and mineral toxins that are known to mimic symptoms. Their intent is to stimulate the body into reacting against the toxins, thereby healing itself. They contend that infinitesimal doses of the poisons work as a catalyst to stimulate not just the body, but also the mind and spirit back to health. More recently, allopathy has been used to describe a traditional approach to medicine in which a physician prescribes a course of treatment that will create unacceptable conditions within the patient's body for the existence of a disease.

*See also:* HOLISM, HOMEOPATHY

## ALMANAC

Astrological books that make predictions relating to the agricultural seasons. They are most popular today in China, giving harvest forecasts, noting lucky and unlucky days, noting the birthdays of the gods and providing a variety of maxims and fortune-telling guidance. Similar books remain influential among some groups in the West. Almanacs have been published for farmers in North America for two centuries. The German agricultural community has particularly set great store by them.

*See also:* ZODIAC

## ALPHA LEVEL

The trancelike state commonly referred to as "altered consciousness," in which the brain is theoretically most receptive to psychic influence. New Age adherents make much of research suggesting that the left side of the brain is the analytical hemisphere, whereas the right side is the creative hemisphere. Supposedly when people are in an alpha state, the objective reasoning of the left brain surrenders to the intuitive imagery and cosmic experiences that occur only in the right side of the brain. This is to allow access to unlimited psychic powers, all-knowing spirit guides, self-healing, and the cosmic enlightenment that unites one with the Universal Mind.

*See also:* ALTERED STATE, WHOLE BRAIN THINKING

## ALTAR ✕

An elevated structure of earth, stones, wood, or a human body, upon which worshipers offer animal sacrifices, burned incense, or carry out religious ceremonies.

**Altar—symbol used by Satanists**

Some pagan cultures have believed that sacrifices made on their altars enable communication with gods and goddesses. Others have viewed the altar as a sacred table upon which venerated deities (represented by fire) consumed their sacrificial meal (represented by the victim). This offering placated the gods in such a way that the soul of the victim could evolve spiritually.

Ancient Israelites used altars extensively in their worship, but with a far different understanding. All of the activities associated with the altar reminded God's people of the necessity of approaching divine holiness through the provision of an acceptable atoning sacrifice. That ultimately was found only in the sacrifice of Jesus. The Old Testament sacrificial system looked forward to Christ's perfect and final atoning sacrifice.

Satanists continue to use altars when they perform the black mass, a neopagan ritual mocking the Roman Catholic celebration of the Eucharist. The altar is often adorned with symbolic imagery and power objects, such as the skull, representing the magical powers of the human consciousness; candles and incense to transmit psychic messages to the heavens; and the pentagram to invoke the spirits. In some satanic cults, rites are practiced upon a naked human body as the altar. Some witchcraft cults believe the altar represents the focal point of life.

*See also:* BLOOD SACRIFICE, POWER OBJECT, SATANISM, SYMBOLISM

## ALTERED STATE

A changed condition of awareness in which the mind seeks to transcend mundane material reality and enter into ethereal dimensions of time and space.

New Age practitioners are eager to achieve an altered state of consciousness, contending that it is a gateway to uncovering repressed capabilities of the mind, body, and spirit. They believe that people in altered states tap into intuitive powers that enable them to experience reality from a new perspective.

Occult leaders advocate the use of altered states to interact with spirit guides, who are then invited to reside within the person under the guise of the "higher self." Achievement of altered states is considered a necessary step in the spiritual evolution of people toward divinity.

Advocates use terms such as "surrender" and "release" "visualize" and "flow" to refer to altered states in which devotees experience lights, colors, and sounds. These are to lead to the ultimate state of existence or enlightenment. Those who achieve this state are said to have realized their innate divinity and unity with the Universal Mind.

*See also:* CONSCIOUSNESS; UNCONSCIOUS, THE; WHOLE BRAIN THINKING

## AMULET

A power object that is used or worn to protect from evil or bring good fortune. Devotees believe some amulets, such as gemstones, are naturally charged with cosmic powers that shield the wearer from danger, disease, demons, and black magic. Other amulets reputedly can be endowed with similar capabilities. For example, by going through a ritual invocation, occultists say they can charge an amulet through psychic means so that it will make the wearer immune to the attack of demons.

Practitioners of sympathetic magic assert that vibrational impulses permeate the universe and that cosmic pulsation in an amulet can be used to deter the conflicting pulsation in a person or entity. Some New Age adherents claim that amulets enable them to realign the vibrational forces of the mind, body, and spirit, that results in holistic health. Others assert that amulets can be used to manipulate the vast psychic forces of the Universal Mind and disclose the mysteries of the astral dimension.

*See also:* COLOROLOGY, POWER OBJECT, QUARTZ CRYSTAL, SYMBOLISM

## ANANDA MARGA YOGA SOCIETY

A religious and Indian political movement in the 1960s and 1970s, declared illegal by Indira Gandhi's government. Damaged by its political strife, Ananda Marga Yoga Society exists with centers in India and the United States, but the number of followers is not known. The Ananda Marga Yoga Society follows a yogic path toward bliss. The path begins with initiation, where a student is privately instructed by a guru. Dedicated followers were celibate.

Prabhat Ranjan Sarkar (b. 1921), known to his followers as Shrii Shrii Anandamurti or Ba'ba, claimed to have been an accomplished yogi at age four and began initiating devotees at age six. He was seen as a Maha-Guru, "God incarnate," a figure who appears every thousand years or so to impart blessings. His followers grew in numbers, and in 1955 Anandamurti gave up his job as a railway clerk to lead the organization. His writings are in the *Ananda Sutra*, that prescribes the group's meditation practices.

Sarkar organized social programs to help the poor, underprivileged, and those in need due to natural disasters. He was also a radical in Indian politics in the 1960s and 1970s, advocating a world government, language, and army. He was jailed for conspiracy to murder during Indira Gandhi's national emergency, and Ananda Marga Yoga Society centers were shut down. Sarkar was convicted and imprisoned from 1975 until he was retried and acquitted in 1978. Members of the movement held rallies that could turn violent, and some burned themselves in protest. In

Calcutta, eighteen devotees were killed by a mob in 1982.

*See also:* ANUVRATA MOVEMENT

## ANARCHY

A utopian society in which enlightened individuals are free from external authority.

This idea is based on the premise that people are innately divine and can determine right from wrong for themselves. Restrictions based on absolute moral standards are unnecessary. All laws and regulations are

**Anarchy—creative disorder imposed upon the old circle of authority**

blamed for deterring the evolutionary advancement of humankind.

Some New Age adherents readily admit that in the absence of any governmental authority, lawlessness and political disorder would result. They argue that this is a necessary step in bringing about the enlightenment of humankind. Supposedly the eradication of all regulatory agencies, viewed as unnecessary and immoral, will destroy the old order and result in a state of anarchy from which the New Order will arise. Some claim that anarchy is the only philosophical movement that recognizes the consciousness of the self and encourages people to reach their full divine potential. Proponents assert that when a critical mass of the earth's population achieves enlightenment, then the establishment of a one-world religion and government under the rule of Lord Maitreya, the New Age messiah, will surely follow. He allegedly will lead the planet to a golden era in which people are free to think and act as they please, engendering such goodwill so as to unite the world in a cooperative social atmosphere.

*See also:* MAITREYA, LORD; ONE-WORLD IDEAL; POLITICS, NEW AGE

## ANCHORING

A neurolinguistic programming technique in which the mind, body, and spirit hypothetically interact as a whole in the treatment of mental and physical ailments. Advocates believe that the natural drive of the human body to heal itself is dependent on individual belief systems. Using hypnotic suggestion, practitioners implant positive messages and experiences and "anchor" them in the individual's mind with sound, touch, and movement. They believe that positive growth is achieved through such programming and is the inevitable result of interaction between the lower self and the elusive but divine higher self.

*See also:* HOLISM, HYPNOSIS

## ANDROGYNY (HERMAPHRODITE)

Someone who has the characteristics and nature of both male and female. Androgyny

fits with the Eastern religious idea that all things possess a cosmic counterpart—such as yin and yang, light and darkness, good and evil. New Age adherents say that the androgyny of the soul represents the absolute oneness of all

**Androgyny—the soul's unity of maleness and femaleness**

entities in the universe.

Androgynous beliefs originally comprised part of the secret traditions of ancient pagan religions. They were based on the concept of deities having the characteristics of both genders. Some believed that the right side of the soul was male, the left side female. According to classic gender division, the male aspect of the deity was helpless unless bonded to the female aspect. Some contemporary thinkers hold that Eve was a complete part of Adam before they became separated, and if humankind ever regains wholeness, the counterparts must be rejoined.

New Age adherents claim that all life requires polarity, and that a person possesses both male and female qualities in the deepest part of the soul. The soul entering the physical realm must emphasize one aspect of its gender and diminish the other. Through innumerable reincarnations, the soul gets to experience both maleness and femaleness. Eventually both the male and female qualities will gain full expression in the soul at the same time. This belief is given as a legitimatization of homosexuality and other sexual practices. These are said to be natural experiences that aid in the evolutionary advancement of the soul.

*See also:* SEXUALITY, YIN/YANG

## ANGEL

The Bible portrays angels as spirit creatures who live in heaven but may be sent to earth by God as messengers (Matt. 22:30; Heb. 1:14). They are mighty and powerful and possess great wisdom (2 Sam. 14:20; Ps. 103:20; 2 Thess. 1:7). Ordinarily they are invisible to us, but they have appeared as humans (2 Kings 6:17; Luke 24:4). Angels do not marry or reproduce (Matt. 22:30). Because they are not subject to death, they will live forever and remain constant in number (Luke 20:36).

Artistic portrayals lead people to believe that angels have wings. But only one reference in the Bible explicitly states that angels have wings (Isa. 6:2). However angels definitely have the ability to fly (Dan. 9:21). Angels also exist in an organized hierarchy (Col. 1:16). Some angels serve God by serving, protecting, and guarding, as well as guiding and helping human beings (Ps. 91:11; Dan. 6:22; 10:13; Acts 8:26; Heb. 1:14).

New Age adherents reject the biblical teaching concerning angels. They claim that angels are the invisible forces of power that ascend and descend between the various levels of human consciousness with messages from the divine self. They believe God is nothing more than the universal essence of collective human consciousness and that angels are nothing more than the vibration of energy that emanates from a higher mental plane of existence. This psychic pulsation of energy supposedly inspires people to recognize their innate godhood and also develops the spiritual evolution of humankind.

Angels are manifested in numerous archetypal images in New Age thought, including imaginary friends, spirit guides, ascended masters, extraterrestrials, and—to those of a Christian bent—angels. New Age guardian angels reputedly appear in a soft, loving light, the warmth of which seems to permeate the soul. Communication with such entities initially requires entering an altered state of consciousness. Some New Age adherents hold that they can identify the master of the angel by the nature of its presence. Others think that if the guidance of the entity is helpful or uplifting, then the source of its origin is irrelevant.

*See also:* ARCHETYPE, ASCENDED MASTER, DEMON, LIGHT, SPIRIT GUIDES

## ANIMISM

The belief that all things in the universe, whether animate or inanimate, possess a personal or impersonal deity, spirit, soul, life force, or mind. The term "animism" comes from the Latin word *anima,* which means "soul" or "breath." Animists tend to believe in a supreme deity, whether a personal being or an impersonal oneness, who exists beyond the intermediate entities in the universe. This deity is so far removed from the world that it uses intermediate entities to communicate for it.

Animists teach that two different kinds of spiritual entities exist—those that were formerly embodied and those that were never embodied. An example of the former would include deceased relatives, while examples of the latter include gods and demons. Because these entities are localized in their presence, their influence is focused in one particular area. Some exert power over the forces of nature, while others make their presence known in the everyday matters of people. The first type makes their presence known in such things as famines and storms, whereas the second type affect such things as family relations and business dealings. Animists pay homage to these entities, hoping to persuade them to intercede favorably on behalf of humankind.

Animism is similar to hylozoism, a view that says that the entire universe is made up of animated or living matter. Animism is also similar to panpsychism, a view that says a spiritual or mental aspect of the universe exists, and that all nature is actively involved in it. New Age adherents use these views to validate their claim that all reality is a complete oneness, which people can manipulate at will in order to create their own reality.

*See also:* HYLOZOISM, KACHINA, MONISM, MOTHER EARTH, SPIRITISM

## ANKH (CRUX ANSATA)

A cross shaped like a lowercase T, but with a loop instead of an upper vertical arm. In ancient Egypt, the ankh was a symbol of life as well as the creative energies of the female and male. Some think the ankh was derived from primitive images of the Mother Goddess and used by worshipers to represent the immortality and sexual union of the deities, as well as the eternal life of their followers. According to some experts in Egyptian hieroglyphics, the term "ankh" also means "hand mirror." This explains its marked resemblance to the symbol of Venus, the goddess of love and beauty, and the creative force from which all life supposedly exists. Like the ankh, the "mirror of Venus" also depicts a circle imposed on a cross, which represents life and sexuality. Some claim that the ankh also symbolizes a key to the secrets of the occult that brings wisdom, knowledge, and peace, as well as prosperity and long life to those who wear it.

Ankh—mirror of Venus

*See also:* FEMINISM, GODDESS WORSHIP, SYMBOLISM, VENUS

## ANTAHKARANA (RAINBOW BRIDGE)

The rainbow is a popular occult symbol that represents humanity's ability to reach a higher level of consciousness, self-empowerment, and personal divinity. In popular New Age teaching, initiates are promised the acquisition of divine powers if they cross over the antahkarana. Supposedly the various colors appearing in this occult symbol represent the cosmic qualities that all should aspire to attain. Proponents believe that by meditating on the colors of the antahkarana, people can achieve an altered state of consciousness, establish a link with the Universal Mind, and reach enlightenment.

## ANTHROPOCENTRISM

The belief that humans are the most significant entity and final aim of the universe. Anthropocentrism says that humans represent the highest rung of the evolutionary ladder. Thus humankind is "the measure of all things" and the final arbitrator of all conduct and morals. This means that reality can only be understood in terms of human values and experiences. Anthropocentrism maintains that people alone determine their fate, whereas the theocentric view holds that God is the omnipotent Overseer of human destiny. New Age adherents agree with the man-centered view. They claim that people are innately divine and have the mental capacities to create their own reality. If a critical mass of enlightened people channel their mental energies, this will create a harmonic convergence in which the entire human race will become enlightened. Proponents contend this is a prerequisite to the dawning of the Aquarian era of peace, love, and joy.

*See also:* GLOBALISM, HUMANISM

## ANTHROPOSOPHY

A mixture of Christian beliefs, Eastern mysticism, and spiritism founded by Rudolf Steiner (1861–1925). Steiner was born in Austria-Hungary and studied science at the University of Vienna in the 1890s. After leaving the Catholic church, this sometime philosopher, scientist, and artist became a prominent member of the Theosophical Society from 1899–1909. After becoming the leader of the German chapter of this occult organization, Steiner began to develop a Christianized version of Theosophy in which he taught that people have the capacity to exercise pure thought apart from engaging the five senses. He established his Anthroposophical Society in 1912 to promote the development of this alleged ability. Today the Society's main office is located in Goetheanum, Switzerland (near Basle), where it propagates its New Age doctrine and practices throughout the world. Their worldwide membership is approximately twenty-five thousand. In addition to Theosophy, Steiner's organization endorses eurythmy (rhythmic order and movement), biodynamic farming (organic gardening techniques), and the Waldorf Schools (psychic development).

The name "anthroposophy" is a combination of two Greek terms, *anthropos* (man) and *sophia* (wisdom). Together they suggest that anthroposophy is concerned with the study of people and their search for wisdom or enlightenment. Advocates maintain that because of greed, the human personality disconnected its higher self (spirit) from its lower self (ego). Allegedly the inhabitants of both the earth and the cosmos are on a journey through time in which they are evolving in their quest to rejoin the higher and lower selves. Adherents claim that history is in the fourth stage of this evolutionary development.

Anthroposophy teaches that people's behavior brings correspondingly positive or negative fruits either in this life or in a future one. These "karmic laws of justice" predetermine the nature of a person's next existence. By cultivating good karma, people can be reincarnated as a higher life form and move closer to spiritual enlightenment. This evolutionary journey through time applies to both individuals and the entire human race.

According to anthrosophy, humanity was at a lower level of cosmic consciousness in other eras. However, the world is now on the verge of global self-enlightenment. The Society advocates that people look within themselves through rigorous meditative exercises to transcend reality. They propose that if enough people practice this, a critical mass will be reached that will lead to the evolutionary transformation of the human race. Devotees view Christ as an *arhat,* or one who has forsaken the world of illusion, achieved enlightenment, and entered nirvana. Like other great arhats, He appeared on the stage of history to show people how they can awaken their higher consciousness and become one with the Universal Mind.

*See also:* CHRIST-CONSCIOUSNESS, ONE-WORLD IDEAL

# ANTICHRIST

According to some interpreters of the Bible, the ruler of the revived Roman empire or confederation of states. Antichrist will establish a peace treaty with Israel that brings to a close the present "church age" and begins a seven-year period known as "the tribulation." Halfway through the tribulation, he will break the peace treaty by desecrating the Jewish system of worship. A series of major military campaigns will ensue, culminating at Armageddon. This climactic battle will take place near the city of Megiddo in the plain of Esdraelon in northern Palestine, the scene of many clashes in Old Testament times. The rulers of the earth will unite under Antichrist's leadership to obliterate Israel in defiance of the God of the Bible. However Christ will return to earth with His glorified church to crush this revolt and to establish His millennial kingdom (thousand year reign) on earth.

New Age adherents claim that the apostle John did not use the term "Antichrist" to refer to the man of lawlessness or to any spirit of rebellion that denies the incarnate Christ. Instead, John was referring to all opponents of the higher self, a contemptible group trying to mislead humankind about the Christ-consciousness within them. New Age adherents assert that Christians, both individually and collectively, are the true "antichrists." They seek to discredit Christianity and show that it has failed.

Occult spirit guides predict the arrival of a great psychic teacher who will descend from an alternate plane of existence to bring a new age of peace and prosperity to a world engulfed in chaos. He goes by many names, including the Master Soul, The One, Krishna, Lord Maitreya, servant of Sanat (Satan), and

Lucifer (the brother of Jesus Christ). Regardless of the name, this christ represents the archetype of humanity's inner evolution. This individual reputedly reveals the esoteric mysteries of those who have spiritually evolved.

At the cosmically appointed time, this liberator will come to cleanse the world of hate, offer miraculous solutions to global concerns, and ultimately usher in a new age and a new race. Those who remain in a lower state of consciousness will be banished to alternate dimensions of existence.

Entities from the astral plane declare that this Aquarian Age leader will create an enlightened community, united both religiously and politically. God and Satan will be reconciled, and the souls of humans will experience a quantum leap in evolutionary development. People living in this New World Order will venerate an androgynous deity, the fusion of the Universal Father and Mother Earth. The yin/yang symbol will represent this cosmic union.

*See also:* ARMAGEDDON, BABYLON, DRAGON, NUMBER OF THE BEAST, YIN YANG

## ANUVRATA MOVEMENT

Indian moral revival movement begun within Jainism in 1948. The movement aims at promoting both individual and national morality through nonviolence, goodwill, tolerance, and universal love. A national center was built at Jaipur in 1984. The movement has had enormous impact on Indian life of the late twentieth century.

*See also:* ANANDA MARGA YOGA SOCIETY

## APARIGRAHA

In Hindu belief, a state of total detachment from desire. In Raja-Yoga aparigrapha is one of the leading virtues of the Great Vow (the Mahavrata), along with satya (truthful living), ahimsa (not hurting others), asteya (refraining from stealing), and brahmacarya (holy living).

## APHRODITE

The Greek goddess of love, beauty, and fertility. Aphrodite was also venerated as the creative and sustaining force of all life, whether vegetable, animal, or human. One legend says that Aphrodite was the daughter of Dione and Zeus, the supreme god and symbol of power, rule, and law. Another legend declares that Aphrodite emerged from the foam of the sea. Greek mythology says that she loved many mortals and gods, two of whom were Adonis, a handsome young god, and Ares, the Olympian god of war. Supposedly she had countless children by them but married Hephaestus, the god of fire and metalworking, instead.

From all indications, Aphrodite originated in the pagan cultures of the East. She possessed many of the same attributes as Astarte, the Phoenician goddess of sexual love and fertility, and Ishtar, the Babylonian and Assyrian goddess of motherhood, love, and war. The Romans identified Aphrodite with Venus. In many ancient cultures, Aphrodite came to symbolize the fertility of the earth. One legend says that the death and resurrection of the male deity she loved symbolized the regenerative power of the earth.

Occult groups continue to worship Aphrodite as the creative force from that all life flows. Sexual rituals are performed in honor of this deity, the goddess of love. She is known as the Queen of Heaven, the Mother Goddess, Mother Earth, Gaea, Wicca, and various other titles. Just as Lucifer, her male counterpart in pagan religions, Aphrodite is also referred to as the Morning Star. Legend tells of an unjust God defeating Lucifer in heaven and banishing him to Venus. Other tales say that Lucifer came to Earth from Venus 18 million years ago to attend to the physical needs of the human race. Satanists portray Lucifer as the hero who makes people aware of their innate godhood. He tells them how to tap into the powers of their divine self, and describes the coming world in which they will be free to express their fullest human potential.

*See also:* BABYLON, DIANA, GAEA, GODDESS WORSHIP, MYTHOLOGY, VENUS

## APOCALYPSE (APOCALYPTIC)

A type of literature characterized by visions, symbols, and dreams. The word "apocalypse" comes from the Greek noun *apokalypsis,* meaning revelation, and from the verb *apokalyptein,* which means "to uncover." In Revelation 1:1, the apostle John used the term *apokalypsis* to describe the contents of the book he was writing. He noted that Revelation is an unveiling, a disclosure of truths that were previously hidden. The apocalyptic literature in the Bible is contained in such books as Isaiah, Ezekiel, Daniel, Zechariah, and Revelation, all of which are accepted as divinely inspired by orthodox Christians.

Noncanonical works, some of which are apocalyptic in subject matter, are called "Pseudepigrapha," a word that comes from a Greek term, meaning "falsely inscribed." Those who created these books ascribed the names of well-known ancient heroes of Israel to their works. These include Enoch, Abraham, and Baruch. A large number of these works are apocalyptic in nature, meaning they contain vivid imagery and symbolism as well as a future-oriented outlook. These works brought comfort to the Jewish people during times of persecution by describing in various ways the impending triumph of the messianic age.

Contemporary apocalyptic literature foretells a time of extreme chaos that necessarily precedes the Aquarian era of peace and enlightenment. Many occult writings predict a time of global purging of negative energies that allegedly impede the transformation of human consciousness. This time of cleansing will occur at the end of the present age. These writings urge people to prepare for the New World Order as it emerges from the anarchy of the Piscean Age by becoming attuned to their divine self and creating individual realities. New Age texts declare judgment upon under-evolved souls who refuse to abandon monotheistic doctrines and acknowledge the divine unity of humankind. Some occult members try to rise above the predicted upheaval by cloistering together in protective groups and creating a utopian environment. Under the firm rule of a charismatic leader, these groups see themselves as an elect community of individuals who will survive the devastation and claim their rightful place as leaders in the new world.

*See also:* ANTICHRIST, ARMAGEDDON, PURIFICATION, SECOND COMING OF CHRIST

## APOCRYPHA

Fourteen books added to the Septuagint, the Greek translation of the Old Testament, that were included in the Latin Vulgate Bible. Because of their dubious authenticity, Protestants consider these books as noncanonical. Roman Catholics and Anglicans also regard these books as noncanonical but give them special status and authority as church tradition.

Some New Age adherents have created a renewed interest in the Apocrypha, as well as the mystical works of so-called "prophets" and "channeled entities." These last two types of books emphasize the virtuous qualities of women. They have gained considerable popularity among goddess and witchcraft cults. Many of these groups believe that patriarchal leaders of the early church failed to acknowledge these works because they were afraid of the "truth" regarding the supremacy of the female principle. Other New Age adherents declare that the writings of Eastern religious cults are divine in origin and thus sacred. They contend that these texts, that endorse reincarnation, were rejected by the leaders of the early church because they wanted to maintain better control of the masses. Some of these occult works are sexually explicit, and one text even suggests that Jesus encouraged the fall of humankind. Though these writings are popular among New Age adherents, they stand diametrically opposed to the clear teaching of Scripture.

*See also:* BIBLE, CANON

## Aquarian Age Gospel of Jesus the Christ, The

A popular New Age bible written by Levi H. Dowling (1844–1911) and published in

1907. *The Aquarian Age Gospel* claims to lay the philosophical basis for the religion of the New Age by providing a historical account of the lost years of Jesus. Dowling was born in 1844 to a pioneer preacher. After pastoring a small church and serving for two years as a Civil War Army chaplain, Dowling finished school and practiced medicine for many years. However his metaphysical interests began years earlier. He claimed that when he was a young boy, he experienced a series of visions in which entities instructed him to "build a white city." Dowling later "translated" these messages and incorporated them into *The Aquarian Age Gospel*. The book allegedly contains the divine revelation of the Akashic Records, which reputedly holds all of humankind's accumulated unconscious thoughts.

Dowling did much of his investigative "research" while in a meditative, trancelike state. He claimed that the vibrational signals of every word, thought, and action of the past, present, and future are recorded within a vast cosmic reservoir of the Akashic Records. Dowling believed that by ascending the levels of human consciousness, people can tap into the Universal Mind and unlock the mysteries of the cosmos. He thought that by attuning himself to this psychic vibration and rhythm pulsating throughout the galaxy, he could telepathically access the historical records of many great esoteric masters, including Jesus of Nazareth.

The christ of Dowling's *The Aquarian Age Gospel* is not the Messiah revealed in the Bible. Dowling says that Jesus is one of many christs who have achieved enlightenment. *The Aquarian Age Gospel* contains a fictitious record of Jesus' life, including his spiritual journey as an initiate in the mystery religions of Tibet, Egypt, and India, as well as Persia and Greece. The christ presented by Dowling is someone who had experienced innumerable reincarnations. This christ overcame his sensual desires, got in touch with his divine self, and reestablished communion with the Universal Mind. *The Aquarian Age Gospel* says that Jesus shows all people how they can recognize and achieve their full

divine potential. Dowling hail his christ as a great avatars, an incarnation of the deity appointed for a certain epoch. Other avatars include Buddha, Muhammad, Krishna, and Lord Maitreya (the New Age christ).

*See also:* AKASHIC RECORDS; AQUARIUS, AGE OF; AVATAR; BIBLE, NEW AGE

## *AQUARIAN CONSPIRACY, The*

One of the most popular New Age volumes, *The Aquarian Conspiracy,* was written by Marilyn Ferguson (b. 1938) and published by J. P. Tarcher in 1980. It depicts the impending evolutionary transformation of humankind. Ferguson based her book on the idea held by astrologers that the hatred and violence of the Piscean Age will soon give way to the love and light of the Aquarian Age. Ferguson states that a powerful network of enlightened individuals are working together to hasten the political, economic, and religious transformation of the world. This coalition supposedly will eradicate the current social laws and values, believed to hinder the development of humanity's full divine potential. Those who belong to this New Age network share, argue, test, and adapt experiences and insights in order to implement their planetary goals.

*See also:* BIBLE, NEW AGE; FERGUSON, MARILYN; ONE-WORLD IDEAL; TRANSFORMATION

## AQUARIUS, AGE OF

An era of global peace, enlightenment, and prosperity under the rule of Lord

Aquarius—astrological symbol

Maitreya, the New Age messiah. Astrology holds that humankind exists within evolutionary cycles that last for about two hundred years. Each cycle is represented by one of the twelve signs of the zodiac. Each one of these epochs supposedly exercises a controlling influence on the present and future characteristics of humankind. Furthermore, astrology claims that the life and actions of people are determined by the cosmic position of the sun, moon, stars, planets in relation to each other.

Astrologers declare that humankind is presently existing in the age of Pisces, characterized by darkness, violence, and ignorance. They believe this will soon be replaced by the age of Aquarius, a time of light, love, and enlightenment. "Aquarius" is the Latin word for "water carrier" or "water bearer" and represents the eleventh sign of the zodiac. Occult leaders claim that when Aquarius dawns, humankind's irrepressible thirst for knowledge will be quenched. The minds of all people will be liberated, and the collective consciousness of humanity will experience a quantum leap in evolutionary development. Unlike people in the Piscean Age, those in the Aquarian Age will be serious, open-minded, intelligent, and powerful, as well as logical, independent, and spiritual. Occult leaders encourage all people to accept and unite with the growing consciousness of the New Age. They advocate the exploration of new and existing esoteric religions for in these the world supposedly will become one with the Universal Mind.

*See also:* CONSCIOUSNESS, NEW AGE MOVEMENT, PISCEAN AGE, ZODIAC

## AQUINO, MICHAEL (b. 1946)

The high priest and founder of a cult named the Temple of Set, organized in 1975. Aquino retired as a lieutenant colonel and a twenty-one-year veteran of the United States Army. After studying at the United States Defense University, Aquino served as an intelligence attaché and expert in international relations with a high national security clearance. At one time he was a member of the Church of Satan, headed by Anton LaVey. Aquino says that he received a vision from Satan to start a new organization that would properly venerate the powers of darkness. Aquino, a student of nazism, incorporated a clear military flavor into the Temple of Set, unlike the Church of Satan.

Aquino is noted for using constitutional law to defend the religious rights of satanists. In his arguments for religious freedom, Aquino equates the philosophical ideology of satanism with the New Age Movement. He cites common beliefs in a universal energy force, self-indulgence, and personal divinity. He and his wife, Lilith (whose name comes from the mythological spirit lover of Adam), describe themselves as decent, law-abiding people whose satanic beliefs reflect a strong moral character.

According to Aquino, Satan's name is derived from the Egyptian god Set-Ham, therefore he named his organization the Temple of Set. The occult leader claims that despite the relatively recent establishment of his group, it finds its roots in the ancient mystery religions of Egypt and Greece. Reputedly the followers of these traditions were among the first to recognize and exalt the divine personification of the human consciousness. The modern priesthood of Set claims a separate and superior identity from the cosmic forces of energy that New Age adherents identify with God. Followers of Set teach that the soul has innate powers, which people can use to manipulate the forces of nature to their advantage.

*See also:* COSMIC ENERGY; SATAN, CHURCH OF; SATANISM; SET, TEMPLE OF

## ARCANE SCHOOL

A meditational organization founded by theosophist Alice Bailey (1880–1949). As one of the largest organizations of its kind, the School has assemblies in most major cities in the United States. Esoteric correspondence courses are offered, with courses in such subjects as the hierarchy of spiritual masters, Eastern mysticism, anti-Semitism, and the plan for unfolding a New World Order. Bailey's works repeatedly glorify Lucifer and his reappearance as the New Age messiah. Before Bailey's death in 1949, she founded three major organizations to spread New Age ideals. World Goodwill covers the political scene, New Group of World Servers brings together the best New Age practitioners, and the Lucis Trust (of which the

Arcane School is a part) publishes and distributes occult information.

*See also:* BAILEY, ALICE ANN; DJWHAL KHUL; LUCIFERIC DOCTRINE; LUCIS TRUST; PLAN, THE; SPIRITUAL HIERARCHY OF LIGHT

## ARCHETYPE

A preexistent image or symbol representing the psychic content of humanity's collective unconscious, as opposed to the personal unconscious. Swiss psychologist Carl Jung (1875–1961) stated that the collective unconscious represents the total of primordial human memories, including recollections of births and deaths, relationships between people, and between people and the divine. This evolving knowledge of the human race is inherited at birth and stored in the brain. Jung claimed that similar archetypes exist in people of all times and places. They are mythological representations of the universal self. These archetypes can be dreams or fairy tales and are manifested in such symbols as the Great Earth Mother, the Sky Father, the hero, and the monster. Jung taught that the "image of God" presented in the Bible is an archetype imprinted in every person. He urged people to make the God image dominant in their personality.

New Age adherents have adopted much of this thinking. They teach that a common psychic nature exists everywhere and in everyone. This collective unconscious, with its many inborn or inherited archetypes, belongs to all members of the human race and is impersonal. Because these latent primordial memories are supra-individual, they eternally preexisted in nature. Every person is linked psychically to the collective unconscious and can draw upon its archetypes through various mind-altering techniques. As people get in touch with their divine self, they can establish communication with the Universal Mind, fathom the mysteries of humanity's ancestral knowledge, gain unlimited human powers, and learn how to manipulate reality.

*See also:* COLLECTIVE UNCONSCIOUS; JUNG, CARL GUSTAV; SYMBOLISM

## AREA 51

Part of a military base near Groom Dry Lake in Nevada, UFO followers cannot go to this off-limits military site, but they are certain that the United States government is hiding proof of extraterrestrial entities there, including bodies of aliens and the alien airship that crashed in the Roswell Incident. So popular is the view that nearby Highway 375 has became a major Nevada tourist attraction. Officially, the U.S. Army does not acknowledge that there is an "Area 51" on the base. Any relationship to UFOs has been consistently denied.

*See also:* ROSWELL INCIDENT, UNIDENTIFIED FLYING OBJECT

## ARGÜELLES, JOSE (b. 1939)

Colorado art historian, sometime amateur archaeologist, and New Age author, Argüelles has a doctorate in Art History from the University of Colorado but is best known for spearheading an event called the Harmonic Convergence, which first occurred in August of 1987. An estimated twenty thousand people gathered at over 350 sites considered sacred. The groundwork for the event was laid by Argüelles's book entitled *The Mayan Factor: Path Beyond Technology*. The purpose was to draw together a critical mass of rainbow warriors, an army made up of New Age groups, organizations, and individuals.

Argüelles claims his first vision of the Harmonic Convergence came while driving down a Los Angeles street. He also says that the use of psychedelic drugs by America's youth in the late 1960s and early 1970s prepared the West for the transformational events to follow. He believes that the Harmonic Convergence launched a five-year world plan during which the people of earth will move toward globalization. He asserts that a minimum amount of human voltage is needed to generate enough energy to establish the infrastructure of a New World Order and to transform the entire human race. Reputedly the Harmonic Convergence marks the last twenty-five years of a five thousand year cycle, a mystical time within which the world will be balanced, cleansed, and evolved before entering the New Age.

He bases prophecies about the emergence of an enlightened world on the wisdom of a space person named Treadwell from the stellar system Actara. Argüelles believes that the ancient Mayan Indians were of extraterrestrial origin. He claims that participants will experience the power of peace as it enters the world, that they will witness incredible examples of cosmic phenomena, and that they will have privileged communication with visitors from parallel universes.

*See also:* HARMONIC CONVERGENCE, MAYANS

## ARICA INSTITUTE (AI)

A New Age organization founded by Oscar Ichazo in 1971. He named the institute after the port city of Arica in northern Chile. AI, which has offices in New York City, Los Angeles, and San Francisco, combines the beliefs of Eastern religions with the teachings of psychotherapy. Ichazo claims that salvation lies within the subconscious, which he says represents the divine essence of humanity, but people are unaware of their innate godhood because of the ego. Over time the ego grows in dominance due to the conflicts that arise between people and the demands placed on them by society.

AI teaches initiates to recognize and destroy the ego so that they realize and cultivate pure essence. This can be accomplished by entering a trancelike state, establishing contact with the subconscious, and bringing about the union of the inner self with the absolute consciousness. AI draws upon various Eastern religious techniques, such as *I Ching*, Zen, and Yoga, as well as Buddhism, Confucianism, and the Martial Arts, to enable practitioners to discover their "essential self." In this way they attain knowledge of salvation or perfect enlightenment. AI espouses the belief that when devotees become aware of the pure essence of their radiant being, all the false guilt they have been carrying will be eradicated. They will also experience a quantum leap in the development of their subconscious, enabling them to realize the fullness of their divine potential.

*See also:* HUMAN POTENTIAL MOVEMENT, SELF-REALIZATION, TRANSCENDENTAL MEDITATION, YOGA

## ARIGO (1918–1971)

A New Age psychic surgeon, Arigo, who was born in Brazil as Jose Pedro De Freitas, received only four years of elementary schooling and was a miner by profession. Arigo claimed that when a German physician named Adolph Fritz died in 1918, the year of Arigo's birth, Fritz's departed spirit took possession of the Brazilian peasant. Arigo asserted that he was the channel for this entity and that this explained how he was able to perform complex medical procedures without the benefit of traditional surgical instruments or anesthetics, and without blood loss or the formation of scar tissue.

Arigo remains one of the most documented psychic surgeons. He reportedly has diagnosed the medical condition of patients from a distance, removed diseased tissue using only a rusty knife, and verbally commanded blood to clot and surgical incisions to close. During his lifetime, he treated as many as three hundred patients a day from all over the world. Arigo credited his psychic "gift" to the power of God. In fact, he recited the Lord's prayer as he performed his "operations." This prayer was also printed beneath a nearby picture of Christ.

*See also:* PSYCHIC SURGERY, TRANCE CHANNELING

## ARMAGEDDON

The location of a climactic battle in the end times connected with the second coming of Christ. Armageddon, mentioned only in Revelation 16:16, literally means "Mount of Megiddo." It refers to an area near the city of Megiddo in the plain of Esdraelon in northern Palestine, the scene of many clashes in Old Testament times. Students of biblical prophecy note that Armageddon signifies more than a geographical locale. It also represents the final apocalyptic conflict that will take place between the forces of evil under Antichrist and the forces of good under the Lord (Rev. 16:14). The Scriptures leave no doubt as to the winner of this battle. When Jesus Christ returns in great power and glory with His glorified church, Antichrist and his forces will be crushed (19:11–21).

New Age adherents define Armageddon in quite different terms. They maintain that the climactic battle will not be fought with physical weapons but with the human mind. Armageddon will be a struggle to achieve a quantum leap of spiritual consciousness. New Age adherents will hail the Beast or Antichrist as the great ascended master of the New World Order, the leader who will usher humankind into a new dimension of peace, love, and harmony. This is to take place amidst the opposing forces of negative energy vibrations emanating from devout Christians who refuse to accept the doctrines of this charismatic world leader.

At some point during this transformational process, the source of these negative energies must necessarily be purified from society. Christians will be banished to another dimension of space and time until they have sufficiently evolved. The 144,000 mentioned in Revelation 14:1–5 are supposedly those who establish a universal mind-link and create the vibrational energy force necessary to bring about a quantum leap in the evolutionary development of humankind.

*See also:* SECOND COMING OF CHRIST

## ARMAGEDDON, CHURCH OF (LOVE FAMILY)

New Age cult founded by Paul Erdmann in the late 1960s in Seattle, Washington. A salesman from California, Erdmann claimed that God spoke to him in a vision and showed him the importance of cultivating mutual love, harmony, and communal living. God had chosen Erdmann as the supreme leader of a new group called the Love Family. He claimed that according to Revelation 16:16, these people would be the true family of God. In keeping with this philosophy, every member is required to renounce all family ties, friend-

ships, and worldly possessions by giving everything they own to Erdmann. This includes giving up their real name. Because Erdmann claims that Israel was the name God used for His people in the Old Testament, all initiates are named Israel as part of their family name. Erdmann himself was known as Love Israel.

In 1971, nearly sixty members of the Love Family occupied seven houses. By 1976, an estimated four hundred to five hundred members had three colonies, a 160-acre ranch in the Seattle area, and groups in Alaska and Hawaii. Instead of growing from this base, the Church of Armageddon became embroiled in internal and legal problems, and over the years the number of adherents dwindled. The centers in Alaska and Hawaii closed in the early 1980s. By 2000, there was little interest in the group, even among cult watchers. It was reported to have fewer than one hundred members.

Erdmann tells his followers they are eternal beings and that he is preparing them for the Day of the Lord, hence the name Church of Armageddon. Part of the preparation process includes making a total break with any former way of life, gathering with others in a commune, and pledging to cultivate harmony and love. Erdmann believes that all earthly problems, including death, will be defeated by showing love. He asserts that he is following the lofty moral example of Christ, whom he says came to earth to gather a small group of disciples out of the world so that they could create a utopian society of kindness and peace. Erdmann's followers reputedly are the true people of God, the Israel of Old Testament days. The cult leader claims that they alone will inherit the original covenant promises the Lord made to Israel.

*See also:* APOCALYPSE

## AROMATHERAPY

The use of fragrant oils, extracted from herbs, flowers, and fruits, to bring about holistic healing and well-being through massages of the body, especially the face. This practice claims a heritage of over four thousand years and is based on the idea that inhaling the scents given off by various substances holds mystical healing powers. Practitioners say that each scent contains psychic vibrational energies that can stimulate and balance corresponding energies within the body to eliminate both physiological and psychological ailments.

Aromatherapists rely on ancient records to show correspondence between healing aromas and the seasons and days, planets and stars. Practitioners also make use of power objects, such as crystals and pyramids, which supposedly enhance the mystical healing powers of the scents. Some aromatherapists focus on what they believe is a physiological connection between a scent and sexual perceptions. Others concentrate on the invocation of aroma-memories, which can be either personal or universal in nature. Some practitioners advocate the use of massage to promote holistic healing, while others place the patient in a vapor room where hot air carries the powers of a specific scent. The average practitioner may wear many scents at the same time, placing them on different parts of the body and inhaling them individually at will.

*See also:* HERBALISM, HOLISM, OIL, POWER OBJECT, VIBRATIONS

## ART, NEW AGE

Mystical, dreamlike images created by advocates of occultic beliefs. The purpose of this art is to provide a glimpse into other dimensions of existence. These alternate universes show images, colors, and lights that touch the human soul. Devotees believe the surreal depictions are echoes of the radiance of higher consciousness. These images reputedly open the minds of viewers to an enlightened recognition of innate divinity. Viewers try to establish contact with psychic energy forces, enabling them to discover hidden but essential qualities of their personalities. Proponents claim the computer generated, mathematically animated shapes and colors are a mirror of nature, which reflects the esoteric complexity of elementary existence.

The transformational powers of the mind-expanding visuals, enhanced by color and light, reputedly are achieved through the infusion of universal energies. These penetrate the soul and bring about the mystical healing of the mind, body, and spirit.

*See also:* COLOROLOGY, LIGHT, TRANSFORMATION

## ARYA-MARGA

Sacred path toward attainment in Buddhism. Four states on this path are (1) the stream-enterer (srotapanna), (2) the once-returner (sakrdagamin), (3) the not-returner (anagamin), and (4) the attainer (arhat).

*See also:* BUDDHISM

## ARYAN RACE

According to legend, one of the seven root races born from the population of Atlantis. After the fabled continent sank beneath the sea around 1500 B.C., the Aryan race scattered through Iran, India, and Europe. The Aryans were the master race who took a quantum leap in consciousness, gaining wisdom and intelligence. The leap circumvented the slower process of natural evolution and resulted in a significant increase in psychic abilities. These supranormal powers were considered a key factor in the Aryan superiority over lesser peoples, giving the advanced race the right and responsibility to exercise absolute rule over the world. To regain their lost powers, the Aryans set up a process called the initiation. Spiritual masters, or god-like beings, taught devotees about the supremacy of the evolved consciousness of the Aryan race.

Adolf Hitler (1889–1945) believed that the Germanic people held the purest form of Aryan blood. He convinced others that, with guidance from the spiritual realm, he could transform the German nation and restore the master race to its rightful place over the world. During his reign of terror, millions were slaughtered by the Third Reich in a crazed attempt to rid the world of so-called inferior races.

The Aryan concept of an elite super race is evident in New Age teaching. Occult leaders claim that the enlightened have reached the highest levels of conscious awareness. Because they are in touch with their divine self, they are forerunners of an advanced race of spirit beings who will usher in the Aquarian era. Some claim that the same ascended masters who once led the Aryan race have returned to earth, assumed human form, and are guiding the planet into an age of peace, harmony, and joy. Lord Maitreya, the cosmic messiah, will rule this utopian society. According to New Age philosophy, he will banish all those who are unenlightened to other dimensions so that the evolutionary advancement of humanity will proceed unimpeded.

*See also:* ATLANTIS, LOST CONTINENT OF; HITLER, ADOLF; JESUS CHRIST; ROOT RACE

## ASAÑÑASATTA

Celestial beings in Buddhism who have attained a state of existence in which mental activity can be stopped for long periods. This is regarded as a dangerous level of attainment, since those who enter it may believe they have reached Nirvana, but they have not.

## ASCENDED MASTER

An entity of an ethereal kingdom known as the fourth dimension. These entities are also called spirit guides, inner selves, higher selves, and angels of light, as well as extraterrestrials, power images, and universal intelligences. They represent the most influential forces of the New Age. Ascended masters claim to have reached the highest level of spiritual consciousness and have returned to earth to guide humans on their evolutionary path to enlightenment. Diverse means of communication with ascended masters reported. These messages tend to teach that God is an impersonal force, that

**Ascension path—the path to enlightenment**

biblical accounts concerning Jesus Christ are myths, and that Lucifer is the divine Morning Star and Light-Bearer.

The title of "ascended master" stems from the Hindu and Buddhist belief that the karmic cycles of reincarnation can be ended by achieving spiritual enlightenment. These disciples have supposedly achieved the highest evolutionary stature. They no longer find it necessary to endure life on the physical plane but have attained the freedom to journey into other dimensions of space and time. Proponents teach that the souls of these entities can either unite with the Universal Mind or retain an ethereal presence on earth to aid others in their pilgrimage to godhood. New Age adherents believe ascended masters have access to the esoteric mysteries of truth that reputedly exist throughout the universe, and they reveal these to selected human hosts called channelers. Some practitioners claim ascended masters can release powerful thought waves directly into the consciousness of these mediums.

Various New Age techniques exist to help people establish contact with spirit guides. For example, the use of Ouiji® boards, tarot cards, and power objects (such as crystals and pyramids) can open communication with these entities. Also popular is the search for a personal guide or "familiar." By using guided imagery techniques, people try to visualize the entity. The most serious form of communication is channeling. That requires practitioners to surrender themselves fully to the control of the ascended master. Most of these methods have infiltrated mainstream Western society. For instance, Ouiji® boards are sold as toys, crystals are sold as jewelry, and the practice of searching for inner guides is occasionally introduced into educational curricula.

*See also:* DEMON, SPIRITUAL HIERARCHY OF LIGHT, TRANCE CHANNELING

## ASCENSION OF CHRIST

The departure of Christ from earth to the presence of His heavenly Father. Jesus' ascension declares His victory over sin and death and points to His present lordship over the events of human history (Luke 24:50–51; Acts 1:9–11; Rom. 1:4; Col. 2:13–15; Heb. 1:3).

Contrary to orthodox Christian beliefs, New Age adherents say that the ascension of Christ is an archetype of every individual's evolutionary advancement to union with the impersonal deity that exists throughout the universe. They depict Jesus as a person who, by perfecting His lower self, was able to evolve to a higher plane of spiritual existence. His ascension allegedly represents the achievement of a divine state of awareness, available to all people. Adherents state that followers of Jesus do not actually worship the *person* of Christ, but rather His *divine qualities* in hope of attaining His status of perfection and enlightenment.

The heaven to which the New Age messiah ascended represents an inner cosmic consciousness. This state of absolute blessedness supposedly releases people from the endless cycles of reincarnation and eradicates the individual consciousness.

*See also:* CHRIST-CONSCIOUSNESS, EVOLUTION, HEAVEN, SELF-REALIZATION

## ASHRAM

The secluded dwellings of Hindu sages. The term "ashram" comes from the Sanskrit word *asrama,* which in turn is derived from *srama,* which means "religious exercise." This etymology fits with the fact that ashrams are often austere places where disciples obtain religious instruction and perform a strict regimen of meditative exercises. They remain under the control of the resident guru who demands divine veneration and total obedience. Initiates share sparse accommodations and perform arduous labor, deemed a necessary step toward achieving enlightenment.

Since the late 1960s, many New Age adherents from the West have visited ashrams in India, hoping to benefit from these spiritual retreats. As the potential for obtaining income from these tourists grew, the leaders of some ashrams made their communes more inviting and less austere. Despite these outward changes, the message has remained the same. In opposition to Christ, Krishna represents the supreme personification of the godhead. In this view, Christ serves as an example of humanity's ability to achieve salvation by removing accumulated bad karma through devotion to Krishna, "Christ's father." Initiates learn that sin is an illusion, that they are inherently divine and that they can escape from the endless cycles of reincarnation through yoga, a form of meditation.

*See also:* GURU, HINDUISM, KARMA

## ASTARTE (ASHTORETH, ASTORETH)

The Canaanite and Phoenician goddess of fertility, sexual love, and war. As the Queen or Mistress of Heaven, Astarte was one of the consorts of Baal, the supreme storm and fertility god of the Canaanites. Astarte's identity parallels Ishtar in Babylonian and Assyrian lore. One Babylonian tale describes the descent of the goddess into Hades in search of her dead husband Tammuz. Another legend makes her the Great Mother, Heavenly Virgin, and the creator of humankind. Egyptian accounts depict the goddess in the nude with horns on her head, riding a horse into battle, carrying either a bow and arrow or a spear and shield. Ancient pagan cults worshiped the goddess through sexually perverse rites performed in temples. In addition, prophetesses would declare oracles to devotees who visited the shrine of the goddess. Some legends portray the deity as representing both the morning and evening stars, giving Astarte an androgynous quality.

Goddess worship continues in many feminist cults of the New Age. Advocates contend that organized religion has ignored the spiritual needs of women for the last five thousand years and has forced them to defer to the spiritual interpretations of male-oriented institutions. The revival of the ancient worship of the Earth Goddess supposedly will enable women to find their roots, rediscover their divine potential, and reclaim their rightful place as leaders of a matriarchal society. This society will be at peace with nature and achieve oneness with the universal life force. Feminist cults seek to dethrone Sky Father and reestablish the rule of Earth Mother over the world.

*See also:* APHRODITE, GODDESS WORSHIP, LUCIFERIC DOCTRINE, VENUS

## ASTRAL BODY

Spiritual counterpart to the physical body in New Age thought. The astral body is said to be the psychic force and ectoplasmic substance that gives life to a a human being. The astral body can separate from the physical body and project itself into other dimensions of space and time known as the astral plane. It remains conscious during altered states, sleep, and even death. New Age advocates encourage the projection of the astral body as a means of achieving spiritual enlightenment and oneness with the Universal Mind.

*See also:* ASTRAL PROJECTION, ETHER

## ASTRAL PLANE

Ethereal realm of existence, distinct from, and beyond the confines of, the physical world. New Age adherents believe the astral plane holds all the knowledge, wisdom, and secrets of the universe. Spirit guides, ascended masters, and other aliens reside there. Entities emerge from the astral plane, come to earth, give willing human hosts unlimited psychic powers, and reveal to them long lost esoteric truths. Initiates obtain these things by entering a trancelike state, leaving their bodies through astral projection, and traveling to the ethereal realm. Entities from the astral plane are usually considered by adherents to be the sources of most New Age literature, programs, techniques, and power objects.

*See also:* FOURTH LEVEL, SHAMBALLA

## ASTRAL PROJECTION

Ability of the soul to leave the body and journey to other dimensions of space and time, known as the astral plane. New Age adherents declare that the physical realm is characterized by illusion and limits, whereas the astral plane is the source of all that is real and boundless. Occult leaders teach their followers to enter trancelike states while using meditative practices and hallucinogenic drugs. By doing so, they can project consciousness into the astral realm, tap into the cosmic consciousness, and obtain the wisdom of the ascended masters.

Special chambers have been designed to create an environment for permitting the rapid release of the astral body from the physical body. They call this an out-of-body experience. Surroundings may include power objects, such as crystals or pyramids, New Age music, subliminal or meditation tapes, or a varied combination of other occult paraphernalia. Once the required trancelike state is achieved, the travelers are said to maintain contact with their physical form through a silver umbilical-like thread.

While some astral projectionists report journeys to distant lands, others claim they traveled to faraway galaxies and parallel dimensions of space and time where they obtain the secrets of the universe. Some say they have reached heaven, were greeted by angels, and were cloaked in radiant light. Others assert they have reached the ethereal realm, met their spirit guide, and received vital guidance.

Some former New Age adherents also report encounters with appalling demons and the paralyzing fear that they would never return to their physical form. Proponents of astral projection explain away these negative experiences as nothing more than necessary stepping stones to achieving enlightenment.

*See also:* ETHER, OUT-OF-BODY EXPERIENCE

## ASTROLOGY

The study of the position and aspects of the celestial bodies (stars and planets, sun and moon) with the intent of predicting their influence on the course of human affairs and terrestrial events. The underlying basis for astrology holds that all things in life are predetermined. For this reason astrologers emphasize the zodiac signs under which people are born to determine their individual character and personality traits. Believers read horoscopes, and birth charts, to predict what might happen to them in the future.

The origins of astrology, and later astronomy, lie sometime around 3000 B.C. and were based on the principle that all heavenly bodies emit forces that in some way dominate human life. By the time ancient Babylon had adopted astrology in approximately 1000 B.C., the zodiac and its symbolic images were well established. The zodiac represented a band of stars that encircled the world and formed the boundary outside of which celestial bodies did not pass. This band was divided into twelve constellations, with each one symbolized by an image fitting the dominant characteristics of the sign it represented. The zodiac was drawn into a horoscope from which astrologers claimed to predict present and future events.

Although astrology originally concentrated on general forecasts, such as the change of seasons and weather patterns, the system later began making predictions about the future of individuals.

Throughout the centuries, astrologers have claimed that the zodiac affects the individual and collective lives of people in a variety of ways. Theoretically each constellation is dominated by the characteristics of its closest or ruling planet, as well as by the qualities assigned to dominating elements, such as the earth, wind, fire, and water. In casting the horoscope, astrologers placed the earth at the center of the solar system, around which all other celestial bodies revolve. The position of each planet, as well as the sun and moon in relation to the earth, supposedly determines detailed personality traits. Astrologers also attribute twelve divisions, called houses, to the earth. Each house represents a different aspect of daily life as well as relationships and death.

In the sixteenth century, the Polish astronomer Nicholas Copernicus (1473–1543) proposed a heliocentric theory of planetary motion. He postulated that the sun was at the center of the solar system and that all the planets revolved around the sun. This cosmological view prompted scientists, mathematicians, and astronomers to question the geocentric assumptions of astrology. Today the overwhelming consensus of opinion views astrology as based on superstition and speculation rather than science. But astrology remains popular among New Age adherents and many publications continue to feature horoscopes. Occult "scientists" assert that the same life-giving energy flows through everything in existence, and thus cosmic interaction is unavoidable. This justifies the necessity for consulting astrological charts on all matters concerning daily living.

*See also:* AQUARIUS, AGE OF; DIVINATION; SCIENCE, NEW AGE; ZODIAC

## ATHEISM

The denial of the existence of God or any supernatural existence. This system of thinking stands in contrast to agnosticism, which says the existence of God and the supernatural cannot be proven. Atheism is philosophically in harmony with empiricism, a theory which states that all knowledge is derived from experience. Empiricists believe that objective information and understanding are derived only from tangible data and activities that are observable and measurable. According to atheists, people do not need to answer to an absolute divine authority because one does not exist. Every person ultimately determines her or his own moral values.

New Age adherents agree with this last point. In fact, they claim that because people are inherently divine, they have the right and responsibility to make their own value judgments on what is proper and improper. And as they link up with the Universal Mind through altered states of consciousness, they discover how to live in harmony with the rest of humanity. Thus they are freed from restrictions imposed on them by absolute moral standards. In fact, they consider all laws and regulations detrimental to the evolutionary advancement of humankind.

*See also:* FAITH, GOD, HUMANISM

# ATLANTIS, LOST CONTINENT OF

Plato (428–348 B.C.) described Atlantis as a vast island-continent west of the Straits of Gibraltar. Atlantis was a peaceful, prosperous people with advanced knowledge who ruled over the surrounding islands and continents. In Plato's legend, the people became complacent and their leaders arrogant, angering the gods, who flooded Atlantis in one day and night.

Plato may have heard an Egyptian story collected by the Greek statesman Solon (630–560 B.C.) of the land of Keftiu. Keftiu was the base for one of the four pillars that supported the Egyptian sky and was the gateway to all of the lands to the far west of Egypt. Egyptians believed that it was submerged in an apocalypse. Historians suggest that the culture of the Minoan civilization of Crete (c. 3000 B.C. to 1400 B.C.) bears a striking resemblance to the descriptions of Keftiu and Atlantis. The island of Santorini, near Crete, was destroyed in 1470 B.C. by a series of volcanic eruptions.

Rudolf Steiner (1861–1925), who founded the Anthroposophical Society, wrote his own account of the history of Atlantis. Helena Petrovna Blavatsky (1831–1891), who cofounded Theosophy, claimed in *The Secret Doctrine* that the Aryans were a master race from Atlantis who took a quantum leap in consciousness to gain wisdom and intelligence.

Edgar Cayce (1877–1945), a clairvoyant and psychic healer, claimed that the lost civilization existed 10 million years ago. Cayce believed that the Atlanteans developed futuristic technologies, such as airplanes, submarines, and wireless communication, as well as atomic power plants and lasers. Cayce described a place where thought projectiles became physical manifestations and mind powers were as refined as technology itself. Cayce believed the continent slowly destroyed itself and broke into three separate islands named Aryan, Og, and Posedia.

During the final phase of the civilization's destruction, the Atlanteans migrated to Egypt, taking with them the worship of Ra, the sun god. According to Cayce, the Atlanteans hid their esoteric records in one of the undiscovered chambers of Egypt's pyramids.

New Age adherents claim that Atlanteans initially worshiped one god, represented by the sun. But as they established new colonies, they eventually worshiped the sun and learned to harness its powers by using a "Great Crystal." Its powers could be used like an oracle to reveal hidden knowledge, or like a shaman to cure terminal diseases magically, or like a weapon to destroy enemies. When they tried to use it to destroy others, the crystal caused a volcano on their island to erupt. In New Age thought, Atlantis is connected with a state of harmonic existence and power. Some believe Atlantis will rise again and its secrets will be revealed in the approaching age of enlightenment.

*See also:* ANTHROPOSOPHY; ARYAN RACE; CAYCE, EDGAR; RAMTHA; ROOT RACE

# ATMAN

In Hinduism, the individual soul of every person. It refers to the principle of life, the breath of life, the innermost essence, and the self that comprises the body, soul, and senses of the entire person. Hinduism teaches that the atman, or individual self, is an extension of Brahman, or supreme universal self. The essence of people is identical to the essence of Ultimate Reality. Because Brahman is eternal and indestructible, so too is the atman. When people die, their atman is reincarnated into the next life. When they reach nirvana, the state of absolute oneness, their atman no longer retains its separate existence.

*See also:* BRAHMA, HINDUISM

# ATONEMENT

The reconciling work of Christ, accomplished for humankind through His death on the cross. Through the substitutionary sacrifice of Christ, the penalty of sin is fully and adequately paid, the demands of God's holy law and its infinite moral requirements are absolutely satisfied, and the believer is completely restored to a relationship with God.

New Age adherents reject the biblical concepts of personal guilt and divine retribution.

Sin is viewed as humanity's ignorance of cosmic oneness with a divine universe. They claim that atonement (at-one-ment) and subsequently salvation is the realization that people are inherently divine. By becoming aware of their innate godhood, people supposedly can discern the wisdom, secrets, knowledge, and powers of the Universal Mind. And because humans and nature are tangible expressions of the impersonal cosmic essence, people have the power to create their own realities and control their destinies.

*See also:* CRUCIFIXION, MONISM, SALVATION, SIN

## AUM

*See:* OM

## AURA

Psychic emanations of the mind or spirit, occurring apart from any physical means and

**Aura—symbol of the astral self**

detected only by mediums. The size and color of each aura reveals different aspects of the physical, psychological, and spiritual condition of the life form. The reading of the auric field is a holistic means of relieving stress and deepening spiritual awareness. Advocates believe that with the proper psychic alignment, all have the ability to see and interpret the human aura.

The auric field emanates from the body in three distinct but coalesced realms. The inner realm glows approximately one-half inch and outlines the human physique. The middle aura emanates an additional three inches, and the outer aura emanates out to a foot or so. Proponents believe that the greater the intensity of the aura, the better the condition of the life form to which it belongs. The dominant color of each auric realm is an additional indication of a person's condition. For instance, a red aura indicates anger, a black aura reveals the presence of stress, and a blue aura indicates peace.

The various colors and intensities of the auric field supposedly can be measured by Kirlian photography, developed by Russian electrician Semyon Kirlian (1900–1980) in 1939. This high voltage photographical process utilizes two electrodes that are energized by a high frequency electrical field. The object to be photographed and an unexposed strip of film are placed between the electrodes. The exposed film registers a phenomena invisible to the human eye.

Scientists think the resulting aura is an ionization of the air from heat generated by a person's body. New Age adherents claim the aura is spiritual radiation emanating from the person's soul. Eastern mystics say the psychic emanations are an astral light that originated in the cosmos, inhabits a human body during its lifetime, and returns to the cosmos after death. Some occultists maintain the aura represents pure energy, the most basic element that produces all life. Still others think the aura is a manifestation of the higher self.

*See also:* CHROMOTHERAPY, COSMIC ENERGY, KIRLIAN PHOTOGRAPHY

## AUTOMATIC WRITING

A phenomenon in which a spirit entity takes control of a human host and causes the medium to write apart from her or his awareness. Automatic writing typically occurs when the medium enters a trancelike state and establishes communication with the entity, such as the spirit of a deceased person.

The sacred writings of most occult groups are usually said to be products of automatic writing. Some New Age psychologists claim that automatic writing is an excellent tool for clearing the unconscious mind and allowing people to get in touch with their higher self. This is regarded as an essential step toward achievement of a state of enlightenment.

*See also:* DEMON, MEDIUM, TRANCE CHANNELING

# AVATAR

In Hindu teaching, the incarnation or embodiment of the impersonal Brahman, or Ultimate Reality, in either animal form (a fish, boar, tortoise, and so on), or human form (Krishna, Buddha, Christ, Muhammad, and others). In particular, the Hindu god Vishnu has reputedly manifested itself as an avatar at least nine times in history. These incarnations occur when a need arises. When the avatar dies, it is reabsorbed back into Brahman. Proponents claim that avatars come to earth to aid people on their spiritual journey and to show them how to attain enlightenment.

New Age adherents reflect this teaching by insisting that Christ is merely one of the manifestations of the impersonal Brahman. Like other avatars, He progressed beyond the law of karma and the need to be reincarnated. Advocates contend that Christ was not resurrected after His death, but rather His essence rejoined Ultimate Reality.

At the dawn of the Aquarian Age, a tenth avatar is to appear, known as Kalki or Lord Maitreya. He will guide an enlightened generation of people into an epoch of unparalleled global harmony, peace, and joy.

*See also:* ANTICHRIST; LOGOS; MAITREYA, LORD; SANAT KUMURA

# AVESTA

The liturgical holy book of Zoroastrianism. Most of this work is regarded as missing, destroyed during centuries of persecution by Islam in Iran. The oldest extant manuscript is from the thirteenth century, but some hymns and bits of writing are of ancient Indian origin, possibly centuries before the birth of Christ. Zoroastrians sing and quote from the prayers each day.

*See also:* ZOROASTRIANISM

# AWARENESS

A heightened state of consciousness in which the mind allegedly realizes the presence of its innate godhood, its oneness with the divine consciousness, and its union with other emanations of the impersonal presence in parallel universes. New Age adherents encourage people to achieve this state of awareness by focusing their mind on a single point of reference, visualizing the deity within them, and chanting a mantra, or sacred sound. Their intent is to attain conscious union with the universal creative principle as well as foster calmness and creativity, peace of mind and spiritual well-being. By regularly entering into a trancelike state, people reputedly can achieve their full human potential, learn to screen out unwanted incoming sensory information, and become more receptive to the greater realities of the universe. These include spiritual entities, cosmic energies, and the inherent divinity of self. The negative side effects of this practice include emotional trauma, mental breakdown, severe depression, and suicidal thoughts or behavior.

*See also:* CONSCIOUSNESS, COSMIC ENERGY, ENLIGHTENMENT

# *AYURVEDA*

In India, an ancient document containing descriptions of diseases and information on the perceived curative qualities of herbs and magic. In keeping with Hindu belief, the *Ayurveda* advocates a system of medicine that attempts to cure the illusion of pain and disease with the realities of health and well-being. Some think this approach is over five thousand years old, which, if true, would make it the "father" of holistic medicine. The *Ayurveda* views people in their universal context, as an indivisible part of a cosmic whole. By adhering to Hindu philosophy and practice, devotees can allegedly achieve a heightened state of awareness, realize their oneness with Ultimate Reality, and experience the elimination of all pain and disease.

Ayurveda healers consider themselves to be invincible spiritual warriors, holding the answers to the universal questions of life and death. Many Hindu devotees think that much of the original wisdom of the *Ayurveda* was lost. This ancient Indian document has given birth to a variety of holistic practices. Some claim that individuals operate in a harmonious balance of interconnected and interrelated parts, united by a divine energy life force that flows through all living things, just as it does throughout the universe. Holistic healers say that people possess the innate ability and responsibility to manipulate this divine force to maintain a harmonious balance of energy within themselves. Physical, psychological, and spiritual ailments are merely the product of improper thinking. However this imbalance of energy is easily corrected once people transcend to a level of consciousness where divine awareness can be utilized.

*See also:* BALANCING, HOLISM

## AYURVEDIC MEDICINE

*See: ayurveda,* MIND BODY MEDICINE

## AZTEC CULTURE

An advanced native American civilization that ruled the central part of present day Mexico through the fifteenth century A.D. The Aztecs developed a warrior/priest culture that was supported by taxation of the farmer, artisan, and merchant classes, as well as by tribute payments from conquered states. The Aztec civilization was marked by the ritualistic sacrifice of people to appease various gods and goddesses. The social status of a warrior was based not on the number of enemies slain but on the number of prisoners captured for sacrificial purposes. According to archaeological research, the ceremonial center of the Az-

tec capital named Tenochtitlán is the site of modern-day Mexico City. Here the Aztecs boasted of skull racks, cleansing pools, and a ziggurat-like temple on which the inhabitants sacrificed some fifty thousand victims a year.

Aztec religious doctrines held to beliefs in reincarnation and karmic laws to justify sacrificing countless numbers of people. Aztec priests believed that the offering of the human heart and blood guaranteed that the gods and goddesses would remain strong. They also believed that anyone who ingested a portion of the victim's body would receive the strength and courage of that person, a concept found in modern satanic cults. In addition Aztec doctors made medicines and magical potions from the bodies of sacrificial victims.

Aztec civilization ended with the arrival of the Spanish conquistadores in 1519 under Hernán (Hernando) Cortés (1485–1547). The Aztec emperor Montezuma II (Moctezuma) (1480–1520) erroneously believed that Cortés and his soldiers were descendants of Quetzalcoatl, the chief Aztec god who ruled over the forces of good and light. In 1520 Cortés razed Tenochtitlán and executed Montezuma II.

Some New Age adherents hold that the Aztecs were a noble race of enlightened warriors and vanguards of a superior race to come. Others have adopted Aztec prophecies as sacred readings. Still others revere the words of channeled Aztec warriors. And some collect bloodstained Aztec artifacts or wear a ziggurat-like Aztec pyramid as a symbol of this ancient culture.

*See also:* BLOOD SACRIFICE, ZIGGURAT

# B

## BABYLON

An ancient city of central Mesopotamia on the Euphrates River about fifty miles south of modern Baghdad. The name "Babylon" comes from the Akkadian term *Bab-ilani,* that means "gate of the gods." The city first became important when an Amorite ruler named Hammurabi, who reigned from 1792–1750 B.C., made it the capital of his kingdom of Babylonia. Around 1180 B.C. Babylonia waned in power and was eventually overrun by invaders from Asia Minor. When Assyria ascended to power in the Middle East in the ninth century B.C., Babylonia (and Babylon) once again prospered as a secondary state within the empire. Although Sennacherib of Assyria destroyed Babylon around 689 B.C., it was soon rebuilt. In 625 B.C., Nabopolassar established the New Babylonian, or Chaldean empire. When his son Nebuchadnezzar became king in 605 B.C., Babylonia reached the height of its power, and Babylon became a metropolis.

The city, which lay astride the Euphrates, had a stone bridge and underground tunnels that connected two fortified towers on either side. Two parallel walls encompassed the city proper, which was about eleven miles in circumference and covered about twenty-one hundred acres. The inner city was accessed by eight major gates, of which the Ishtar gate was the most extensively decorated. The layout of Babylon was symmetrical, and a number of main boulevards linked the city gates. The capital had three main palaces and at least nine temples, the largest of which was the temple of Marduk, the patron deity of Babylon. The Temple Tower, or ziggurat, was located in the center of the city. The tower had the form of a pyramid with receding outside staircases and a shrine at the top of the structure. The Hanging Gardens of Babylon were one of the seven wonders of the ancient world.

In 586 B.C., Nebuchadnezzar destroyed Jerusalem and exiled many of the Israelites to Babylon (2 Kings 25). After Nebuchadnezzar's death in 562 B.C., Babylonia and Babylon experienced a gradual decline. In 539 B.C., a coalition of the Medes and Persians succeeded in overthrowing the empire and capturing Babylon (Daniel 5). In the aftermath of the Babylonian empire's fall, Cyrus the Persian allowed the Jews to return to their homeland (2 Chron. 36:22–23). In the centuries that followed, the once great city of Babylon declined in importance, was gradually deserted, and eventually fell into ruins.

In the book of Revelation, Babylon represents the corrupt political, social, and religious system of the world that will prevail in the end times (Rev. 17:5). Some think the notorious ancient city will be rebuilt as the capital of a great world empire headed by the Antichrist. If this interpretation is correct, Scripture reveals that the city and the pagan system it represents will be destroyed by God (Rev. 14:8; 16:19). The Bible portrays all forms of satanic power, deception, and rebellion meeting their doom at the second coming of Christ (Rev. 18:2, 10, 21).

New Age thought adopts the sort of pantheism popularized by Babylon. Pantheism says that the supreme being is neutral, impersonal, and one with the material world—that all power, activity, and life are brought forth by the power, activity, and life of the Universal Mind.

Babylonian religion honored numerous trinities, whether they were masculine, feminine, or androgynous in nature. Worshipers of the Queen of Heaven, symbolized by the triangle, performed rituals involving human sacrifices, temple prostitution, and self-mutilation. The goddess cult also emphasized divination through astrology, sorcery, and magic. Because they considered knowledge sacred, it was monopolized by the priestly class and revealed only to those who obtained "godhood" through initiation into the mystery religion. The Babylonians taught and perpetuated ideas such as spiritual evolution, the innate divinity of people, and reincarnation. These concepts prevail in New Age circles today.

*See also:* MYSTERY, NEW AGE MOVEMENT, TRIANGLE, ZIGGURAT

## BACH, RICHARD

Twentieth-century New Age fiction writer. Richard Bach contends that people are innately divine and that by getting in touch with their higher self, they can convert fantasy into reality. He claims that much of his work was dictated to him by a disembodied spirit from the astral plane. This powerful force allegedly refused to free Bach until he completed the dictation. Bach holds that the world is merely an illusion and that people have the ability to look beyond it to see what is real. Through various mind-altering techniques, they can manipulate the waves of destiny, or Ultimate Reality.

Bach tells his readers that what they foresee in their minds, such as good health, untold riches, and endless freedom, is displayed in their lives. Initiates learn that any law or belief that inhibits the mind in any way, such as absolute morality, should be set aside. The only true sin is limiting the endless potential for ideas to pour forth from the mind. For Bach, heaven is not a specific place for the redeemed in glory, but rather a state of being to which people must aspire. In his writings, Bach sets forth his opinion about how they can attain it through the application of psychic techniques.

*See also:* AUTOMATIC WRITING, BIBLE, HEAVEN, TRANCE CHANNELING

## BACKMASKING

Recording messages on the reverse track of a cassette tape, record, or compact disk (CD). The intent of backmasking is to communicate subliminal messages to listeners. Although hearers are not consciously aware of the message, supposedly the unconscious mind receives the messages. Some trace backmasking to British occultist Aleister Crowley (1875–1947). His self-styled Satanism, incorporating sex and drugs, reached legendary status within the rock music industry. Based on the occultic Law of Reversal, Crowley demanded that his followers learn to do things backward— walking and talking, reading and thinking, as well as listening to music. This was to reveal esoteric messages about the future.

*See also:* CROWLEY, ALEISTER; ROCK MUSIC; UNCONSCIOUS, THE

## BAHA'I

A religious movement that emphasizes the spiritual unity of all humanity. The Baha'i faith is a doctrinal outgrowth of Islam, especially Shi'ite Islam. In particular, Baha'ism traces its origins to a Shi'ite sect that followed a Persian named Sayyid Ali Muhammad, who was born in 1819 in Shiraz (a city in present-day Iran). He declared himself to be the "Bab," which means "Gate of Truth." The Bab proclaimed himself as the divine manifestation whom God had sent to remind religious leaders throughout the world of their common origin and shared religious truths.

In 1844, the Bab asserted that he was to fulfill a special work of divine importance. His followers heralded his messages throughout Iran. In 1848, the Babi leaders separated themselves from Islam and announced that the Bab was a new prophet who had succeeded Muhammad. But this message was rejected by many Iranians. In 1850, the authorities imprisoned the Bab. On July 8, upon orders from the Shah, he was executed by religious zealots called *mujtahids*. Babis claimed their leader died as a martyr, accompanied by miracles and cosmic disturbances. Before his execution, the Bab chose Mirza Yahya to succeed him. The new leader adopted the title "Subh-i-Azal," that means "Morning of Eternity." In 1852, some Babis failed in their attempt to assassinate the Shah, who then ordered the extermination of all leaders and followers of this religious movement. However Subh-i-Azal and his brother Baha escaped and fled to Baghdad.

In 1863, another Babi named Husayn Ali declared himself as the Bab's rightful successor, the Greater One about whom the martyr had prophesied. Ali, who was born in 1817 in Tehran, Persia, adopted the named Baha'u'llah, meaning "Glory of God." He declared that God had given him special revelations, and that he was the fulfillment of all prophecies and pledges made by all the religious leaders of the world throughout history. The Persian government eventually expelled Baha'u'llah. In 1868, the Ottoman Empire banished him to Akka in Palestine. Until his death in 1892, Baha'u'llah wrote numerous books and received many pilgrims to his palace. Through his influence, the Baha'i faith spread throughout Iran and the rest of the Middle East.

Baha'u'llah appointed his son, Abbas Effendi (1814–1921), as his successor. Effendi adopted the name Abdu'l-Baha, which means "Servant of the Glory." Devotees of the Baha'i faith dubbed him "Master," and regarded him as the sole authority for interpreting and explaining the sacred writings and teachings of Baha'i. He introduced the Baha'i faith to Europe and the United States. Abdu'l-Baha chose as his successor a grandson named Shoghi Effendi (1897–1957). He selected twenty-seven people, called the Hands of the Cause of God, to succeed him. Their job was to provide leadership, stability, and direction for the Baha'i faith. In 1963, they founded the Universal House of Justice at the Baha'i World Center in Haifa, Israel. From their headquarters, various leaders have overseen the growth of Baha'i into a religion having almost 6 million followers.

The Baha'i faith teaches the unity of all religions and the equality of men and women. This religious movement advocates universal education, world peace, and the establishment of an international language and government. The Baha'i faith says that God is infinite and unknowable. Yet He has sent various human messengers at different times throughout history to make Himself known to people. These divinely appointed representatives include Moses and Krishna, Zoroaster and Buddha, as well as Christ and Muhammad. The last and greatest messenger is Baha'u'llah. They revere him as the Blessed Perfection, the hope of the world, the one whose teachings will unite the earth in peace and harmony. His writings, as well as those of the Bab and Abdu'l-Baha, supposedly comprise the final message revealed by God.

The Baha'i faith views Christ as one great religious teacher among many. His death does not represent atonement for sin, but demonstrates that the life of the spirit is eternal. They claim that because of the prophet Baha'u'llah and his followers, a new age of spirituality will dawn and lead to global enlightenment. The Baha'i assert that people are inherently good, not sinful, and that they are perpetual emanations of God, along with everything else in the universe. Such things as strife, hatred, and injustice are simply "imperfections" that can eventually be eliminated through education. They teach that when people die, they continue in the spiritual state of enlightenment attained while in this life. People can better their situation in the next life. Baha'is are encouraged to pray for the forgiveness and spiritual advancement of those who have died.

*See also:* ONE-WORLD IDEAL, SUFISM

## BAILEY, ALICE ANN (1880–1949)

Theosophist and writer. Alice Bailey spent her early childhood in Montreal with her father. When he died, she was raised by relatives. Throughout Bailey's adolescence, she was exposed to Christianity. As a young adult, studies took her to India where she came in contact with Eastern mysticism. After returning from India, Bailey married an abusive Anglican clergyman. She and her children eventually moved to California.

Bailey broke all ties with her Christian family and heritage to pursue the occult beliefs of Theosophy. She asserted that her spirit guide Djwhal Khul dictated her nearly twenty books. She claimed this Tibetan master was a spiritually evolved being who had returned with others to assist people on their journey to higher consciousness. Djwhal Khul resides in the astral kingdom of Shamballa and relays the wisdom of his master, Lucifer. Topics of Bailey's writings include the divinity of people, reincarnation, anti-Semitism, symbology, and prophecies concerning a new world order, as well as disarmament, religious wars, and the cleansing of Christians from society. Bailey's writings also glorify Lucifer as the New Age messiah, declare the sacredness of his number (666), and assert that his mark is an initiation into godhood.

Bailey established the Lucifer Publishing Company, or Lucis Trust, to print her works, and the Arcane School to disseminate her teachings. Bailey also founded the New Group of World Servers, an elite fraternity whose members see themselves as custodians of The Plan, an occult blueprint for world domination. In addition, she started World Goodwill, a political lobbying group that promotes the establishment of global unity as key to building a New World Order.

*See also:* ARCANE SCHOOL; DEMON; DJWHAL KHUL; ESOTERIC PHILOSOPHY; LUCIFERIC DOCTRINE; LUCIS TRUST; NEW GROUP OF WORLD SERVERS; PLAN, THE; THEOSOPHY

## BAISAKHI (VAISAKHI)

Hindu New Years and spring harvest festival, celebrated around April 13. The festival has become especially important to New Age Eastern religionists in Britain.

## BALANCING

The realignment of the universal energy flow that allegedly permeates all living things and instills life, health, and well-being. This energy, also known as *ch'i, ki,* and *prana,* is generated by the interplay of forces in the universe. These accumulate within the human body in odd proportions, causing infirmities. Proponents believe these can be healed by any number of holistic methods that bring the energy flow into balance with nature. Other therapists claim that the balancing of energy has nothing to do with any religious, magical, mystical, psychic, or medical phenomena. This practice does fit, however, with the New Age premise that all thought, matter, and even the human soul emanate from a universal, impersonal energy force. Balancing also agrees with the occult idea that people are inherently divine, have unlimited psychic powers, and are one with the cosmic consciousness.

The idea of balancing finds its roots in the Hindu belief of the karmic law of justice. Devotees claim that people are bound to an endless, repeating cycle of birth, death, and rebirth. The nature of people's next existence is supposedly determined by the ethical consequences of their present life. The ideal situation calls for maintaining a healthy balance between good karma and bad karma. Hinduism urges people to cultivate simplicity and balance in order to achieve harmony with the ebb and flow of the universal way. People maintain equanimity by realigning themselves with the all-pervasive cosmic energy. By nurturing and enhancing this universal life force, they achieve inner tranquillity and promote societal harmony.

*See also:* COSMIC ENERGY, HOLISM, POLARITY THERAPY

## BAPHOMET

An androgynous goat-headed deity with large wings. Baphomet was originally worshiped by the Knights Templar, a religious and military fraternity established in Jerusalem during the Crusades. In contemporary satanic cults, Baphomet is usually depicted in a sitting position, its piercing eyes staring out from

**Baphomet— occult sign for divine blessing**

the goatlike face of a beast. The deity's protruding horns represent its alleged sexual potency and mental prowess. The fingers of Baphomet form the occult sign of divine blessing—the index finger, middle finger, and thumb represent the magic mother, phallic father, and son respectively. From Baphomet's cloven hooves to the fiery torch that protrudes from between its horns, the deity symbolizes the destructive force of all that is evil.

*See also:* BLACK SABBATH, GOAT OF MENDES, PENTAGRAM, ROCK MUSIC, SATANISM, SYMBOLISM

## BEAST

A demonic entity that stands opposed to God, His representatives, and the message they proclaim. Two prominent views pertain to the Beast who will emerge from the sea in the end times (Rev. 13:1–10). Some regard the Beast as the embodiment of wickedness found in the evil world system. Ancient Rome would be one example of a human system that endorsed the persecution of believers, the spread of immorality, and the proliferation of heretical ideas. Adherents of this view say that, in the end times, some kind of human system will promote these goals in a heightened way (1 John 2:18, 22; 4:1–4; 2 John 1:7).

Others teach that the creature of Revelation 13:1 is a real person, commonly known as the Antichrist. This individual not only deceives the earth but also seeks to control it through the military, economic, and religious systems of the world. While history comes replete with despots, many think this false messiah will appear during the end times to spread wickedness, persecute believers, and gather the world in rebellion against the Lord (Dan. 7:19–25; 2 Thess. 2:1–10; Rev. 19:19).

Biblical teaching concerning the Beast are, of course, unpopular in occult and New Age circles. These believers claim the Beast represents the negative process of involution. Their Beast represents a perversion of the higher self that inhibits the spiritual evolu-

tion of the soul. The Beast is the animal nature of lower consciousness, focused solely on human desire, that impedes people from recognizing their inherent divinity. The Beast archetype embodies the concentrated evil of all root races and past incarnations, except for the New Age super race of the enlightened who have discovered the wondrous secrets of the cosmic consciousness.

Some adherents maintain the Antichrist includes all who refuse to accept Lord Maitreya, the leader who will usher humankind into a new age of peace and harmony.

*See also:* ANTICHRIST; BABYLON; MAITREYA, LORD; NUMBER OF THE BEAST; SANAT KUMURA

## BEDWARDITES

Jamaican racial purity cult begun by Alexander Bedward (1859–1930). Bedward was reputed to be a great spiritual healer, whose Pentecostal-style version of Christianity was replaced in 1891 by the declaration that he was the Christ and that all whites must be killed. Bedward was arrested and confined in an institution for the mentally ill, but a small band of followers continued a century later.

*See also:* CARGO CULT

## BELENUS

Belenus was a central Gaelic deity, whose name literally means "bright one," leading some to suggest a connection with sun worship. He was particularly worshiped on Beltaine in a spring fertility ritual. Modern nature worshipers in the Celtic tradition still honor Belenus.

*See also:* BELTAINE, CELTIC PAGANISM

## BELL

An occult symbol and power object. Some think its arched shape represents the infinite expanse of the cosmos, while others maintain that the shape of the bell symbolizes the vulva of the Mother Goddess. Its hanging position represents the magical passageway between heaven and earth.

Many occult groups believe the ringing of a bell represents creative power, mystical occurrences, and communication with the spirits.

*See also:* BLACK MAGIC, POWER OBJECT, SATANISM, SYMBOLISM, WHITE MAGIC, WITCHCRAFT

## BELTAINE (BELLTAINE, BEALTINNE, CÉTAMAIN)

An ancient day of Celtic celebration on May 1, that included sexual magic rituals and the blessing of cattle. It was first recorded in about 900 B.C. and is still celebrated in some forms in areas with a strong Gaelic tradition. It was adopted by the Anglo-Saxons as May Day. Beltaine is regarded as particularly significant to various occultic groups that draw on the Celtic tradition. It is a holy day of the Witches' Calendar.

*See also:* CELTIC PAGANISM, SOLSTICE

## BERG, DAVID BRANT (1919–1994)

The founder of a cult named the Children of God (COG). Berg was the son of a pastor/college administrator/evangelist within the Christian and Missionary Alliance. After the U.S. Army discharged him in 1941, Berg married in 1944, became ordained as an Alliance pastor, and helped start a church in Arizona in 1949. After leaving the pastorate, Berg assisted a Pentecostal evangelist named Fred Jordan in his radio ministry. In 1958, Berg moved to Huntington Beach, California and worked with a group called the Teen Challenge Coffeehouse.

At this time, Berg fell under the sway of a radical religious group that rejected orthodox Christianity and the traditional family. They also advocated communal living and authoritarian control of would-be initiates. After gaining a cult following of his own, Berg started an organization called "Teens for Christ" that attracted numerous young people who felt alienated from and disillusioned by society. He pressured them to defect from their churches, homes, and jobs to join his commune. He and about seventy disciples then relocated, first to Tuscon, Arizona and then to various others parts of the United States and Europe. In Europe, COG renamed itself the Family of Love. By 1967, Berg had changed his name to Moses David and claimed that a gypsy king, who had lived over a thousand years ago, was his spirit guide.

Throughout the 1970s, nagging legal problems and controversies forced Berg to uproot continually and relocate his organization. He was accused of separating teens from their families and brainwashing them with COG propaganda. He reputedly pressured new converts to give all their money and possessions to him, as well as permit his leaders to open all their correspondence. The authorities subsequently charged Berg with polygamy, kidnapping, and tax evasion, among other things.

Every member of COG supposedly belonged to the Royal Family, which Berg himself controlled. New converts were called babes and placed in the babe's colony. After a sufficient amount of time, these people were moved to another group that typically had about twelve disciples. One of the primary duties of these smaller colonies was to sell COG literature, videos, and audio tapes and to recruit young people into the cult.

During the 1980s, repeated clashes and divisions within COG eventually caused Berg to segregate himself from immediate contact with followers, and communicate directly with only his top leaders. He also published numerous letters, called Moses Letters or Mo Letters, in which he discussed COG teachings. His writings contained lewd sexual instructions and espoused radical political philosophies. In 1994, Berg died at the age of seventy-five. Despite the problems COG has experienced since the early 1980s, the organization continues to remain popular in such places as Brazil and the Philippines.

## BESANT, ANNIE WOOD (1847–1933)

The former head of the Theosophical Society, an occult organization founded by Madame Helena Petrovna Blavatsky, Helen

Hahn (1831–1891), and Blavatsky's husband, Henry Steel Olcott (1832–1907). Born in London, Besant was a radical, outspoken advocate of free thought and birth control. After joining the Theosophical Society in 1889, she became an avid student of Blavatsky who taught that a universal philosophy unites all the world's religions. All the sacred texts contain an outer and an inner significance, or exoteric and esoteric meaning. Blavatsky urged her followers to devote themselves to these texts, discovering their hidden meaning so that all people might come to realize their innate divinity and union with the cosmic mind.

Theosophy's eclectic blend of Hinduism and the occult profoundly shaped the thinking of Besant. She spent most of her life in India, and took over the International Theosophical movement when Olcott died in 1907. Besant continued to spread the Society's main creed that all people should unite. Like her predecessors, Besant emphasized Eastern religion, reincarnation and karma.

In 1925, Besant claimed that an Indian mystic named Krishnamuati, whom she had adopted as her son, was the messiah and would lead the world. Despite the time, money, and effort she expended to groom Krishnamuati for such a lofty destiny, he renounced the plan in 1931. During Besant's time at the helm of the Society, her political power in India grew. She founded the Central Hindu College and the Indian Home Rule League. She also became president of the Indian National Congress. Under the pen name "Ajax," she wrote two books entitled *Ancient Wisdom* and *Esoteric Christianity,* both of which are favorite reading among New Age adherents today.

Upon Besant's death, the Society was led by George Arundale and C. Jinara Jodosa. Since then, Theosophy has experienced considerable growth in Europe and the United States.

*See also:* ESOTERIC CHRISTIANITY; ESOTERIC PHILOSOPHY; KRISHNAMUATI, JIDDU; THEOSOPHY

## BESHARA

Mystical Islamic movement founded in London in 1970 and predominantly Sufi in orientation. The group follows an esoteric regimen of meditation and study, mainly looking to the ancient Sufi writers. It claims to have no leaders. The goal of Beshara is to bring people to full and constant awareness of Allah.

*See also:* SUFISM

## BHAGAVAD GITA

A sacred Hindu devotional work. The name "Bhagavad Gita" is a Sanskrit phrase that means "Song of the Blessed One." It refers to Krishna, the eighth avatar (or incarnation) of Vishnu, the preserver god of the Hindu triad. The Bhagavad Gita is one of the classics of Hinduism and was incorporated into the Mahabharata, a Sanskrit text that was written between 200 B.C. and A.D. 200. The Mahabharata contains eighteen volumes that detail the dynastic struggle and civil war in the kingdom of Kurukshetra.

The Bhagavad Gita is contained within this epic and relates the philosophical dialogue between Lord Krishna and Prince Arjuna on the threshold of the battle of Kurukshetra. It states that Arjuna was distressed upon discovering that his kinsmen and friends were in the opposing army. Krishna tells him about the nature of spiritual wisdom and that by demonstrating selfless action, knowledge, and devotion, Arjuna can become united with Ultimate Reality. Krishna is able to persuade him to fight in the battle.

The Bhagavad Gita is one of the most revered and popular of Hindu scriptures. The document claims authority as the sacred revelation of humankind's essential nature, their environment, and their relationship with God. The Bhagavad Gita is said to possess instruction in morality superior to the ethics of all other religions. During the countercultural movement of the 1960s in the United States, the Bhagavad Gita was widely distributed on college campuses. As New Age beliefs and practices have been incorporated within the life of mainstream America, the Bhagavad Gita has achieved an even wider distribution and acceptance.

*See also:* BIBLE, NEW AGE; HARE KRISHNA

## BHAGAVAN SRI SATHYA SAI BABA (b. 1926)

An Indian Hindu mystic deemed to be divine by his followers. Satyanarayana Raju took the name Bhagavan Sri Sathya Sai Baba and is usually called Sai Baba. He claims to have paranormal powers and mainly shows them in conjuring miracles that are much like stage magic shows.

## BHAKTIVEDANTA SWAMI PRABHUPADA, A. C. (1896–1977)

The founder and leader of the Hare Krishna movement in the United States. Bhaktivedanta was born in Calcutta, India, and studied business and economics, philosophy and English at both the Vaisnava school and Scottish Church College. He became a disciple of a Hindu guru named Siddartha Goswami, who emphasized the teaching of Krishna Consciousness. One of the main features of this sect calls for chanting Krishna's name to obtain a higher state of awareness.

In 1922, Goswami initiated Bhaktivedanta into Bhakti Yoga, characterized by meditation and chanting of mantras or sacred sounds. Bhaktivedanta devoted himself to the study and propagation of a sacred Hindu text called the Bhagavad Gita. In 1944, Bhaktivedanta published a magazine entitled *Back to Godhead.* In 1950, he abandoned his wife and five children in order to devote more time to his writing and religious work. In 1959, he began work on a multivolume translation of Bhagavad Gita. He also wrote a popular New Age text, *Easy Journey to Other Planets.* In 1959, Bhaktivedanta also took the vows of Sannyasin, or Samyasin, by which he renounced all family ties, friendships, and worldly possessions to join himself to Hare Krishna, the Hindu deity of love and devotion.

In 1965, Bhaktivedanta came to the United States to teach Americans about Krishna. He soon attracted a large following of young people, many of whom were disillusioned with life and hooked on drugs. Within a short time Bhaktivedanta founded the International Society for Krishna Consciousness (ISKCON) in New York. Throughout the rest of the 1960s and into the early 1970s, the movement spread across the United States and Europe. In 1968, Bhaktivedanta established a Vedic community in West Virginia, and in 1972, he started a school in Texas. Many of his Hindu concepts have been adopted into the curriculum of American public schools under the label of "alternative teaching methods." Despite Bhaktivedanta's death in 1977, ISKCON continues to flourish among ashrams (the secluded dwellings of Hindu sages), schools, temples, and farm communities throughout the world.

*See also:* BHAGAVAD GITA, HARE KRISHNA, PEACE

## BIBLE

The collection of the sacred writings of the Old and New Testament that are officially recognized and used in Christian churches. Various other world religions have their collection of religious writings, sometimes referred to as their "bible." However from the Protestant Christian point of view, this term is restricted to the sixty-six books of the Old and New Testaments. These alone are regarded as God's inspired, infallible, and authoritative written Word.

As in many aspects of New Age teaching, a certain ambiguity enters the discussion about the Christian Bible. Many New Age advocates argue that the Bible contains numerous myths, errors, and contradictions. Yet these same advocates often cite passages from the Bible, arguing that it supports the concept of a universal, albeit impersonal God, Christ-consciousness, and the deity of humankind. New Age adherents generally view the Bible as a prime example of the psychological return of humans to the godhead, as seen in the spiritual progress of Jesus. Bible verses are often quoted out of context or run together with others in an attempt to validate New Age beliefs. Other verses are paraphrased or simply fabricated in an attempt to support unorthodox views.

Some New Age thinkers credit the Bible's inspiration to the "Holy Spirit," as defined by New Age theology. But most others hold that it was inspired by ascended masters from other spiritual dimensions who came to teach concepts from ancient mystery religions to humankind. Other parts of the Bible, such as those that speak about judgment and hell, are considered shallow and meaningless, the product of the human ego. Some New Age critics argue that the Bible was written for another time and has lost creditability in its various translations.

The most popular, and perhaps the most dangerous form of Bible manipulation, lies in esoteric interpretations advanced by different occult groups. Advocates of the New Age teach that the true meaning of the Bible can only be understood by the spiritually enlightened. They maintain that Jesus became Christ only after becoming one with the universal God-force. Supposedly humankind must enter altered states, like Jesus, in order to find the God-force deep within them, thereby attaining Christ-consciousness. Only then will the divine interpretation of the Holy Bible be revealed and understood.

While New Age thought generally downplays the significance of the Christian Bible and attacks its theology, many "gospels" and "bibles" are issued by New Age publishing houses. The writers of these documents most often claim to have received divine revelations from angels or other spirit beings during altered states of consciousness.

*See also:* BIBLE, NEW AGE; ESOTERIC CHRISTIANITY

## BIBLE BELIEVERS, INC. (BRANHAMISM)

A small antitrinitarian, millenarian Pentecostal sect, found in the southern United States. William Marion Branham's (1909–1965) healing ministry began May, 1946. Small groups meet worldwide under the name Bible Believers, Inc. There are several organizations that distribute literature and taped sermons by Branham. Branham's followers identify him as the prophetic Elijah of Malachi 4 and the seventh angel of Revelation 10. This claim lost some of its luster in 1977 when the United States was not destroyed as he had predicted.

Born in 1909 in a log cabin in Kentucky, Branham had no formal Bible education, but from age seven he claimed to experience visions from an angel, including the commission to be forerunner for the Second Coming of Christ, for which he received the gifts of healing and of the "word of knowledge." He adopted doctrinal positions of the Jesus-Only Pentecostals, a sect that denies the Trinity. Branham taught a form of modalism. Jesus is alone God, though at times in history He has been the Father, the Son, and the Holy Spirit. Proper baptism in the name of Jesus is needed to avoid the "Mark of the Beast" of denominational churches and escape the danger of missing the Rapture. The group holds other doctrines in common with the Identity Movement and the Unification Church.

*See also:* BEAST, UNIFICATION CHURCH

## BIBLE, NEW AGE

Any number of literary works describing how to usher in the Aquarian Age of personal and social transformation. Such works allegedly contain the wisdom of ascended masters who have come from the ethereal realm to aid people on their journey to divine consciousness.

Many New Age sects portray the Christian Bible as an inaccurate composition of narrow views that have imprisoned humankind for centuries. Occult leaders believe that there are many helpful guides to achieve self-awareness. Some psychics foresee the day when the enlightened, under the inspiration of spirit guides, will create a single New Age bible. This text will contain the combined learning of past generations and represent the truths and ideals common to all world religions. Such a document will be used to establish a single creed for all people. This ecumenical framework is necessary to inaugurate the coming era of peace under the leadership of the New Age messiah.

*See also: AQUARIAN CONSPIRACY, THE*

## BIOFEEDBACK

A method of learning that increases the ability to control involuntary biological responses of the body.

In the 1960s, Dr. Elmer Green of the Menninger Foundation observed the physiological functions of Hindu yogi and Zen masters while they were in trancelike states. He then used this information to develop biofeedback procedures. Eventually clinicians began using a wide variety of medical instruments such as the electroencephalograph (EEG) and the electrocardiograph (EKG) to monitor patients. Medical personnel then trained these patients to reach deepened states of consciousness so that they could regulate their autonomic nervous systems.

Sophisticated instruments, such as an oscilloscope, are used to measure physiological processes, such as heartbeats, blood pressure, or brain waves. By using the results, practitioners try to change and control these responses without the help of monitoring devices. New Age adherents claim that by entering altered states of consciousness, people can reduce stress by relaxing certain muscles, eliminate headaches by adjusting blood flow to the brain, and enable the paralyzed to walk by sending electrical signals through the spinal column. New Age adherents have applauded these developments as a step forward in human evolution.

*See also: HOLISM, TRANSCENDENTAL MEDITATION, TRANSPERSONAL PSYCHOLOGY, YOGA*

## BIORHYTHM (BIOLOGICAL RHYTHM)

An inherent cyclical pattern of biological changes within organisms connected to regularly occurring environmental changes. For example, certain flowers open and close in response to daylight. Certain nocturnal animals become active at night. Different species of birds and animals follow migratory and mating patterns at certain seasons of the year. Scientists are not exactly sure what triggers these changes in physiology and activity, but they attribute some to gravity, light, and temperature.

New Age adherents claim they can predict how people will behave and what will occur in their lives by using a biological graph of each person's numerology. A German doctor named Wilhelm Fliess first developed the biorhythmic graph to chart human potential, growth, and development. He based his graph on the theory that certain numbers contain physical, emotional, and intellectual significance. For example, starting from one's birthday, three numeric cycles are plotted onto a graph whose indicators represent high and low energy levels. When one, two, or three lines intersect the midcycle at any given point, the person supposedly experiences a critical day. Adherents claim these indicators reveal the future occurrence of such things as creativity, productivity, and emotional traumas. New Age adherents see biorhythms as one more way to control the personal destiny of the individual.

*See also: NUMEROLOGY; SCIENCE, NEW AGE*

## BLACK MAGIC

The attempt to produce harmful results, such as misfortune or death, through such methods as curses, spells, the destruction of dolls representing enemies, and alliances with evil spirits. Magicians try to compel a god, demon, or spirit to work on their behalf, using a pattern of occult practices to bend psychic forces into doing their will. Black magic is usually identified by satanic rituals, symbols, and invocations that boldly call on the demonic realms for assistance. In contrast, white magic attempts to undo curses and spells, and to use occult forces for seemingly good purposes.

Practitioners of black magic contend that all magic is demon-invoked. However others claim that magical powers are not generated from demonic realms, but from the universal forces that permeate all life. Still others assert that magic, like all occult practices, summons its powers from entities in alternate dimensions, and invokes spiritual laws to which all are subject, including God. Contemporary witches, occultists, and spiritists believe that the essence of magic lies in an interactive bond of divine cosmic energy, in which hidden realities of forgotten powers that exist in the human soul are explored.

*See also:* DEMON, OCCULTISM, SATANISM, SORCERY, VOODOO, WHITE MAGIC, WITCHCRAFT

## BLACK MUSLIMS (NATION OF ISLAM)

Black racial identification and purity movement founded loosely around Islamic theology by Wallace D. Fard (1877–1934?) in Detroit, Michigan, in the 1930s. Fard proclaimed himself the Supreme Ruler of the Universe and the black race as the founder of all civilization. He called for the destruction of both Christianity and all those with Caucasian blood lines. Fard disappeared and is presumed to have died in an organizational power struggle. Elijah Muhammad (1897–1975) took control of the movement, eventually choosing Malcolm X (1925–1965) to be his successor. However, Malcolm X broke away from the Nation of Islam in 1963 to found the Organization of Afro-American Unity. Malcolm X was killed in 1965, evidently in retaliation for his break with the organization.

Black Muslims were a radicalizing factor in the civil rights struggles of the 1960s in the United States. Beginning in the 1970s, however, leaders began to preach a return to purer Islamic theology and a community-ordered program. In general the Nation at the end of the century was heavily involved in African cultural awareness among African-Americans, including the establishment of Kwanza as a Christmas season celebration of African roots in North America. Some leaders still proclaimed antipathy toward all

caucasians, and one offshoot New Age twist looked for UFOs to come to take the black race from planet earth to a new Edenic land.

## BLACK SABBATH (BLACK MASS)

The ritual celebration of occult holidays. Black Sabbaths are held one to four times a year to worship Satan and the forces of darkness, and to desecrate symbols of Christianity. Satanist groups observe Black Sabbaths on Christmas, Easter, Thanksgiving, and/or Halloween, possibly combining groups for these occasions. More active cults also include four additional celebrations of blood rituals to commemorate the seasons. Through the sacrilegious liturgy of the Black Sabbath, members strive to renew their devotion to Satan, to attain purification, and to seek additional demonic powers. Because the ceremonies are intended as blasphemous caricatures of parallel Christian holy days, observing the calendar of occult rituals is essential to any satanic group.

The Black Mass is a parody of the Roman Catholic observance of the Eucharist. The Black Mass also incorporates rituals that appeared in the ceremonies of various ancient pagan religions. The contemporary structure of the satanic service is based primarily on rites that were first adopted during the Middle Ages by the Knights Templar and the Tanat cults. Satanic groups today have integrated the sexual rituals of the Tanats, the blood sacrifices of the Knight Templars, and other pagan practices.

The Black Mass is the focal point of satanic worship. A main feature of the ceremony is an altar which can either be an object, a person, or an animal. The altar is surrounded by occult symbols such as an inverted cross, a baphomet (an androgynous goat-headed deity with large wings), a pentagram (a figure of a five-pointed star, usually made with alternate points connected by a continuous line appearing within a circle), a chalice, and a dagger. Cult members, whether cloaked or naked, form a circle around the altar to enhance the power of the group.

Satanists vehemently deny some of the

more lurid descriptions of their rituals, and in the loosely defined movement practices vary widely. In the classic Black Mass ritual, a naked woman often serves as the initial altar of the Black Mass, and various sexual acts are performed upon her to enhance the spiritual power of the participants. The service can include the blood sacrifice of either an animal or a human being on the altar. Adherents believe that the death of the victim will release living energy into the satanic circle of worshippers. Reputedly the more intense the torture and pain experienced by the victim, the more power will be released. After performing blasphemous acts against the Christian God, participants expect to receive a greater reward from Satan. Blood and skin, urine and feces may be collected from the victim to enhance the communion ritual to follow. The sacramental wine is mixed with any number of fluids from the victim's body, and the sacramental bread is mixed with the victim's flesh.

The participants join in the demonic communion as a way of sharing in the powers of Satan. The Black Sabbath may continue from one to three days, and may end with a sexual orgy or sexual magic rituals.

*See also:* ALTAR; BAPHOMET; BLOOD SACRIFICE; GOAT OF MENDES; PENTAGRAM; *Satanic Bible, The;* SATANISM; WITCHCRAFT

## BLAVATSKY, HELENA PETROVNA (1831–1891)

A Russian spiritist medium. Born in the Ukraine, Helen Hann was twelve when her mother died. At age seventeen, she married Nikifor V. Blavatsky, who was a middle-aged Russian general. Their marriage lasted only three months. For the next quarter century (1848–1873), Blavatsky lived a promiscuous lifestyle in Paris, London, Greece, Mexico, India, and the United States. She was also addicted to hashish, represented herself as a medium of sorts, and claimed to have a spirit guide named John King.

In 1872, Blavatsky arrived in the United States where she met and married Henry Steel

Olcott (1832–1907). They established the Theosophical Society in New York in 1875. At first, their organization met with lackluster interest in America. This prompted the couple to leave the states in 1879 and move to India. In 1882, they relocated the headquarters of the Theosophical Society to Adyar, where the international branch for the movement has remained ever since. As the organization grew in popularity, Blavatsky began to travel to Europe and Great Britain. She eventually left India and settled in London where she remained for the rest of her life.

The name "Theosophy" is derived from two Greek words: *theos* and *sophia,* that mean "god" and "wisdom." Theosophy claims to teach wisdom about God. Theosophy portrays itself as the great unifier and peacemaker in religion. It embraces select teachings of various creeds, philosophies, and sciences. Blavatsky's prominent works are *Isis Unveiled* (1877), *The Secret Doctrine* (1888), and *Key to Theosophy* (1889). She wrote that a universal philosophy unites all the world's religions.

The occult ideas advocated by Blavatsky are almost universally endorsed by New Age adherents. They practice trance channeling spirits and achieving altered states of consciousness to become one with the universal spirit. Blavatsky's writings and teachings had a profound impact on such people as Annie Besant (1847–1933), Alice Bailey (1880–1949), and Adolf Hitler (1889–1945). Hitler was an avid fan of *The Secret Doctrine*, from which he extracted the Aryan race theory along with an intense hatred of Christianity.

*See also:* ARYAN RACE; BESANT, ANNIE WOOD; LUCIFERIC DOCTRINE; *Secret Doctrine, The;* THEOSOPHY

## BLOOD OF CHRIST

In Orthodox Christianity, the death of Jesus on the Cross paid the penalty for the sins of humankind (John 19:24–27; 1 John 2:2). New Age adherents reject this concept presented in Scripture. They make a distinction between the man Jesus and a state of Christ-consciousness achieved by Jesus and all the enlightened. Adherents teach that the blood of Christ is a life-giving force inherent in all people, enabling them to realize the full potential of their godhood. They assert that by using psychic means to tap into the cosmic flow of Christ's blood, people can recognize their divine self and achieve oneness with universal reality.

*See also:* ATONEMENT, CRUCIFIXION, SALVATION, SIN

## BLOOD PACT

The surrender of the soul to the service of Satan by signing a contract in blood, the life-giving force. Satanic cults promise initiates physical fulfillment, amazing mental powers, and membership in the fraternity of the Devil. Over a period of time, the standard methods of indoctrination, such as ingesting hallucinogenic drugs, and sensory deprivation begin to alter the thoughts and actions of initiates. During an official ceremony, participants denounce the existence and power of Christ. To symbolize the surrender of their life to Satan, new devotees use their own blood to sign a pact with the Devil.

These followers learn that self alone stands as the ultimate authority, that they have the ability to alter reality, and that they can invoke spiritual entities from astral realms of existence. Their indoctrination presents Christianity, Christians, and the Bible as the chief obstacles that prevent humankind from achieving its fullest potential.

*See also:* SATANISM

## BLOOD SACRIFICE

The practice of torturing, murdering, and/or eating an animal or human being during an occult ritual to release living energy into the circle of worshipers. The more intense the torture and pain experienced by the victim, the more powerful are thought to be the forces released. It is also believe that the participants will receive a greater reward from Satan. Remains of the victim are sometimes converted into magical powders, medicine, jewelry, or even sacramental food. Both ancient and modern satanic cults have asserted that the gods and goddesses require the continual spilling of sacrificial blood to maintain stability in the universe. Rituals are carried out to attain psychic powers, send messages to the dead and receive answers back, exact revenge on enemies, and obtain protection.

Occult leaders claim that blood is the all-powerful source of life-energy, the bioelectric vibrational force that feeds the earth, and maintains the natural balance of universal energies. The cruelest practices of ancient pagan societies have found a respectful following among New Age adherents. For example, some occult groups are enthralled by the channeled spirits of Mayan warriors, as well as Aztec art depicting the altars on which innocent blood was shed. Other groups have adopted the ancient pagan idea of sacrificial blood providing the only means for meeting material and spiritual needs, as well as bringing harmony with the universe.

*See also:* ALTAR, AZTEC CULTURE, DRUIDS, SATANISM, VAMPIRE

## BODHISATTVA

In Buddhism, those who attain enlightenment, but refuse to enter nirvana in order to guide the unenlightened to absolute blessedness. The bodhisattvas claim the physical world is an illusion from which they have escaped. By experiencing numerous deaths and rebirths, they have overcome attachment to the self and ignorance about Ultimate Reality. Out of compassion for the unenlightened masses, the bodhisattvas remain on earth as avatars. They work to relieve suffering and guide others down the path of salvation.

Adherents reflect this thinking in teaching about the New Age christ. Jesus was not the Christ at birth, but rather a pious man who attained christhood by following the path of enlightenment set forth in Buddhist tradition. Like other great bodhisattvas, Jesus refrained from entering final nirvana. Instead, He chose to remain in this world to help others achieve union with cosmic consciousness.

*See also:* AVATAR, BUDDHISM, COSMIC CONSCIOUSNESS, ENLIGHTENMENT

# BODYWORK

Holistic healing techniques based on the premise that the mind, body, and spirit are an interconnected triad. Bodywork practitioners teach that illness and pain should be diagnosed and treated as a comprehensive "whole." They also believe this discomfort is an accumulation of unbalanced energy that is easily corrected by realigning the vibrational forces of the mind, body, and spirit. Practitioners teach that psychic powers can be translated into physiological change by entering an altered state of consciousness that supposedly releases the universal life force permeating human existence. New Age adherents claim that bodywork exercises lead to the acquisition of unlimited psychic powers, agelessness, and spiritual fulfillment. However, patients treated through these techniques repeatedly report encounters with demonic oppression, terrifying physical manifestations, and insanity.

*See also:* COSMIC ENERGY, HOLISM, VIBRATIONS, YOGA

# BOOK OF CHANGES, The
*See: I Ching*

# BOOK OF Mormon, The
*See: Mormon, The Book of*

# BOOK OF SHADOWS, THE
*See:* SHADOWS, THE BOOK OF

# BRAHMA (BRAHMAN)

The Hindu creator. With Vishnu and Shiva, Brahma is the father figure of a Hindu trinity. Vishnu is a more minor deity but the one most worshiped, because his role is to preserve the earth. Shiva is the destroyer, remaker, and purifier.

The earliest writings connected with Brahma worship come from before 500 B.C. The main temples are in India at Rajputana and near Mount Abu. Idols and reliefs usually show Brahma with four heads, facing the four compass points, and with four hands. He is said to be the source of the Vedas. Brahma came into being from the side of the life force and he is the essence of all living things. Hindus believe change constitutes illusion, so they consider Brahma to be the only true reality. Because of its perfection, he is impersonal and cannot be approached by people, who do change. Brahma also is the Creator of all things. Because creation is complete, there is no need to worship this god. Hindu worship tends to be pragmatic, with goals of appeasement and manipulation. For this reason, Judeo-Christian and Islamic monotheism's worship of a Brama-type god has seemed illogical to the Hindu.

While powerful, Brahma is not highly regarded. Creation of the living world arose from an act of incest with his daughter Vach. He is said to have a consort, the goddess of wisdom, Sarasvati, but also a mistress, Gayatri. He is thought to be drunk much of the time. It is Brahma who with Shiva destroys and recreates the universe every 4,320,000 years. Shiva more than Brahma will play a prominent role in the purification process of the great new age, according to New Age thought.

The gods, especially Vishnu manifest themselves on earth from time to time in human form. These "avatars" account for the special holiness in people such as Jesus and some of the greater gurus. Some Hindu believe that Vishnu and Shiva are themselves avatars of Brahma, which would make a triune three-in-one god of sorts. The concept of avatars is not recorded until the sixth century A.D., when Christian teachings had been in India for centuries.

*See also:* CREATION, GOD, HINDUISM, SHIVA, VISHNU

# BRAIN DRIVE

Mechanical paraphernalia used to expand brain activity and enhance the creativity, intelligence, and powers of the mind. By regulating electrical stimulation to the brain, people can supposedly leave the tension-filled Beta state of normal consciousness and exist in the Alpha state of altered consciousness. New Age adherents claim that these devices can increase the subconscious awareness level of people, thereby intensifying their psychic potential, mental dexterity, and natural instincts. They promise initiates that once they achieve an altered state of consciousness, they will feel extreme peace and relaxation, enjoy an out-of-body sensation, and gain personal insight. Some zealous enthusiasts claim brain drive devices exercise the cranium, increase its size, and create new cerebral cells.

Practitioners seek a state of "whole brain integration" by entering a trancelike state. Occult leaders urge their followers to use meditative practices and hallucinogenic drugs to journey to the astral realm, tap into the cosmic consciousness, and obtain the wisdom of ascended masters. They encourage devotees to set aside their logical thinking processes, and let their psychic intuition take control of them. New Age adherents purport that this is the only way they can perceive what is real, recognize their divine self, and attain enlightenment. They claim that successful brain drive experimentation will result in a superrace of whole-brain individuals whose evolutionary leap into the New Age will secure the survival of humankind.

*See also:* ALTERED STATE, BIOFEEDBACK, WHOLE BRAIN THINKING

## BRANHAMISM
*See:* BIBLE BELIEVERS, INC.

## BRITISH ISRAELISM
A racial purity belief that the Anglo-Saxon peoples that predominate in the United Kingdom, and to some extent Canada and the United States, are the remnant of the ten lost tribes of Israel and so are directly referred to in Revelation prophecies about the twelve tribes. The view has been most influential through the work of Herbert W. Armstrong and his Worldwide Church of God and the nationally distributed *Plain Truth* magazine. The Worldwide Church of God has now distanced itself from the doctrine. In the prophecy reading of "British Israelism," the tribe of Ephraim becomes Great Britain, Manasseh is the United States, and the throne of David is the throne of England. British Israelism claims that the stone under England's coronation chair in Westminster Abbey is the "pillar stone of Jacob" that was transported by Jacob, and finally by Jeremiah to the British Isles. Doubt was cast upon this doctrine when the stone was analyzed and found to be sandstone from Scotland.

## BUDDHA
*See:* BUDDHISM; GAUTAMA, SIDDHARTHA

## BUDDHISM
An Eastern religion founded by Siddhartha Gautama (563–483 B.C.). Gautama was born into the warrior caste of a tribe in northeastern India (part of modern-day Nepal). His father was a wealthy rajah, or ruler. According to folklore, Siddhartha's father dreamed of the day his son would succeed him, becoming a great king. To encourage Siddhartha to this end, his father shielded him from all that was ugly and painful and surrounded him with great wealth and pleasures. But one day Siddhartha decided to leave the confines of the palace and see the world. During his journey, he saw four kinds of suffering (old age, sickness, death, and poverty), and he grew disillusioned with wealth and political power.

Tradition says that at the age of twenty-nine, Siddhartha renounced the future his father had planned for him. Siddhartha's encounter with suffering convinced him to leave his home, wife, and child in search of enlightenment. The former prince was reduced to begging and roamed from place to place in search of the source of suffering and how to eliminate it. Siddhartha eventually came to a town called Bodh Gaya, and sat under a fig tree along the bank of a river for seven days. He then went into a deep state of meditation, resisted the temptations of Mara, or evil one, and attained nirvana, the highest state of god-consciousness. He emerged from the experience as Buddha, or the enlightened one. He vowed to devote the rest of his life to the spread of truths he learned while under the bodhi (bo tree), or tree of wisdom. Today Buddhists consider the Bodh Gaya as the most sacred of their shrines.

By the time of Buddha's death, his converts numbered in the thousands and lived in communities called Sanghas. As Buddhism spread from its base in northern India, many individual sects began to appear, such as the Theraveda (Way of Elders) and Hinayana (Lesser Vehicles). One of the most popular sects is Mahayana (Great Vehicle) that developed in East Asia. The Mahayanans instituted the belief in many reincarnated buddhas. This group also introduced gurus, mantras, and visualization techniques to the Americas.

Buddha taught that the Middle Way is the path to enlightenment. He conjectured that suffering in life was caused by two different extremes—affluence and asceticism. Supposedly the way to eliminate anguish and hardship and to attain enlightenment was to avoid luxury at one extreme and self-torture at the other. This spiritual teacher declared that those who held to this philosophy would gain insight, acquire knowledge, experience calm, and eventually reach a state of absolute blessedness, or nirvana.

Buddha emphasized Four Noble Truths. The first says that suffering exists everywhere, and that no one can deny the pain associated with disease and old age. The second noble truth states that suffering is caused by excessive longing for things, such as happiness and prosperity that are temporary and ever-changing. The third noble truth expresses that the way to eliminate suffering is to renounce the craving for things that are temporary—completely extinguishing the presence of all passion and desire for such things. The fourth noble truth suggests that following the Eightfold Path will end all pain.

The first of the Eightfold Path teaches followers to cultivate *Right Views* by accepting the Four Noble Truths and the Eightfold Path. Second, develop *Right Resolve* by renounc-

ing pleasure, harboring no animosity toward others, and refusing to harm any living creature. Third, cultivate *Right Speech* by refusing to lie, slander, or participate in idle conversation. Fourth, practice *Right Behavior* by not committing any unlawful sexual act, not stealing from others, and not destroying any living creature. Fifth, engage in *Right Occupation* by earning a living in a way that brings no harm to others. Sixth, practice *Right Effort* by abandoning all evil qualities and cultivating good qualities in life. Seventh, employ *Right Contemplation* by becoming freed from all desire and sorrow, and by remaining alert and observant. Eighth, exercise *Right Meditation* by entering into heightened states of awareness through concentration exercises.

Buddha taught that each step included others. He viewed them as dispositions and actions fulfilled simultaneously and concurrently, not consecutively. Buddha also declared that right understanding leads to right thought, and that both of these lay the foundation for wisdom *(Panna)*. This leads to right speech, action, and livelihood, and these form the foundation for proper ethical conduct *(Sila)*. Finally, right effort, awareness, and meditation round out the equation for mental discipline *(Samadhi)*.

The goal in Buddhism is to attain freedom from the cycle of death and rebirth *(Samsara)*. *Samadhi,* or entering a deep state of consciousness, is supposedly crucial in this process. Through regular meditative exercises, adherents allegedly can prevent evil thoughts from entering their minds, gain awareness of all the events occurring in their lives, and eventually attain the bliss of enlightenment. Buddhism bases this teaching on the understanding that the universe is temporary and illusory. Enlightenment comes when devotees release themselves from the realm of illusion. This leads to a release from the endless cycles of reincarnation and the extinction of individual consciousness.

Buddhists consider God as an impersonal and abstract Void, not a personal, transcendent, and immanent being. They claim that Jesus was an enlightened spiritual Master, like Buddha. Buddhism teaches that people are a collection of impermanent entities in the process of achieving enlightenment. They define sin *(tanha)* as the desire for that which is temporary. This causes people to remain under the illusion that their individual self exists. Deliverance lies in eliminating all desire for that which is impermanent. Permanence comes when people realize the nonexistence of the self. Buddhism also teaches that people should cultivate their ethical character by following the Middle Way, the Four Noble Truths, and the Eightfold Path. The result is that people will enter nirvana, where the self is extinguished.

Mahayana Buddhists also teach the doctrine of bodhisattvas. This refers to those who have attained enlightenment, but refuse to enter nirvana in order to guide the unenlightened to a state of absolute blessedness. The bodhisattvas claim that the physical world is an illusion from which they have escaped. They also claim to have overcome attachment to the self and ignorance about Ultimate Reality by experiencing numerous deaths and rebirths. Out of compassion for the unenlightened masses, the bodhisattvas remain on earth as avatars. They work to relieve suffering and guide others down the path of salvation, as defined by these precepts.

Buddhists call their sacred scriptures the *Tripitaka,* or *Three Baskets. The Basket of Disciplines* contains rules and regulations for Buddhist monks, while *The Basket of Discourse* mostly presents sermons for study and memorization. *The Basket of Higher Dharma* sets forth additional Buddhist doctrine that was developed later. *Dharma,* or moral law, and *Tripitaka* were brought together in Sangha, the ideal Buddhist community, inhabited by the spiritually advanced. Life in this commune includes the worship of Buddha, the study of *dharma,* and the practice of meditative techniques. Practitioners who follow their prescribed religious and ethical duties will earn merit toward higher rebirths, thus escaping the laws of karma.

*See also:* BODHISATTVA; DALAI LAMA; DHARMA; GAUTAMA, SIDDHARTHA; KARMA; MIDDLE WAY; NIRVANA; ZEN BUDDHISM

## CABALA (CABBALA)
*See:* KABBALAH

## CAMPBELL, JOSEPH (1904–1987)

A prolific author and lecturer, Campbell was one of the most influential minds behind the New Age relativism of the late twentieth century and the concept of "political correctness." His works were required reading in most college and university religion, literature, and philosophy courses and in New Age, neopagan and Gaea environmentalism circles.

Joseph Campbell's studies dealt with the meaning of "myth," from which he removed any discussion of truth and falsehood. He discovered some of the same motifs in mythology, whether of Native Americans or ancient Anglo-Saxon or Greek. Campbell limits the concept of myth to the symbolic level, making all religions, including Christianity, purely subjective, separating myth from notions of historical truth. He was warmly sympathetic toward any nonabsolute religious view but remained vehemently opposed to Christianity and other groups proclaiming an absolute reality and a transcendent view of truth.

Campbell's own religion was a pantheistic, subjectivist view of religious experience. He taught that consciousness and energy are the same thing. The "vegetable world" is conscious. Modern humanity's responsibility is to get back into accord with the wisdom of nature and realize brotherhood with the animal and oceanic worlds. God as a world entity is unknowable and unknown.

Campbell's theology of impersonal pantheism permeated culture through students who attended his popular classes at Sarah Lawrence College in Bronxville, New York. Such students as George Lucas and Steven Spielberg portrayed Campbell's thought through the "Star Wars" films.

Campbell's views extended to a doctrine of "absolute relativism," which stated with full understanding of its own internal illogic that anyone who believes in only one ultimate truth, or in only one way to God, is automatically narrow-minded and wrong. Only Campbell's own statements were allowed to bypass that criterion of reality.

Campbell sometimes personifies nature and the earth as a divine, conscious organism from whom everything evolves. "We are the fruits of an intelligent earth," says Campbell. Paradise exists in the here and now, and mankind already lives in a magnificent garden. The key to enjoying this garden is to rise above the suffering world by becoming one with the God within. This ecology myth excited Campbell so much that he often mentions it as the one myth that modern society should wholeheartedly embrace.

*See also:* NEW AGE MOVEMENT

## CANDLE

A source of fire that gives light, heat, or scents in religious ritual. In some pagan religions, the candle was linked to purification and preservation of the soul, as well as the illumination of the divine qualities believed to exist within all people. In other pagan religions, devotees honored the Earth Mother goddess as the "Mother of Light." They viewed God as a pervading life force energy. The candle symbolized the psychic nature of humankind, while the flame represented the glory of the divine spirit. Some contemporary pagans celebrate an annual candle service in tribute to the goddess of fire, inspired by the belief that the earth's energies will bring them gifts throughout the year. Satanist and witchcraft groups regard the candle as a primary power object, symbolizing the light of truth present in the human soul.

Adherents view candle magic as one of the most effective forms of sympathetic sorcery. This involves casting a spell or curse on an object representing a person or entity to bring about the desired results. Some witches claim that the occult use of candles enables them to tap into the unlimited resources of universal energies by activating supernatural powers within the psyche. They use the particular shapes, colors, and aromas of candles to produce a corresponding magical response. They use a green candle to produce money, a red candle to engender love.

Some New Age adherents practice candle gazing. They believe energy will produce enlightenment by reverberating into the "third eye." They consider this "eye," that allegedly exists on the center of the forehead, to serve as the center of their spiritual vision. Candles also play a prominent role in satanic rituals and adorn the sacrificial altar. These candles are usually black, are often carried during the ceremony, and are sometimes used to light ritual fires for blood sacrifice. By placing a candle in the hand of the sacrificial victim, Satanists believe they ward off evil spirits.

*See also:* ALTAR, COLOROLOGY, GODDESS WORSHIP, POWER OBJECT, SATANISM, SYMPATHETIC MAGIC

## CANON

From the Greek *kanon,* referring to a carpenter's measuring stick. *Kanon* may also be related to the Hebrew *qaneh,* meaning a "reed" or measuring rod. Over time *kanon* came to mean a rule or standard of faith, then an accepted list or catalogue, and finally a collection of sacred texts. In orthodox Christianity the canon of Scripture is the sixty-six books accepted by leaders of the early church and deemed supernatural in origin. They set the standard rule of faith and practice for all Christians. Most, if not all, contemporary religions and New Age cults have their own collection of writings regarded as divinely inspired, authoritative, and normative.

*See also:* APOCRYPHA, BIBLE

## CAPRA, FRITJOF (b. 1939)

A university physicist and a New Age mystic. In his most famous work entitled *The Tao of Physics,* Fritjof Capra held that the monistic ideology of ancient mysticism was similar in many ways to that of modern physics. This idea came to him in 1969 while in a drug-induced meditative state on a California beach. As Capra focused his thoughts on the rhythm of the waves against the shore, he claims that the entire world around him exploded into a cosmic dance of universal elements. He claims to have seen and heard elemental atoms interacting with those of his own body. He also reported seeing cosmic energy rain down from outer space, in which particles were continually created and destroyed in rhythmic surges. Capra said that the "oneness" he felt with the Universal Mind permanently changed the way he thought about life. He believed it was now his responsibility to bring about a fundamental change in society's worldview. He said that the philosophical, cultural, and spiritual implications of research that united physics and mysticism would create a paradigm shift in humankind's thinking and bring about a quantum leap in their evolutionary development.

Most scientists say there are few, if any, similarities between modern physics and ancient mysticism. They note that mystics generally deny the reality of anything outside of the mind, whereas physicists maintain that the external world is a real part of existence. Also, physicists tend to underscore the importance of empirical, objective data before coming to any conclusions, whereas mystics stress conjectural, subjective impressions to formulate opinions about life. Despite these significant differences, Capra has gained a substantial following among New Age adherents.

*See also:* KUHN, THOMAS; MYSTICISM; SCIENCE, NEW AGE

## CARGO CULT

A peculiar twentieth century form of animism that is centered in the Melanesian Islands northeast of Australia (though not exclusively). Cargo cults led by prophets claiming a new revelation first appeared in the late Nineteenth century. They captured world attention when they contributed to a revolt in New Guinea in 1919. They proliferated as industrialization began reaching the islands in the 1930s and the islanders were exposed to the outside world suddenly in the Pacific theater of World War II.

Adherents believe that a new age of blessing has been initiated by the tribal divinities. This "cargo" of blessings can be observed in the material blessings that foreigners bring to the islands. Sometimes the military and colonial transports of these cargo blessings are considered to be helping the gods. Sometimes the foreigners are accused of interfering with the shipments of blessings that the gods have intended for the native people. In areas where beliefs are strong, the construction of port facilities and warehouses can bring life on the island to a standstill. People stop working in expectation of the arrival of blessings. Tribal customs and worship to ancestral gods intensify. New social practices that imitate what the islanders know of the foreigners' customs may be introduced. Because of the potential economic loss that can result, governments have repressed cargo cults. On the other hand, they have often been unintentionally encouraged by missionaries who speak of the coming millennium.

# CARTOMANCY

The divination of the secrets of humankind and the universe through the archetypal images printed on tarot cards. This set of seventy-eight playing cards, including the twenty-two picture cards, is used in fortune telling and as a trump in tarot games. Some New Age adherents claim the cards represent the universal elements of life. Supposedly when the tarot are dealt out to players, the different combinations of cards are open to interpretation and manipulation. Occultists maintain that the tarot serve as a psychic point of contact between participants and the astral realm. Allegedly the cards have the ability to awaken extrasensory powers of perception so that Ultimate Reality might be controlled, extraterrestrials might be contacted, and lost civilizations, such as Atlantis, might be revisited.

*See also:* DIVINATION, OCCULTISM, SPIRITISM, TAROT CARDS

# CASTANEDA, CARLOS (b. 1925)

An American anthropologist, New Age channeler, and best-selling author. Castaneda claims to have served as a sorcerer's apprentice to Don Juan, the spirit of a Yaqui Indian warrior. Supposedly Don Juan taught Castaneda that the "warrior" must be versed in the occult arts in order to deal with the dangers of the spirit world. Castaneda says that under the entity's tutorage, he explored parallel dimensions of space and time. He states that he used a variety of hallucinogenic drugs to transcend reality, come in contact with spirit guides, and receive esoteric wisdom. He maintains that such psychic experiences flourished long before the Europeans came to America.

Castaneda's objectivity and credibility as an anthropologist was widely questioned when he adopted shamanistic beliefs and practices. Nevertheless, he has written a number of books popular among New Age adherents. These titles include *The Teachings of Don Juan: A Yaqui Way of Knowledge* (1968), *Journey to Ixtlan* (1972), *The Fire Within* (1984), and *The Power of Silence* (1987). A common mystical theme in these books is that people keep each other in bondage by demanding adherence to traditional thoughts and actions. Although Castaneda offers freedom to those who follow his philosophy, he warns that the cost is high. The best-selling author avoids publicity and is rarely seen in public.

*See also:* ALTERED STATE, PEYOTE, SHAMAN, SPIRIT GUIDES, SPIRITISM

# CASTE SYSTEM

A hereditary order of social classes within Hindu society. There is a hierarchy of five castes or *jatis,* and each is separated from the others by restrictions placed on occupation, marriage, religious practice, and tribal affiliation. These five social classes include the Brahmans (priests and scholars), the Kshatriyas (warriors and rulers), the Vaishyas (farmers and merchants), the Sudras (peasants and laborers), and the Hariyan (untouchables or outcasts who perform the lowliest of tasks).

Hinduism teaches that as a result of Karmic laws, every person is born into a particular station in life. Those who are members of a lower caste allegedly committed horrible crimes in a former life. The widespread fear of violating karmic law prevents members of the lower castes from moving upward in the social classes. And the lack of interaction between people in different castes has perpetuated the hunger, poverty, and misery suffered by those in the lowest rungs of Indian society.

*See also:* BUDDHISM, HINDUISM, KARMA, REINCARNATION

## CAULDRON

A Wiccan symbol drawn from Celtic mythology. In Celtic belief, cauldrons represented the Irish god Dagda and the Welsh goddess Cerridwen. Dagda's cauldron provided sustenance in time of need and possessed powers of rejuvination. Cerridwen's cauldron represented the source of artistic inspiration. Because of the significance, cauldrons have always been a part of Druid religion and witchcraft.

## CAYCE, EDGAR (1877–1945)

A clairvoyant, psychic healer, sometime photographer, and founder of the Association for Research and Enlightenment (ARE). Cayce was born near Hopkinsville, Kentucky, and showed an interest in spiritual things at an early age. As a child, Cayce heard many stories about the psychic abilities of his grandfather, and reported seeing him many times after his death. At the age of eight, Cayce allegedly was visited by an entity. When he was thirteen another entity promised to grant him what he desired most. The young boy supposedly said he wanted to be able to help others, especially ailing children.

Despite his diligence in reading, Cayce was initially a poor student who could not even spell simple words. The story is that Cayce fell asleep on his spelling book following one of these visions. When he awoke, he knew all the material in the text. He then began to pray regularly to the entity, and soon he was at the top of his class. Cayce's first reported psychic healing occurred when he was fifteen. He remembered being struck at the base of his spine with a baseball. He claimed that while he was in bed, he accurately diagnosed his problem and prescribed the solution.

Cayce asserted that these sorts of experiences were evidence of his ability to diagnose illnesses, read past lives, predict future events, and speak numerous foreign languages fluently while in an altered state of consciousness. He maintained that when he was in a trancelike sleep, he received supernatural revelations. For this reason, he has been called "the sleeping prophet."

In 1923, Cayce met Arthur Lammers, a Dayton, Ohio, printer. Lammers introduced him to the teachings of the occult, Theosophy, and other Eastern philosophies. This led Cayce to mix such pagan beliefs as reincarnation and the laws of karma with Christian concepts. In 1931, he founded the Association for Research and Enlightenment to preserve his teachings and make them available to others. The organization incorporates occult practices into its psychic research. Its national headquarters is in Virginia Beach, Virginia.

The god of Cayce is an impersonal spirit and creative energy that exists everywhere. This god is both masculine and feminine in essence. As people set goals, devise plans, and then bring goals to fruition, they are expressing the god-force within them. Cayce taught that Christ was the reincarnation of four previous well-known individuals from history—Adam, Melchizedek, Joshua, and Zen (an early leader of Zoroastrianism). He also maintained that Christ was one of the world's great avatars, an incarnation of the deity appointed for a certain epoch. Other avatars include Buddha, Muhammad, and Krishna.

Cayce believed that the spirit of Christ is present throughout every age and exists to lead spiritual truth seekers to enlightenment. By entering a trancelike state, people can gain access to the light of the Christ spirit, unleash the god-force within them, and be rejoined to the divine universal presence.

*See also:* ATLANTIS, LOST CONTINENT OF; DREAM; PSYCHIC; REINCARNATION; RESEARCH AND ENLIGHTENMENT, ASSOCIATION FOR

## CELTIC PAGANISM

A revival religion that tries, through research and some creative interpretation of literature and symbols, to recreate the ancient Northern European spiritism and polytheism. The Celtic tradition has influenced New Age beliefs, but true Celtic pagans draw careful distinctions. Because so little is known about actual Druidic and Celtic religion as practiced in ancient times, modern Celtic groups vary among themselves in their beliefs.

Although there is considerable disagreement over what comprises Celtic religion, there are three popular modern forms of Celtic paganism: Celtic Wicca, Witta, and Celtic Druidism. Purists scoff at these groups, however, and call themselves Druidic, Welsh, Scottish, and Irish Celtic Reconstructionalists. In general the beliefs center around the Celtic "Three Realms" of sky, land, and sea and honor a number of pre-Christian Celtic deities. They follow the traditional Celtic Calendar, with its four "Fire Festivals," Samhain, Imbolc, Beltaine, and Lœnassadh. As spiritualists, Celtic pagans try to connect or channel with ancestor and land spirits, that make them avid environmentalists. They have a passion for genealogical research and archaeological study of ancient cultures.

The Celtic moral code stresses truthfulness, honor, and personal responsibility. There is a strong bent toward feminism. Modern Celtic Pagans do not use ceremonial magic or traditions influenced by it, such as those used in Wicca. Rituals focus on connecting with the spirits and world forces to create a sacred space. Dancing, singing, drumming, and meditation are parts of the Celtic pagan ritual. Many pagans today combine religious traditions from a variety of sources to form an individual religious expression. Celtic pagans, however, demand a more disciplined and culturally pure worship.

A triskele is a rounded spiral with three arms radiating from a central point, turning counter-clockwise and representing the three realms of sky, sea, and land in Celtic religion. The triskele or triad is a frequent theme of New Age beliefs most frequently drawn from ancient Northern European origins.

*See also:* BELTAINE, WICCA, WITCHCRAFT

## CENTER

The physical, emotional, psychic, and spiritual home of the human body. New Age adherents claim that the center is the essence of human s existence. Witches describe the center as the convergence point for energy, time, and light. Occult leaders maintain that the center is the source of unlimited psychic powers, a calm, comfortable place where people can enjoy an intimate encounter with the Cosmic Consciousness, accessed by entering a trancelike state. This reputedly enables people to experience reality from a new perspective. They learn about their innate divinity and oneness with Ultimate Reality. They also discover how to tap into repressed abilities of the mind, body, and spirit.

"Centering" exercises comprise a fundamental part of the New Age educational process, allegedly creating the ideal conditioning environment for teaching occult ideas and practices. Children are taught through relaxation and breathing techniques, as well as chanting and imaging routines, to reach their "center." They are then encouraged to create a detailed image of their "center," a safe place where they can retreat in times of confusion, depression, or anger. They are also encouraged to seek out a personal spiritual guide in the center. These entities might claim to be the higher or inner self, or they might be manifestations of the subconscious. The children are taught to allow the spirit guide to remain their constant companion who answers all of life's questions.

*See also:* CIRCLE, GUIDED IMAGERY, HIGHER SELF, SPIRIT GUIDES, TRANSFORMATION, UNIVERSAL MIND

## CERNUNNOS (HORNED GOD)

A popular Neo-Druidic symbol, originally representing a Pictish deity. The Celtic Cernunnos has stag antlers instead of some of such other variations as goat or bull horns. The stag antlers can be seen as tree branches, and therefore can represent fertility. Some of the earliest carved symbols in the British Isles are of this stag-antlered god.

## CHAKRA

According to yoga philosophy, any of the seven centers of psychic energy in the human

**Chakras—seven mystic energy points**

body. These energy points are supposedly located in ascending order along the human spine. The first chakra is at the base of the spine and referred to as *Muladhara,* or "Root Support." It represents the earth and house of the sleeping Kundalini, the cosmic life force of the goddess Shakti. This force lies coiled at the base of the spine until activated and then transmits stimulation to the brain for the enlightenment process. The practice of Hindu yogic exercises arouses this dormant energy, enabling people to tap into the powers of the inner self.

The second chakra lies in the genital area and is called *Svadhisthana,* or "Her Special Abode." This represents water, as well as the core of all sexual desire. The third chakra, *Manipura* or "City of the Shining Jewel," is in the area of the navel and represents fire and sacrificial rituals. The fourth chakra is located at the heart and represents air. This is called *Anahata* and refers to the mantra, or sacred sound "om." This mantra contains all the primal vibrations of the universe.

The fifth chakra is located at the larynx and called *Vishuddha,* or "Gateway of the Great Liberation." It represents the Logos, or spiritual insight and intelligence of Lucifer. The sixth chakra is called *Ajna,* or "Command Kundalini." It activates the Logos at the third eye, or center of psychic vision. The seventh chakra is at the crown of the head and extends upward into infinity. This is called *Sahasrara,* or "Thousand Petaled Lotus of Light."

Once Kundalini is awakened, it uncoils upward through the other chakras of human energy. As Kundalini moves up along the spine, the last three chakras leave the material realm and release spiritual knowledge. The yogic life force then moves through energy channels wound in a double spiral on either side of the human spine. As Kundalini progresses upward, energy is released until the last chakra is reached. Here Shakti and Shiva, the Hindu gods of destruction and regeneration, join in psychosexual union. The devotee then experiences enlightenment and is separated from Brahman, the Hindu three-in-one God, by only a thin veil. This goal of achieving enlightenment remains a fundamental aim of the New Age Movement.

*See also:* COSMIC ENERGY, ENLIGHTENMENT, HINDUISM, KUNDALINI, PSYCHIC, SHIVA, TANTRA

## CHALICE

A drinking cup or goblet used for ceremonial purposes by various religious groups. Some New Age adherents say the chalice represents invisible psychic forces. It helps people to channel their mental powers and establish contact with entities from the astral plane. Others maintain that the chalice is a receptacle of life-giving blood that can ensure youthfulness, heal the infirm, and intensify magical powers. Satanic cults use the chalice as part of their Black Mass, a parody of the Roman Catholic observance of the Eucharist. Witchcraft cults say the chalice is a receptacle of water that they regard as the mother element of life and joy. Some occult leaders claim the chalice symbolizes the immortal principle through which people can ascend to incorruptible perfection. Part of this process reputedly includes leaving behind the lower self and achieving an enlightened awareness of the higher, or divine, self within.

See also: ALTAR, POWER OBJECT, SYMBOLISM

## CHANT

As a verb, to recite a sound, word, or phrase in a monotonous repetitive tone. As a noun, an occasion at which devotees seek enlightenment by chanting together. Chants are recited to achieve an altered state of consciousness, establish contact with entities from the astral plane, and awaken the innate divinity that reputedly exists within every person. The chant may take the form of a long poetic piece, short drawn out words, or mystical syllables. One or many people might recite the chant. Sometimes a leader will start the chant, and the group will continue or finish it. An entire piece may also be recited by the leader, backed by the low chant of other voices.

One of the largest chants ever recorded was at the Harmonic Convergence in August of 1987. This global peace meditation took place at sacred sites around the world. The purpose was to draw together a critical mass of rainbow warriors, an army made up of New Age groups, organizations, and individuals. The resulting Harmonic Convergence launched a five-year world plan for moving people toward globalization and the transformation of humanity that necessarily precedes the dawning of the Aquarian Age of peace.

See also: CRITICAL MASS, HARMONIC CONVERGENCE, MANTRA, VIBRATIONS

## CHARM

An occult object or incantation used to protect against harm or to promote good fortune. The charm gives users the power to cast spells, induce magical healings, as well as to summon demons and evil spirits.

Contemporary goddess cults use charms during sacred rituals to assure the presence of a particular evil spirit. During this pagan ceremony, they summon the powers of darkness to project an image on the charm. Then the object is passed through breath, smoke, water, and salt, which represent four various aspects of earth deities.

See also: AMULET, MAGIC, POWER OBJECT, TALISMAN, WITCHCRAFT

## CHEN TAO (GOD'S SALVATION CHURCH)

An apocalyptic Buddhist cult, based mainly in the United States. Hon-ming Chen (b. 1955) founded Chen Tao in 1993 in Pei-pu, Taiwan. He claimed to have learned in a vision that Pei-pu is the only spot on earth where "the inexhaustible light of the Grand Way" flows from heaven. Further messages from heaven told of new sources of energy as about 140 members of the group were directed to Southern California in 1995. They moved to Garland, Texas, in 1997 and to Lockport, New York, in 1999, though most followers had abandoned the group by then and returned to Taiwan. Media reports in 1998 alleged that members had paid large sums of money to join the cult and travel to the United States. It was also charged that the group was bound by a mass suicide pact. Chen and his followers have emphatically denied that suicide is an option should their prophecies fail. They missed two 1990s deadlines without incident, March 25, 1998, when God was to take over channel 18 television broadcasts around the world, and April 22, 1999, the date for a great tribulation when war and devils would strike down millions.

The tenets of Chen Tao draw on Buddhism, Taoism, and Taiwanese folk religion, as well as UFOlogy and a millenarian worldview. Chen Tao eschatology describes an ancient earth on which four civilizations have been destroyed by nuclear annihilation, and predicts a fifth early in the twenty-first century. The goal of life is to achieve purity by reincarnation until the individual is reunited with the source of life. Spiritual life energy, the essence of being, can be measured by degrees. Small animals have less than 2 million degrees of spiritual life energy; humans have as much as 9 million. Once a human being achieves 9 million degrees, the soul reunites with the Taoist spiritual essence of being. The process of purification requires about ten reincarnations, and the soul must escape dangers and surmount obstacles to advancement. Spiritual vampires, called "outside souls" and devils can only survive by feeding on the spiritual light energy of a human being, prolonging that person's journey toward unity.

## CH'I

In Taoist philosophy, the breath, or essence, of life. Ch'i reputedly is one of three life principles, while ching (semen) and Shen (spirit) are the other two. Ch'i represents the essence of yang, the active, positive, masculine cosmic element. In turn, this combines with yin, the passive, negative, female cosmic element. Ch'i represents the primal energy and psychic forces of the cosmos that permeate all action and instills life, vitality, and health in every living thing.

Taoists teach that ch'i flows through a series of twelve pathways, or meridians, on each side of body. The ancient Chinese believed meridians channeled through the deep tissues of the body and only on occasion touched the surface. They attributed disease to an imbalance in the energy flow of the body and concluded they could cure these diseases where the meridians surfaced. By inserting needles in these various points, acupuncturists claimed they could remove excessive pressure, break down blockages in the energy flow, and restore perfect balance throughout the body.

*See also:* COSMIC ENERGY, TAOISM, YIN/YANG

## CHILDREN OF GOD (FAMILY OF LOVE)

A cult founded by David Brant Berg (1919–1994). The Children of God (COG) teaches that Berg, who changed his name to Moses David, was the Lord's spokesperson,

and that his writings, called the Moses Letters or Mo Letters, are the infallible Word of God. In fact, the Mo Letters are reputedly more inspired than the Christian Scriptures, thereby making the Scriptures obsolete. Although Berg affirmed the existence of God, he rejected the doctrine of the Trinity. He ascribed both evil and good to God, whom he claimed is the wellspring of life. COG renounces the deity of Christ, whom they say was the product of the sexual union between God and Mary. Jesus showed the "love" of God by having intercourse with such women as Martha and Mary Magdalene. Also, the Holy Spirit is not the third Person of the Trinity, but rather God's feminine quality that permeates all of life and manifested itself through sexual intercourse.

COG teaches that orthodox Christian churches belong to the Devil. Berg taught his followers that these congregations were filled with hateful, self-righteous, and deceitful people. He taught his converts to abandon their families, churches, and jobs as a prerequisite for obtaining salvation and joining COG. Initiates must also give all their money and possessions to the organization in order to remain right with God. The Mo Letters espouse reincarnation, anti-Semitism, anarchy, and sexual immorality. COG teaches that God permits group sex, husband and wife swapping, polygamy, and other assorted practices. Berg claimed such perversions were an expression of God's love. In fact, God's love supposedly can only be experienced in its fullest and truest sense through copulation. Mo Letters were often laced with pornographic texts, pictures, and diagrams. They also contain references to astrology, witchcraft, and other occult practices.

Today COG maintains an international office in Zurich, Switzerland. Membership in the United States has declined, perhaps due in part to various legal problems COG has experienced since the early 1980s. Worldwide, the cult still has tens of thousands of followers and continues to remain popular in such places as Brazil and the Philippines.

*See also:* BERG, DAVID BRANT; SALVATION; SEXUALITY

## CHIROMANCY (PALMISTRY)

The practice or art of fortune-telling, or reading a person's character or future, from the lines, marks, and patterns on the palms of the hands. Chiromancy, or palmistry, is one of the oldest and most highly developed forms of divination. References to palmistry can be found in the writings of Aristotle, the ruins of ancient Eastern cultures, and the religious practices of Babylonia. New Age adherents claim the study and interpretation of the hand can reveal hidden knowledge of past, present, and future events to those who use psychic means to get in tune with their inner powers. Some holistic healers assert that the palm, properly used, can focus psychic energy on various parts of the body to treat ailments.

Those who practice divination say various portions of the palm represent the seven mountain planets and can reveal artistic, and leadership qualities. Practitioners believe the development of the mount corresponds directly with the strength of character to which it is associated. For example, the Jupiter mount, just below the joint of the index finger, would reveal ambition and pride. The Venus mount, just below the thumb, reveals the capacity for love.

Those who practice divination are also trained to recognize the main creases of the palm. These include the life line (representing the length and physical quality of life), the heart line (indicating emotional disposition), the head line (revealing mental capabilities such as intelligence and imagination). Other lines mark destiny, marriage, and health. Palmists also study such conditions, as the color, shape, or size of the hand, muscular reactions, nervousness, or the condition of the finger nails. Each of these conditions adds a dimension to the reading.

*See also:* ASTROLOGY, DIVINATION

## CHIVIDILAS FOUNDATION

An American-based organization founded to continue the work of Bhagwan Shree Rajneesh following his deportation from the United States in the late 1980s. Rajneesh was a prominent Indian guru whose Eastern mysticism, combined with Western therapeutics, gained him considerable popularity during the human potential movement of the 1980s. The Chividilas Foundation publishes his discourses as well as keeps active Sannyasins, his followers, informed on topics of interest. Since Rajneesh's death, his influence continues to be felt in the New Age Movement. Richard Price, the founder of the Esalen Institute and a leader in the human potential movement, was one of Rajneesh's followers.

*See also:* ASHRAM; RAJNEESH, BHAGWAN SHREE; REINCARNATION

## CHOPRA, DEEPAK (b. 1947)

Deepak Chopra established the American Association of Ayurvedic Medicine in 1991. In 1995, he opened the Chopra Center for Well Being in La Jolla, California. Deepak Chopra studied medicine in India and interned at a New Jersey hospital. After further study in the United States he became a specialist in internal medicine and endocrinology. He taught medicine at Tufts and Boston University and became chief of staff at New England Memorial Hospital. Dissatisfaction with his life and Western technology led Chopra to Ayurveda, an ancient holistic Indian healing theory. By the year 2000, Chopra's following was quite large, and he had published nineteen books. Ten million were sold in English alone. He also successfully marketed seminars, audio and video tapes and interactive computer programs.

*See also:* AYURVEDA, MIND BODY MEDICINE

## CHRIST-CONSCIOUSNESS

A psychic state of heightened awareness that supposedly lies within the reach of every person. New Age adherents claim that by entering a trancelike state, people can achieve Christ-consciousness and become aware of their true identity, referred to as the God Within, the higher self, or the Oversoul.

Proponents maintain that once people achieve Christ-consciousness, they have successfully crossed the Rainbow Bridge, the illusory gap between themselves and Ultimate Reality.

New Age adherents teach that Jesus became Christ when He realized His oneness with the Universal Presence. By attaining this heightened state of awareness, Jesus liberated Himself from a lower form of existence and became His own savior. They claim the subsequent ascension of Christ refers to an archetype of every individual's evolutionary advancement to union with the impersonal deity that exists throughout the universe. Once a critical mass of people achieve Christ-consciousness, a quantum leap in human evolutionary development will occur and usher in the Aquarian Age of love, peace, and joy.

*See also:* ANTAHKARANA, HIGHER SELF, JESUS CHRIST, QUANTUM LEAP

## CHRISTIAN SCIENCE

The church founded by Mary Baker Eddy in Boston, Massachusetts, in 1879. In 1892, she reorganized and renamed it The Mother Church, the First Church of Christ, Scientist. Eddy led the church until her death in 1910. Historians say that membership peaked at about three hundred thousand in the 1930s, but had decreased to two hundred thousand by 1979. Christian Science has about three thousand branches in more than fifty countries. Their most well-known and successful publishing enterprise is the daily newspaper *Christian Science Monitor.* The *Monitor* has gained wide acclaim for the high journalistic standards it maintains. Other publications include the *Christian Science Quarterly* (daily Bible study lessons), *The Christian Science Journal* (a monthly magazine), and the *Christian Science Sentinel* (a weekly magazine).

The fundamental teaching of Christian Science maintains that the spiritual world is real, good, and eternal, whereas the material world is illusory, evil, and temporal. This is a form of dualism, which says that the universe is under the dominion of two opposing principles or forces. Advocates claim one is virtuous and the other is corrupt—immaterial reality versus material reality. Eddy taught that the mind and the body are completely distinct and unrelated entities. She believed the spiritual realm mattered, whereas the physical realm did not. The presence of strife, misery, and death in the material world are the result of distorted views about the universe. She also believed that people would never get sick if they only realized that ill-health was a figment of their imagination.

Eddy said that God is Infinite Mind and Pure Spirit. He is the universe and the universe is Him, a pantheistic view. This means that God neither governs the world nor decrees events. Eddy made a distinction between Jesus and Christ. She claimed the former was merely a person who lived in Palestine some two thousand years ago, whereas the latter is an archetype of the divine Mind. Eddy advocated that during Jesus' time on earth, He taught that all infirmities are an illusion. In fact, His death on the cross was apparent, not real. The cross simply symbolizes the power of the divine idea and the goodness of God.

Eddy called Christ the divine idea of God, whereas the Spirit is the divine principle. She promoted Christian Science and the Spirit as one and the same. To accept one meant to receive the other. The Spirit (or Christian Science) saves people by liberating them from false notions about the universe. People learn they are not really flesh and bones, but rather the manifestation of pure mind and spirit—emanations of the truth and love of God. Eddy taught that evil and death, heaven and hell are not material realities, but rather states of mind. By accepting the teachings of Christian Science, adherents become pure representations of God's truth and love.

*See also:* EDDY, MARY BAKER; QUIMBY, PHINEAS PARKHURST

## CHROMOTHERAPY

A New Age healing technique in which the spiritual diagnosis of patients is determined by the color and intensity of their aura. Auras reputedly are psychic emanations of the mind or spirit, occurring apart from any physical means and detectable only by mediums. Supposedly only certain people are enlightened by psychic means to the point of detecting the presence of auras and deciphering their meanings. Proponents claim that each color, vibration pattern, level of brightness, and intensity of auras symbolize the physical and mental, emotional and spiritual well-being of people. Their color response allegedly determines the success or failure of the diverse treatment programs suggested by clairvoyant counselors.

Chromotherapy is based on the belief that the human body radiates a vibrational energy force, manifested in color and light. Supposedly the body selects the colors it needs to maintain a proper psychic alignment from sunlight. One way of influencing this process is to project predetermined colors directly onto the body. Other methods might require patients to eat correctly colored fruits and vegetables, to breath in air enhanced by colored light, or to apply clear color gel over a personal photograph. Each chromotherapeutic color allegedly possesses a host of properties that work best when applied to specific portions of the mind, body, or spirit.

*See also:* AURA, COLOROLOGY, KIRLIAN PHOTOGRAPHY, LIGHT, MIND BODY MEDICINE, VIBRATIONS

# CHURCH OF ARMAGEDDON
*See:* ARMAGEDDON, CHURCH OF

# CHURCH OF JESUS CHRIST OF LATTER-DAY SAINTS
*See:* MORMONISM

# CHURCH OF SATAN
*See:* SATAN, CHURCH OF

# CHURCH UNIVERSAL AND TRIUMPHANT
*See:* UNIVERSAL AND TRIUMPHANT, CHURCH

# CIRCLE

An ancient symbol of eternality, infinity, and wholeness. According to Egyptian and

Wheel—universe of endless cycles as seen in the heavens

Roman mythology, the circle represents various aspects of sun deities, especially those of the feminine spirit. Many early civilizations believed that the essence of the universe was represented in the round shape of the circle, causing all things in the world to act interdependently. Some groups believed this concept was evident at significant points during the circle of a person's life. Proponents see roundness in childbirth, the breast of nourishment, and the culmination of life in death.

Hinduism has a similar doctrine in which the wheel of reincarnation is represented by an eternal circle of life in an eternal circle of the cosmos. A Hindu god known as the One is also symbolized by an unbroken circle and represents the political and religious unity of humankind. Many circular symbols remain a conspicuous part of the New Age Movement. This is particularly true of the peace symbol with its broken, upside down cross within a circle.

The circle also plays a significant role in the practice of ritualistic magic. Some satanic cults boast about the tremendous powers of full demonic possession acquired by stepping into the circle. Contemporary witches believe that the circle provides a ceremonial space in which alternate realities can intersect and share their divine powers. By gathering coven members into a circle, they claim that the divine energy of the goddess within each member can be contained and manipulated to bring about the heightening and transference of magical powers. Most contemporary witches deny any negative aspects of this demonic activity, but ritualistic texts repeatedly refer to the circle as a protective barrier from the spiritual forces conjured up.

*See also:* CENTER; MANDALA; ONE, THE; PENTAGRAM; REINCARNATION

# CLAIRAUDIENCE

The ability to perceive psychic vibrations that are inaudible. Clairaudience supposedly is an inherent gift that is manifested as an inner voice. Proponents claim it is the most difficult of the extrasensory perceptions to ignore and the one most commonly experienced. Clairaudience abilities are developed by entering the realm of psychic awareness through the use of occult meditative techniques. Some believe that only in this altered state of consciousness can the vibrational messages be gathered, sorted, and translated into mental sound waves.

Some practitioners use mantras (sacred sounds) to balance their psychic energies while others rely on music to enhance the reception and transmission of psychic communication. Adherents claim clairaudient powers communicate, guide, and teach people in a manner similar to messages from the inner self, spirit guides, ascended masters, and other voices heard in an altered state of consciousness.

*See also:* ALPHA LEVEL, ALTERED STATE, SPIRIT GUIDES, VIBRATIONS

# CLAIRSENTIENCE

The perception of past, present, or future knowledge through psychic abilities. Clairsentience supposedly manifests itself to people in an enhanced state of awareness, in which they experience an intuitive knowledge of unseen thoughts or ethereal presences. Unlike other extrasensory perceptions, clairsentience does not rely on inner voices or visions, but on instantaneous flashes of insight unfettered by time or distance.

Clairsentience operates on the belief that centers of psychic energy, or chakras, exist along the human spine. The seventh, or last, chakra reputedly is located at the crown of a person's head and extends into infinity. Proponents assert that the crown chakra is the receptor point for psychic vibrations. They teach initiates who wish to develop clairsentience powers to focus the vibrational impulses of the universe through their crown chakra. This occult exercise is to un-

lock the secrets to higher consciousness, universal knowledge, and evolutionary development.

*See also:* CHAKRA, INTUITION, PSYCHIC, VIBRATIONS

# CLAIRVOYANCE

The ability to discern something about inanimate objects or events, whether past, present, or future, apart from the five senses. Viewing the past through psychic means is called *retrospective* clairvoyance, whereas inklings about the present are called *telaesthesia*. The most commonly identified clairvoyant ability, precognition, involves foretelling future events. Practitioners claim this supranatural ability to transcend the physical realm and journey along the dimensional plane of time occurs while in a trance-like state. Clairvoyants maintain that they are unaffected by conventional limitations as they exercise their gift.

Some assert that all people have the ability to exercise clairvoyance. They say that everyone occasionally experiences clairvoyance, but people fail to recognize it or use it at will. Others claim that clairvoyance is passed down genetically from one generation to the next. Still others maintain that their powers emanate from the spiritual realm and are controlled by entities who can see beyond the limitations of their human host. Some telepaths identify the third eye as the reception point for transmitted cosmic vibrations. This eye supposedly is located at the center of spiritual vision existing in the center of the forehead. By learning to transcend the levels of consciousness, initiates allegedly learn to reach a heightened state of awareness where psychic frequencies can be received and translated into visual symbols.

*See also:* PSYCHIC, SPIRITISM, THIRD EYE

# CLUB OF ROME

A globalist organization comprised of some of the world's wealthiest and most influential people. The Club of Rome was founded in 1968 by former Olivetti executive Aurelio Peccei. The organization's globalist aims include the implementation of drastic population control methods. The Club's published report, entitled *The Limits to Growth,* contains a futuristic interpretation of the world. Abortion and euthanasia are presented as viable population control measures—one for birth control, the other for eliminating the elderly and unproductive from society.

The Club holds to a New Age vision of international economic cooperation. Its leaders contend that humankind lives in a world divided into rich and poor, and literate and illiterate. What is needed is a new philosophy, or one-world religion, which will enable the concepts of a global village and economic unity under a single governmental body to become reality. The first step is to prepare the world for an economic collapse which will inevitably occur. The second step is to familiarize people with the concept of achieving fiscal recovery by means of a new world currency. The Club predicts that when financial panic strikes, the nations of the world will plead for a leader to restore law and order. The Club also claims that when the economic collapse occurs, every country will be placed within an organization that will oversee the global recovery. The United States, the European Community, and Japan allegedly will be the most powerful members of this globalist confederation.

*See also:* ABORTION, ILLUMINATI, ONE-WORLD IDEAL

# COLLECTIVE CONSCIOUSNESS

Humankind's state of awareness as a race. In New Age thought, the collective consciousness has been gradually progressing toward global enlightenment. While humanity's spiritual evolution has occurred over the centuries, the pace now has quickened with the dawning of the Aquarian era. Supposedly this quantum leap is necessary in order for humanity to burst forth in insight, achieve cosmic consciousness, and create an environment of peace, love, and harmony.

*See also:* CRITICAL MASS, NEW AGE MOVEMENT, QUANTUM LEAP

# COLLECTIVE UNCONSCIOUS

In Jungian or analytical psychology, the total of all primordial human memories. These include recollections of births and deaths, as well as relationships between the sexes and the divine. This ancestral knowledge of the human race lays dormant in the human brain, has evolved over time, and is inherited at birth. Swiss psychoanalyst Carl Jung (1875–1961) theorized that preexistent images or symbols, called archetypes, exist within every society and culture, and that these archetypes represent the psychic contents of the collective unconscious.

Jung experienced periodic visions and dreams that contained vivid religious and mythological features. These experiences motivated Jung to study myths, dreams, and the psychology of religion. He sought to explain the existence of spiritual entities as manifestations of the collective unconscious. He claimed that spirits, ghosts, and demons are exteriorizations of the fears, anxieties, and complexes of the human psyche. These involuntary and sometimes unfamiliar manifestations are evolved representations of ideas created in dreams and fantasies. He believed that manifestations that cannot be explained within the realm of personal consciousness are part of the historical development of the collective unconscious inherited from ancestral sources.

New Age adherents have adopted much of this thinking. They claim that a common psychic nature is present everywhere and in everyone. They purport that this collective unconsciousness, with its many inborn or inherited archetypes, belongs to all members of the human race and is impersonal. And because these latent primordial memories are supraindividual, they eternally preexisted in nature. Advocates teach that every person is psychically linked to the collective unconscious and can draw upon its archetypes through various mind-altering techniques. As people get in touch with their divine self, they can establish communication with the Universal Mind, fathom the mysteries of humanity's ancestral knowledge, gain unlimited human powers, and learn how to manipulate reality.

*See also:* ARCHETYPE; JUNG, CARL GUSTAV; PSYCHE

## COLOROLOGY

A New Age holistic healing practice. Colorology is based on the belief that certain colors can affect the emotional, physical, and spiritual health of people. Devotees usually practice color therapy in conjunction with occult paraphernalia and philosophies, including crystals, astrology, and numerology, as well as meditative mantras, chakras, and psychic readings. The intent is to induce an altered state of consciousness within patients. Once they ascend the levels of human consciousness, these patients supposedly will encounter swirling images of intensified colors. Proponents claim that as they focus their thoughts on kaleidoscopic images, all negative influences will be eliminated from their mind, thus leading to psychic enlightenment.

Depending on the particular occult philosophy, the significance and powers associated with different colors may vary. Some say that the colors of the rainbow represent the Seven Rays of Initiation, with each hue symbolizing certain godlike qualities worth acquiring. Others maintain that various colors represent yogic chakras, or spiritual energy centers of the human body, through which powers are transmitted through psychic means. Some avid disciples even believe that color is the cosmic manifestation of Lucifer's separation from the godhead. They claim that Lucifer formerly manifested his presence in a pure white light, but was forced to divide into a trinity of color—with red symbolizing the will, blue representing love, and yellow symbolizing wisdom. Proponents say the rainbow, or Lucifer, represents the evolutionary journey of humanity to the white light of enlightenment and godhood.

Some New Age colorologists associate certain hues with specific days of the week. Others say that each day is vastly different and must be individually divined through numerology. If they consider a certain day to be represented by an unsuitable color, the disciple can simply compensate by dressing in opposing colors. Supposedly, if Monday is a blue day (soothing), devotees may dress in red for stimulation. If Monday is a green day (invigorating), avid colorologists may dress in yellow to add inspiration to the surge of expected psychic energy. Traditional colorologists associate red with strength and sexual love, danger and charity. Blue represents tranquillity and understanding, truth and devotion. Yellow symbolizes charm and confidence, comfort and joy. And green represents finance and fertility, as well as luck, energy, and growth. Various occult techniques align the color attributes differently and slant the attributes to the targeted response desired within the mind, body, or spirit. Both the science and medical communities acknowledge that colors can be used to soothe or invigorate patients, though any divinational qualities of colors are, of course, not accepted.

*See also:* ANTAHKARANA, AURA, CANDLE, CHAKRA, FENG-SHUI

## COMMUNITY CHAPEL AND BIBLE TRAINING CENTER

Community Chapel and Bible Training Center is a Bible college and church in King County, Washington, with about twelve satellite churches (down from twenty-two at the height of the church's influence in the 1970s and early 1980s). The movement appealed to new believers who had been in the counterculture of the 1960s and especially those who had been involved in drug use. In the late 1960s Donald Lee Barnett taught that the end of the world was at hand and that his Community Chapel was being groomed to be "the bride of Christ," part of an elite work of God to win the world to Christ in the final days. Chapel members were told to "purify" themselves by total submission to the church and the teachings of Barnett.

During the Community Chapel's theological wanderings, spiritual life in the group began to overwhelm family and other commitments, and members were continually told of new "movements of God" they must take part in to purify themselves. These included physically falling down in the power of the Spirit and casting out demons. Anger and doubt were regarded as demons to be rebuked. Spiritual dancing and connections, usually involving adulterous relationships, began breaking down families in the mid 1980s. Charges of child abuse and neglect have been leveled against the church. Those who left the church were ostracized by former friends and family.

## CONFLUENT EDUCATION

A pedagogical system designed by Beverly Galyean, who believed that students need to learn that they possess an innate divine nature. Through use of New Age exercises, children learn that sin does not exist, that Christ is obsolete, and that "God" lives within. Galyean's underlying assumption is that every child holds the answers to the universe. If students are unable to solve their own problems, they are introduced to their own personal spiritual guide who will lead them throughout their lives. Some of the more popular exercises used in confluent education are visualization, guided imagery, and role playing, as well as meditation and journaling.

*See also:* GALYEAN, BEVERLY; SIN; VALUES CLARIFICATION

## CONSCIOUSNESS

The quality, state, or condition of being self-aware. Personal identity is obtained through reflecting on information received from the five senses. Sigmund Freud (1856–1939), the father of psychoanalytical theory, held that an unconscious aspect of human self-awareness contained the total scope of a person's existence. The unconscious realm of the human psyche recorded all the erotic images, archetypes, and experiences that the conscious mind suppressed. Freud claimed that these suppressed thoughts were responsible for all mental and physical diseases within society.

Swiss psychotherapist Carl Jung (1875–1961) took this a step further by saying an even deeper level of awareness existed, called the collective unconsciousness. He maintained that the collective unconscious was the total of all the primordial human memories, such as recollections of births and deaths, and relationships between the sexes and the divine. This ancestral knowledge of the human race lays dormant in the brain, has evolved over time, and is inherited at birth. The collective conscious connects the psyche of the human race with the Universal Mind.

New Age adherents assert that when people transcend the levels of consciousness, they are able to discover their repressed thoughts, realign the vibrational forces of the mind, body, and spirit, and holistically heal themselves. Dozens of occult techniques teach people how to reach these altered states of consciousness. As initiates transcend each level, new revelations are supposedly revealed that allow for easier access to the next level. By raising the self-awareness of each person, New Age adherents claim they will usher in the transformation of the world in a Consciousness Revolution.

*See also:* ALPHA LEVEL; ALTERED STATE; COLLECTIVE UNCONSCIOUS; FREUD, SIGMUND; JUNG, CARL GUSTAV; SCIENCE, NEW AGE

## CONSCIOUSNESS REVOLUTION

The New Age call for an upheaval in psychic self-awareness that will result in a new way of perceiving and experiencing life. This shift in awareness is sometimes called the "Second American Revolution." The intent of this radical change in thinking is to free people from the chains of traditional values, to convince them of their innate divinity, to indoctrinate people into believing they are all joined to an impersonal force called Ultimate Reality, and to inculcate the idea that the only way the planet can survive is by establishing a one-world religion and government. If enough people enter an altered state of consciousness, a critical mass of psychic power will be reached, thereby initiating the Consciousness Revolution. Global holidays, such as the Harmonic Convergence, Earth Day, and Great Invocation Days, are celebrated to usher in the upheaval in psychic self-awareness.

New Age adherents say that the consciousness of the human race began to evolve as more and more people discovered their divine self and their oneness with the cosmic life force. This ongoing process allegedly began to accelerate at the dawn of the Aquarian era, an idea popularized in the countercultural movement of the 1960s. Radicals in the West claimed that the establishment did not have the ability to solve humanity's social problems. They proposed an upheaval in psychic self-awareness as the solution. Proponents stated that people could create and implement the agenda for social change by looking within themselves.

Human self-awareness, combined with scientific and mystical means to explore the psyche, would create a revolution in thinking. Some occult leaders assert that those who stand in the way of Global Consciousness, such as Bible-believing Christians, must be purged or purified, from society. After they are banished to an astral plane of existence, they presumably will gain enlightenment and then return to earth.

*See also:* AQUARIUS, AGE OF; CONSCIOUSNESS; GLOBALISM; ONE-WORLD IDEAL; PURIFICATION

## COSMIC CHRIST

The psychic entity that inhabited Jesus during His time on earth. A Dominican priest named Matthew Fox (b. 1940) popularized this idea. He claimed that the cosmic christ is the life force within all living things. This entity is available to all people and exists to guide the human race on its journey to enlightenment. New Age adherents teach that those who allow this spiritual being to indwell them will discover their divine self, recognize their one-

ness with the universal whole, and attain enlightenment.

*See also:* COSMIC ENERGY; FOX, MATTHEW; GOD; JESUS CHRIST

## COSMIC CONSCIOUSNESS

A state of enlightenment in which people recognize their innate divinity and oneness with the universe. New Age adherents claim that the individual self is an extension of the supreme universal self. The essence of people is identical to the essence of Ultimate Reality. Because New Age adherents consider the Cosmic Consciousness to be eternal and indestructible, so is the inner soul. When people die, their psyche is reincarnated. Upon reaching nirvana, the state of absolute oneness, the inner soul no longer retains its separate existence. It merges with the Cosmic Consciousness.

Devotees achieve a state of enlightenment by repeatedly transcending the levels of human consciousness through mystical or occult practices. Within each altered state of awareness, new revelations are revealed until cosmic consciousness is attained. Practitioners claim to have encountered unusual lights, colors, and sounds, as well as felt an invisible energy source flow through the center of their being. New Age adherents maintain that this energy source is god, a psychic awareness available only upon attaining cosmic consciousness.

*See also:* ENLIGHTENMENT, GOD, INTERCONNECTION

## COSMIC ENERGY

The life force that is thought by some New Age groups to permeate all life, instilling health and well-being. Metaphysical enthusiasts say this energy flow originates from within the depths of the universe, flows through all people, and returns to the cosmos. In this way, proponents claim that all of creation is divinely linked. New Age adherents maintain that cosmic energy is responsible for the existence of life, and is the essence of the divine nature within people.

See also: BLOOD OF CHRIST; GOD;
METAPHYSICS; NEW AGE MOVEMENT

## COUNCIL OF FOREIGN RELATIONS (CFR)

A nongovernmental organization founded in 1921 by globalist Edward Mandell House (1858–1938). The CFR believes that the impending New World Order, in which the world's governments, economies, and religions cooperatively work together, represents an evolutionary leap for humankind. The CFR has repeatedly called for the creation of a Council of Wise Persons, or a Global Watch Committee, comprised of elite leaders. They would function as global decision makers and have the power to override the political authority and sovereignty. CFR claims to function only in an advisory capacity, but critics argue the CFR and similar organizations have exercised considerable political clout in promoting their New Age agenda around the world.

See also: ONE-WORLD IDEAL;
POLITICS, NEW AGE; UNITED NATIONS

## COURSE IN MIRACLES, A

A three-volume New Age series written by atheist and Columbia University psychologist Helen Schucman over a seven-year period (1965–1973). She claims that one day a spirit named "Jesus" dictated to her A Course in Miracles. The result was a 622-page textbook, a 478-page workbook, and an eighty-eight-page teacher's manual, all of which were published in 1976 by the Foundation for Inner Peace. Over 160,000 of the sets have been sold without the benefit of advertising, and more than three hundred American organizations have been founded based on the information in these materials.

A Course in Miracles rejects the biblical idea that God is a personal, loving Creator. Schucman presents "God" as an impersonal oneness to which all belong. She also rejects the scriptural teaching concerning the divinity of Jesus. She categorizes Jesus as a great moral teacher who recognized the Christ-consciousness within himself and all people. She reasons that since everyone is inherently divine, they cannot sin. Schucman sees sin, guilt, and separation from God as an illusion, thereby negating the need for atonement and redemption. A Course in Miracles asserts that all paths, except Christianity, lead to God because they all emphasize the importance of universal love and oneness. The three-volume set is popular among New Age adherents and successfully presents occult ideas in Christian-sounding phrases. Some say that A Course in Miracles should be used as a companion to the Bible. Others say the series should replace the Scriptures entirely, since the Bible is obsolete.

See also: AUTOMATIC WRITING; BIBLE, NEW AGE; JESUS CHRIST; SCHUCMAN, HELEN

## CRAFT, THE

Neopagan practices involving the ritualistic use of magic to invoke supernatural powers. The Craft is also called the Old Religion and is associated with Ecofeminism. Practitioners depict themselves as a benign cult of gentle souls who worship the primordial image of the Mother Goddess. They claim that with the dawn of the Aquarian era of love, joy, and peace, the deity has once again given her benevolent powers to humankind.

See also: GODDESS WORSHIP, MAGIC, WICCA, WITCHCRAFT

## CREATION

According to Genesis 2–3, God's act of bringing matter, the various forms of life, and the world into existence out of nothing (see Heb. 11:3). The Bible teaches that the Creator is personal and loving, all-powerful and distinct from the universe He created. By way of contrast, evolution teaches that the universe and various types of animals and plants had their origin in other preexisting types and that the distinguishable differences are due to modifications in successive generations.

Evolution presents humanity as gradually emerging by chance through progressive change and development.

Various creation stories exist in New Age thought. One involves the Great Mother Goddess who was complete within herself. According to New Age lore, she caught the reflection of her own light, was filled with sexual desire, and made love to herself in the darkness of the universe. The resulting waves of ecstatic energy created the world and spirits, who then became human beings. The radiance of her pure light became the sun, symbolized as the great horned god who ruled the underworld. Other occult legends say that the universe began in an empty state of chaos. Mother Earth reputedly arose from this primordial disorder and commanded the world into existence with one supreme syllable, identified by some as "om," the popular meditative mantra of Eastern religions.

Eastern religions and occult groups maintain that the individual, not God, is sovereign and exists at the center of an ever-evolving universe. Unlike more classic theories of evolution, New Age adherents believe that all souls are extensions of an eternal celestial energy called God. This entity exists in countless other dimensions of space and time and flows through all people, giving them the freedom and ability to create what they want. When people enter heightened states of awareness, the Force enables them to traverse the realms of consciousness and cause reality to manifest itself in three-dimensional material existence.

This means that reality exists primarily in the perfect, invisible universe of thought and that the physical world is only an illusion. Some occult groups teach that soul-like emanations from the Force created material extensions of themselves, became obsessed with the experience of physical existence, and consequently forgot the existence of their divine nature. Through a variety of means, such as transcendental meditation, hallucinogenic drugs, and so on, people can rediscover the divine self within and can regain the power to manipulate reality.

*See also:* EVOLUTION; FALL OF HUMANITY, THE; LOGOS; MYTHOLOGY; QUANTUM LEAP

# CREME, BENJAMIN (b. 1922)

A Scottish artist and a lifelong disciple of Theosophy. In 1959, Creme asserted that he received the first of many messages from a channeled spirit named Lord Maitreya, whom Creme said was the christ of the New Age. Through telepathic "overshadowing," Maitreya instructed Creme regarding his key leadership role in the emergence of a spiritually evolved global community. In 1980, Creme moved from London to Los Angeles where he founded the Tara Center. This organization is dedicated to the dissemination of New Age information, including the social, political, and economic agenda of a New World Order under the rule of Lord Maitreya.

In April 1982, the Tara Center ran full page ads in twenty major newspapers under the headline "The Christ Is Here Now." While unable to produce this christ on demand, Creme continued to publish his occult messages in a magazine entitled *Share International*. This publication explained that the world was not yet ready for the emergence of Maitreya who would lead the enlightened into a state of godhood. Therefore the New Age christ was working behind the scenes to prepare the nations, leaders, and citizens of earth for the inauguration of the Aquarian era. This age reputedly will be characterized by a new social structure devoid of the negative vibrations of stress, death, and individuality.

Creme says that the ultimate destiny of humankind lays in the wisdom of ethereal masters. He also claims that these are spiritually evolved souls who have come to earth to help people in their journey to godhood. In his book entitled *The Reappearance of Christ and the Masters of Wisdom,* published by the Tara Center in 1980, Creme describes Maitreya as the most evolved of the spiritual hierarchy. He purports that Christ is not a person, but a state of existence attained through enlightenment. Maitreya is the greatest and last of the world's avatars. Other avatars, the incarnation of the deity appointed for a certain epoch, include Buddha, Muhammad, Krishna, and Jesus.

*See also:* MAITREYA, LORD; OVERSHADOW; *REAPPEARENCE OF CHRIST AND THE MASTERS OF WISDOM, THE;* SHARE INTERNATIONAL; TARA CENTER; THEOSOPHY

## CRITICAL MASS

The minimum number of humans needed to trigger the transformational process that will lead to the establishment of the New World Order. The individual minds of people are all a vital part of a universal mind that, when properly energized, can be shifted to reflect the imagination of the critical mass. New Age adherents assert that if the critical mass of the world's population focuses on a particular thought, that thought will become instinctive knowledge and result in a quantum leap in cosmic consciousness.

Adherents claim that everything is an interrelated part of the Universal Mind. This explains why global peace events, such as the Harmonic Convergence, attempt to create a human mind-link strong enough to change the consciousness of the human race. New Age adherents believe that if only 1 percent of the earth's population establishes a mind-link, it will create a pulse of psychic energy to reach eleven percent of the population and instill within them the vision of global peace. Ultimately, this will cause an ever-widening ripple effect and usher in the Aquarian Age of universal peace, love, and unity.

*See also:* GLOBALISM; HUNDREDTH MONKEY THEORY, THE; QUANTUM LEAP; TRANSFORMATION

## CROSS

A Christian symbol used to depict the crucifixion of Jesus Christ. Throughout church history, various cults have perverted the true intent of the cross. In the Middle Ages, witchcraft cults inverted the cross to demonstrate their derision for Christ and the church. Satanists represent their alleged dominion over Christ by placing the cross with broken or bent

arms within a circle or triangle. New Age adherents depict a cross beneath a rainbow to symbolize the ecumenical harmony of humankind on the path to godhood. Some say the cross is a divine light, representing the division of the spiritual and physical realms. Others think the coss is the symbol of divine unity between the spiritual and physical realms, the ego and self, and the East and West, as well as the male and the female, or god and the individual.

*See also:* CRUCIFIXION, JESUS CHRIST, MYSTERY, PEACE SYMBOL, POWER OBJECT, SYMBOLISM

## CROWLEY, ALEISTER (1875–1947)

British occultist Aleister Crowley's parents were members of the Plymouth Brethren church and tried to rear him in this religious tradition. However, Crowley detested Christianity to such an extent that he was dubbed the Great Beast of Revelation. At the age of twenty-three, Crowley joined the Order of the Golden Dawn, an occult group whose teachings are identified with the worship of Thoth, the Greek name for the Egyptian god of learning, wisdom, and magic (otherwise known as Djhowtey). Crowley attained the title of "magus," the highest position possible within the Order. But due to a major conflict with its leader, MacGregor Mathers, Crowley was expelled from the group.

This incident prompted Crowley to start his own occult organization, called the Order of the Silver Star. Crowley spent most of his life in Boleskine, a large castle located on the rocky cliffs of Loch Ness, Scotland. Hidden passages and secret chambers beneath the castle provided the ceremonial center for the Order. Crowley also belonged to a secret German occult group called the Ordo Templi Orientis (OTO), which he joined in 1912. He eventually became the leader of the OTO chapter headquartered in England. In 1920, Crowley started an occult group named Abbey of Thelema in Cefalu, Sicily. Black magic and sexual orgies were the hallmarks of the abbey.

During the next twenty years, Crowley continued to spread his occult philosophy through writing, teaching, and demonic rituals. The Black Mass that commemorated his death in 1947 was attended by devoted followers who, at Crowley's request, recited his hymns to Pan, the goat-horned sex-god of nature. After the ceremonial cremation of Crowley in Brighton, England, his ashes were sent to the United States, where followers continued his satanic traditions. Rock musician Jimmy Page later bought Crowley's abandoned castle at Boleskine.

Crowley believed his life mission was to research, enhance, and proliferate the practice of evil. He maintained that an entity named Aiwaz, or Aiwass, gave him revelations, which he recorded in a work entitled *The Book of the Law* (1906). This text and a later work entitled *The Equinox* (1909) are the foundation for the beliefs and practices of modern Satanism, especially as seen in Anton LaVey's *The Satanic Bible*. Crowley's writings instruct readers about magic, sorcery, hedonism, and paganism, along with instruction on perverted sexual acts, drug abuse, and blood sacrifice.

In *The Book of the Law,* Crowley announced the dawn of a magical new age in which the Law of Thelema, "Do what thou wilt," would be the prevailing creed. He advocated that people should have the right to live the way they wanted, unbound by the moral limitations imposed by society. Crowley asserted that the subconscious mind is activated through repetitive invocations. He therefore practiced the Law of Repetition, used in satanic worship services. Participants would chant demonic prayers to conjure up evil spirits to manipulate people and circumstances. Crowley also taught the Law of Reversal, which says that good is evil, and evil is good. He encouraged students to learn to walk, talk, read, think, and listen to music backward. He claimed this would reveal esoteric messages of the future.

*See also:* PAN; ROCK MUSIC; *Satanic Bible, The;* SATANISM; SPIRIT GUIDES; WITCHCRAFT

## CRUCIFIXION

A means of torture and execution that was invented in the East and adopted by the Romans who used it for slaves and the lower class. Victims of Roman crucifixion typically would carry the crossbeam to the place of execution. They or someone else would also often carry a tablet citing the charge against the offender, and this placard was sometimes nailed to the top of the cross. At the execution site, the crossbeam would be attached at or near the top of a longer beam, or stake, while it was lying on the ground. The victims' hands, and sometimes their feet, would be affixed to the cross by nails. Then the cross would be lifted and dropped into a hole.

Victims sometimes lived for two or three days, finally succumbing to death due to poor blood circulation, heart failure, or asphyxiation. If the executioners wanted to make their victims last longer, they would first outfit the cross with a block of wood as a seat or a footrest to serve as a support. If the executioners wanted to do away with their victims quickly, they would break their legs, thereby removing the victims' ability to support themselves with their legs.

New Age advocates believe that Jesus allowed Himself to be crucified to teach people that they should not fear persecution because their innate divinity makes them indestructible. Occult leaders say that the significance of Jesus' execution lies not in the death itself, but in the releasing of His life force into the cosmos. This allows every person to discover the Christ-consciousness within their soul. Some New Age adherents claim that the death of Jesus was staged, while others believe that Lord Maitreya (Satan) engineered the entire episode. Still others assert that the Bible denies the blood sacrifice of Christ.

*See also:* ATONEMENT, JESUS CHRIST, RESURRECTION

## CRYPTOMNESIA

Ability to recall the thoughts and ideas buried in the almost perfect memory of the subconscious mind. Cryptomnesia is derived from two Greek words that, when combined, mean "hidden recall." New Age adherents assert that the ability to recall memories that would otherwise remain undetected by the conscious mind is due to extrasensory perception or other occult powers.

*See also:* EXTRASENSORY PERCEPTION, PAST LIVES THERAPY, SUBCONSCIOUS

## CRYPTOZOOLOGY

The study of creatures whose existence has not been proven, based on legends, folklore, physical proof, and reports of sightings. Among subjects of cryptozoological study are "big foot" and the Loch Ness monster, both of which have been suspected by some New Age groups of having spiritual significance.

## CRYSTAL

In occultic thought, an object that can be used as a focal point for psychic energy. These objects range from naturally occurring crystalline structures to cut glass and even round "crystal balls." They are usually translucent or light refractive in some way. For centuries, quartz crystals and gemstones have been considered to have magical healing or paranormal properties. They are commonly used by New Age healers or carried as talismans or future telling stones. The theory is that crystals channel good energy and ward off bad energy. With the popularity of personal computers, crystals began to be marketed as a "bioelectric shield" against harmful forces emitted from computer monitors, cellular phones, microwave ovens, and even other people. They resonate with healing frequencies, work with the chakras and help balance yin and yang. Crystals allegedly affect the emotions and can be used for achieving emotional harmonization. Crystal wands are used to heal auras in auratherapy.

*See also:* CRYSTAL BALL, CRYSTAL SKULL, POWER OBJECT, QUARTZ CRYSTAL

## CRYSTAL BALL

An object through which the seer visualizes psychic pictures. Some historians think seers first used a clear pool of water to practice crystal gazing. As time went on, they began using metallic and other reflective surfaces to divine the unknown. Traditionally crystal gazing is cloaked in a colorful ritual that creates a mysterious, eerie atmosphere.

The crystal ball is usually mounted on a gold, ivory, or ebony pedestal that is often engraved with the astrological signs of the occult and is sometimes covered with a layer of oil. The crystal ball remains covered until the psychic reading begins. Any given session may be accompanied by dim lights, candles, chants, rhythms, and repetitive movements as the seer enters a trancelike state of psychic accessibility. Once the seer makes contact with the ethereal realm, a cloud appears within, and sometimes surrounding, the crystal ball. Some maintain that this cloud represents the potential outpouring of divine truth through a permeable source like light through a crystal. Others say the cloud is *raith* energy, an elemental force that is projected from the human consciousness. The clouds apparently dissipate as the reading ensues, only to return when the seer is finished.

The images appearing in the crystal ball reputedly symbolize the past, present, and future of any person. Some fortune-tellers claim that the pictures actually appear within the crystal, while others assert that the ball's state of transparency aids in the transmittance of telepathic thoughts and vibrations. In either case, the seer seeks to enter an altered state of consciousness by restricting sensory awareness to one unchanging source of stimulation. This allows the seer to interpret images visible only to the third eye, the center of spiritual vision at the center of the forehead. Some fortune-tellers claim they have an inherent power of psychic vision, while others say they obtain their visions and esoteric wisdom from the spirit world. Those in the latter group might pray incessantly, consecrate their ball, and chant a sacred sound to compel entities from other realms to manifest their presence and reveal their sacred knowledge.

*See also:* CLAIRVOYANCE, DIVINATION, POWER OBJECT, PSYCHIC, SÉANCE, TELEPATHY, TRANCE CHANNELING

## CRYSTAL SKULL

Stone or quartz carvings in the shape of human skulls. Some stone skulls are genuine artifacts from ancient cultures, notably the Aztecs, though they have been found in other parts of the world. New Age crystal skulls are said to have come from Atlantis or an extraterrestrial source and are endowed with magical powers. Modern interest dates to the 1920s when a young woman, Anna Mitchell-Hedges, was alleged to have discovered a clear quartz skull on an excavation of Mayan ruins. Her claim was disputed by the archaeologists on the dig, and the true origin of the small skull is not certain. It was marketed by Anna's father, Mike, as an indication that the site was the ruins of Atlantis. He founded the Crystal Skull Society, which still seeks and studies these skulls.

*See also:* ATLANTIS, LOST CONTINENT OF

# D

## DALAI LAMA (TA LE' LAMA)

Leader of Tibetan Buddhists and in the late 1900s a popular figure among Western followers of Buddhism and Eastern religion generally. In this era the Dalai was Tenzin Gyatso (b. 1935), who has remained in exile because of pressure from the Chinese government, which ruled Tibet as a satellite nation. In fact, forced resettlement of Chinese in Tibet has made the Tibetan people a minority in their own country. In 1989 Gyatso received the Nobel Peace Prize for his efforts to keep peace and negotiate better conditions for the Tibetan people. Taking advantage of the New Age interest in all things Eastern, the Dalai Lama was a heroic and charming figure who was the subject of numerous books and several popular films.

Traditionally, Tibet is a theocratic state, ruled by the Dalai Lama. *Dalai* is a Western mistransliteration that is more precisely transliterated *Ta Le'*.

Within the theology of Buddhism, the Dalai Lama is considered to be a reincarnated emanation of Avalokitesvara, the bodhisattva of compassion. This makes the person who holds the office a supernatural being, though not a god. Most who have held the office have carefully avoided being called a god, though they are frequently revered as one.

*See also:* BODHISATTVA, BUDDHISM

## DANCE OF SHIVA

A dance of celebration associated with Shiva, one of the three major gods in the Hindu trinity, the other two being Brahma, the Creator, and Vishnu, the Preserver. Shiva represents the Destroyer and is worshiped for its power in eradicating the old to make way for the new. The dance associated with this Hindu deity symbolizes the destruction and creation of elemental particles and the ever-existing change asserted to be necessary for existence. The rhythmic beat of the dance is to emit life-giving energy. And the cosmic pulses of light represent the spiritual flame that burns away layers of illusion, eliminates all fears and memories of past lives, and makes participants aware of their mystical connection with Ultimate Reality.

The Dance of Shiva was popularized by Fritjof Capra, a university physicist and New Age mystic. He claims that the idea for the dance came to him in 1969 while he sat in a drug-induced meditative state on a California beach. As Capra focused his thoughts on the rhythm of the waves against the shore, he asserts, the entire world around him exploded into a cosmic dance of universal elements. Capra says that the "oneness" he felt with the Universal Mind permanently changed the way he thought about life. This experience prompted him to write *The Tao of Physics*. In his book, he attempts to unite ancient mysticism with modern science. He believes this will create a paradigm shift in people's thinking and bring about a quantum leap in humanity's evolutionary development.

*See also:* CAPRA, FRITJOF; HINDUISM; LIGHT; QUANTUM LEAP; SCIENCE, NEW AGE; VIBRATIONS

## DAOISM

*See:* TAOISM

## DEAD SEA SCROLLS (DSS)

Ancient papyrus and leather manuscripts discovered in caves along the northwestern shore of the Dead Sea between 1947 and 1956. One of the greatest recent archaeological finds, the collection has generated significant interest among biblical scholars. The scrolls were written in Hebrew, Aramaic, and Greek and left there by the Essenes, a Jewish religious community that lived an ascetic agricultural life between the second century B.C. and the second century A.D. While the scrolls include a few intact complete manuscripts within the collection, most of the documents are in fragments. Researchers have examined the scrolls to further their understanding of the Hebrew text of Old Testament, the rise and development of early, or intertestamental, Judaism, and the cultural backdrop of the New Testament.

New Age interest in the DSS stems from the assertion that both John the Baptist and Jesus received Essene training. They base this claim on similarities in teachings and practice. Like members of this sect, John and Jesus denounced sinners, called for repentance, quoted from the Old Testament, and baptized converts. New Age adherents see John and Jesus, like their Essene compatriots, as preparing for an age of righteousness in which lessons about love, light, and karmic law would be practiced. Some maintain that after Jesus received Essene training, He was initiated into Egypt's ancient mystery religion at the great pyramid of Alexandria. He then underwent a symbolic crucifixion of self in the tomb of His soul.

It is further claimed that Mary, Joseph, and Elizabeth, the mother of John the Baptist, were members of the Essenes. Mary, like her mother before her, was allegedly chosen at the age of four as a potential channel for the coming messiah. She was then mentally, physically, and spiritually trained for the role she would fulfill at the age of seventeen. New Age adherents also claim the DSS reveal unexpected revelations on the meaning and way to salvation. These Lord Maitreya, the New Age messiah, will use to synthesize all religion into a spiritual whole for the coming Aquarian era.

*See also:* BIBLE, JESUS CHRIST, MARY, NEW AGE MOVEMENT

# DEATH

The cessation of physical life (Gen. 2:16–17; 3:19; 5:1–31). Death also signifies temporal and eternal separation from God (John 8:24; Rom. 5:12ff.; Eph. 2:1–3; 4:18–19; 2 Thess. 1:7–9; Rev. 20:11–15). The occurrence of death implies a changed relationship between a person and God, and ultimately impacts every dimension of existence. From the biblical perspective, death is not an unconscious state of existence, rebirth into another form of life, or the absorption into cosmic universal reality. Neither is it the pathway through which every individual will experience unending paradise, or the absolute end to personal human existence.

New Age adherents reject the biblical teaching on death. Some claim that death is nothing more than a learning experience in love before reentrance into another, and hopefully more advanced, life form. They say that the death experience is determined by the individual who, as a divine part of the universal whole, creates the destiny that best serves karmic justice. Life reputedly is a temporary suspension from the power and freedom of the discarnate realm. They see death as a transformational doorway to the ethereal dimension. Although the spirit separates from the body at death, they believe the spirit continues its existence as part of the universal energy force, adding to it another lifetime of wisdom and knowledge. New Age adherents view death as the source of spiritual and physical life as well as the liberating agent of light, love, wisdom, and rebirth.

*See also:* ABORTION, BLOOD SACRIFICE, FALL OF HUMANITY, KARMA, REINCARNATION, ROCK MUSIC, SUICIDE

# DECLARATION OF INTERDEPENDENCE

An official document drafted by the World Affairs Council in 1975. The Declaration claims that future objectives cannot be measured by individual accountability, but by the cosmic contribution every person makes to the universal whole. Because portions of the Declaration address legitimate concerns, some highly respected global leaders have endorsed the entire document. Among other things, the Declaration asserts the following: "To establish a New World Order of compassion, peace, justice, and security, it is essential that humankind free itself from the limitations of national prejudice and acknowledge that the forces that unite it are incomparably deeper than those that divide it."

*See also:* GLOBALISM; ONE-WORLD IDEAL; POLITICS, NEW AGE

## DECREE

A high speed chant in which participants affirm the deity of their inner self. Decrees are part of the worship services observed by members of the Church Universal and Triumphant (CUT), a New Age cult founded in 1958 by Theosophist Mark L. Prophet (1918–1973). Since his death, the group has been led by Elizabeth Clare Prophet (b. 1939). She claims that each "decree" surrounds participants in the Violet Consuming Flame through which their karma is purified. Both color and sound are given special spiritual significance, and these are the standard tools practitioners use to induce altered states of consciousness. Once the mind is brought to this point, inherent defense mechanisms are shut down and devotees are much more susceptible to demonic control.

*See also:* CHANT; LOGOS; UNIVERSAL AND TRIUMPHANT, CHURCH

## DEEP ECOLOGY

A New Age environmental philosophy popularized in 1973 by Norwegian Ecologist Arne Naes. Deep ecologists claim that the earth is a living organism of which people are an interrelated part. They also assert that all species possess intrinsic value to the global community. They believe the future of humankind can only be assured by the careful examination and alignment of life, society, and nature.

*See also:* ENVIRONMENTALISM, GLOBALISM, MOTHER EARTH

## DEGUCHI NAO (1836–1918)

Japanese shaman and founder of the syncretistic Japanese-Christian religion Omotokyo. Deguchi Nao first became prominent at age 55 by proclaiming a radical millennialism that struck out at government policies. Most of her writings were scratched out with a nail in a form of spirit writing. At about the turn of the century, she declared that her new son-in-law, Ueda Kisaburo, was the Messiah. He became a perennial enemy of the emperor and was jailed in 1921 and 1935. After World War II, the movement became known as Aizenen, "the community of love and virtue." While the movement itself did not experience spectacular growth, it did influence other, more successful, Japanese religious developments in the twentieth century.

*See also:* AUTOMATIC WRITING

## DEISM

A system of thought in which adherents deny that God, the Creator, interferes with the laws of the universe. Even though God is ever-present outside the visible realm of creation, He is not active in it in a supernatural way. Instead, the world operates by natural and self-sustaining laws established by the Creator. Deists deny most of the tenets of Christianity.

Deism was popularized in the mid-eighteenth century during the Era of Enlightenment by the Frenchman Francois-Marie Arouet (1694–1778), who wrote under the pen name of Voltaire. He asserted that living in accordance with reason was the only true form of religion. The knowledge of God supposedly comes through humankind's rational inquiry and creative thinking. Deistic thought later became a major influence in the development of modern secular humanism and the New Age Movement.

*See also:* BIBLE, ENLIGHTENMENT, HUMANISM, SIN

## DÉJÀ VU

The feeling of having already experienced scenes and events that are being experienced for the first time. *Déjà vu* is a French adjective that means "already seen." The experience is an illusion of memory, not of the senses. Some New Age adherents claim that déjà vu offers proof of reincarnation (past-life existences), while others maintain that it provides evidence of the presence of parallel universes. Still others assert that déjà vu reflects the subconscious conversion of psychic thought into reality.

*See also:* REINCARNATION, SUBCONSCIOUS

## DELPHIC ORACLE

A temple in Delphi, a town located in Phocis, Greece, on the southern slope of Mount Parnassus. The ancient Greeks regarded Delphi as the abode of Apollo, the god of prophecy, medicine, and purification, as well as music, poetry, and the pastoral arts. The oracle (meaning "womb of the Earth") was associated with the worship of Gaea, the primal goddess and mother of all things. Both Oedipus and Socrates reputedly consulted the oracle. The Delphic oracle also advised teachers, travelers, sages, and statesmen, thereby making the temple one of the most influential powers of ancient Greek religion, economics, and politics.

Greek mythology says that Apollo murdered the high priestess of Delphi and stole the oracle from Gaea. Nevertheless, statues of the python representing the goddess continued to guard the cave-like temple. And women, known as pythonesses, continued to serve as the vehicle through which Apollo allegedly spoke. These pythonesses were often chosen at an early age and trained in the meditative arts of trance channeling. Once in the shrine, the pythonesses were seated on a tripod, the official seat representing a trinity of prophetic spirits.

The devotees would practice meditative breathing techniques, as well as ingest potions and herbs to induce a hallucinogenic state. This process was accompanied by uncontrollable trembling, grotesque facial contortions, and a frenzy of hysterical, unfathomable sounds. Priests would interpret these oracular messages, which were usually vague and hard to dispute.

New Age adherents maintain a continued interest in the Delphic oracle. Some say that the shrine still emits an abundance of cosmic energy, and that by absorbing this energy, people will unite with the universe and become aware of forgotten divine secrets. Others claim that the Oracle is the home of a channeled spirit, supposedly a disembodied entity representing the psychic contents of humanity's collective unconsciousness. This ancestral knowledge of the human race lays dormant in the brain, has evolved over time, and is inherited at birth. New Age adherents maintain that, by consulting the Delphic oracle, people can get in touch with their divine self, establish communication with the Universal Mind, fathom the mysteries of humanity's ancestral knowledge, gain unlimited human powers, and learn how to manipulate reality.

*See also:* MOTHER EARTH, PSYCHIC, TRANCE CHANNELING

## DEMON

Supernatural being who strives to deceive people, thwart the will of God, and undermine the work of the church (Matt. 12:22–29; 1 Cor. 10:20–21; Eph. 2:2; 6:12; 1 Tim. 4:1; James 2:19; Rev. 9:20; 16:14). Because of Christ's atoning sacrifice, Satan and his demonic cohorts are defeated foes (Luke 10:18; John 12:31; 16:11; Col. 2:15; Heb. 2:14). They await certain doom (Matt. 25:41; 2 Peter 2:4; Jude 1:6; Rev. 20:10). At the end of the age, they will be forced to bow to the lordship of Christ (Matt. 22:44; Phil. 2:10; Heb. 1:13; 10:13).

Some modern views claim that demons are benevolent entities from alternative planes of existence who have come to aid people on their evolutionary journey to enlightenment. Others say that demons are the personification of an innate intelligence within humankind. Still others assert that demons are a hallucination of the unconscious mind, manifested in thought and action. The last view claims that humanity's collective unconscious contains all the past, present, and future realities of all people. Humankind's negative nature supposedly is projected to the outside world in archetypal images called "demons." Because these latent primordial memories are supraindividual, they eternally preexisted in nature. New Age adherents teach that every person is linked to the collective unconscious through psychic means and can draw upon its archetypes through various mind-altering techniques.

Some witchcraft cults say that demons are the dark side of a primordial energy force that permeates all living things. Although they believe these evil energies can be manipulated through ritual magic, practitioners recognize and fear the powers with which they are dealing. Occult groups refuse to differentiate between demons and angels, simply designating them as immaterial beings that represent both good and evil. Demons, as well as angels, supposedly possess the wisdom and knowledge of the ages and make this information accessible to those who are willing to serve them.

*See also:* ANGEL, ENTITY, EVIL, EXTRATERRESTRIAL INTELLIGENCE, LUCIFERIC DOCTRINE, SPIRIT GUIDES

# DHARMA

In Hinduism and Buddhism, the religious and ethical duties of the individual. Proponents say that dharma emanates from the Universal Mind, is implanted within each living soul as natural laws, and guides people to ethical behavior. People who follow their dharma live in harmony with the universe and are assured of a favorable rebirth. Dharma represents the path by which people can eliminate attachments to the material world, gain peace, and attain nirvana, the state of absolute oneness.

The dharma emphasizes the Middle Way, a Buddhist philosophy that declares that suffering in life is caused by two different extremes—affluence and asceticism. Initiates learn that by avoiding luxury and self-torture, they can supposedly eliminate anguish and hardship, as well as attain enlightenment. The dharma also includes an emphasis on the Eight-Fold Path of Right Living. This consists of eight points arranged in three categories. The first category contains wisdom *(Panna)* and includes right understanding and right thought. The second category teaches about ethical conduct *(Sila)* and includes right speech, right action, and right livelihood. The third category addresses mental discipline *(Samadhi)* and includes right effort, right awareness, and right meditation. New Age adherents say that those who follow these prescribed religious and ethical duties will earn merit toward higher rebirths and escape the laws of karma.

*See also:* BUDDHISM, EIGHTFOLD PATH, HINDUISM, MIDDLE WAY

# DIANA

According to Roman mythology, the goddess of chastity, hunting, and childbirth, as well as the earth and moon. The Latin word "Diana" literally means moon goddess, and is identified with Artemis, the Greek goddess of wild animals, wild nature, and fertility. Legend says that Artemis was the daughter of Zeus, the supreme deity of the Greek pantheon, and Leto, the daughter of the giants Coeus and Phoebe. Lore also indicates she was the twin sister of Apollo, the god of prophecy, sunlight, poetry, and music. Roman folklore portrayed Diana as the beautiful virgin huntress who traveled through the mountains and forests accompanied by nymphs. She was widely worshiped as the protector of deserving mortals. Temples dedicated to her service were scattered throughout the oak groves of ancient lands. By the Middle Ages, Diana had become widely known as the Queen of the Witches, a title used by several pagan cults of the New Age Movement.

The ancient Romans worshiped Diana by sacrificing humans in pagan temples. In contrast, modern-day cults proclaim a gentle goddess of unconditional love. Yet these same occult groups also teach that one day Diana will eradicate all forms of "negative energy" from the earth. This ambiguous phrase refers to the removal of Christians from society. Most of the Diana cults practice feminist separatism and prohibit men from becoming official members of the coven. Although such groups give prominence to the female aspect of the goddess, they also venerate the Great Horned God that allegedly rules the underworld. They consider him to be Diana's consort and male counterpart. Occult leaders assert that the Horned God provides such positive male qualities as strength and courage. In contrast, Diana is the supreme wisdom presiding over the astral plane. She possesses such positive female qualities as passion and pleasure, and liberates her followers from bondage by allowing them the open expression of their sexual and spiritual love.

*See also:* GODDESS WORSHIP, MARY, MYTHOLOGY, PURIFICATION, WITCHCRAFT

# DIANETICS

A New Age form of counseling that probes into a person's past to remove the harmful influence of engrams, the excruciating memories of bygone experiences. Dianetics owes its origins to L. Ron Hubbard (1911–1986). He was a science fiction writer, the founder of the Church of Scientology, and author of the best-selling book entitled *Dianetics: The Modern Science of Mental Health.* Initiates into Scientology attend therapy sessions in order to experience past life regressions and relocate their divine self. Counselors called auditors work with them to subdue their engrams and increase the power of their analytical, or conscious, mind. This "cures" the patients of their psychosomatic and emotional illnesses, leading to a dramatic improvement in their quality of life.

Hubbard believed that the human mind was composed of analytical and reactive portions. The reactive part was responsible for the destructive vibrations that preclude untapped human potential. Dianetics is the process for enhancing the innate powers of the analytical mind while subduing the influence of trauma from past life experiences. Once the reactive mind is eliminated, the analytical mind would function without fault, release unlimited personal powers, create a harmonious sense of self, and pave the way for tapping into people's latent deity.

*See also:* HUBBARD, L. RON; HUMAN POTENTIAL MOVEMENT; SCIENTOLOGY; VIBRATIONS

# DISCARNATE

The state of being incorporeal, or having no physical body. Occult leaders use the term "discarnate" to refer to disembodied entities who reveal themselves to unsuspecting initiates. While some claim these entities are earthbound spirits, others say they are spirit guides or ascended masters who emanate from an alternate dimension. They supposedly have come to earth to aid in the transformation of humankind and guide the population of the planet into the Aquarian era of peace, joy, and love. Still others maintain that discarnate entities represent the survival of human consciousness after death, a stepping-stone on the road to spiritual evolution.

*See also:* ASCENDED MASTER, DEMON, ENTITY, KARMA, SHAMBALLA, SPIRIT GUIDES

# DISCORDIANISM (ERISIANISM)

A philosophical "audience cult," that reveres chaos as the universal principle. Audience cults have no concept of organization or leadership, and they constantly change. Some devotees treat their organization with utmost seriousness, while others use participation as an avenue of tongue-in-cheek creativity. The audience cult has the best chance of succeeding in a closed artistic culture or over an interactive medium such as the Internet. For these reasons, audience cults are disregarded or distrusted by more conventional faiths.

Greg Hill (Malaclypse the Younger) and Kery Thornley (Omar Khayyam Ravenhurst) founded Discordianism over coffee in a San Francisco, California, bowling alley in 1958. The two men said that they suddenly realized that they had stepped out of time, so that all action in the bowling alley was frozen around them for a period. They decided to write their experience as a book, *Principia Discordia*, a collage of sayings that has been remarkably successful.

Discordians push aside the veneer of order to see the true state of universal confusion. They believe world problems are the result of the imposition of order where it does not work. The Discordians developed their own Greek goddess of chaos, Eris, and invented the Sacred Chao, a yin-yang symbol that incorporates a pentagon and the golden apple of their Eris mythology. The Chao represents the endless cycle of order and disorder. Particularly active on the Internet, a variety of discordian groups have emerged, some connected with drug use and such odd groups as the Church of the Sub-Genius.

# DIVINATION

The art or practice of foretelling events or discovering occult knowledge by means of supernatural powers and the interpretation of omens and oracles. Divination operates under the assumption that all things are predecided, that every object and incident (regardless of how random it might appear) has cosmic significance, and that the course of the future can be discerned by examining them. Divination has been practiced by mediums, such as a sibyl, prophet, or shaman, throughout history. Rulers and dignitaries consulted them about the prospects of war, the outlook for harvesting crops, and the best time to construct a shrine, as well as the choice of laws to pass, and the selection of persons to appoint for public office. The ancient Chaldeans studied the flight of birds, patterns left in water, and the entrails of animals to deduce the future or the unknown. In contrast, the ancient Greeks interpreted dreams, observed signs, and examined the actions of people who were in a trance.

Modern practitioners claim that divination is a window into the self and the universal consciousness beyond the self. The influence of Eastern religions and occult groups has convinced seekers that the alteration of human consciousness is the only viable means to maintaining spiritual and psychological equilibrium. They promise that entering a trancelike state will heighten the innate powers of perception, and provide the universal knowledge necessary to make the most difficult decisions in life. New Age adherents divine the future and try to make sense out of the present through such practices as tarot cards, runes, *I Ching,* tea leaves, and entrails, as well as dowsing and pendulums, crystals or mirrors. Other techniques may include astrology (stars), numerology (numbers), phrenology (head bumps), and necromancy (communicating with the dead), as well as capnomancy (fire), causiomancy (burns), or chiromancy (palms).

*See also:* ASTROLOGY, CRYSTAL BALL, *I Ching,* NUMEROLOGY, RUNE, TASSEOGRAPHY

# DIVINE LIGHT MISSION (ELAN VITAL)

A form of Sikhism that borrows heavily from Hindu thought. It is notably found in the United States and other Western countries. The Divine Light Mission was founded in the 1920s by Shri Hans, the first Guru Maharaj Ji. Shri Hans was trained in the "way of the saints" tradition and established an organization in Dehli after his master's death. Leadership passed to his own sons, though they were children when he died in 1926. The mission was suddenly thrust into prominence in the 1960s when Americans seeking spiritual enlightenment in India discovered the movement. The new Guru Mahara Ji was Prem Pal Singh Rawat (b. 1958), a boy of thirteen when he was invited to the United States in 1971.

The American Divine Light Mission was founded in Colorado during this visit and immediately became popular enough to give India a boost in pilgrim tourism. The headquarters eventually were moved from Delhi to Denver, Colorado. Followers believed that they were launching a new era of world peace. However, their festival Millennium 1973 in

Houston, Texas, which was to begin a thousand-year reign of peace, was a failure. The young Maharaj Ji then married an American woman and broke ties with his mother, a leading force behind the organization. The organization became more Western in orientation, ashrams closed, and members drifted away. In the late 1970s Maharaj Ji revitalized the organization, with more Eastern thought and elaborate entertainment at programs. The headquarters were moved to Miami, Florida. In 1983, when the renewal seemed doomed, a new organization, Elan Vital, was established to spread the guru's teachings. The Maharaj Ji eventually augmented the media efforts of Elan Vital with an aggressive speaking schedule. Most connections with Indian religion are downplayed. According to Maharaj Ji's web page, there was some involvement in 1998 by nearly five hundred thousand people in eighty-one countries.

According to cult teachings, the ultimate spiritual experience is reception of the "Knowledge." This Hindu concept refers to the highest possible spiritual experience. This knowledge is entrusted by Maharaj Ji to his mahatmas, or chosen few, who then dispense it to premies, or devotees. Like many westernized Hindu cults, the Divine Light Mission advocates meditation as the path to spiritual enlightenment. The mahatmas teach that the divine light of knowledge will purify the soul only if the mind is clear of all external thoughts.

Premies are initiated into the cult through a four-step meditative program that allegedly assures spiritual advancement. To receive the Light, premies are placed in a darkened room and then touched by the mahatma. The divine light that appears within supposedly holds the Knowledge. Devotees are then instructed to meditate on its brilliance for hours at a time. During the next meditative phase, premies are instructed to focus on "divine music" with the right, or spiritual, hemisphere of the brain. (They say the left hemisphere is mortal and therefore evil.) The divine nectar, a cosmic potion allegedly taken from the brain, is the third focal point. This represents the sweetness of total devotion to Maharaj Ji. Finally, devotees are given mantras, or sacred sounds, to chant in order to enhance their meditative worship.

*See also:* GURU, HINDUISM, TRANSCENDENTAL MEDITATION

## DIVINE PRINCIPLE, THE

The sacred text of the Unification Church founded by Sun Myung Moon (b. 1920) in 1954. *The Divine Principle* was first published in 1957. According to Moon, biblical history is divided into an Old Testament age, a New Testament age, and a Completed Testament age, beginning in 1960. During each epoch, God allegedly reveals only the spiritual and intellectual truths that people are ready and willing to accept. Moon claims that during the present age, the Bible is outdated and needs to be supplemented with further revelations that God has given him. Moon also asserts that *The Divine Principle* records new truths for a New Age. Those who are capable of understanding its revelations will supposedly respond positively. Moon maintains that as spiritual awareness grows, *The Divine Principle* also will grow to reveal higher and higher levels of cosmic existence.

*See also:* ESOTERIC PHILOSOPHY; MOON, SUN MYUNG; NEW AGE MOVEMENT; UNIFICATION CHURCH

## DJWHAL KHUL

A reputed ascended Tibetan master from a spiritual kingdom known as Shamballa. Djwhal Khul claimed to have returned to earth to assist people on their spiritual journey to higher consciousness. This spirit channeled his messages through the well-known theosophist and writer Alice Ann Bailey (1880–1949). In her more than twenty books, Bailey outlined how humankind could be transformed in preparation for the coming New Age. Her books also describe how to remove the negative forces of Christianity from the earth and how to glorify Lucifer as the New Age christ.

Djwhal Khul guided Bailey to start a number of organizations to disseminate satanic information. She established the Lucifer Publishing Company, or Lucis Trust, to print her works and the Arcane School to distribute her teachings.

*See also:* ASCENDED MASTER; BAILEY, ALICE ANN; SHAMBALLA

## DOLPHIN

The New Age belief that dolphins are the reincarnation of ancient human souls and endowed with the divine intelligence of an advanced race of god-men. Environmental scientists appear to legitimatize this concept by suggesting that dolphins are capable of advanced reasoning processes. Adherents claim that dolphins are the repositories of ancient wisdom that can be telepathically communicated to those who are receptive on the psychic level. The dolphins' ability to produce high-frequency sound pulsations beyond the range of human hearing reputedly is the evolutionary achievement of an advanced life-form that has become one with its environment. Spiritual masters proclaim dolphins as the guiding light to intergalactic communication and the mystical relay to alien intelligences. These creatures supposedly possess the peaceful, gentle, and compassionate qualities that signify a harmonious union with the divine.

*See also:* EXTRATERRESTRIAL INTELLIGENCE, REINCARNATION

## DOUKHOBORS

Ancient Russian Quaker-like sect with great influence traditionally upon peasants, especially in the area of the Caucasus Mountains. The name means "spirit wrestlers" and was originally meant to be derogatory. They prefer to call themselves simply "the people of God." While influenced by an adoptionist Christian theology, the Doukhobors believe in transmigration of the soul. The group did not fare well under the communist government, and most now live in Cyprus and Canada.

*See also:* TRANSMIGRATION

## DOWSING (WATER WITCHING)

The occult practice of using a fork-shaped branch or tree limb to seek water underground. Ritual magic textbooks contain complete instructions on how to dowse. Practitioners hold a forked branch horizontally as they walk across an open area. The tip of the rod allegedly will dip down suddenly, signaling the spot where water exists beneath the surface of the ground.

The first documentation of dowsing appeared in medieval Germany, but cave drawings of dowsers date back thousands of years. One occult theory is that small magnetic fields in the earth stimulate sensors in the dowser's adrenal glands, which in turn signal the brain to move the arms holding the rod. This movement is intensified by the stick, which "leads" the dowser to the underground substance. Another theory is that the rod is responding to some kind of psychic power being channeled through it.

## DRAGON

In mythology, a huge, forked tongue, fire-breathing, venomous creature. Various cultures depict the dragon in different ways. Some picture dragons with the head of a camel or horse, the horns of a deer, and the neck of a snake. Others show the body of a serpent, crocodile, or clam. Still others display the legs of an eagle or the feet of a lion. While some dragons have the scales of a fish and reside in the water, others are depicted as having the wings of a bat and flying through the air. Still other dragons reside in wild, remote lands. Regardless of the details, this creature is known universally for its invulnerability, fierceness, and magical powers.

The dragon most often symbolizes evil, though in ancient China, the creature sometimes represented benevolence. In Revelation 12:3–4, the creature symbolizes the Devil, the archenemy of God and His people. The creature's blood-red color represents Satan's murderous character, while the dragon's other features represent the Devil's cunning, strength, and influence over nations and peoples.

Ancient alchemists believed that the dragon symbolized prophecy and wisdom, and presided over the earth, the elements, and the weather. To the Buddhist, the dragon is the defender of the law. To the Hindu, the creature is only one of a super race of reptiles. To the Taoist, the dragon symbolizes heaven, fortune, and virtue. A few Chinese assert that the dragon represents the way to spiritual perfection, as well as protection from evil spirits in the coming year.

Some New Age adherents claim that the dragon represents the negative forces of the psyche closing in on itself. Others say that in the old (Piscean) age, the dragon represents eternal wisdom or divine self, and lays hidden in the darkness of the unconscious. But in the new (Aquarian) age, the dragon will emanate forth and lead humankind to cosmic consciousness.

*See also:* BABYLON, LUCIFERIC DOCTRINE, SATAN, SERPENT, SYMBOLISM

# DREAM

Thoughts, images, or emotions that occur during sleep and in which divine revelation is sometimes communicated (Gen. 20:3–7; 1 Kings 3:5–15; Dan. 2:4; 7:1; Matt. 1:20–24; 2:12; 27:19; Acts 2:17). Austrian psychologist Sigmund Freud developed the therapeutic use of dream interpretation, suggesting that hidden messages exist within dream symbols. These thoughts are unacceptable to the human consciousness and disguised in psychic language. By unraveling the subconscious messages, the therapist could disclose the innermost thoughts and feelings of the patient.

Swiss psychologist Carl Jung disagreed with Freud, suggesting that the symbolic elements of dream evolved not only from the repressed emotions of the individual, but also from the collective unconscious of the human race. Jung said that the unfolding message portrayed in universal symbolism, revealed ancient wisdom, knowledge, fears, and powers. These emphasized the link between humanity's divine inner self and the Universal Mind.

New Age adherents claim that the dream state is a vital doorway to interdimensional communication. While some think dreams are a confused display of legitimate memories, other say that dreams reflect a cosmic link between the unconsciousness and Ultimate Reality. This connection is revealed in the demonstration of innate psychic forces such as clairvoyance, precognition, and spiritual communication, as well as telepathy, holistic healing, and astral travel. With the right preparations, according to New Age belief, dreamers can plan, control, and recall their dreams and thereby gain spiritual insight.

*See also:* CAYCE, EDGAR; COLLECTIVE UNCONSCIOUS; DREAM THERAPY; DREAMWORK; UNCONSCIOUS, THE

# DREAM JOURNAL

A book in which dreams are recorded, analyzed, and interpreted for later use. The journal helps people to focus on the emotional response they had to their dreams. Proponents believe that as people meditate on the thoughts recorded in their dream journal, they can reexperience a dream, take control of its development, and manipulate its outcome. Some New Age adherents claim that dreams are the repressed memories of the unconscious mind or the innate memories drawn from the Universal Mind. Others assert that dreams symbolize the events of life, and that people can learn to manipulate the realities of the conscious state through their dreams.

*See also:* DREAM, DREAM THERAPY, DREAMWORK

# DREAM THERAPY

An analytical approach to dream interpretation that attempts to translate unconscious messages into words that can be understood in the conscious state. The heart of dream therapy lies in interpretation. This is an ambiguous process that uses numerous analytical formulas, but it ultimately relies on subjective conclusions drawn by the interpreter. Therapists maintain that some dreams are the repressed memories and emotions stored in the unconscious mind as a complex series of veiled symbols. These symbols, when brought to the conscious state of awareness, reveal patterns of desire or fear that exist within the deepest recesses of a person's psyche. Adherents claim that when people analyze their dreams, they obtain profound insights into their divine self. They can then use this information to enhance their potential for human growth.

Sigmund Freud formulated a system of dream therapy characterized by three important elements: condensation, in which many characters are represented by one composite person; displacement, in which the object of projected feelings shifts from one entity or person to another; and symbolization, in which ideas are represented by metaphors and allegories. In analyzing dream symbols, Freud taught that symbols are a sign representing its literal meaning, or an emblem representing what is known only to the individual, or a concept representing the psychic memories of humanity's collective unconsciousness. New Age adherents claim that as people get in touch with their dreams, they can establish communication with the Universal Mind, fathom the mysteries of humanity's ancestral knowledge, gain unlimited human powers, and learn how to manipulate reality.

*See also:* DREAM; FREUD, SIGMUND; PSYCHOANALYSIS; SYMBOLISM; UNCONSCIOUS, THE

# DREAMWORK

The use of the dream state to gain access to higher dimensions of existence and to exploit the psychic forces of the mind. New Age adherents claim that dreams link the human mind to the collective unconscious, a cosmic source of universal knowledge and power. The symbols, images, and forces encountered in the dream state symbolize the fears, desires, and complexes of the human psyche and represent the keys to the spiritual evolution of humankind. Advocates claim that the successful manipulation of dreams enables people to fathom the mys-

teries of the universe, achieve unlimited spiritual growth, and master such psychic powers as telepathy, clairvoyance, and holistic healing.

Scientific research indicates that adults experience from three to five dreams a night, with each dream lasting from five to thirty minutes and occurring at ninety-minute intervals. Dreamwork attempts to enhance the subconscious experience by training initiates to preplan their dreams, take an active role in controlling them, and recall them later for interpretation. Some participants make use of dream journals, pillows, and mantras, as well as occult meditations and power objects, to induce a balanced dream state on the psychic level. Dreamwork promises to enable initiates to journey to alternate dimensions of space and time, to communicate with spiritually evolved entities, and to acquire knowledge, powers, and truths far beyond the realm of human consciousness. Negative effects can include demonic manifestations and control, severe physical and mental disorders, and the loss of perceptive and comprehensive brain functions.

*See also:* ARCHETYPE, COLLECTIVE UNCONSCIOUS, MANTRA, POWER OBJECT, PSYCHE

# DRUG

A substance taken into the body through digestion, injection, or absorption that interacts with tissue or body chemistry. In occult practice, a substance used to control others or alter the state of the mind. South American Indian tribes long have used hallucinogens to recall mythological events. African shamans use narcotics to achieve a trancelike state and to divine omens. Hindus have used morphine and opium to probe the unconscious mind and establish contact with ascended masters. Various practitioners regard their experiences as legitimate spiritual journeys.

Some New Age adherents ingest such hallucinogens as lysergic acid diethylamide (LSD), peyote, and psilocybin to produce a mental state in which to experience alternate dimensions of space and time. The sensory changes encountered are accompanied by vivid imagery, a bright array of colors, and overwhelming emotions. Through these effects, users seek a new understanding of the divine self and its union with Ultimate Reality.

Despite the medical risks associated with drug abuse and addiction, some within the New Age movement continue to tout the benefits of using chemicals to alter the mind or body. If drugs can raise the psychic awareness, their restraint may slow the evolutionary advance of humanity. These drug use advocates believe that use of mind altering drugs helps one acquire the unlimited mental powers and divine knowledge believed necessary to facilitate personal and global transformation. The "bad trip," or toxic psychosis (characterized by terrifying auditory and visual hallucinations, as well as nausea and chills), is dismissed as a temporary negative effect of this step on the road to enlightenment.

*See also:* ALTERED STATE, CONSCIOUSNESS REVOLUTION, LYSERGIC ACID DIETHYLAMIDE, MARIJUANA, PEYOTE

# DRUIDS

The priestly upper class among the ancient Celts living in Britain, Ireland, and Gaul (France) who functioned as prophets and sorcerers, wizards, and magicians. The druids were renowned for their knowledge of astrology and medicine. They venerated the sun god and believed in the immortality of the human soul, once it was ceremonially cleansed and released into the spiritual realm by certain entities. To this end, the druids established the Feast of Samhain on October 31. This celebration honors the god of the dead and his demonic cohorts. Druidism was reestablished in the late seventeenth century by pagans who were interested in their heritage. By the nineteenth century, Druid beliefs and practices were incorporated into the organizational structure of secret fraternal orders.

*See also:* CELTIC PAGANISM, HALLOWEEN, SATANISM, SYMBOLISM

# DUNGEONS AND DRAGONS (D AND D)

An occult fantasy game in which players assume the role of characters endowed with magical powers who battle their way through obstacles while acting out a scenario invented by the leader. Although many similar fantasy role-playing games are now on the market, D and D was among the first and most popular. Gary Gygax, the creator of D and D, based the game on J. R. R. Tolkien's *Lord of the Rings*.

Because D and D is a fantasy game, participants make extensive use of their imagination. The Dungeon Master tosses dice to assign different roles to each player and to unfold the drama of the game. The leader invents complex worlds of dungeons and tunnels, swords and sorcery, dragons and demons through which players can obtain adventure, treasure, and magical power. Participants might adopt the persona, character, or even the gods of a witch, wizard, troll, cleric, or demon, using all the spells, incantations, or conjurations available within the context of the role. Most of the deities, rituals, practices, and traditions were not created by Gygax, but stem from ancient witchcraft, voodoo, and pagan cults.

When D and D loses its challenge, participants may continue to develop the game further. They might discard the game board and use only their imaginations to create and enact the desired fantasy. Players might incorporate events and actions from everyday life. This blurs the distinctions between fantasy and reality.

Estimates place D and D players at 4 million, most of whom are between the ages of eight and twenty-seven. Countless others play the hundreds of fantasy role-playing games currently on the market. The market also capitalizes on this occultic interest by offering game pieces, power objects, costumes, and literature, all of which are intended to enhance the "adventure."

Despite the objections of concerned parents, religious leaders, and mental health professionals, advocates of occult fantasy games and their derivatives assert that the immediate benefits far outweigh the perceived dangers. Advocates insist that such games teach children to reason through problems, use their imagination, and conquer fears, as well as bolster self-esteem, and overcome learning disabilities. They believe that role-playing firmly implants achievable objectives in the participants' minds and motivates them to accomplish each goal chosen by the game's master.

Critics of occult role-playing, however, believe that such practices expose participants to emotional and spiritual danger. Younger players may over-identify with their character and become obsessed with the world of the occult. Participants may come to think that they can manipulate reality through visualization techniques, and alter the present and future through the use of their mind.

*See also:* AMULET, ILLUSION, MAGIC, MYSTICISM, OCCULTISM, SYMBOLISM

# E

## EAR ACUPUNCTURE

A holistic healing practice. Ear acupuncture is based on the premise that ill heath is the result of an unbalanced or obstructed energy flow in the human body. Therapists claim this psychic force travels through the human body by way of invisible channels, all of which come together at the ear. Because the ear roughly resembles a fetus in the womb, it supposedly contains acupoints for the entire body. Practitioners use appropriately inserted needles to unblock and redirect the flow of cosmic energy, resulting in the restoration of health and well-being to the patient.

*See also:* BALANCING, COSMIC ENERGY, HOLISM

## ECKANKAR (ECK)

A cult founded in 1965 by Paul Twitchell (1908–1971). He was born in Paducah, Kentucky, attended Western State Teacher's College, and served in the U.S. Navy. After leaving the Navy, Twitchell worked as a writer, editor, and journalist in the New York and Washington, D.C., areas.

Twitchell's increasing fascination with Eastern religions paved the way in 1950 for his joining the Self-Realization Fellowship (SRF), a Hindu religious group founded in 1914 by Paramahansa Yogananda. At some point, Twitchell edited the group's flagship publication entitled *The Mystic Cross.* When Twitchell was forced to leave SRF in 1955, he became a follower of an Eastern guru named Kirpal Singh. This guru led a cult named *Ruhani Satsang,* meaning "Divine Science of the Soul." Twitchell also studied the teachings of other mystics and gurus, such as Dr. Julian Johnson, author of *The Path of the Masters,* and L. Ron Hubbard, founder of Scientology. By 1964 he had disassociated himself from Singh.

In 1965, Twitchell asserted he was the incarnation of God, and the Living Eck Master. He also proclaimed himself to be a Mahanta, a divine being who had become all-powerful, all-knowing, and above human laws. In 1967, Twitchell published a book entitled *The Tiger's Fang,* a plagiarized version of Johnson's earlier work. Twitchell maintained that he had experienced out-of-body soul travel and that only through him could people know what is real. He asserted that ECK was the oldest religion on earth, having been founded by Gakko, a former inhabitant of the planet Venus who had come to earth some 6 million years ago.

After Twitchell's death in 1971, Darwin Gross became the leader of ECK. Ten years later, Gross was succeeded by Harold Kemp. Under these and other leaders, ECK has recruited tens of thousands of members worldwide. Their marketing program for recruiting new members into the cult includes a variety of advertisements, lectures, magazines, and books.

ECK combines elements of Hinduism, Gnosticism, and spiritism, as well as the occult, mysticism, and Christianity. ECK teaches that God, named Sugmad, is an impersonal totality of all that exists. Everything, including people and evil, supposedly is an extension of God who dwells in Anami Lok, the highest celestial plane. ECK espouses the belief that people bring karmic debt upon themselves when they become greedy, immoral, or wicked. This debt can be eliminated only through many reincarnations, but the path to enlightenment can be dramatically abridged by becoming a disciple, or chela, of ECK. The cult asserts that it is the only true path to God.

ECK teaches that the soul is eternal in its existence and does not need the body to survive. The cult also maintains that soul travel is the most direct route to divine self-realization, as well as attaining the level of a genuine coworker of Sugmad. They base this idea on the premise that the physical realm is characterized by illusion and limitedness, whereas the astral realm is the source of all that is real and boundless. Religious leaders such as Buddha, Christ, Hare Krishna, and Muhammad were Eck Masters who practiced soul travel. Cult leaders urge their followers to enter a trancelike state so they can project their body to the astral realm, tap into the Cosmic Consciousness, and obtain the wisdom of the ascended masters. They encourage initiates to use telepathy, dream-states, hypnosis, and meditation to travel out of the body.

*See also:* ASTRAL PROJECTION, SELF-REALIZATION, TRANCE CHANNELING, VENUS

## ECOFEMINISM

Belief that divine feminine powers exist within environmental elements and can be harnessed to enhance human potential. Ecofeminists claim that under the reign of the universal male principle, or Sky God, a patriarchal society has abused both the environment and the women who exist within it. Ecofeminists say that Mother Earth is a divine, living entity from whom all people have originated. They assert that the survival of humankind depends on the spiritual, mental, and physical transformation of the human consciousness into a harmonious union with Mother Nature. Once people are aligned with her divine energy, which permeates all living things, they will achieve a higher evolutionary state. This will liberate the human spirit and unleash boundless personal powers.

*See also:* DEEP ECOLOGY, ENVIRONMENTALISM, FEMINISM, GAEA, GODDESS WORSHIP, MOTHER EARTH, WICCA, WITCHCRAFT

## ECOTHEOLOGY

A neopantheistic belief that the biblical teaching of humanity's domination over nature places Christianity at the heart of the current environmental crisis. Ecotheologists assert that belief in a God who exists apart from nature will do little to preserve and protect the environment. The idea that people are distinct from the world only encourages them to exploit and destroy it. The proposed solution is to discard the Christian worldview and replace it with a new way of thinking. This enlightened worldview will unify God, humanity, and nature into one, thereby assuring ecological balance. This new consciousness is the reemergence of ancient paganism, contemporary witchcraft, and goddess cults—all of which claim the earth as the mother of creation.

*See also:* ENVIRONMENTALISM, GAEA, GLOBALISM, GODDESS WORSHIP, MOTHER EARTH, PANPSYCHISM, PANTHEISM

## ECTOPIA

A New Age novel written by environmentalist Ernest Callenbach. *Ectopia* depicts a fictional new country in which humans and nature attain a perfect balance. This ecological utopia is created after Washington, western Oregon, and northern California secede from the rest of the United States. The unfolding drama is seen through the eyes of a skeptical newspaper reporter, the first visitor allowed within the boundaries of the new country during the first twenty years of its existence.

Callenbach envisions a harmonious society in which a matriarchal government eradicates pollution, overpopulation, and deforestation. This theme has widely appealed to an assorted group of New Age adherents. *Ectopia* reflects the sentiments of those who advocate planetary unity, as well as bringing together diverse alternative social and political movements to achieve common environmental goals. *Ectopia* was first published by a small, independent press, but the novel soon became a classic among New Age environmentalists. They claim that such works as *Ectopia* will help transform the collective unconsciousness of humankind and pave the way for the Aquarian era of peace, love, and joy.

*See also:* COSMIC CONSCIOUSNESS, GLOBALISM, GODDESS WORSHIP, GREEN, MOTHER EARTH

# ECTOPLASM

A substance thought to be produced when an immaterial entity, such as a spirit, assumes material form. Ectoplasm is described as milky white, with an odor. Some say ectoplasm is a living ethereal substance emanating from the elements that clothe the medium in a slightly luminous matter while in its primary state. Others claim that ectoplasm floats out of the pores and mouth of the body after the spiritualist enters a trancelike state. Depending on the stage of the substance's condensation, it allegedly can be solid, liquid, or gas. The spirits of the dead supposedly use the ectoplasm to take on bodily forms, ranging from hands to vocal chords to an entire person.

*See also:* DEMON, GHOST, PARAPSYCHOLOGY, POLTERGEIST, SPIRITISM

# EDDY, MARY BAKER (1821–1910)

The founder of Christian Science, Eddy was born in Bow, New Hampshire. She grew up in frail health and was the youngest of seven children. During adolescence, she joined a Congregational church in Tilton, New Hampshire, but was repulsed by such Calvinistic doctrines as predestination. In 1843, she married George W. Glover, a local businessman. The following year he died from yellow fever while in Charleston, South Carolina. She was pregnant at the time, and her husband's death caused her great anguish. In 1853, Eddy married a dentist named Daniel Patterson, but was quite unhappy in this marriage. In 1873, she divorced Patterson on the grounds of desertion. In 1877, she married Asa G. Eddy, an active Christian Scientist who died of coronary thrombosis in 1882.

Throughout her life, Eddy's domestic problems were eclipsed only by her ill health. In 1862, she met a metaphysical healer from Portland, Maine, named Phineas P. Quimby (1802–1866). He allegedly healed her of "spinal inflammation." One month after Quimby's death in January 1866, his new disciple claimed to have taken a fatal fall. Eddy supposedly was miraculously delivered from the injury and divinely endowed with the sacred writings of a new religion called Christian Science. Although she claimed that the principles of Christian Science had cured her of all illness, she continued to struggle with sickness and pain. In fact, she often took morphine to deaden the pain and frequently sought out physicians and dentists for relief from her ailments.

Quimby's philosophy runs throughout Eddy's book, *Science and Health with the Key to the Scriptures* (1875). The book sets forth the argument that all sickness is mental rather than physical. Ironically, Eddy not only denied Quimby's influence on her written work, but also derided him as an "unlearned" man. Quimby's writings played an influential role in the development of the New Thought movement which stresses the power of the mind to heal disease and improve life. This laid the foundation for many of the beliefs and practices of the New Age Movement.

In 1879, Eddy founded the Church of Christ, Scientist (or Christian Science) in Boston, Massachusetts. In 1892, she reorganized and renamed her organization The Mother Church, the First Church of Christ, Scientist. She continued as its leader until she died in 1910. Historians say that membership peaked at about three hundred thousand in the 1930s, but by 1979 had decreased to two hundred thousand.

*See also:* CHRISTIAN SCIENCE

# EIGHTFOLD PATH

According to Buddhism, the steps for attaining nirvana, the state of absolute oneness. Advocates maintain that following the Eightfold Path will end the existence of all pain. They also teach that each step of the Eightfold Path includes the others. These steps are not performed in any particular order, but rather are dispositions and actions performed simultaneously and concurrently.

The first of eight steps teaches followers to cultivate *Right Views* by accepting the Eightfold Path. Second, develop *Right Resolve* by renouncing pleasure, harboring no animosity toward others, and refusing to harm any living creature. Third, cultivate *Right Speech* by refusing to lie, slander, or participate in idle conversation. Fourth, practice *Right Behavior* by not committing any unlawful sexual act, not stealing from others, and not destroying any living creature. Fifth, engage in *Right Occupation* by earning a living in a way that brings no harm to others. Sixth, practice *Right Effort* by abandoning all evil qualities and cultivating good qualities in life. Seventh, engage in *Right Contemplation* by becoming freed from all desire and sorrow, and remaining alert and observant. Eighth, practice *Right Meditation* by entering into heightened states of awareness through concentration exercises.

*See also:* BUDDHISM, MIDDLE WAY

## ELAN VITAL
*See:* DIVINE LIGHT MISSION

## ELECTROENCEPHALOGRAPH (EEG)

An instrument that detects and records brain waves. By attaching electrodes from the EEG to the scalp of the patient, scientists monitor how nerve impulses in the brain change with varying levels of consciousness. The normal level of consciousness, represented by the beta wave, produces small, fast oscillation patterns at a rate of thirteen to thirty per second, whereas the delta wave, representing a state of deep sleep, produces large, slow oscillation patterns. The most popular level of consciousness to New Age adherents is the alpha state at a rate of eight to twelve oscillations per second. Proponents claim that practitioners in this state are more relaxed, spiritually aware, and open to cosmic enlightenment.

## ELECTROMAGNETIC HEALING (EMH)

An occult therapeutic technique, Electromagnetic Healing is based on the idea that an electromagnetic field surrounds all living things. Advocates claim that illness and pain are an accumulation of unbalanced energy,

corrected by realigning the electromagnetic forces of the mind, body, and spirit. Once the body's vibrational energy force is recognized, it supposedly can be stimulated or stabilized, transmitted or modified to enhance the health and healing of the mind, body, and soul.

Some New Age adherents assert that people have biologically evolved to carry and transform the healing energy surrounding their body into electromagnetic waves, or photons of light. People use a variety of devices to manipulate these waves. Quartz crystals are a popular power object used to summon psychic forces and promote holistic healing. Adherents maintain that the light waves emanating from the crystals produce spiritual illumination, whereas the x-rays coming from the object penetrate the skin to balance the vibrational frequencies of the body. When soaked in various solutions, crystals supposedly magnetize the liquid, which then creates elixirs rich in healing energies. Others use the electromagnetic field unit to align a patient's energy field with that of the earth. This procedure is to reduce pain and stress, alter consciousness, and enhance communication with entities in other dimensions of space and time.

*See also:* MIND BODY MEDICINE, POWER OBJECT, QUARTZ CRYSTAL

## ELEMENTS OF MAGIC
*See:* PENTACLE

## ELIADE, MIRCEA (1907–1986)

As a historian of religions, Mircea Eliade helped popularize the concept of *myth* in postmodern Western culture. He attempted to trace all mystical phenomena to a small number of primordial myths. Eliade studied Eastern religions and philosophy in India and lived in a Himalayan ashram for a time. At the University of Bucharest he taught the history of religions and Indian philosophy until he had to flee the Holocaust in 1939. After World War II, he taught at the Sorbonne in Paris and in 1956 took a position at the University of Chicago, where he remained. In 1961 he founded the journal *History of*

*Religions.* Eliade considered religious experience to be rooted in *hierophanies* (manifestations of the sacred). In later life he was particularly noted for his work in occult spirituality and wrote a three-volume work, *A History of Religious Ideas* (1978-85). He was editor-in-chief of the sixteen-volume *Encyclopedia of Religion* (1987).

*See also:* CAMPBELL, JOSEPH

## ENDORPHINS

Neurotransmitters occurring naturally in the brain and affecting the perception of pain, changes in mood, learning, and memory retention. Neurotransmitters send electrical impulses across a junction called a synapse. These separate one nerve cell, or neuron, from another nerve cell or muscle. Endorphins, which were discovered in the 1970s, are chemically similar to narcotics derived from opium. New Age adherents claim that endorphic research is a westernized, scientific version of such Eastern practices as acupuncture. Acupuncture is a Chinese therapeutic technique in which fine metal needles are inserted into the skin at designated points to alleviate pain or combat disease.

Scientists know that pain can be blocked from conscious awareness. The levels of endorphins released by the body do not always correspond to the actual amount of pain or stress experienced. Holistic healers assert that by entering a trancelike state, people can regulate production of endorphins. The more endorphins released by the brain, the greater the feeling of euphoria and sense of enlightenment. Advocates claim that endorphin therapy can induce greater self-awareness, sexual libido, social bonding, and well-being. They say it reduces pain, stress, loneliness, anguish, and fear in the mind/body/spirit continuum.

*See also:* ALTERED STATE, DRUG

## ENGRAM

According to Scientology, an excruciating memory of past experiences that confuses the reactive, or unconscious mind. Trained counselors, called auditors, work with patients to subdue the engrams and increase the power of their analytical, or conscious, mind. This "cures" the patients of their psychosomatic and emotional illnesses, leading to a dramatic improvement in their quality of life. By going through this process, patients are freed from negative forces and can tap their latent deity. Successful completion supposedly brings a quantum leap in spiritual powers and awareness.

*See also:* DREAM THERAPY; HUBBARD, L. RON; SCIENTOLOGY

## ENLIGHTENMENT

A state of pure mystical awareness in which Ultimate Reality is attained. When devotees achieve enlightenment, their sense of personal identity vanishes, they are released from the realm of illusion, and they realize their innate divinity. Enlightenment may be referred to in a variety of ways. These include illumination, transformation, or intervention; as well as eureka, satori, or gestalt formation. Other labels include quantum leap, peak experience, or left-brain shift; and also grace, the miracle, or being born again. A sense of oneness with the cosmic consciousness supposedly is attained through a variety of mind-altering techniques. Those who become enlightened acquire unlimited psychic powers and can manipulate the past, present, and future.

*See also:* CHRIST-CONSCIOUSNESS, PEAK EXPERIENCES, SALVATION, SATORI, SELF-ACTUALIZATION, SELF-REALIZATION

## ENNEAGRAM

An ancient occult symbol of interlocking triangles, nine points of which touch an outer circle. These nine points represent the Egyptian belief in the Great Ennead, a family of nine gods and goddesses, including Osiris, Isis, and Horus. Occult groups claim the number nine (9) represents fervency, impulsiveness, and power, as well as authority and the perfected form of the unholy trinity (in other words, 6 + 6 + 6 = 18; 1 + 8 = 9). Because of the enneagram's association with the number nine, occultists consider it an important symbol.

New Age numerology teaches that the number nine and the enneagram symbolize the nine orders of hell and the nine divine masters. The latter have come from the astral dimension to guarantee the evolutionary progress of humankind. Some say these masters control powerful networks of New Age workers who will usher in the leader of the Aquarian era. Others maintain that the enneagram has the power to identify and describe basic personality types of people, their compulsions, and their abilities to interrelate. Devotees also assert that the enneagram provides humankind with the keys to unlocking ancient mysteries. Those who unravel these secrets will obtain power and riches.

**Enneagram— perfected form of the unholy trinity**

*See also:* POWER OBJECT

## ENOCH

The son of Jared and the father of Methuselah (Gen. 5:18, 21). Enoch lived seven generations after Adam and prophesied about the coming day of the Lord (1 Chron. 1:2–3; Jude 14–15). Enoch was an upright person who trusted and obeyed God during his 365 years on earth. This righteous man never died, for God took him directly to heaven (Gen. 5:24; Heb. 11:5).

In New Age thought, Enoch symbolizes human spiritual evolution, proving that people have the ability to leave the confines of the illusory world and attain the reality of the astral plane. Concerning his prophecy recorded in 1 Chronicles and Jude (and in the pseudepigraphic First Book of Enoch), some believe Enoch based this material on an apocryphal gospel discovered in 1773. This document allegedly contains a series of messages that ascended masters revealed to Enoch detailing the nature of life. Proponents claim that Enoch obtained these secrets while on mystical journeys into heaven and hell.

Occult leaders also assert things about Enoch that contradict the clear teaching of Scripture. Aria Jaeger has written an occult book entitled *The Keys: Enoch's Teachings Simplified,* published in 1995 by Reincarnation Books. The author maintains that sixty-four keys open cosmic doors and link people to the infinite powers of the universe. *The Keys* describes a plan for using genetics, physics, and holography, as well as laserology, communications, and other technological advances to bring about a quantum leap in the evolutionary transformation of the world. The main character in *The Keys* claims to have been translated into heaven and given the sacred texts for a New Age. These documents are written in a coded language and can be used to unlock the gate of the ascended masters of the Great White Brotherhood. This group proclaims the coming of an Aquarian era of higher consciousness.

*See also:* BIBLE, NEW AGE; ENLIGHTENMENT; GREAT WHITE BROTHERHOOD; TRANSFORMATION

## ENTITY

In New Age thinking, a being so advanced that it has escaped the illusion of material existence and transcended to the astral plane. These entities are known as spirit guides, ascended masters, inner selves, higher selves, and angels of light, as well as extraterrestrials, power images, and universal intelligences. New Age adherents believe these beings come to earth to aid people on their evolutionary journey to enlightenment. They also claim these entities are personifications of the innate intelligence within humankind.

According to the latter view, these entities exist independently of physical form and represent a psychic form of higher consciousness created in the mind. Some maintain that entities are an archetype of the divine self, while others assert they are a reflection of the universal soul present in all people or a primordial image of the psychic contents of humanity's collective unconsciousness. Through diverse means of communication, these entities allegedly bring their messages to New Age initiates. They teach that God is an impersonal force, that biblical accounts concerning Jesus Christ are myths, and that Lucifer is the divine Morning Star and Light-Bearer.

*See also:* ARCHETYPE, AVATAR, DEMON, PARAPSYCHOLOGY, SPIRIT GUIDES, TRANCE CHANNELING

# ENTROPY

The measure of energy that is lost or no longer usable in a closed thermodynamic system. The greater the entropy, the less energy is available with which to do useful work. Entropy also measures the amount of disorder or randomness within a system. According to the second law of thermodynamics, entropy in the universe is increasing. Matter and energy in the universe continuously degrade until they reach a state of inert uniformity. Entropy also means that all processes within a system undergo the loss of energy. The presence of these inefficiencies indicate that closed thermodynamic systems will run down over time, or move toward greater uncertainty and disorder.

New Age adherents argue that entropy exists only within the physical realm; the second law of thermodynamics does not govern the operation of psychic energies in the universe. The values, vision, and ideologies emanating from the human mind determine how people interact with their environment. This determines the actual amount of entropy existing on the planet. Such Christian doctrines as sin and eternal damnation are considered negative influences that increase the world's entropy. Banishing Christians to other dimensions of space and time will bring about the transformation of human consciousness. This will then decrease the world's entropy and spark a quantum leap in humankind's evolutionary development.

*See also:* COSMIC ENERGY, ENVIRONMENTALISM, GLOBALISM, INTERDEPENDENCE, TRANSFORMATION

# ENVIRONMENTALISM

A movement that advocates the preservation and improvement of the natural environment. Environmentalists strive to educate the public on ecological dangers, such as air and water pollution, wasteful use of resources, and excessive human encroachments. They also encourage action among alternative groups to achieve common goals, based on the idea that humankind and nature are inseparably linked.

Since the late 1960s, the surge in New Age spiritualism has increased public support for private organizations that have placed real and imaginary environmental concerns at the center of the political arena. Many maintain that a huge environmental crisis looms, and that only a one-world government with absolute authority can solve it. An increasing number of goddess cults have also joined New Age environmentalist groups to establish the earth as a sacred entity, inhabited by humans playing an interdependent role.

*See also:* ECOFEMINISM, GAEA, GLOBALISM, GREEN, MOTHER EARTH

# ERDMANN, PAUL

*See:* ARMAGEDDON, CHURCH OF

# ERHARD, WERNER HANS (b. 1935)

The founder of the Erhard Seminars Training (EST/Forum). Originally named John Paul Rosenberg, Erhard changed his name in 1960. In the ensuing years, Erhard engaged in a number of enterprises, including selling cars, magazines, and encyclopedias. During his travels, he studied Scientology, Zen Buddhism, and Mind Dynamics, which teaches that the mind has the potential to achieve unlimited things. Those who learn to exploit the mind's infinite powers can achieve untold health and wealth.

In 1963, Erhard asserted that his life was transformed by a psychic experience in which he became enlightened. He continued to immerse himself in Eastern mysticism— hypnosis, yoga, psychocybernetics, and transpersonal psychology. He claimed permanent enlightenment in 1971, the year he established EST. The main theme of EST is that people have the innate power to transform themselves and experience life to the fullest. He bases this on the premise that the mind is a source of infinite possibility and has the power to shape and determine what is real.

According to Erhard, a supreme, personal God simply does not exist, and people are their own gods. He holds to a pantheistic view that *God is everything, and everything is God*. Initiates are indoctrinated to believe in no moral absolutes and that the world contains no determining truths. People reputedly must look within themselves to discover morals and truth and to experience genuine liberation from life's problems. Avid disciples believe that sheer willpower can improve their health, save their marriages, and increase their finances. Enlightenment comes when initiates accept the fact that their rational and objective view of the world is an illusion. Reality exists only within the mind and is created by the mind.

EST consists of a sixty-hour training seminar designed to teach participants how to assert themselves. The seminar involves locking participants into a room, with no bathroom facilities, while trainers systematically break down their personalities. Trainers repeatedly address participants with obscenities and ridicule. Then they attempt to rebuild the shattered personalities by teaching manipulation and assertion techniques. Participants reach the point of rejecting the ideas of right and wrong. Reality is chosen at will, regardless of how it affects the world around them.

EST had more than five hundred thousand graduates in the first thirteen years of operation. By the mid-1980s, interest had dwindled, and Erhard took his seminars to the business word. He founded the Forum, claiming that just as the people of the 1970s wanted to "get it together," people of the 1980s wanted to "make it happen." Since the Forum was directed more toward the business community, verbal abuses, deprivations, and degradation were exchanged for an informal dialogue between leaders and participants, laced with catchy phrases, songs, and dances.

Through the four sixteen-hour sessions of the Forum, EST still promised to put participants in touch with their "being," the dimension they use to either limit or expand their creativity. Trainers told initiates how to shape their action, performance, and results, being responsible for no one but themselves. The Forum held that, in order to genuinely reach their "being," people must realize that they are gods in their individual universes.

*See also:* PSYCHOTHERAPY

## ERISIANISM
*See:* DISCORDIANISM

## ESALEN INSTITUTE

A major think tank for the promotion of Eastern mysticism, the revival of occultism, and the introduction of the Human Potential Movement in America. The Esalen Institute was cofounded in 1962 by Michael Murphy and Richard Price in Big Sur, California. Esalen claims that human potential can be beneficially incorporated into education, politics, and health care, as well as the interconnected relations among people around the world. A primary goal is to research religion, philosophy, and physical science, placing emphasis on the value of human spiritual potential. Esalen has become a repository of New Age thought and regularly introduces occult ideas and practices to the public. The institute boasts an impressive list of visitors, many of whom have become leaders in the Human Potential Movement.

In 1979, Michael Murphy discovered that Soviet society was receptive to New Age thinking. Under the auspices of Esalen, he began the Soviet-American Exchange Program in which citizens from the U.S. and Russia collaborated in consciousness research. The Institute is best known for such controversial techniques as sensitivity training and encounter groups, in which participants are invited to release suppressed thoughts and feelings. Initiates are trained to use occult practices, such as channeling, to obtain wisdom from entities from the astral dimension. They also learn how to use transcendental meditation techniques to help them explore their higher self and to become one with Universal Reality. Physical program studies include bodywork, skilled touching (massage), and yoga. Because of the pioneering work of Esalen, these practices have become popular within the New Age Movement.

*See also:* ONE-WORLD IDEAL; POLITICS, NEW AGE

# ESOTERIC CHRISTIANITY

The search for hidden knowledge and secret or veiled truths within Christianity. This information allegedly has been preserved in occult traditions until humanity is ready for full revelation. Esoteric Christianity was popularized by theosophist Annie Besant (1847–1943). Advocates maintain that they embrace all that is best in the world's creeds, philosophies, and sciences. They also contend that all people can unite, regardless of their race, gender, ethnicity, or faith.

Proponents seek to unveil the hidden meaning of all the sacred texts of all the world's religions, allowing everyone to realize their innate divinity and union with the cosmic mind. They claim the Bible is an esoteric text, complete with secret symbols and hidden meanings, and can be fathomed only by the spiritually advanced. Esoteric Christians believe God is a human being, Jesus is an ascended master, Christ is an attainable state of mind, and Lucifer will one day appear as the world's messiah.

*See also:* BESANT, ANNIE WOOD

# ESOTERIC PHILOSOPHY

A system of thought maintaining that all knowledge and truth remain hidden or obscured from casual observation. Only those who have been properly initiated can accept or fathom such ideas as the innate divinity of people, the necessity of uniting humanity under a one-world government and religion, and the certainty that a New World Order will eventually arise. Ascended masters from other dimensions of space and time allegedly assist devotees in their interpretations. These entities claim they have come to earth to aid people on their evolutionary journey to enlightenment.

New Age adherents use esoteric philosophy to understand the enigmas of history, science, and mathematics and to explain the meaning of life, especially as it pertains to people and Ultimate Reality. Such ideas occur commonly in occult documents, books, and manuals, written by those using their so-called psychic giftedness. Many claim their work is the result of automatic handwriting. Therefore deliberate inaccuracies, strange symbols, and unfamiliar semantics can only be understood by the enlightened.

*See also:* NEW WORLD ORDER

# ESP

*See:* EXTRASENSORY PERCEPTION

# ESP CARDS

*See:* ZENAR CARDS

# ETHER

According to ancient Greek philosophy, a divine substance of the heavens, the stars, and the souls of those who are spiritually evolved. Mystics later claimed that ether exists in all matter, including the light-body of the inner person. Practitioners developed techniques to help people transcend their physical body and unite with their etheric body. Some maintain that the ether cannot be seen or felt. Other mystics say the human aura is composed of ether and manifested in the emanation of psychic light energy. New Age adherents assert that a person's astral body is composed of ether and can be released from the physical body to wander through other planes of existence, a phenomenon known as astral travel. They also claim that ether is the common life fluid that joins people with Ultimate Reality. Occultists use this idea to support their teaching that a divine spark exists within every person and is ready to be ignited.

*See also:* ASTRAL PLANE

# EVIL

Throughout history, philosophers and theologians have debated the existence and cause of moral and natural evil in the world. Christian scholars have made at least seven key observations regarding this.

First, much physical evil is a consequence of human choice, whether remote (by reason of Adam's past fall into sin, as well as the past free choice of demons to rebel against God) or immediate (the result of current mistakes or flawed judgment). Second, when physical evil occurs, it falls on both the wicked and the righteous. Third, evil serves as a reminder that this fallen world is ultimately a training and proving ground for the perfect world to come (Rom. 5:3–5; 2 Peter 1:5–7). Fourth, evil serves to engender a sense of perspective in God's people by causing believers to realize that, when compared with the evil they experience in this life, a far better world and life await them in the future (Rom. 8:18). Fifth, evil serves to foster hope. God's people know that their focus is heavenward (Col. 3:1–2). The evil of this world prompts them to long for the future kingdom of God (Heb. 11:13–16). Sixth, evil serves to wean believers from their sinful tendencies. Christians who have experienced the malicious attacks of the wicked no longer have a desire to live as their antagonists do, but gain an increased desire to do the will of God (1 Peter 4:2). Seventh, evil serves to underscore the care, preservation, and power of almighty God (Rom. 8:38–39). The Lord deals with the existence of evil in this present world, not just in the world to come, and He directly answers the prayers of saints for deliverance.

New Age adherents reject all seven observations. They claim that the universe exists as a great energy mass, generated by equal yet opposing forces. These are complementary and reciprocal, and permeate all living things. Evil is a state of illusion, a condition of energy imbalance in the evolutionary knowledge of human development. The illusion of evil (sickness, fear, violence, demons, and death) is merely a matter of personal perception, and therefore only as real or as powerful as each individual wants it to be.

Evil is regarded as a positive force because it encourages growth toward a state of higher cosmic consciousness. Because they see people as innately divine and therefore good, no moral absolutes or truths exist. They claim all morality and truth is relative to the preferences and determinations of each person. Because evil is reputedly nothing more than an illusion, it can be eliminated through the transformation of human consciousness.

*See also:* CHRIST-CONSCIOUSNESS; FALL OF HUMANITY, THE; GUILT; HOLISM; LUCIFERIC DOCTRINE; SIN; YIN/YANG

# EVOLUTION

The process by which change occurs in the genetic makeup of plant and animal species. Popularly the term is used to refer to the theory of naturalistic evolution, which explains the diversity of species on earth as a product of chance occurrences over enormous spans of time. Evolutionists believe that plants and animals naturally change to adapt to their environment. Those that do not adapt die. The modifications in the surviving members over successive generations eventually cause species to become more complex forms of life. A basic tenet of naturalistic evolutionary theory is materialism. The material world is all that exists, and life operates within a closed universe. A creating God who rules over and maintains creation is unneeded.

To avoid misunderstanding, creationists—who do most emphatically posit the necessity of a creating and governing God—carefully distinguish between macroevolution and microevolution. The theory of naturalistic evolution promoted (though not developed) by Charles Darwin (1809–1882) involves macroevolutionary processes, by which one species changes into something different. Creationists accept microevolution, through which successive generations change within species to adapt to environment while remaining in all essentials the same species. All selective breeding of plants and animals and modern forms of genetic research aim at microevolutionary change.

Some theists do believe in a Creator while also accepting most aspects of macroevolutionary theory. These "theistic evolutionists" believe that the processes of evolution have been superintended by God over long expanses of time.

New Age philosophy has faced a similar problem to that of theists in deciding how to maintain belief in a spiritual universe in the face of materialistic evolution assumptions. New Age adherents generally accept most teachings of materialistic science uncritically. They do, however, organize their understandings of these processes around a pantheistic worldview. Modern movements such as Wicca and Goddess Worship look for an earth mother that is the living womb of all things. Their beliefs are driven in part by a desire to spiritualize the atheistic presumption of evolutionary processes. New Age evolution offers a natural process that is guided in some fashion by the life force within the organic and inorganic realms.

Reincarnation itself is a spiritual evolutionary worldview, and the journey of a soul toward enlightenment is similar to the New Age expectations that humanity is moving toward new, higher forms of spiritual life in the Age of Aquarius.

*See also:* MOTHER EARTH; REINCARNATION; SCIENCE, NEW AGE; WICCA

## EXPERIENCE

Mystical states, such as enlightenment, divine awareness, psychic visions, and extraterrestrial contacts, occurring in altered states of consciousness. New Age adherents claim that these experiences signify a religious or mystical encounter with the Universal Mind. People become enraptured with the cosmic consciousness and have a sense of profound understanding, ineffability, and transiency. Advocates say that after such experiences, people have a greater awareness of their innate divinity and are more receptive to the wisdom and guidance of ascended masters.

They learn from their mystical encounter that evil does not exist—that it is merely an illusory variation of the great cosmic force that permeates life.

*See also:* ENLIGHTENMENT, MYSTICISM, PEAK EXPERIENCES

## EXTRASENSORY PERCEPTION (ESP)

The ability to receive, understand, and respond to past, present, and future knowledge apart from the aid of the five senses. Such knowledge is obtained from other people's minds or from objects and events in the outside world. Advocates of ESP maintain that energy fields in the universe stimulate the psychic senses. Since these senses are not bound by physical laws, practitioners are able to transcend both time and space using their psychic abilities to gain access to the past, present, and future in the minds and lives of others.

The three primary categories of ESP are telepathy, clairvoyance, and precognition. These psychic abilities, as well as psychokinesis, remote viewing, and psychometry, are investigated in the field of research known as parapsychology. In the 1930s, noted biologist J. B. Rhine conducted the first scientific investigations of ESP at Duke University. For the next thirty years, parapsychologists depended upon elementary tests, such as the percentage ratios produced by subjects using cards and dice, to measure psychic ability.

During the countercultural movement of the 1960s, psychic research greatly increased. Innovative testing methods, using computer-enhanced technology, were developed. Since then, New Age adherents have made ESP into a multibillion dollar industry. Hundreds of programs, techniques, and paraphernalia were designed to help initiates transcend their consciousness and establish contact with their divine self. Initiates are led to believe that through ESP, they can tamper with time, journey to parallel universes, and eventually merge their consciousness with the cosmic consciousness.

*See also:* CLAIRVOYANCE, PSYCHIC, PSYCHOKINESIS, ZENAR CARDS

## EXTRATERRESTRIAL INTELLIGENCE (ETI)

Interplanetary visitors who allegedly come to earth to aid people on their psychic journey to higher consciousness. Some New Age adherents say that in previous lives they were aliens. Others assert they are able to communicate telepathically with ETIs. Still others maintain that ETIs chose them as special messengers to earth, and that they received esoteric knowledge while on UFOs. Such alien revelations include claims that humankind is on the verge of experiencing a quantum leap in evolutionary development, that a time of turmoil followed by an epoch of peace will soon come, and that a dynamic leader will emerge and usher in the New World Order.

*See also:* UNIDENTIFIED FLYING OBJECT, UNIDENTIFIED FLYING OBJECT EXPERIENCE

## EYE OF HORUS

The center of spiritual vision that is said to exist in the middle of the forehead of the Egyptian god Horus, who was traditionally depicted as entombed in the underworld. His soul is watchful while awaiting rebirth. Folklore relates that Horus was the son of Osiris, god of the underworld, and Isis, the Mother Goddess of Egypt. Horus represents the new age christ, whose soul waits in the underworld to be cloaked in the light of rebirth. Occult leaders urge initiates to meditate on the eye of Horus, for then they will gain insight into the Universal Mind and become enlightened.

**Eye of Horus— the god within awaiting rebirth**

Through the influence of Freemasonry in United States history, the eye of Horus came to be depicted on the reverse side of the paper currency of the U.S. dollar.

*See also:* FREEMASONRY, PYRAMIDOLOGY, TRIANGLE

# F

## FAIRY

In folklore, a being with magical powers. Throughout history, most stories involving fairies center around the souls of the dead. Some legends depict small, mischievous creatures with transparent wings and magic wands. Other myths present fairies as the lingering souls of the evil dead, the souls of unbaptized newborns, or the guardian souls of deified ancestors, such as the Fairy Godmother. In the Middle Ages, people believed fairies were real women of ordinary size who possessed secret knowledge as disciples of the Mother Goddess (Gaea, Diana, and Venus), from whom all life began.

Ancient myths describe fairies as having the power to transform a person into an animal or stone ,to disappear and to reappear at will, and invoke the universal powers of the mother spirit. Some suggest that fairies lived in the burrows, mushrooms, and river banks of the woodlands. Others say they reside in an astral realm between heaven and hell and are accessible only to mortals who can manipulate the extrasensory powers that lie dormant within all people. Legend claims that fairies travel in groups and are usually more concerned with their own lives than with those of humans. If people want the aid of a fairy, they must apply to the entity's chief, to the Devil, or to the fairy queen. Even then the fairy's volatile nature, nasty temper, and tendency toward mischief might do more harm than good. Many New Age adherents have incorporated the concepts and descriptions of these creatures into their occult beliefs and practices.

*See also:* DEMON, DIANA, GAEA, GODDESS WORSHIP, MAGIC, MYTHOLOGY, VENUS, WICCA

## FAITH

In religious usage, belief or trust *in* and loyalty *to* a being transcendent to oneself. Faith includes cognition (mental awareness), comprehension (understanding), conviction (acceptance), and commitment (unswerving fidelity—Acts 16:31; Rom. 4:1–25; 9:30–33). Hebrews 11:1 relates that faith has to do with spiritual realities, unseen by human eyes.

In Christian usage, faith can be defined as dependent certainty in the promises revealed by God in Scripture. Through faith in Christ and His atoning sacrifice comes salvation in the Christian view (John 1:12–13; 3:16; Rom. 10:9–13; Eph. 2:5–10).

Other religious faith systems reject all or part of the biblical concept of faith. In Eastern mysticism, for example, faith is a confidence in the psychic ordering of the universe, a hunger or spiritual instinct for the christ within, or the higher self taking control of the inferior, lower self. New Age initiates focus faith on themselves as a divine being. Jesus supposedly is one of many incarnated christs who can open their consciousness to the presence of the divine light within. The object of faith is immaterial, as long as it enables enhancement of paranormal experiences. Faith is a tool for entering altered states of consciousness to reach the astral plane, for rediscovering the divine self, for getting in touch with the Universal Mind, and for receiving esoteric truths.

*See also:* CHRIST-CONSCIOUSNESS, EXPERIENCE, LIGHT, SALVATION

## FALL OF HUMANITY, THE

The phrase Christian theologians use to describe humankind's tragic descent from a state of moral perfection and innocence to one of sin and guilt. With the Fall came the presence of guilt, shame, sin, and death. The Creator and His creatures were alienated and separated from each other. The creation itself was subjected to deterioration. All of humanity was plunged into a never-ending cycle of corruption and degradation. Scripture teaches that these things occurred when Adam willfully disobeyed God's specific command in the Garden of Eden (Gen. 2:15–3:24; Isa. 59:1–2; Rom. 3:1–23; 5:12ff.; 8:18–23; Gal. 3:22; Eph. 2:12).

New Age adherents reject the biblical account concerning the fall of humanity. Some claim it was the point at which humans forgot their oneness with the universe. When the serpent encouraged Adam and Eve to eat from the Tree of Knowledge, they say he was setting humanity back on the true spiritual path. New Age adherents teach that when people left their conscious mind of Eden, they began their evolutionary journey toward divine consciousness.

Other New Age adherents believe the human race began as disembodied souls or extensions of a cosmic energy force, and roamed about exploring the multidimensional universe. After discovering creative mind powers on Earth, these souls became so obsessed with the sensations of material existence that they took on physical form. Then the entities began to develop a consciousness. As their self-awareness grew, their divine awareness became buried deep in the recesses of their memory. Then the Universal Mind sent Adam and Eve to rescue these lost souls, but they somehow forgot they were divine. Therefore Lucifer, the New Age Bearer of Light, came to redirect confused and lost humanity back to the path of enlightenment.

*See also:* SALVATION, SATAN, SIN

# FAMILIAR

A physical manifestation of a demon in animal form sent to aid in the practice of witchcraft. (In some cultures, people view the familiar not as a demon, but as an incarnation of their soul or as a guardian spirit sent by the gods.) Although traditionally associated with the black cat, familiars take the form of toads, turtles, dogs, bats, or beetles. Occultists presented these entities to a witch upon her initiatory blood pact with the Devil. Although the familiar served as a companion or attendant to the witch, the demon was empowered by the Devil to report if the blood pact had been broken.

According to legend, the familiar alone held the keys to the Grimore (a collection of magical incantations and rituals) and was therefore instrumental in casting spells, concocting potions, and divining spirits. Cats were especially good at grounding negative energies, while dogs were prized as an unlimited source of elemental energies. Familiars are often welcome at coven gatherings but are not allowed within the circle of power where psychic energy is reserved for members.

*See also:* SATANISM, WITCHCRAFT

# FAMILY OF LOVE (CHILDREN OF GOD)

*See:* CHILDREN OF GOD

# FEATHER

Throughout history, the feather has played an important part in ceremonial magic. In ancient Egypt, the feather symbolized truth. It was believed that each soul was weighed against the feather of *Maat,* the Mother of Truth, to determine its burden of sin at the time of death. In some cultures the feather was the sacred symbol of the air or wind, where the reincarnated souls of the dead allegedly roamed. In other cultures, the feather symbolized faith and contemplation, while its quill represented the divine Word, the delineator of all things.

Today some occult groups believe the feather can be used to control mystical powers. They wear the feather as an adornment of protection or use it in foretelling the future. Some New Age adherents regard the feather as a symbol of the lower self, whose awareness of justice and law reputedly proves its inability to acknowledge the divine character of the soul.

*See also:* NATIVE AMERICANS, POWER OBJECT, SYMBOLISM

# FELDENKRAIS METHOD

A system that combines physics, psychology, and the realignment of the structure of the body to release tension and to restore bodily functions. Moshe Feldenkrais (1904–1984), an Israeli scientist who was crippled by a soccer injury, believed that through exploratory learning techniques people could train their consciousness to control the body and mind thereby attaining a higher state of awareness. Despite its alleged benefits, the Feldenkrais method can also produce serious side effects.

*See also:* ALTERED STATE, BIOFEEDBACK, HOLISM

# FEMINISM

A movement that advocates the political, social, economic, and educational equality of women with men. Throughout history, most cultures have considered women as an inferior appendage of men. In America's history, a woman's place was in the home, not in institutions of higher learning, nor the workplace, and certainly not in the voting booth. But by the mid-1800s, the fight for the rights of women to control their person, property, and politics became widespread in both Europe and the United States. By the end of the century, numerous feminist goals had been realized. Many feminists believe the true turning point in American history occurred in 1920 when the suffrage movement won the right for women to vote.

Feminism found a new voice in the countercultural movement of the 1960s. Advocates joined civil rights leaders in their demands for economic, social, educational, and political equality. Powerful feminist organizations began to call national attention to the growing dissatisfaction of the contemporary woman. Feminists demanded the rights to abortion, birth control, equal opportunity, and pay. Some radicals called for the eradication of traditional gender roles as a means of advancing humanity's evolutionary progress toward becoming an asexual species. The latter is based on the idea that all humans are composed of complementary forces, or principles, called yin and yang. Yin represents the passive, negative, female cosmic element, whereas yang symbolizes the active, positive, masculine cosmic element.

In recent years, feminist cults have emerged, teaching that women are influenced by powerful inner forces emanating from the universal unconsciousness represented in the archetypal Earth Mother Goddess. Members of these groups spurn Christianity as a male-dominated religion, claiming that men were responsible for humankind's alienation from God, as well as for the suppression of yin. They believe that by developing such feminine principles as intuition, sensitivity, cooperation, and introspection, people can achieve a new depth of understanding, thereby transforming the collective human consciousness. Only then will people be able to reestablish a relationship with the universal forces of nature and its untapped psychic potential.

The occult elements of the movement foresee the liberation of the feminine spirit as a catalyst for the expansion and transformation of human consciousness. They advocate feminine superiority and believe that people will realize their full human potential and innate divine powers only by transcending male/female polarities and by awakening the universal feminine principle. The sheer number of those involved makes occult forms of feminism one of the most significant New Age factions. The emphasis on a matriarchal society has helped to revive goddess cults, ancient paganism, and contemporary witchcraft.

*See also:* GODDESS WORSHIP, POLARITY, WICCA, WITCHCRAFT

# FENG-SHUI

The art of manipulating the Universal Life Force (ch'i) so that it flows smoothly from our surroundings into and within our bodies. In the 1990s, Feng-shui became extremely popular in the Western workplace, school, and home for its use of architecture, color, and even furniture placement to affect well-being. As an Eastern philosophy,

Feng-shui is closely aligned with Tantric (Tibetan) Buddhism, Chinese astrology and spiritualism. It seeks to restore balances in a space that may have become out of balance through the vibrations left by former tenants, spirits, or other influences.

*See also:* CH'I

## FERGUSON, MARILYN (b. 1938)

Brain researcher and New Age leader Marilyn Ferguson wrote *The Aquarian Conspiracy*. Published in 1980, this New Age bible examines the role of the enlightened in the impending global transformation. She bases her claims on the observation that various occult disciplines are equally influential in expanding the psychic abilities of people. Such techniques as accelerated learning, heightened awareness, insight, power imagery, and memory recall led Ferguson to examine the social implications of unrestricted human potential.

In 1975, Ferguson began publishing the *Mind-Brain Bulletin*. This newsletter examined the advancement of New Age theory and practice. She received an avalanche of responses that further convinced her of the existence of a powerful, but leaderless, network of enlightened people. Despite their diversity, they recognize and share a heightened sense of human potential. Ferguson claimed this awareness would spark the inevitable evolutionary transformation of humankind.

*See also: AQUARIAN CONSPIRACY, THE;* BIBLE, NEW AGE; CONSCIOUSNESS REVOLUTION; GLOBALISM; TRANSFORMATION

## FILMORE, CHARLES (1854–1948)
## FILMORE, MYRTLE (1845–1931)

Leaders in the New Thought movement of the late nineteenth century and cofounders of Unity School of Christianity (USC). Myrtle Filmore was raised in an New England Methodist home where, as a young school teacher, she first became interested in transcendental philosophy. In 1884, she moved to Kansas City, Missouri, and in 1887 she converted to Christian Science. Charles Filmore grew up as an agnostic with an intense interest in spiritualism, Hinduism, and the occult. Through the influence of Myrtle, Charles became a convert to Christian Science.

In 1889 the couple rented a small hall in Kansas City and began USC to teach their own blend of occult, Christian Science, and New Thought. The organization they founded has remained popular and at the end of the twentieth century, more than 2 million people worldwide have some level of involvement. The basic belief system remains that of the eclectic Filmores, though part of the organization's success has been its low-key proclamation of its own strange mix of doctrines, especially to outsiders. USC is open to other faith traditions and most of its members have other religious affiliations.

*See also:* CHRISTIAN SCIENCE, NEW THOUGHT, TRANSCENDENTALISM, UNITY SCHOOL OF CHRISTIANITY

## FINDHORN FOUNDATION

A community founded in 1963 by Peter (1917–1993) and Eileen (b. 1917) Caddy. Located forty miles east of Inverness in northern Scotland, the Findhorn community boasts two hundred permanent residents who believe in the creation of a new world through increased universal consciousness. The model community offers a continuing education program on spirituality and world unification. Initiates learn about a cosmic energy source, and about the essence of all creation, as well as the powers of the universe revealed within the elements of nature.

Communal residents believe that Devas, or divine spirits, inhabit all of nature, which they believe is an organic manifestation of Cosmic Consciousness. All plant life possesses emotion and intelligence and is to be worshiped as a significant part of divine nature. In return, the Devas channel "great truths" to initiates about the evolution of human nature, as well as the new civilization this evolution will bring. According to these spirits, communication between people and nature will energize cosmic forces, raise humanity's collective consciousness, and eventually bring about total unification of the world's population.

## FIRE-WALKING

The ancient practice of walking over a bed of hot coals or stones. For thousands of years, people have practiced fire-walking to prove their faith in a deity, to purify themselves, or to prepare themselves for a fertility ritual. Some New Age groups perpetuate fire-walking as a way to channel psychic power to themselves. They believe an intense meditative session, accompanied by music and chanting, will allow initiates to transcend the levels of consciousness and release powers that defy physical reality. Advocates speculate that successful fire-walking is the result of an auric shield, innate power over the elements, intuitive secretion of protective chemicals, or supernatural intervention.

Despite the occultic connotations, many arguments suggest that fire-walking is nothing more than an elaborate parlor trick designed to develop confidence in the individual. Scientists have proposed several explanations. One theory is the Leidenfrost Effect, which says that a wet foot will form an insulating layer of steam the moment it hits the hot coals. Another theory, proposed by physicist Bernard Leikind in 1984, contends that the secret to fire-walking lies in understanding the distinction between temperature and heat, not in the spirits. The porous lava-type rock usually used in pagan rituals is an extremely poor conductor of heat. Even if the temperature hits twelve hundred to two thousand degrees Fahrenheit, participants will not be burned if they step lightly and quickly.

## FIRST EARTH BATTALION

A New Age militia group whose warrior monks are trained to resolve conflict through New Age psychic and meditative techniques. First Earth was conceived by Army Lieutenant Colonel Jim Channon and an unconventional military think tank called The Delta Force. First Earth represents those who believe that true power lies in the transformation of human consciousness. The mission of warriors belonging to this occult militia is to create harmony out of conflict by using meditative techniques, martial arts, and telepathy, as well as astral projection, psychokinesis, and other psychic powers. The self-proclaimed defenders of truth, who are sometimes referred to as the Natural Guard, train from an operation manual entitled *Evolutionary Tactic*. This book claims that cultivating the inner divinity of people is the key to establishing paradise on earth.

*See also:* CONSCIOUSNESS REVOLUTION, PURIFICATION, TRANSCENDENTAL MEDITATION

## FLOTATION TANK

A water chamber used in sensory deprivation exercises to isolate an individual from all outside stimulation and induce an altered state of consciousness. Flotation cylinders, often containing saline solutions for added buoyancy, keep the individual in a weightless state. This supposedly simulates a womb-like ambiance and the illusion of cosmic awareness. Through sensory isolation, the patient transcends the levels of human consciousness and experiences age regression, out-of-body flight, hallucinatory visions, and spiritual enlightenment. Sensory deprivation is one of the most commonly used techniques in cult programming, making the individual highly susceptible to brainwashing techniques.

*See also:* ALTERED STATE, SENSORY DEPRIVATION

## FORGIVENESS, DIVINE

The act of the god or gods to remove whatever human actions or weakness has made anger. Achieving forgiveness from spirits and ancestors is a major preoccupation in animistic religions. Christian faith has both an unlimited view of the human offense against God, so that human-initiated acts cannot gain forgiveness, and an unlimited act of God Himself in Christ to make forgiveness possible (Rom. 3:21–25; 5:1–11; 8:1; 1 Cor. 6:11; Eph. 1:7; 4:32; Col. 2:13–14; 3:13; 1 John 2:12).

Eastern religions have no concept of a need for forgiveness, since all physical reality is an illusion and there is no conscious divine being or spirits to placate. If people themselves are innately divine, they are not ultimately subject to moral sanctions, though their actions may slow their progress of self-realization. Feelings of guilt (and the need for forgiveness) in themselves are a hindrance in this path, and they must be overcome so that godhood may be realized.

New Age adherents consider sin as a deception perpetuated by the lower consciousness, separating people from the divine awareness of their higher consciousness. They urge initiates to reject concepts such as sin, guilt, and forgiveness, and to acknowledge the presence of their godlike self.

*See also:* EVIL, GUILT, JESUS CHRIST, SALVATION, SIN

## FORUM, THE
*See:* ERHARD, WERNER HANS

## FOURTH LEVEL
A phrase used to describe the altered states of consciousness advocated by proponents of the New Age. Consciousness, sleep, and dream states allegedly are followed by this trancelike condition, in which secrets to the universe are unlocked and the unlimited potential for personal divinity is realized. New Age adherents claim that all contact with ascended masters, spirit guides, and extraterrestrial beings occur at the fourth level.

*See also:* ALTERED STATE

## FOX, MATTHEW (b. 1940)
A Dominican priest who developed creation spirituality. Fox became a Dominican in 1960 and was ordained to the priesthood in 1967. He went on to earn a doctorate degree in the history and theology of spiritual-

ity from the Institute Catholique de Paris. In 1977, he established the Institute of Culture and Creation Spirituality at Holy Names College in Oakland, California. He also launched a bimonthly magazine entitled *Creation.* Between 1984 and 1987, Fox and his Institute came under sharp scrutiny by Church leaders. Despite sanctions against him for his views, both his popularity and distribution of his writings continued to grow.

Fox espouses a form of mysticism in which he believes that an awareness of Ultimate Reality can be gained through a heightened state of mental perception and excitement. The goal is to become awakened to the deity within and united with the universal life force. Four paths lead to direct communication with this inner god. Each path interweaves and interconnects with the others in an ascending spiral of increasing mystical awareness.

The first path is called *via positiva,* representing a love for Mother Nature and all that exists within it. The second path, called *via negativa,* entails the discovery of the mystery, darkness, suffering, and emptiness of nature. The third path, known as *via creativa,* signifies the realization that people are cocreators with Ultimate Reality. Fox urges people to cultivate the hemisphere of the brain where imagination, intuitiveness, and artistry reside to enhance their creative potential. The fourth path, referred to as *via transformativa,* advocates the creation of a new world order, characterized by justice and peace. Fox asserts that the survival of humanity depends on the establishment of a new epoch of joy and creativity.

Fox, who is pantheistic, says God is in everything and everything is in God. Although the universe supposedly is part of the reality of God, Fox would say that God is more than the universe. He calls the Spirit the feminine principle of God and the Mother Goddess of the New Age. Fox sees Jesus as a principle of divine potentiality and an ideal person who realized the presence of the cosmic christ located in the unconscious mind of all people. Fox believes everyone can come to a realization of full creative potential by looking to Jesus and becoming joined to the cosmic christ of the New Age. He claims people can achieve oneness with Ultimate Reality through such practices as listening to music, dancing, and sexual intercourse, as well as fasting, yoga, and transcendental meditation. If more and more people come to an awareness of their divine self, then a critical mass will be reached and usher in the Aquarian era of enlightenment.

*See also:* COSMIC CHRIST, GODDESS WORSHIP, ONE-WORLD IDEAL

## FREEMASONRY

An international fraternal organization. Statisticians consider the Masonic Society to be the largest worldwide organization of its kind. A belief in God is the primary requirement for membership. Freemasons affirm that all people are children of one God and are related to each other. The Society also affirms that service to people is the best way to worship God. In keeping with this belief, Freemasons typically involve themselves in social and charitable activities.

Many researchers believe that the society emerged from the guilds of stonemasons that existed in Europe during the Middle Ages. The lodge forms the basic organizational unit of the Freemasons, and each lodge is joined together by a system of common principles and practices. Of the approximate 4.8 million Freemasons belonging to lodges around the world, about 3 million live in the United States. The Shriners are perhaps the best known of the distinct Masonic groups, gaining notoriety for their charitable support of hospitals and hosting festive parades.

Each lodge issues three degrees—Entered Apprentice, Fellow Craft, and Master Mason. Two groups of advanced freemasonry award additional degrees. The York Rite confers twelve higher degrees, while the Scottish Rite confers thirty higher degrees. Because of the common structure of these fraternal organizations, initiates in either rite must advance through similar phases of indoctrination. They learn the various secrets associated with each degree and are required to demonstrate their allegiance to the orga-

nization before they can advance any further.

Much of Masonic practice is characterized by occult philosophies, rituals, and symbols. Freemasons learn that all the diverse world religions adhere to certain basic moral truths and therefore can be united under a common deity. The Masonic motto "out of chaos, order" affirms the ideal that dissimilar groups will one day achieve enlightenment and live in peace. As initiates advance through higher degrees, they are exposed to additional occult ideas drawn from the mystery religions of ancient Egypt and Greece.

*See also:* ILLUMINATI; ROSICRUCIANS; SYMBOLISM; WEISHAUPT, ADAM

## FREUD, SIGMUND (1856–1939)

An Austrian psychiatrist and founder of psychoanalysis, Freud was born to Jewish parents in Freiberg, Moravia, presently known as Pribor in the Czech Republic. In 1881, he graduated with an M.D. from the University of Vienna and became a resident in the General Hospital of Vienna in 1882. After completing his residency in 1885, Freud traveled to Paris and studied with a neurologist named Jean-Martin Charcot (1825–1893). Freud also began collaborating with an Austrian physician named Josef Breuer (1842–1925) on the use of hypnosis in the treatment of hysteria. In 1886, Freud returned to Vienna, married Martha Bernays, and opened a private practice.

Freud concluded that psychotherapeutic techniques could be used successfully to treat symptoms of hysteria. In 1889 Freud returned to Paris and in the course of his work over the next six years refined his psychotherapeutic technique. He determined that hysteria and other mental disorders were caused by the memories of repressed traumatic experiences. He claimed that these psychological disturbances could be treated by reversing suppression of the patient's unconscious memories and the affects caused by these disagreeable experiences. Based on clinical work and self-analysis from 1895 to 1900, Freud concluded that sexual factors were a major cause of mental disorders. He maintained that all people have an Oedipus complex, an unconscious yearning toward the parent of the opposite sex, as well as an intense jealousy of the parent of the same sex.

In 1899 Freud declared that dreams represented the camouflaged expression of unconscious desires people wished they could fulfill. He also stated that neurosis was caused by the compromises people made between their fantasies and reality. Freud claimed that the repeated behavior patterns of parents were transferred to their children. Between 1900 to 1926 Freud developed his theory of the mind. He postulated that the psyche is made up of the id (the unconscious source of vital energy), ego (the conscious mediator between a person and reality), and superego (the internalization of the parental conscience and the rules of society).

Freud's ideas have had a tremendous influence on New Age thinking. Advocates claim the psyche is the locus of human existence and holds secret powers and wisdom. They also maintain that there is a "collective unconscious," a dimension of reality that contains the symbols and memories of the entire human race. The spiritually advanced can tap into this incredible source of knowledge, which explains why the exploration of the human psyche has become a high priority. It holds the key to spiritual evolution.

*See also:* DREAM; JUNG, CARL GUSTAV; MASLOW, ABRAHAM; PSYCHOTHERAPY

# FULLER, R. BUCKMINSTER (1895–1983)

An architect, inventor, and author, as well as ecologist, philosopher, and New Age futurist. Born in Milton, Massachusetts, Fuller was essentially self-educated. As an architect, Fuller is best known for his innovative design of the geodesic dome, a large, lightweight, prefabricated enclosure that he perfected in 1947. From 1959 until his death in 1983, Fuller was a professor at Southern Illinois University.

Fuller believed that "God" is the driving force of cosmic evolution, the power through which people can bring harmonic order from the chaos of unleashed energy present in the universe. He developed a theory of technological innovation in which he claimed that people have unlimited potential for creativity. He said that by tapping into this virtually limitless capacity for innovation, people could maximize the limited resources of the earth without exhausting them. Fuller referred to the planet as Spaceship Earth. He claimed that as humanity's awareness of their cosmic evolution grew, they would come to accept globalism. This view states that advances in technology have created a world community in which distance and isolation are drastically reduced.

*See also:* COSMIC ENERGY, ENVIRONMENTALISM, GLOBALISM

# G

## GAEA (GAIA, GE)

In Greek mythology Gaea is the daughter of Chaos (the disordered and unorganized state from which primordial matter arose), the primal goddess, and the mother of all things. Gaea is derived from the Greek word *Gaia,* which means "personification." This is derived from the word *ge,* which means "earth." Gaea is the mother and wife of both Uranus (the god of the sky) and Pontus (the god of the sea). With Uranus as father, she also is the mother of the Titans (twelve primeval deities who were overthrown by the Olympian gods), the Furies (three horrifying, winged goddesses of vengeance with serpentine hair), and the Cyclopes (one-eyed giants). With Pontus as father, she gave birth to the five sea deities.

New Age adherents have revived the worship of Gaea under a theory called the "Gaea Principle." This hypothesis was popularized by James E. Lovelock in a book entitled *Gaea,* published by Oxford University Press in 1979. Lovelock claimed that all living matter is part of a cosmic whole, a single living organism. The elements (earth, air, and water) allegedly work together with life to create a coherent whole, and each element is unable to exist without the other two. As long as all the world's components remain in balance, life can exist. However, if the balance is disturbed at any time, it threatens the existence of Gaea and humankind.

New Age adherents maintain that the only way to restore harmony to the current global imbalance is through a united human consciousness. Gaea has been seriously injured by the growth of human civilization. The increase of volcanic and earthquake activity reputedly is Gaea's warning to humankind that devastating consequences will arise if her need for atonement is not met. Entities from the astral plane insist that world peace can only be achieved by removing negative elements (i.e., Christianity) from the earth. Then the enlightened of the world will be free to tap their godlike powers and appease Gaea.

*See also:* MOTHER EARTH

## GALYEAN, BEVERLY

A Californian educator, Galyean designed confluent education, also known as holistic, transpersonal, and humanistic, as well as psychological or New Age education. This educational approach is based on pantheism. Galyean initially oversaw three federally funded confluent education programs in the Los Angeles area. She eventually spearheaded the development of international curriculum models, of which various forms have been adopted in public schools throughout the United States.

Galyean noted that the ancient mystery religions all utilized intuition and inner guides, dreams and visions as their source of wisdom and knowledge. She concluded that an exploration of occult techniques could result in the development of unlimited human potential. Galyean devised a multisensory approach to education that combined the logical elements of learning with emotion and intuition.

Confluent education operates on the premise that learning from within can create heightened intellectual capabilities. Her system integrates Eastern philosophies and techniques into all aspects of the curriculum. Galyean claims that the key to education is providing the environment and tools that will enable children to search out and release their inner divinity. These include such things as guided imagery and meditation, affirmation and spiritism. Supposedly when enough children recognize their innate godhood, there will be a mass unleashing of human consciousness resulting in a quantum leap in humanity's evolutionary development.

*See also:* CONFLUENT EDUCATION, GUIDED IMAGERY, HUMAN POTENTIAL MOVEMENT, TRANSPERSONAL PSYCHOLOGY

## GARRETT, EILEEN (1893–1970)

One of the most famous mediums in the history of contemporary spiritism. Because of her many celebrity followers, Garrett was known as an aristocrat of the psychic world. Evidence of her paranormal capabilities reputedly were first demonstrated in early childhood. After the suicidal death of both of her parents, Garrett earnestly set forth on what became her life mission, investigating the nature of psychic ability. Her journey began as a young woman in London. While attending a seance, she suddenly lapsed into a spontaneous hypnotic trance and began to channel the "wisdom" of an entity named Ouvani.

Over the next thirty years, Garrett would channel a variety of spirits, all of whom would propagate familiar New Age doctrines. These included the divine interconnectedness of all life and the survival of human consciousness beyond death. Garrett was skeptical of her psychic powers, and reluctant to believe that foreign entities could enter her body at will. In an attempt to discover more comforting truths, Garrett established and supported the Parapsychology Foundation, in which she allowed her alleged abilities to be extensively investigated.

Garrett channeled four basic entities. She claimed that each was a progressively higher order of guiding intelligence. Some think they represent the evolutionary stages of her development as a spiritualistic medium. The two principal entities—Ouvani and Abdul Latif—appeared to act as controllers by consistently dominating Garrett's channeling sessions. Ouvani, who was the first to reveal himself, claimed to have been an Arab soldier who died in battle. In contrast, Latif described himself as a well-traveled Muslim physician who at one time served in the court

of the sultan of Egypt. Latif allegedly was a knowledgeable conversationalist in medicine, history, theology, and physics, as well as music, mineralogy, and anatomy. He reputedly channeled New Age doctrines to many mediums throughout the twentieth century. Garrett depicted her final two spirits, Tahoteh and Ramah, as godlike figures. She claimed they were entities of a higher form who were unable to channel without a inquisitor who possessed an equally receptive level of psychic attunement.

*See also:* COLLECTIVE UNCONSCIOUS, DEMON, PARAPSYCHOLOGY, PSYCHIC, SPIRITISM, TRANCE CHANNELING

## GATEWAY VOYAGE

A New Age mind/brain therapy in which the two halves of the cerebrum are integrated to enhance mental skills, using a series of audio tapes that allegedly contain the necessary sound pulses to achieve this integration process. When these sound pulses are repeatedly exposed to the brain, certain electrical patterns result. This process supposedly allows participants to leave their bodies and travel to alternate planes of reality.

*See also:* ASTRAL PLANE

## GAUTAMA, SIDDHARTHA (563–483 B.C.)

The founder of Buddhism. Gautama was born into the warrior caste of a tribe in northeastern India, or part of modern-day Nepal. His father was a wealthy rajah, or ruler. According to folklore, Siddhartha's father dreamed of the day his son would succeed him and become a great king. To encourage Siddhartha to this end, his father shielded him from all that was ugly and painful, and surrounded him with great wealth and pleasures. But one day Siddhartha decided to leave the confines of the palace and see the world. During this journey, he saw four kinds of suffering—old age, sickness, death, and poverty—that disillusioned him concerning wealth and political power.

Legend says that at the age of twenty-nine, Siddhartha renounced the future his father had planned for him. His encounter with suffering convinced him to leave his home, wife, and child, and live as a beggar in search of enlightenment. The former prince now roamed from place to place looking for the source of suffering and how to get rid of it. Folklore says that Siddhartha eventually came to a town called Bodh Gaya and sat under a fig tree along the bank of a river for seven days. During this time, he went into a deep state of meditation, resisted the temptations of Mara (the evil one), and attained nirvana (the highest state of God-consciousness.) He emerged from the experience as Buddha, or the enlightened one. He vowed to devote the rest of his life to spreading the truths he had learned while under the bodhi (the bo tree, or tree of wisdom). By the time of Buddha's death, thousands of his converts lived in communities called Sanghas.

*See also:* BUDDHISM, ENLIGHTENMENT, ZEN BUDDHISM

## GELLER, URI (b. 1946)

Israeli psychic best known for his telekinetic demonstrations. In his most popular performances, Geller demonstrated the ability to bend spoons without physical contact, and to draw items without visual contact. Some think that Geller's alleged psychokinetic powers emanated from the depths of his unconscious, while others say his psychic abilities were produced by tapping into the collective unconscious of humankind. Still others maintain that his powers were genetically passed on to him by his parents. Geller asserted that his abilities emanated from supernatural entities from a neighboring planet.

Throughout his career, Geller faced a barrage of criticism and examinations, making believers of some and skeptics of others. Some claimed that the spoons Geller bent were made out of a heat-sensitive alloy, while others said that he bent the objects on his chair or table while the attention of onlookers was directed elsewhere. A knowledgeable and talented magician named James Randi wrote a book entitled *Truth About Uri Geller* (Prometheus Books, 1990) in which he maintains that Geller was a clever and talented fraud.

*See also:* EXTRASENSORY PERCEPTION, PSYCHOKINESIS

## GEMOLOGY

The use of precious and semiprecious gems for occult purposes. Current interest in gemology focuses on the alleged mystical value of gems in healing the mind, body, and spirit. Some mystics claim that gemstones were placed in the rocks of the earth as the seeds of a higher intelligence who sought the spiritual advancement of humankind. They believe that pulsations of energy and light emanating from the gems correspond with the vibrational patterns of astral planes and open the channels of communication to spirit guides. These energy pulses are discernible only in altered states of consciousness, and provide access to unlimited powers of healing, telepathy, and clairvoyance, as well as precognition and retrocognition.

Occult gemologists meditate upon and carry, wear and even ingest gems to manipulate their psychic powers. Sympathetic magic attributes mystical powers to the stones according to their color. (Sympathetic magic means casting a spell or curse on an object representing a person or entity, allegedly bringing adverse effects.) "Gem and tonic" and "liquid consciousness" identify the tint produced by grinding the gems into a powder, and then mixing it into a drink.

The quartz crystal is a popular gem among New Age adherents. They claim that it has healing, as well as psychic and prophetic powers. Other popular stones used in mystical gemology include the ruby, emerald, amethyst, and amber (fossilized resin). Although the value of these stones may be quite high, their quality is not necessarily important to their ritualistic use. Some believe a less precious stone of the same color often possesses many of the same occult powers.

The ancient Hindus attributed the red of the ruby to the blood of the Great Goddess. They believed the stone had the power to prevent bloodshed and cure blood illnesses. The ancient Burmese inserted the ruby beneath the skin to become invulnerable to disease. Contemporary mystics advocate wearing the ruby on the left side of the body to protect the heart. The vibrational energies of the ruby supposedly cleanse the blood, and are used in the treatment of AIDS, leukemia, and other terminal diseases. Purportedly, the ruby is also a valuable tool in communicating with entities from the astral realm.

In ancient times, the emerald was identified as the most sacred stone of the Mother Goddess because its color represented the earth to which she gave birth. Some claim that the emerald fell from Venus in a green bolt of light. Others maintain that the stone has the power to dissolve the eyes of snakes and expel demons. The emerald supposedly has the power to relieve all nerve-related illnesses, including stress, pain, and eye strain. Contemporary mystics assert that the emerald is the living energy field of universal intelligence, and has the power to balance negative vibrations within the mind, body, and spirit.

For centuries mystics have maintained that the amethyst has the power to determine right from wrong, to change the molecular structure of matter, and to transmit subliminal messages to devotees of the occult. The stone supposedly emits the highest psychic vibrations of all gems. They claim that the amethyst can absorb negative forces and repel them to other dimensions, bringing health and well-being to the entire planet.

Some pagan cultures thought that amber symbolized the tears of the Mother Goddess, while others said it represented the souls of tigers. Amber was often burned in purification rituals, and ground into powder to create elixirs of immortality. Mystic healers believed that amber could cure jaundice, urinary and sinus problems, and neurological diseases. New Age philosophers contend that the electric pulsations of amber resonate directly with brain wave patterns, and this creates a powerful magnetic flow that can purify the entire body.

*See also:* CRYSTAL, POWER OBJECT, QUARTZ CRYSTAL

# GESTALT THERAPY

An existential approach to mental and emotional health first developed by Frederick S. Perls (1893–1970). Perls based Gestalt therapy on the idea that people are responsible for what they are thinking, feeling, and doing. An emphasis is placed on the client's perceptions of reality, especially the present. All abstract discussions about past and future concerns are brought into the present so the client can immediately and directly experience them. Proponents claim this approach increases the clients' awareness of what they are experiencing and doing. This leads to greater self-understanding and the knowledge of how they can change. Rather than waiting passively for the therapist to provide insight and solve problems, clients are expected to do their own sensing, feeling, seeing, and interpreting.

Gestalt therapy uses a wide range of techniques to intensify a client's experience of the present and to facilitate an integration of conflicting feelings. The therapist might use confrontation, dialogue with polar opposite emotions, and role playing, as well as staying with feelings, reaching an impasse, and reliving and reexperiencing unfinished business. Self-awareness reputedly can be achieved through dream analysis and entering alternate states of consciousness. New Age adherents promote Gestalt therapy because it gives them a set of ideas and techniques for doing self-exploration, establishing contact with alien entities, maximizing their full human potential, and getting in touch with the godlike self believed to dwell within every person.

*See also:* DREAM THERAPY, PSYCHOTHERAPY

# GHOST

Commonly thought to be the disembodied spirits of the dead who have returned to cause mischief, take revenge, or impart profound wisdom, ghosts are usually categorized by spiritists as the ancestral protector, the mischievous poltergeist, the malevolent returning to avenge a violent death, or the benevolent who is summoned back to aid humankind.

The transparent or shadowy images with humanlike form and gaunt, empty faces reputedly swoop, hover, and make various strange noises. Some attribute the activity of spirits to either the release of psychic energy, the projection of the human unconscious, or a manifestation of the collective conscious, a universal source of wisdom. Others think the ancient practice of contacting, acknowledging, and even worshiping the dead stems from people's innate need to seek verification of life after death and the immortality of the soul. Common techniques include the trance channeling of ascended beings, as well as the meditative search for inner guides through altered states of consciousness.

See also: ASTRAL BODY, DEMON, PARAPSYCHOLOGY, POLTERGEIST, SPIRITISM

## GLOBALISM

A comprehensive ideology of human existence based on the belief that the survival of the earth ultimately depends on the interdependence of its inhabitants, and implemented by redetermining values and objectives and by redistributing all global resources. The movement toward globalism is both political and religious in nature. Although the reasons and means for achieving globalism vary according to allegiances, all proponents agree that a world devoid of religious and political barriers will ultimately result in peace. Globalists advocate the unilateral disarmament of all nations, the establishment of a unified monetary system, the abolishment of the traditional family, and the elimination of moral absolutes and racial barriers. Adherents believe all these things impede world peace and the evolutionary advancement of humankind.

Globalism is based on a belief in the inherent wisdom and goodness of humankind. Advocates claim that through the unification of the political, spiritual, and scientific aspects of life, through the transformation from individual consciousness to global consciousness, and through the interplanetary cooperation of ideas and organizations, a new, evolved human race will arise and welcome in the New Age. Part of this plan includes using educational institutions to indoctrinate a new generation into the global perspective deemed necessary for the future existence of humankind.

The Aquarian globalist talks about a New Age arising from the ashes of the old worldview after people have completed their mystical journey to the peak of higher consciousness. This journey begins with global awareness, wherein every person discovers their innate divine potential and union with the cosmic consciousness. Proponents assert that when a critical mass of the enlightened harmonically converge their psychic awareness, a paradigm shift in global consciousness will occur. This will produce a quantum leap into the New Age of peace and harmony.

See also: DEEP ECOLOGY; ENVIRONMENTALISM; INTERDEPENDENCE; PEACE; PLAN, THE

## GNOSTICISM

A heretical concept that appeared in the early years of the Christian church and flourished by the beginning of the third century A.D. Gnosticism is derived from the Greek word *gnosis,* which means "knowledge." This system of thought and practice advocates that all forms of matter are evil. The goal of the gnostics was to become free from evil material existence and to enter a pure spiritual life. They believed this liberation came only through gaining knowledge of profound and mysterious spiritual truth. Such knowledge is limited to a select group of "initiated," those specially chosen souls entrusted with the secrets of the universe, and who possessed unlimited powers to reunite with the divinity from which they emanated.

Many New Age adherents reflect a gnostic view of life. They claim that humanity's flesh represents a lower form of existence, whereas the spirit represents a higher form of reality. They view the physical body as an evil hindrance to the evolutionary advancement of the soul. They say this present world is an illusion, and that Ultimate Reality lies in higher states of consciousness. Only those who are enlightened can receive and understand these truths.

*See also:* ESOTERIC CHRISTIANITY

## GOAT OF MENDES

The head of a goat appearing within the satanic star, embroidered on altar cloths and used in the Black Mass. Although the Goat of Mendes allegedly communicates its presence through demonic eyes, Satanists deny it has demonic overtones. Many claim the image characterizes the goat god of ancient paganism. *The Satanic Bible* depicts this god as the Luciferic alter ego of Satan, known as Pan. Satanists often display the Goat of Mendes when performing their rituals. In the New Age Movement, the goat has developed into a symbol of the higher self, which emanates from a supreme energy force. New Age adherents say the goat brings the desires of the unconscious mind to new levels of awareness, deemed essential to the cosmic evolution of the soul.

**Goat of Mendes, whose head appears within inverted pentagram**

*See also:* BAPHOMET, HIGHER SELF, PAN, PENTAGRAM, SATANISM, SYMBOLISM

## GOD

The ultimate reality in any worldview system. This may be a sentient physical or spiritual being, a nonsentient spiritual force, or the material universe. In pantheist systems there is a blurring of the physical and spiritual aspects of deity, so that everything is now God or is potentially in the future. Most modern occult and New Age theology accepts some form of pantheism.

Theists in general, and orthodox Christians in particular believe that God is an eternal Spirit who is infinite in His being and independent in His self-existence (Exod. 3:14; 6:3; John 4:24). He is perfect in power, wisdom, and goodness, and worthy of worship as the Creator and Ruler of the universe.

There are diverse New Age and occult definitions, though at their most basic level these religions almost invariably find some form of Universal Mind, Collective Unconscious, Creative Force, Ultimate Reality, or Cosmic Nothingness.

Those who would move in a more atheistic direction define the ultimate reality as neutral, impersonal, and one with the material world. Those in occult religions frequently see this ultimate as an animistic entity or pantheon of entities, manifested in the spirits of people, places, and things. Another assertion is that God is the archetypal Mind, containing the collective memories of humankind. This flow of expanding consciousness is the source of the universe and a directing influence on humanity.

Platonic idealism has influenced many of these concepts. Usually the material world is viewed as an illusion, and Ultimate Reality lies in higher states of consciousness.

New Age adherents maintain that, only by recognizing the divine nature of their inner self and their mystical union with the Christ-consciousness, can people truly understand God. Enlightenment comes by relinquishing the powers of reason and by journeying to heightened states of awareness. When initiates reach this state, their sense of personal identity vanishes and they are released from the realm of illusion. They are masters of their own destiny, able to create their own realities by using the psychic powers of their godlike Self.

*See also:* BUDDHISM, CHRIST-CONSCIOUSNESS, ENLIGHTENMENT, NEW AGE MOVEMENT, SALVATION, SATORI, SELF-REALIZATION

## GODDESS WORSHIP

The veneration of the female deity or principle that exists in nature and rules the cosmos. For centuries, pagan worshipers have paid homage to such feminine attributes as reproduction and fertility. The original Great Goddess reputedly is Semiramis, the wife of Nimrod and Queen of Babylon. Also referred to as the Queen of Heaven, Semiramis established the mystery religions in ancient Babylon that used human sacrifices and perverse sexual rituals. After Semiramis's death, her fame continued to spread around the world.

Semiramis was also known as the prophetic Virgin whom Nimrod impregnated. Nimrod was the incarnation of Ra, the sun god. According to legend, Semiramis bore a son named Tammuz. After Tammuz was killed by a wild boar, Semiramis fasted for forty days, until Tammuz rose from the dead. Other folktales refer to Semiramis as the "goddess of ten thousand names." The Romans called her Venus, and the Greeks referred to her as Aphrodite. In yoga, she is Kali, the Kundalini serpent, and New Age adherents refer to her as Gaea, the Mother Earth Goddess.

Mother Earth allegedly is a benevolent benefactress who is responsible for the creation of all life. She offers everlasting peace and love to her followers. Wiccan practitioners believe they hold the spiritual key to the evolution of Mother Earth. One of their major goals is to remove the Sky God of the current patriarchal system and replace him with the Mother Goddess of the matriarchal system in the Aquarian era. By following a ritualistic schedule according to the cycles of Gaea, Wiccans believe they can tap into her divine energies, which will supposedly bring global transformation.

*See also:* GAEA, MOTHER EARTH, WICCA

## GOD'S SALVATION CHURCH
*See:* CHEN TAO

## Gospel of Jesus, the Christ of the Piscean Age, The
*See: Aquarian Age Gospel of Jesus the christ, The*

## GRAHAM POTENTIALIZER
An electrically-charged device worn on the head and designed to create an electromagnetic field. A Canadian electrical engineer named David Graham developed the potentializer. When electric currents pass through the device, it supposedly alters the wearers state of consciousness, creates a mystical experience of inner peace, and provides insights into the soul.

## GRAPHOLOGY
The analytical study of handwriting as it pertains to an individual's physical, psychological, and spiritual condition. In the past, the pseudo-scientific diagnosis of handwriting was readily accepted in European countries. Handwriting analysis has now gained a significant following in the psychoanalytical sects of the New Age. Proponents claim that pen strokes can mirror the personality, and reveal things unrecognized by the conscious mind.

Each separate feature of handwriting is thought to reveal characteristics of human thoughts and actions. Adherents claim narrow spacing suggests the need for close proximity with people. Large handwriting reveals ambition, while small handwriting reflects modesty. A left slant points to defensive passivity, while a right slant indicates the demonstrative rule of the heart. By way of contrast, no slant illustrates a calm, self-reliant poise. A disciplined life is reflected in the regularity of slants and strokes, while erratic characters suggest an eccentric lifestyle and character. Tendencies toward up and down strokes illustrate respective optimism and pessimism, while narrow and broad strokes demonstrate the liberal and conservative nature of the individual.

*See also:* CHIROMANCY, PALMISTRY, TRANSPERSONAL PSYCHOLOGY

## GREAT INVOCATION
As a New Age prayer, the Great Invocation is designed to invoke the coming of the

cosmic christ, who supposedly will lead the world into the oneness and fellowship of all living things. Advocates claim that each recitation of the prayer strengthens the New Age army, and opens the eyes of the world to psychic enlightenment.

World Goodwill first distributed the Great Invocation in 1945. It has been translated into more than eighty languages. The Great Invocation contains basic ideals that are to transcend the different religions of the world, uniting all devout people. Advocates say this occult prayer can open the channels into human consciousness through which spiritual energies flow. They claim this prayer will gradually transform the world and create an era of peace and love.

The Great Invocation reads as follows:

From the point of Light within the
Mind of God,
Let light stream forth into the minds
of people,
And let Light Descend on Earth.
From the point of Love within the
Heart of God,
Let love stream forth into the hearts of
people,
And may Christ return to Earth.
From the center where the Will of God
is known,
Let purpose guide the little wills of
people,
The purpose that the Masters know and
serve.
From the center that we call the human
race,
Let the Plan of Love and Light work
out,
And may it seal the door where evil
dwells.
Let Light and Love and Power restore
the Plan on Earth.

"Light" refers to people's innate awareness of their divinity. "God" is a cosmic energy force created by the subconscious mind of all people. "Masters" refers to avatars, or embodiments of Ultimate Reality, such as Christ, Buddha, and Muhammad who have tran-

scended the endless cycles of reincarnation. "The Plan," the ultimate goal of the New Age Movement, is the establishment of a one-world government, economy, and religion.

*See also:* ONE-WORLD IDEAL, WORLD GOODWILL

## GREAT WHITE BROTHERHOOD (SPIRITUAL HIERARCHY OF LIGHT)

A cosmic power structure made up of ascended masters, archangels, and angels, as well as extraterrestrials and spirit beings. The Brotherhood is led by christ, also known as Sanat Kumura, or Lucifer. This entity claims responsibility for destroying Eden, thereby starting people on their journey to enlightenment, or the realization of their innate divinity. The Great White Brotherhood claims to work with an intergalactic federation to control all aspects of nature.

Members of the Great White Brotherhood claim they are highly evolved, have attained spiritual perfection, and have returned to earth to guide humanity toward enlightenment. The entities of this celestial fraternity also assert that they are the divine authorities of the coming New Age. They identify themselves as spirit guides and ascended masters who can channel profound revelations to receptive agents, and teach the world new methods for achieving a higher consciousness of Light. Some people believe the Great White Brotherhood is the highest state of existence people can reach by themselves. Initiates receive marks on their lower body until the time when global consciousness is reached and the New Age masters ascend to power.

*See also:* ASCENDED MASTER

## GREEN

A New Age political movement particularly strong in Europe. Green challenges traditional politics and emphasizes a transformational vision in which humankind reestablishes its unity and balance with nature. Since the early days of the countercultural movement, advocates of Green have sought to establish a synergetic collaboration of interconnected people, services, and organizations. Those who belong to this New Age network share, argue, test, and adapt experiences and insights in order to implement their planetary goals. They have joined forces with other New Age proponents to stress that humankind's relationship to the environment is the most important aspect of evolutionary transformation. Advocates seek to establish a planetary consciousness that recognizes the interconnected web of biological life. Environmental issues, such as global warming, ozone depletion, overpopulation, deforestation, and wetlands loss are presented as political concerns critical to the survival of humankind, and therefore are addressable only from a global perspective.

Those involved in the Green movement call for a paradigm shift in the environmental consciousness of the world's inhabitants. Only those who have become aware of their universal oneness with their planet are capable of such an evolutionary step. Some advocates try to reach alternate states of awareness through a diverse array of mystical and magical techniques. Others choose to worship the Earth Goddess, and assert that the survival of humankind depends on the spiritual, mental, and physical transformation of the human consciousness into a harmonious union with Mother Nature. They believe this can only be achieved through economic redistribution and the establishment of a New World Order.

Proponents of Green personify the earth as a sacred being who seeks vengeance for the disrespect and abuse it has suffered at the hands of unenlightened people. They blame Christianity for the current environmental crisis existing throughout the world. The problem can only be solved by banishing Christians to alternate dimensions of space and time, as well as unifying the rest of the world's religions. They believe humans are an interrelated part of nature and see nature as the divine creator. When people align themselves with the earth's energies, they liberate the godlike self within, and thereby evolve to higher consciousness. According to Green, the purpose of humanity is to recognize their divine potential, and to use these newfound powers to create a better environment.

*See also:* CONSCIOUSNESS REVOLUTION; ENVIRONMENTALISM; GODDESS WORSHIP; MOTHER EARTH; POLITICS, NEW AGE

## GRIMORE

*See:* SHADOWS, THE BOOK OF

## GUIDED IMAGERY

The process by which images are conjured up in the imagination through the help of a psychic guide. Guided imagery is based on the idea that all people have the innate ability to create and manipulate their own reality. Advocates claim that by tapping this divine power, people can discover the secrets of the universe and solve the riddles of life. New Age beliefs and practices associated with guided imagery are derived from the Hindu concept of maya. This theory says the visible world is an illusion that prevents people from realizing that all reality is an absolute oneness. New Age adherents claim that through guided imagery, as well as other mind-altering techniques, people can rediscover their union with the cosmic consciousness and the existence of their divine self.

*See also:* HINDUISM

## GUILT

From the biblical perspective, the state in which people are declared to have violated some legal code, and deserve punishment as the just penalty. New Age adherents reject the biblical teaching about guilt. They see guilt as nothing more than the negative by-product of an archaic system of absolute morality. They also reject guilt on the basis it is an illusory concept, perpetuated by Christianity to prevent people from realizing their innate divinity, their full psychic potential, and their union with Ultimate Reality.

*See also:* FALL OF HUMANITY, THE; FORGIVENESS, DIVINE; SIN

# GURU

In Hinduism, a personal religious guide, spiritual teacher, or psychic master. New Age adherents assert that gurus point the way to Christ-consciousness within each person. They also claim that gurus are agents of enlightenment who show others how to attain nirvana, the state of absolute blessedness. Gurus often claim to have mystical insight into the soul of their devotees.

*See also:* ENLIGHTENMENT, HINDUISM

# GYATSO, TENZIN
*See:* DALAI LAMA

# H

## HADITH

Islamic traditions that have exerted more practical influence on folk Islam than has the Qur'an itself. Muslims look to the Hadith as the original record of the Prophet Muhammad's teachings and actions. In fact, the work is a compilation of thousands of legends and oral traditions, which were written down over the ninth through the eleventh centuries. Most of the legal code of Islam comes from the Hadith, as well as the practical code of conduct for interpersonal relations. Some may have been influenced by the spiritualistic polytheism of the cultures in which Islam arose. One of the elements of conflict between the Sunni and Shi'ite Muslims arises from disagreements over which Hadith sayings are to be accepted. In everyday Islamic life, Hadith sayings are the source of considerable mysticism and questionable practice.

## HALLOWEEN (SAMHAIN)

Celebrated at night on the thirty-first day of October, Halloween is the most revered of all occult holidays—when the veil between the physical and spiritual worlds is lifted. Halloween originated in the Celtic tribes of Great Britain, Northern France, and Ireland some two thousand years ago as the Feast of Samhain, a pagan festival honoring the god of death. Upon deciding that people must be cleansed after death, Celtic priests called druids orchestrated a ritual in which the soul of the individual was transferred into sacred animals.

The Feast of Samhain marked the Celtic New Year, the transition from the light of summer to the darkness of winter, which they believed was governed by the Lord of Death. On this night, enchanted souls were set free from their animal guardians and ancestral spirits and were allowed to pass between worlds to join the celebration. In preparation, the druids built great bonfires of sacred wood. Individual hearths were extinguished and relit to welcome the spirit entities. In an attempt to intimidate the spirits, villagers disguised themselves as hideous creatures and went from house to house gathering food, using lanterns carved from beets, potatoes, or turnips to light their way. They believed that if the feast adequately placated Samhain, the spirits would appear amiable by bringing gifts to the children, revisiting their homes, granting interviews, or bestowing mystical powers. Some adherents laid on the graves of the dead to receive spiritual revelations. Others participated in blood rituals in which they divined the future from the writhing of the sacrificial victim in the fire or from the entrails cut from his or her body.

Despite the influence of the conquering Romans and the later arrival of Christianity, the festival of the dead, combined with affiliated Roman holidays, continued for several hundred years. By the mid-ninth century, the Roman Catholic Church had established All Saint's Day (in England known as All Hallows; thus All Hallow's Eve shortened to Halloween) in an attempt to shift the focus of the pagan holiday from departed spirits to departed saints. By continuing to include traditional pagan rituals into the proposed Christian holiday, however, the church unwittingly propagated the holiday that would be brought to the New World by early American settlers. Although the strict religious code of early America banned the holiday rituals, Irish and Scottish immigrants had reintroduced Halloween to the masses by the mid-nineteenth century, and once again it became a popular celebration of death.

In occult circles, Halloween has regained much of the philosophical and ritual significance inherent in ancient pagan practices.

Although contemporary witchcraft cults publicly deny any demonic connotations, they continue to celebrate Halloween as the time when the Great Horned God rises to rule during the darkness of winter. Dabblers in the occult are encouraged to take advantage of this time by using various techniques such as Ouija boards, crystal balls, and mirrors to communicate with the spirit world. This supposedly helps to eliminate personal weaknesses and enhance personal powers. Other witchcraft cults believe that Halloween is the night of the sacred goddess who takes revenge on her children's enemies. The rituals of horror and perversion associated with Halloween in some satanic cults rival the most hideous evils of ancient paganism.

Although the self-styled cults of the New Age Movement develop individual traditions, Halloween is the prevalent celebration of death and the most "holy" of satanic holidays.

*See also:* BLACK SABBATH, CELTIC PAGANISM, DRUIDS, WITCHCRAFT

# HANDWRITING ANALYSIS
*See:* GRAPHOLOGY

# HARE KRISHNA (ISKCON)

The International Society for Krishna Consciousness (ISKCON), better known as Hare Krishna, was founded in 1956 by Indian guru A. C. Bhaktivedanta (1896–1977). Established in a New York City storefront, the Krishnas proposed to spread "spiritual enlightenment" to Western civilization. Based on Vedanic scriptures, this Hindu sect believes it is possible to break free from the painful laws of karma by living a good and pure life, totally devoted to Lord Krishna.

From the moment people devote themselves to the cult, their lives cease to be their own. Leaders immediately begin breaking all ties to the outside world and immersing these devotees in the teachings of the sect. Initiates pledge all their worldly possessions, their minds, and their bodies to the group. A strict regime of work awaits them both inside and outside the commune. Worship consists of hypnotic chants,

songs, and literature, while food consists strictly of fruits and vegetables. Members of the Krishna movement are best known for their colorful robes, shaven heads, book selling, and chanting the Krishna mantra in airport lobbies. Through continuously chanting the names of God, Krishnas believe they can obtain spiritual bliss, as well as everlasting peace and happiness.

The leaders of ISKCON claim that Krishna is the supreme personification of the godhead. "Christ," the son of Krishna, serves as an example of humanity's ability to achieve salvation. Despite Bhaktivedanta's death in 1977, ISKCON continues to spread among ashrams, the secluded dwellings of Hindu sages, as well as in schools, temples, and farm communities throughout the world.

*See also:* BHAKTIVEDANTA SWAMI PRABHUPADA, A. C.; HINDUISM

# HARMONIC CONVERGENCE

One of the largest-ever global peace meditations that occurred simultaneously at sacred sights worldwide. The Harmonic Convergence followed in the wake of the World Healing Event of 1986. The convergence first took place in August of 1987, when an estimated twenty thousand people gathered at more than three hundred fifty sites that were considered sacred. Inspired by New Age guru Jose Argüelles's book *The Mayan Factor: Path Beyond Technology,* the purpose was to draw together the critical mass of rainbow warriors, an army made up of New Age groups, organizations, and individuals. The resulting Harmonic Convergence was to launch a five-year world plan, during which the people of earth would move toward globalization. Globalists believe a minimum amount of human voltage is needed to generate enough energy to establish the infrastructure of a New World Order and to transform the entire human race.

Argüelles, a Colorado art historian, claimed to receive his first vision of the Harmonic Convergence while driving down a Los Angeles street. He believes that the convergence marks the last twenty-five years of a five-thousand-year cycle, a mystical time in which the world will be balanced, cleansed, and evolved before entering the New Age. Argüelles promised that participants would experience the power of peace as it enters the world, witness incredible examples of cosmic phenomena, and have privileged communication with visitors from parallel universes.

*See also:* ARGÜELLES, JOSE; CRITICAL MASS; GLOBALISM; NEW AGE MOVEMENT; TRANSFORMATION

## HATHA YOGA

One of the most popular meditative techniques in America. Hatha Yoga is most widely recognized by its meditative positions and stretching exercises. Because of its benign Western front, Hatha Yoga has become an accepted practice in sports, education, entertainment, and community events.

*See also:* TRANSCENDENTAL MEDITATION, YOGA

## HEAD

In Celtic and some New Age beliefs the seat of the soul and the source of divine inspiration. Therefore, the head is symbolic of divinity and otherworld powers. This is a probable explanation why human sacrifice in Druidic religion was frequently by beheading, and the skull remains a key element of occultic magic.

*See also:* BLOOD SACRIFICE, CELTIC PAGANISM

## HEALTHY, HAPPY, HOLY ORGANIZATION (3HO)

An Americanized Sikh movement founded in 1969 by an Indian-born teacher named S. S. S. Harbhajam Singh, who is better known as Yogi Bhajan. Combining Hindu Kundalini yoga and Islamic traditions, the 3HO cult hosts a membership numbering several thousand. They boast in their readiness for the transition from the Piscean to the Aquarian Age, from the material to the spiritual, and from the individual to the universal consciousness. In an attempt to attune to the forces of change in religious consciousness, the 3HO seek spiritual enlightenment through communal living. In the search for divine peace, cult members use a vegetarian diet and various New Age mediative techniques, including the chanting of holy music taken from ancient Sanskrit.

*See also:* AQUARIUS, AGE OF; CONSCIOUSNESS REVOLUTION; PEACE; SIKHISM; VEGETARIANISM; YOGA

## HEAVEN

The concept of a place or state of reality corresponding to the Christian concept of "heaven" differs drastically from religion to religion and even among Eastern and New Age teachings. The Christian Scriptures view heaven as a spiritual but very real place where God dwells with the spiritual beings of angels and those whose sins have been covered by the death of Jesus Christ. Christians believe that heaven is where one exists in intimate fellowship with God (see Deut. 26:15; Matt. 5:45; Rev. 21:1–4).

No non-Christian religion has the same conception. In Judaism, heaven is simply where God is, since belief in a life with God after death is not fully developed. The Kabbalah views God as a Gnostic series of emanations, so heaven is a correspondingly complex set of spiritual realms. Islam views heaven as a beautiful sensual paradise for the faithful.

In Eastern teachings, the closest corresponding concepts both come from Buddhism. Ultimately, one seeks to reach Nirvana, where personal consciousness is absorbed into the Cosmic Consciousness. A place of relative bliss, the Pure Land, which was created by Buddha to reward those who show great devotion. This place of "utmost bliss," as its name can be translated from East Asian languages, is chiefly revered because it opens the way to a more rapid ascent into nirvana.

The Western versions of Eastern religion in the New Age movement usually have a less well defined belief unless firmly within the Buddhist orbit. Heaven often is simply equated with a state of mind. If people are gods, they have the right to create their own "heaven." This right represents the very core of human existence, which is manifested in the individual morality of human nature. In this conception, heaven lies within people, who are responsible to perfect their own heaven while on earth.

Because New Age philosophy denies distinctions between good and evil, gaining heaven depends upon the ability of people to open heart and mind to enlightenment. New Age adherents experience heaven in temporary moments of oneness with the universal whole, just as they experience hell in the painful moments of separation from that whole.

*See also:* HELL, NIRVANA, SATORI

## HEAVEN'S GATE

A UFO cult associated with mass suicides in the late 1990s, particularly during the period of the appearance of Comet Hale-Bopp. Cult members were well educated computer professionals, who lived a communal lifestyle. They believed they had originally been aliens who had come to earth to fulfill a particular task. By killing themselves they would shed their human bodies and rendezvous with space ships that were following the comet. Marshall Herff Applewhite, who helped popularize New Age channeling of psychic communication from the dead, founded the group and was among those who committed suicide.

*See also:* UNIDENTIFIED FLYING OBJECT

## HEGEL, GEORG WILHELM FRIEDRICH (1770–1831)

A German philosopher and teacher whose lectures on the nature of truth and reality influenced the thinking of such prominent individuals as Mary Baker Eddy, the founder of the Christian Science Church, and Adolf Hitler.

Hegel believed that the human mind progresses through forms of consciousness, with one idea (thesis) challenging another idea (antithesis) and ultimately producing a new idea of greater significance (synthesis). Hegel contended that truth does not exist in matter and that what we perceive as reality is nothing more than the manifestation of the spirit, or the Infinite Mind. Hegel also taught that people should not be bound by the illusion of moral absolutes (unchanging truths) but should realize that truth and morality are relative, depending on the circumstances of any given time or place.

*See also:* CHRISTIAN SCIENCE; EDDY, MARY BAKER; HITLER, ADOLF

## HELL

According to the Bible, a place of separation and torment originally prepared by God for the Devil and his cohorts (Matt. 25:41). The Bible also teaches that at the end of the age, God will judge the wicked and condemn them to the eternal lake of fire (Rev. 20:11–15). Hell is characterized by "unquenchable fire" and "blackest darkness" (Matt. 3:12; Jude 13).

New Age hell represents a state of mind rather than a place. Generally speaking, New Age adherents consider hell as a necessary, but temporary, stage of evolutionary development on the spiritual path to heaven, or godhood. They assert that people receive endless chances to achieve heaven and ascend the negative consciousness levels of hell through the process of reincarnation.

*See also:* FALL OF HUMANITY, THE; HEAVEN; SIN

## HERBALISM

A belief in the beneficial properties of plants for medicinal and mystical purposes. Even in the most primitive societies, human dependence on vegetation for the subsistence of life has elevated the discipline of herbal science to a sacred position of power. As the oldest healing art known to humanity, the ancient herbalist grew, collected, studied, and administered plants (both externally and internally) to enhance the body's natural healing process and to cure minor illnesses.

Herbalism finds its roots in the mystery practices of ancient Babylonian priests, Arabian alchemists, and Eastern magicians, all of whom believed that the possession of a perfect knowledge of natural things was the key to spiritual powers. This concept easily translates into New Age philosophy. Some herbalists believe that each plant has its own personality and power that emanates in vibrational energy patterns. This energy is transmitted to the psychic center of the individual who, through altered states of consciousness, can interpret the relative response of people to colors, sounds, and actions. Once the power of nature and the power of the person unite in universal understanding, then it is possible to create, direct, or alter reality.

Some herbalists, particularity those of pagan religions, believe that the aromatic properties of plants contain magical power to bridge the natural and supernatural worlds. Since herbal aromas are thought to be sacred to individual spirits, both good and bad, these aromas are used in invocation rituals according to their particular powers. In addition to spirits, herbal additives have ritual significance with angels, gods, goddesses, seasons, and planets, as well as colors, senses, animals, tools, and rules of witchcraft. Aromatics may be used in amulets, charms, incense, oils, lotions, or infusions. The purpose is to achieve a visionary or trancelike state, obedience, or levitation, as well as invisibility, transformation, or to invoke the healing or hexing powers of life and death. Proponents often use sweet-smelling sacred herbs in veneration rituals, whereas strong, foul-smelling herbs are reserved for evil incantations.

*See also:* AROMATHERAPY; HOLISM; MEDICINE, NEW AGE; SYMBOLISM

# HERMAPHRODITE
*See:* ANDROGYNY

# HEXAGRAM
A six-pointed star depicted by intertwined triangles. Ancient Eastern religions revered the hexagram as the perpetual sexual union of a god and goddess, whom they believe are responsible for maintaining all life within the universe. Some New Age occultists believe

**Hexagram— merging triangles of god and goddess**

the hexagram has the power to protect practicing members and control demonic activity, while others think the emblem enables them to divine future events through the ancient art of *I Ching*.

*See also:* CHARM, *I Ching,* POWER OBJECT, SYMBOLISM

# HIGHER CONSCIOUSNESS
A state in which people transcend, or rise above, the normal levels of consciousness. Adherents maintain that the deeper the state of consciousness achieved, the higher the degree of awareness that can be experienced.

*See also:* ALPHA LEVEL, ALTERED STATE, HIGHER SELF, TRANSCENDENCE

# HIGHER SELF
A sliver of the divine whole, represented by the soul, which supposedly exists deep beneath the conscious awareness. According to New Age adherents, the higher self originates from a universal energy source traditionally recognized as "God."

In a cosmic explosion, slivers of consciousness became human souls, manifesting themselves as three dimensional images on earth. The New Age Movement contends that in becoming three-dimensional thinkers, these divine souls forgot their fourth dimension, or godhood, represented by the higher self. They believe that the higher self lies within the collective unconscious of all people but is only recognized by the spiritually enlightened.

Many New Age techniques reputedly can facilitate the initial introduction to the higher self. These are designed to delve into the depths of the soul, where initiates can choose an image that will manifest the higher self. To those from a Christian background, the spirit guide may even take the form of Jesus Christ in a proverbial garden within the person. New recruits learn to practice making contact with their higher self in happiness, sadness, anger, or frustration. Because the spirit guide has direct access to the collective unconscious, it holds the keys to unlimited wisdom and knowledge, human potential, and psychic powers.

*See also:* CONFLUENT EDUCATION, HIGHER CONSCIOUSNESS, SPIRIT GUIDES, SUPERCONSCIOUSNESS

## HINDUISM

The dominant religion of India. Although its founder is unknown, historians trace Hinduism back to around 1500 B.C., making it one of the oldest existing religions. Experts say that Hinduism is the predecessor of all Eastern religious beliefs. The Hindu wheels of reincarnation, laws of karma, and meditative practices have also become influential in recent Western history, helping to propagate New Age philosophy.

Hinduism claims Brahman as its infinite and absolute supreme being or god. Brahman reputedly is the eternal Trimutri, a three-in-one god, who is unchanging and represents the essence of all living things. Because change supposedly constitutes illusion, Hindus consider Brahman as the only true reality. And because of its perfection, the Hindu supreme being is impersonal and cannot be approached by an imperfect people.

Hinduism advocates the worship of many gods as a pathway to understanding Brahman. The great triad of Hindu gods is comprised of Brahma, Shiva, and Vishnu. Brahma is believed to be the creator of all things. Because creation is complete, they rarely worship this god. They worship Shiva, the destroyer, because of its power to eradicate the old to make way for the new. They believe Shiva, and its representative gods, play a prominent part in the purification process preceding the global transformation into the New Age. The final and most popular aspect of the Hindu triad is Vishnu, the preserver. They believe Vishnu is Brahman incarnated into avatars (such as Krishna), who come to earth to aid people on their spiritual journey. Hindus choose to follow only one aspect of Brahman, as well as the many lesser gods they represent.

According to Hinduism, the ultimate purpose of the soul is to unite with Brahman in an unchanging state of eternal bliss. Only when bad deeds are balanced against good, which is impossible to accomplish in one lifetime, can adherents reach this unity. Hindus believe the soul must be born and reborn in reincarnation until this balance is achieved. Karma is the force generated by the actions of people. According to the laws of karma, the soul is not subject to death, but simply transmigrates to the next state of existence upon death. They believe the actions of people in one life will determine their station in the next. While bad karma may be balanced against good in any given life, more bad karma inevitably results.

Hinduism advocates living a life characterized by the disciplined purity of the mind and body, accomplished through devotion, meditation, and performing good deeds. This life of discipline includes the study of Hindu sacred writings, written in Sanskrit and compiled over the centuries. The Vedas (1000 B.C.) are written in lyrical prose and describe the powers and worship of nature. The Brahmanas (800–600 B.C.) teach that people can tap into supernatural powers through the ritualistic worship of gods. The Upanishads (600–300 B.C.) teach about the unity of the universe. The Laws of Manu (250 B.C.) contain the legal code of Hindu life. The Bhagavad Gita (A.D. 1) teaches devotional methods of meditation and faith and is the most revered Hindu text, as well as the most popular one in America today. The last of the sacred writings are the Epics and the Puranas (200 B.C.–A.D. 250), which present the entire Hindu lesson in narrative form.

The laws of karma ultimately led to the establishment of the caste system in India. This binding hereditary social order exists out of fear of disturbing the equalizing karma (or life force) of the universe. This system, and the sacred writings that promoted it, eventually led many to reject Hinduism in favor of various sects. Hindu offshoots, such as Buddhism, were a major influence on Eastern religions, as well as the American countercultural movement of the 1960s.

*See also:* BRAHMA, CASTE SYSTEM, KARMA, REINCARNATION, SHIVA, UPANISHADS, VISHNU

## HITLER, ADOLF (1889–1945)

The leader of the National Socialist German Worker's Party (Nazi) in Germany before and during World War II. Hitler is most remembered for ordering the slaughter of more than 12 million people, half of whom were European Jews. Commonly depicted as a charismatic madman, Hitler did not originate his philosophy, nor did it end with his death.

Adolf Hitler was an early initiate into the ancient mystery religions at the heart of the New Age Movement today. As a young child, he attended a Benedictine monastery where an abbot, who believed man could achieve the powers of God, initiated him into the occult. As a young artist in Vienna, Hitler continued his intense study of the occult with friends and was particularly fascinated with the metaphysical side of humanity. He practiced ascending states of consciousness by using Eastern religious techniques such as yoga and supplemented this practice with drugs.

In one of these drug induced, trancelike states, Hitler claimed to have journeyed to the Akashic Record, a collective account of all human thoughts and actions. Hitler believed that, with guidance from the spiritual realm, he could transform the German nation and restore the master race to its rightful place in world affairs.

His National Socialist German Workers Party struggled for acceptance in the early 1920s. But by 1932, it had gained so much strength that it prevented its opponents from forming a majority in the Reichstag, the lower house of the German parliament. This enabled Hitler and his Nazi party to take control of the country in 1933. By 1934 Hitler eliminated all his political opponents who were within the Nazi party and assumed the title of führer, or supreme commander. An elaborate terror and propaganda apparatus allowed the Nazis to maintain absolute control of Germany. In defiance of the world community, the Nazis rearmed the nation in 1935, remilitarized the Rhineland in 1936, annexed Austria in 1938, and acquired all of Czechoslovakia in 1939. From 1939 to 1945, Hitler and his Nazi party immersed Germany and all of Europe, northern Africa, and western Russia in war.

During his reign of terror, Hitler injected occultism and mysticism into the youth culture and into his own private army. He established an elite party guard known as the SS, an abbreviation for *Schutzstaffel* that means "protection echelon." This regiment included an extensive bureau dedicated solely to the research and practice of occult methodology. Like an esoteric cult, the SS was set up to reveal only certain knowledge to its initiates, adepts, and masters. Members were initiated into the organization and swore blood oaths. They received instruction in witchcraft, evolution, karma, and reincarnation, as well as the domination theory of the Aryan race. Hitler promised them a significant role once his objectives were realized.

Although Allied forces eventually defeated the Third Reich and ended the Fascist era in Germany, Nazism did not die. Since World War II, neo-Nazi parties have sprung up in continental Europe, Britain, Russia, and the United States. These groups espouse white supremacy and anti-Semitism and are heavily influenced by New Age thinking. Those wanting to join neo-Nazi groups typically must take blood oaths, as well as undergo initiations into the occult. As members, they learn about Satanism, witchcraft, and astrology, as well as evolution, karma, and reincarnation. They embrace the goal of transforming enlightened humankind into a superrace. Their indoctrination says this objective can only be achieved through racial purification and the attainment of global consciousness.

*See also:* EVIL, LUCIFERIC DOCTRINE, PURIFICATION, TRANSFORMATION

## HOLISM

The belief that the universe operates in a harmonious balance of interconnected and interrelated parts of a greater whole. New Age adherents contend that by transcending the levels of consciousness, the individual can learn to balance the divine energy forces that circulate through all living things. They encourage people to harmonize their mind, body, and spirit, thereby integrating themselves with the universal energy forces, or the New Age.

*See also:* BALANCING, COSMIC ENERGY

## HOLISTIC HEALTH

A method of treatment based on ancient metaphysical and occultic beliefs. Practitioners claim that the mind, body, and spirit are an interconnected triad, deserving of diagnosis and treatment as a comprehensive "whole." They believe illness and pain are an accumulation of unbalanced energy, easily corrected by realigning the vibrational forces of the mind, body, and spirit. Psychic powers reputedly can be obtained while in altered states of consciousness and then translated into physiological change by tapping into the universal life force that supposedly permeates human existence.

In holistic health, the philosophical beliefs of the East are mixed with the ritualistic practices of ancient Babylon and, more recently, the metaphysical thought of the twentieth century. The resulting philosophy contends that the individual, just as the universe, operates in a harmonious balance of interconnected and interrelated parts, united by a divine energy life force that flows through all living things. Holistic healers claim that people possess both the innate ability and responsibility to manipulate this divine force to maintain a harmonious balance of energy within themselves. They view physical, psychological, and spiritual ailments as simply the product of thinking improperly. According to their philosophy, this imbalance of energy is easily corrected by transcending to a level of consciousness where divine awareness can be utilized.

The success of holistic health treatments is often temporary. Practitioners usually demand that the patient continue therapy while learning the revelations of ancient pagan belief systems. Some popular holistic healing practices include power crystals, homeopathy, iridology, and electromagnetic healing, as well as therapeutic touch, kinesiology, visualization, aroma-therapy, and acupuncture.

*See also:* AROMATHERAPY; BALANCING; MEDICINE, NEW AGE; QUARTZ CRYSTAL; VIBRATIONS

## HOLOGRAPHIC THEORY

A theory that depicts the human brain as a functioning hologram. Invented in 1947 by Dennis Gabor, the hologram is the projection of a three-dimensional photographic record, created by illuminating an object with lasers. The light from the object itself and from a beam deflected by a mirror image of the object reflects onto a photographic plate. A laser then reconstitutes the image, resulting in the three-dimensional likeness. Scientists have found that any one component of a hologram can hold the information necessary to reproduce the whole object.

In 1966, Stanford professor Karl Pribram proposed the holographic theory. He pointed out that both the brain and the hologram have the capability of storing infinite quantities of information and that any given part can recall the information of the whole. Pribram suggested that, like the hologram, our brains construct reality by interpreting frequencies from an unknown dimension. This universal hologram, which transcends time and space, is made up of the bioelectric frequencies of all human brains, and their interaction creates what we perceive as reality.

Based on this information, Pribram claimed that transcendental experiences are able to give people access to a "new" dimension of reality. They supposedly enter into an altered state of existence, resulting in psychic phenomena. Pribram says that such experiences have remained unexplained because they occur at primary levels of reality in a dimension that transcends time and space. This is also why, he argues, ancient religions have encountered the same spiritual experiences throughout time.

*See also:* HOLISM; SCIENCE, NEW AGE; TRANSCENDENTALISM; UNIVERSAL MIND

# HOLOTROPHIC BREATHING

A breathing technique developed by clinical psychiatrist and John Hopkins University of Medicine professor Stanislav Grof (b. 1931). As a research leader on the effects of psychedelic drugs on human consciousness, he conducted more than four thousand lysergic acid diethylamide (LSD) experiments. He also had access to the records of eighteen hundred additional cases. (LSD is an organic compound that induces psychotic symptoms.) Grof concluded that psychedelic drugs allowed easy access to an altered state of consciousness through which the mysteries of the universe could be realized. He also concluded that the same effects could be achieved through other means.

As a resident scholar of the Esalen Institute, Grof developed the holotrophic breathing technique in which subjects engaged in intense, rapid deep breathing exercises. Through holotrophic breathing, subjects allegedly experienced visions, vibrations, and color trails of molecular particles, as well as past life regressions and various encounters with the spiritual dimension. Most importantly, some subjects reputedly lost themselves in the realm of the Universal Mind, experiencing a sense of unity with the cosmic whole, or New Age enlightenment. Time and space seemed limitless, matter was transformed into an illusory pattern of energy, and physical laws no longer had any meaning. The adventures of the human consciousness were manifested in an illusionary world that was previously perceived as reality.

Although most holotrophic breathing experiences claim to result in a deeper understanding of the self and the universe, the benefits are short-lived. Initiates must continually return to these altered states to retain the sense of universal unity. The negative effects of transcending human consciousness were substantial. The numerous reports of a "transpersonal crisis" led Grof and his wife Christine to found the Spiritual Emergency Network (SEN) in 1980. The increasing number of negative effects included apparent demonic manifestation and control, severe physical and mental disorders, and the loss of perceptive and comprehensive brain functions.

*See also:* CONSCIOUSNESS, DRUG, ENLIGHTENMENT, ESALEN INSTITUTE, LYSERGIC ACID DIETHYLAMIDE

# HOMEOPATHY

A holistic technique devised by Samuel Hahnemann (1755–1843). Minute doses of natural poisons are introduced into the system in an attempt to stimulate the healing processes of the human body. Literally translated "similar disease," homeopathy operates on the premise that if too much of a substance causes a particular symptom, then minute amounts will alleviate it.

Unlike similar treatments in traditional medicine, homeopathy looks to treat only the symptoms, rather than discovering the organisms or mechanisms that cause an illness. Practitioners work with an elaborate collection of plant, animal, and mineral toxins that are known to mimic symptoms. The intent is to stimulate the body into reacting against the toxins, thereby healing itself. Holistic healers contend that traditional medicine works to suppress the body's natural healing processes by treating only selected symptoms of the interrelated mind, body, and spiritual whole. Practitioners of homeo-pathy believe that infinitesimal doses of a substance work as a catalyst that stimulate not just the body but also the mind and spirit to health.

*See also:* HERBALISM, HOLISTIC HEALTH

# HOMONOETICUS

A new species said to emerge from human-kind's quantum leap forward into a new dimension of instant spiritual consciousness. Proponents believe the New Age person is the product of centuries of spiritual evolution toward divinity. They also believe this race is nearing perfection with the closing of the Piscean Age. The pace of this evolutionary change supposedly has quickened. When a critical mass is reached and a large enough segment of humankind is ready, the Aquarian Age of homonoeticus will dawn.

*See also:* AQUARIUS, AGE OF ; ASCENDED MASTER; PLAN, THE; QUANTUM LEAP

## HOUSTON, JEAN

A Jungian psychologist and author who holds a doctorate in psychology and religion. Houston has served as president of the Association of Humanistic Psychology and as director of the Foundation of Mind Research. She advocates the use of techniques and rituals from ancient mystery religions to help people adopt the beliefs and practices of the New Age Movement. In this system, the superior powers of the mind, experienced in the spiritual realm, permanently replace the powers of ordinary consciousness and physical technology.

As a result of her belief in a universal source of power and wisdom, Houston has written a number of books on self-induced altered states, self-healing, and the art of psychic development. In 1972, Houston joined with Robert Masters to write *Mind Games,* a step-by-step manual showing how the mind can serve as a stargate to a larger world of universal unity. In true Jungian form, Houston believes that spiritual entities are the projections of a collective unconscious, or parts of the self that have taken on an acceptable form in order to communicate. Her book introduces an educational game, which she claims is harmless, where a team of children work together to bring an entity into existence that can be touched, seen, and heard. Although Houston concedes that some entities may originate in alternate dimensions of existence, she advocates trust as a means of protection. She believes that such exercises should be and will be a routine part of the educational system.

Houston is also known for coining the term *Therapeia,* which she says means "work of the gods." These are workshops used to aid participants in transcending consciousness and regressing to past prehuman

existences by using theatrical devices. Houston believes that the human brain still retains the chemical patterns of its reptilian, mammal, and neomammal ancestry. Houston leads people into an altered state specifically designed for receptivity to suggestions. She allegedly helps them to achieve awareness of these ancient memories, gain insight into their personalities, clear away emotional blocks, and open memories into the future. In an attempt to restore the sacred status to the psyche, Houston tells her initiates that Jesus Himself taught that God dwells in every person, that every person is bound only by their own ethics, and that sin and guilt are nothing more than the ignorance of the individual's greatness within.

*See also:* CHRIST-CONSCIOUSNESS; GUIDED IMAGERY; HUMANISTIC PSYCHOLOGY; JUNG, CARL GUSTAV; PAST LIVES THERAPY

## HUBBARD, BARBARA MARX (b. 1930)

A New Age author, teacher, theorist, and cofounder and director of the Global Family. Hubbard helped to introduce the concept of spiritual futurism, which she claims is a new universal species of higher consciousness, brought about by humanity's recognition of the savior within themselves. Hubbard's spiritual journey began with a pseudo-Christian religious experience, in which she claims Jesus imparted pantheistic/naturalistic messages to her. She describes Jesus as an evolutionary entity who developed enhanced abilities to attune to an impersonal, universal force known as "god."

Hubbard believes that as global problems grow, so does the potential for human development. She also believes that in the face of crises, New Age networks, which are dedicated to expanded awareness, will eventually join in a quantum leap of consciousness. She says this radical evolutionary transformation will produce a new suprahuman species. In preparation, Hubbard advocates the use of altered states of consciousness to contact the higher self and channeled entities, both of which are believed to expound on the nature of humanity's transformation.

*See also:* ALTERED STATE, CHRIST-CONSCIOUSNESS, DEMON, HIGHER SELF, QUANTUM LEAP

## HUBBARD, L. RON (1911–1986)

A science fiction writer and author of the best-selling book *Dianetics*. In the 1950s, Hubbard founded the Church of Scientology on the belief that people are forgotten gods. His philosophy is a mixture of Eastern mysticism, psychotherapy, and science fiction. Initiates pay large sums of money for therapy sessions that promise to help them experience past life regressions and relocate their divine.

The Church of Scientology grew to more than 6 million members before declining due to problems with the FBI and IRS. Hubbard claimed that governmental agencies were attempting to suppress Scientology. Despite Hubbard's promises of magical powers and total knowledge, Scientology members were unable to reach a divine state, although many claimed incredible growth.

*See also:* DIANETICS, SCIENTOLOGY

## HUMAN POTENTIAL MOVEMENT

A euphemistic phrase used to describe the New Age Movement of the 1970s. During this decade, belief that the destiny of the world lay in the innate powers of untapped human potential became very popular. The human potential movement followed the idealistic search of the 1960s subculture and was initially characterized by a concern for self-improvement. But by the middle of the 1970s, it had become a search for self-divinity.

The ideological elements of Theosophy (divine knowledge through direct occult experience) and Eastern religions (eternal truth through transcendental discipline) joined humanist psychology to develop a new perspective on the divine potential of humankind. Suddenly transpersonal therapies, behavior modification techniques, training

seminars, and mystical experimentation exercises flooded the market. All of these concepts invited initiates to face their feelings, touch the inner self, and unleash the latent powers and abilities existing within the unconscious mind. They claimed that anything the mind could believe, it could also achieve. By commanding the cosmic forces of the universe to obey personal thoughts, every individual could now take responsibility for the creation of their own realities. With the potential of developing into a superior race of beings, people considered themselves as the vanguards of an emerging New Age.

*See also:* HOMONOETICUS, NEW AGE MOVEMENT, THEOSOPHY, TRANSCENDENTALISM, TRANSPERSONAL PSYCHOLOGY

## HUMANISM

The belief that humankind is the ultimate ideal, that people are complete within themselves, the highest rung of the evolutionary ladder and the measure of all things. Humanists deny the existence of God, as Creator and Supreme Being. They believe that moral and ethical standards should be determined by human experience, relative to what society currently regards as acceptable behavior. Since society is constantly changing, humanists disregard moral absolutes held by biblical Christianity. Spiritual humanists assert that the limitless, untapped potential of the human spirit holds the key to all existence, whereas cosmic humanists express theories of an eight-dimensional universe based on the integrated principles of life. Secular humanists maintain that intellectual, creative, and moral freedoms represent the exaltation of the human life, while spiritual humanists assign to people the role of god, an alleged divine heritage of universal forces.

During the Enlightenment Era of the eighteenth century, a solid outline of humanist beliefs began to take form. Christianity came under direct attack by Western intellectuals who claimed that organized religion existed only to put unjust moral restraints on society and that it was incompatible with humanist values. Although the nineteenth century boasted a widespread Christian revival, the implications of secular humanism continued to grow. This movement dedicated itself to expunging all religious influence from society. The advancement of technology, psychology, and science contributed to the strength of the humanist movement in which each supported the theory that humanity's existence was influenced by environment, not by God. Despite its influence, humanism had a minimal effect in America until the antiestablishment movement of the 1960s. Suddenly traditional values and religious morality were once again under attack. But this time, the tenets of Eastern mysticism, occultism, and belief in unlimited human potential had merged with humanism.

See also: ENLIGHTENMENT; *Humanist Manifesto, the;* HUMANISTIC PSYCHOLOGY

## HUMANIST MANIFESTO, THE

A publication issued in 1933 by the American Humanist Association. This document proclaimed the creed for a new religion in which people alone were deemed responsible for the condition and conservation of the universe. Although the manifesto did not flagrantly deny the existence of God, it denounced the doctrines of traditional Christianity as being unresponsive to the needs of contemporary humanity. The document reflects the pseudo-scientific approach of secular humanism by maintaining that the supernatural has been supplanted by the natural, absolute morality has been rejected for subjective experience, divine worship occurs through social cooperation, and eternal salvation is achieved by cultivating personal potential.

In 1973, *The Humanist Manifesto II* was issued, proclaiming itself as an international statement of human objectives and laying the foundation for a planetary civilization. In many cases, the document simply reiterated the tenets of its predecessor, but the voice of outrage had grown bolder. The manifesto said traditional Christianity was detrimental to so-ciety because it held people back from attaining salvation. Salvation was defined as something achieved through logic, intelligence, and the complete realization of human potential. It also called for the abolishment of all sexual distinctions and introduced the new tenets of sexual exploration, birth control, and abortion. *The Humanist Manifesto II* recognized supernatural occurrences as alternate dimensions of the natural realm, all of which could be harnessed by humankind. Above all, the document called for transcending religious and political divisions and proclaimed the coming New Age of humanity and the establishment of a system of global unity.

See also: HUMANISM, NEW AGE MOVEMENT, SALVATION

## HUMANISTIC PSYCHOLOGY

The study of mind and behavior based on humanistic tenets and practices. Sometimes referred to as the third force of human psychology, the humanist approach was developed by Abraham Maslow (1908–1970) in opposition to existing psychotherapies. Contrary to the thinking of his day, Maslow believed that human disorders were not caused by the environment or by unconscious repressions but by personal values and choices. He advocated the fulfillment of untapped human potential as a means to achieve mental and physical stability.

Humanistic psychology places humanity at the center of the universe and seeks to unite the human race with universal forces. Although this system of thought appears compatible with Christianity, it denies the existence of sin and people's need for redemption. Based on the premise that people are basically good, humanistic psychology teaches that evil is merely the failure to grow or the failure to fulfill the innate potential for greatness. This system of thought urges people to resist externally imposed moral values in favor of those they themselves have created or chosen. These values are determined by experiences and feelings and are enhanced through altered states of consciousness achieved during mystical and occultic sessions.

*See also:* EVIL; MASLOW, ABRAHAM; PEACE; SCIENCE, NEW AGE

## HUMANISTIC PSYCHOLOGY, ASSOCIATION FOR (AHP)

A New Age organization founded by Abraham Maslow (1908–1970). With headquarters in San Francisco, AHP focuses on the exploration of human potential and holistic healing through trances achieved in occult and mystical practices. Sometimes called the "network of people for a New Age," AHP provides a worldwide link between New Age thinkers and institutions. Those who belong to this occult network share, argue, test, and adapt experiences and insights in order to implement their planetary goals. Advocates believe that the ability to communicate with others over this complex web will generate a metaphysical power that will one day bring fragmented clusters together and trigger a paradigm shift in human consciousness. This will lead to a global transformation and usher in the Aquarian Age of peace, joy, and enlightenment under the rule of Lord Maitreya.

*See also:* HUMANISTIC PSYCHOLOGY; MASLOW, ABRAHAM; PSYCHOTECHNOLOGY

## HUNDREDTH MONKEY THEORY, THE

The hypothesis that originated from a 1953 study of macaque monkeys on the Japanese island of Koshima. This theory erroneously reported paranormal activities among the observed subjects. According to project researcher Lyall Watson, scientific evidence proved that when a specified percentage of the total monkey population adopted the same behavior, it became the instinctive behavior of the remainder of the species. Watson reported that when a female monkey was lured into observation with a sweet potato, the animal rinsed it in the sea before eating it. He also noted that other nearby monkeys began to rinse their sweet potatoes, until eventually one hundred monkeys had adopted the behavior. Watson contended that when this critical mass of the total population had been reached, the entire race of macaque monkeys were paranormally infused with the concept, including those on the mainland and on other islands.

Although Watson admitted fraud when later challenged by the scientific community, the hundredth monkey theory has continued to flourish within New Age circles. Author Ken Keys has offered a popularized version of the hypothesis. He suggests that when the critical mass of the human population is able to focus their minds on any given subject, they can alter reality by creating a cosmic shift in the consciousness of all humankind. The underlying belief suggests that the individual minds of people are all a vital part of a universal mind that, when properly energized, can be shifted to reflect the imagination of the critical mass. New Age leaders endorse global mind-link events, suggesting that each person may represent "the hundredth monkey," the necessary energy force to tip the scales toward global peace.

*See also:* CRITICAL MASS; KUHN, THOMAS; QUANTUM LEAP; TRANSFORMATION

## HUNGER PROJECT

A charitable organization founded by Werner Erhard (b. 1935) in 1977 and popularized by musician John Denver. Despite the name, the program's purpose is not to feed the hungry, but to raise public awareness to the problem of global hunger. New Age advocates believe people already have the resources to end world hunger, but the goal will only be accomplished if the world reaches the conviction that the goal is possible. Their purpose is to force a shift in the thinking of all humanity.

Leaders in the organization encourage participants to become "teachers" by enlisting others into the project, who in turn enlist others. These new recruits send money, which is used to enlist more people. If enough participants believe that world hunger can be ended, then supposedly it will become a reality.

See also: ERHARD, WERNER HANS; ONE-WORLD IDEAL; VISUALIZATION

## HUXLEY, ALDOUS (1894–1963)

A utopian novelist and mystic best known for his book *Brave New World* and for advocating the use of drugs as a means of altering consciousness to open the doors of human perception. Huxley believed that a divine reality permeated all things, including humanity. While he acknowledged that many paths led to the god within, he suggested that drugs provided the easiest and most direct access to the liberation of the mind. Huxley maintained that, while intelligence could lead us to the brink of experience, it had served its purpose. The time had come to put aside finite, systematic reasoning in order to change the level of consciousness through the use of drugs.

See also: COSMIC CONSCIOUSNESS, DRUG, PERENNIAL PHILOSOPHY

## HYDROCHROMAPHY

The mystical attempt to charge a glass of water with color power to produce a particular effect in the individual who drinks it. A glass bottle of the appropriate color is filled with pure spring water and set in direct sunlight to absorb rays for one hour. Because hydrochromaphy is an inexact practice, believers say that it can also be done with a colored plastic container, tap water, and artificial light.

See also: COLOROLOGY

## HYLOZOISM

An animistic view that personifies or ascribes sentient life to all matter. Hylozoism is closely related to the New Age worldview belief that a life force pervades the universe. It is one reason that Christian missiologist and social critic Harvey Conn has said that it is a mistake to regard late twentieth century philosophy as atheistic or even humanistic at its core principle. Rather, Conn said, popular modernity is animistic.

Hylozoism is an ancient aspect of primitive religions that interprets all existence by human self-awareness. The Ionians, early Greek philosophers, conceived of the universe as animated and closely manipulated and watched over by various gods.

This gave way to a materialistic view of the universe, but at about the time of Christ the neoPlatonism taught in North Africa was resurrecting an animistic view that a spiritual principle emanating from God inhabited all things as a "world soul," an idea coined by the stoic philosophers. Since physical reality is by nature either illusion or evil in the thought of Platonists, the world soul raised all existence above the inferiority of matter.

Pantheistic hylozoism quickly developed within Platonic thought. All that is good in material being proceeds from a distinct principle, the soul. The universe is an immense organism. Everything is animated. Though life is distinct from matter, life was imparted to all material beings. Pantheistic hylozoism was part of medieval Jewish and Arab philosophy, and entered Western thought with the Renaissance study of nature, and classical Greek literature. Its popularity was increased because it serves as an excuse for a sensual morality.

When Jewish philosopher Benedict de Spinoza (1632–1677) combined atheistic materialism with pantheistic hylozoism, he offered the possibility of a godless spirituality as well as a hedonistic morality.

Much of New Age science is actually a scientific hylozoism. This is a protest against a mechanical view of the world, though a protest that still allows for the denial of God and the mechanistic processes of naturalistic macroevolution.

See also: ANIMISM, MONISM, MOTHER EARTH, PANPSYCHISM

## HYPNOSIS

An induced state of relaxation in which the mind is receptive to suggestion. Through the trancelike state the reasoning functions of normal consciousness can be bypassed to a limited extent, and the hypnotist can plant ideas in the subconscious. Eastern religions try to induce hypnotic states in order to increase psychic awareness.

Hypnotic trance states have been described as part of religious ritual since at least the ancient Egyptians. By the late eighteenth century, the practice was given some level of scientific credibility in studies conducted by the German physician Franz Anton Mesmer (1734–1815). Researchers have since tried to discern what kinds of changes are induced in the brain. It has been determined that the physiological and psychological effects depend largely on the subject's ability to focus concentration and on the person's willingness and motivation.

Hypnosis is used to treat a variety of physical and psychological problems, and it remains a field of psychological experimentation. Its primary advocates are those who study psychic phenomena. Holistic healers contend that hypnotic suggestion can induce the release of healing energy, blocking pain and altering biological functions. Psychotherapists insist that hypnotic suggestion can be used to modify behavior, help uncover repressed emotions and encourage healthy ways of thinking.

The most controversial use of hypnotism has been to legitimize reincarnation by regressing a subject into memories of past lives. Hypnotic regression is a psychotherapeutic technique in which patients are hypnotically influenced to search out repressed memories of the past—including former lives. Hypnotherapists believe that the accumulation of suppressed negative emotions stems from the unresolved pain of past lives manifested in current fears and phobias. They believe that by retrieving and dealing with these memories on a conscious level, patients will obtain a new understanding of current life patterns, characteristics, preferences, and fears.

Advocates of hypnotism make staggering claims of the unlimited psychic abilities that potentially could be unlocked. Substantiation of claims that hypnotised people have super creative abilities or hypernormal thinking processes has not been forthcoming. Advocates contend that patients can unblock psychic barriers and develop a wide range of divine powers by transcending the levels of consciousness. By feeding suggestions to the subject, the hypnotist seeks to enhance visualization, sensory perception, and dreams, as well as clairvoyant and telepathic abilities.

*See also:* ALTERED STATE; HOLISTIC HEALTH; MESMER, FRANZ ANTON

# I

## I Ching

A collective work believed to contain the wisdom of the ages and the secrets of the universe. Also known as *The Book of Changes, I Ching* originated during the Han Dynasty in China and became one of the country's most revered texts. People believed that by consulting the book, they could gain divine insights into the self, as well as the power to predict the future.

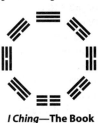

*I Ching*—The Book of Changes

*I Ching* is based on the principle of yin/yang. This concept promotes the essential unity of all things, including opposites such as good and bad, light and darkness. All material objects are made up of a combination of positive and negative forces. *The Book of Changes* contains sixty-four hexagrams (a six-pointed star) and eight trigrams (combinations of three whole or broken lines). Each symbol represents certain psychic principles. By tossing yarrow stalks and dividing them into piles, the intuition of their spirit foresees how they land. *The Book of Changes* then interprets the meaning.

*See also:* DIVINATION, YIN/YANG

## IATROGENIC

Literally translated "doctor-caused," iatrogenic is the term used to describe the disease and suffering that are the direct result of medical treatments. In some cases, iatrogenic pain and sickness may be due to incompetence, such as unnecessary medical treatments, surgical complications, or misprescribed medication. In other cases, iatrogenic illness may be the inescapable by-product of those in the medical profession who have become apathetic to the needs of their patients. New Age adherents like to focus attention on iatrogenic illness to underscore the perceived benefits of holistic health.

*See also:* HOLISM; HOLISTIC HEALTH; MEDICINE, NEW AGE

## ILLUMINATI

An elite organization of wealthy people believed to be responsible for a massive conspiracy designed to result in world domination. Although the organization reputedly has existed for centuries throughout the upper echelons of European society, the Order of the Illuminati was formally founded in 1776 by Bavarian professor Adam Weishaupt (1748–1830). He believed that by manipulating politics, the economy, and religion, a select group of people could be elevated into positions of global leadership. Weishaupt also believed that by bringing all occult groups under the control of a single organization, they could generate the power necessary to dominate the world.

Once established, the small secret organization quickly garnered support from the aristocracy, believing they descended from superior bloodlines. Incorporating their paganistic philosophies and practices into the Order assured Weishaupt the necessary funds to keep his organization operational. To avoid public detection and enhance membership, the Order of the Illuminati infiltrated the well-established and respected Continental Order of Freemasons in 1782. This created what Weishaupt termed "Illuminated Freemasonry." The influence of the Masonic Order enabled Weishaupt to place many members in top European governmental positions, but an overwhelming defeat in the French Revolution seemed to kill the Illuminist dream of a New World Order.

However the Illuminati was not to be dismissed so easily. Less than a century later, the same principles and practices resurfaced in various secret societies. According to some today, these form a global network functioning as the shadowy inner circle of an elite fraternity.

*See also:* FREEMASONRY; GREAT WHITE BROTHERHOOD; LUCIFERIC DOCTRINE; WEISHAUPT, ADAM

## ILLUSION

Misleading appearance, impression, idea, or belief that does not correspond to reality. Since the beginning of time, philosophers and scientists have pondered the ambiguous questions of existence. They have searched for a key piece of information that will once and for all distinguish illusion from reality. Christians believe that the ultimate answers to life are found in the Bible. Many others devote themselves to science and psychology for answers to life's enigmas.

Modern forms of Platonic idealism build upon the supposition that existence itself is illusion. Some suggest that the world is a visible manifestation of the unseen spiritual dimension, a mere breath of smoke reflecting the patterns that originate in a higher plane of existence. Mary Baker Eddy, the founder of Christian Science, reasoned that the spiritual realm was real and the material world was not real. Therefore all matter must be an illusion—beautiful yet transitory. Others suggest that if people can imagine an ideal world, then it must already exist. When the purpose of the present world of illusion has been fulfilled, the world will pass away, allowing the real world that lies beyond the facade to be unveiled.

In this concept, the true nature of humanity never left heaven and never fell from grace. Rather, it waits within the inner self to be rediscovered and reclaimed. This divine self within is the only true reality because it has no need for change and growth, only enlightenment. Because the world is an illusion, sin and evil are also illusions. They are misguided concepts that originated from an unenlightened religious community. Christianity enslaves people to a false concept of guilt and prevents them from achieving godhood. If people would only listen to the inner voice of their Christ-consciousness, they could be freed from the world of illusion (hell) and brought into a world of reality (heaven).

*See also:* CHRISTIAN SCIENCE; EDDY, MARY BAKER; SCIENCE, NEW AGE; THEOSOPHY

## IMAGINATION

The ability to form a mental image of something not directly derived from the senses. Imagination is also the ability to join dissimilar experiences or objects to produce new metaphors and symbols.

In New Age thought, the imagination represents an unbounded source of revelation, a gateway to an expanded dimension of learning. Through such "imagineering" techniques as visualization and guided imagery, initiates are promised that they can expand their mind and enhance their potential for greatness. Imagineering further promises to develop their intuitive (or psychic) abilities as they ascend the levels of human consciousness and tap into the vast reservoir of universal knowledge. Whatever they can picture mentally, they can turn into a reality because they are an interrelated part of the divine whole, thereby capable of creating and controlling whatever exists in their world.

*See also:* CONFLUENT EDUCATION, GUIDED IMAGERY, HOLISM, ILLUSION, VISUALIZATION

## IMMORTALITY

The quality or state of having unlimited length of life. Immortality indicates freedom from any kind of decay and death, the negative side of the concept, and living an eternal divine life, the positive side of the concept. Christianity holds that only God has eternal life within Himself, He alone is the source of immortality (Ps. 36:9; John 5:26; 1 Tim.

1:17; 6:13, 16). Though fallen humanity is mortal, God graciously gives immortality to those who trust in Christ (John 3:16; Rom. 2:7). Scripture describes physical immortality, not as a present possession, but as God's future gift (1 Cor. 15:52–54).

New Age adherents believe the soul, or "life force," is inherently immortal through reincarnation. The soul is successively reborn into new life forms, either human or nonhuman, on its journey to perfection. The soul's aim is to join itself to the universal spirit, whereby self-awareness ceases to exist as the soul enters into a state of eternal, harmonic bliss.

*See also:* DEATH, REINCARNATION

## IN-BETWEEN PLACE

Places between places and times between times are traditionally sacred themes of occult religions and are drawn from Celtic observances. Such places are bridges between sacred and secular or one realm and another. For this reason, many rituals in religions drawing on Celtic traditions involve trees (between sky and earth) and are held at dusk or dawn (when it is neither day nor night). Solstices are in-between times (between winter and summer).

*See also:* SOLSTICE

## INCANTATION

Words that, when recited or sung in a particular order, have magic power to cast spells or summon demons or evil spirits. Ancient sorcerers thought that by penning their incantations in ink or joining letters that had a particular shape, they could enhance their manipulation of the powers. Because these powers intensified with repetition of the incantation, the special sequence of words themselves possessed magical qualities. However others thought the words were powerless unless spoken by those who were attuned to the powers of darkness. Ancient pagans believed the great Mother Goddess possessed all power behind written and spoken charms. This explains why incantations

are often associated with women. In contemporary goddess cults, devotees chant mystical hymns and prayers during sacred rituals to assure the presence of a particular spirit.

*See also:* CHANT, LOGOS, MAGIC, MANTRA, SORCERY, WITCHCRAFT

## INCARNATION

The biblical teaching that Jesus, the Second Person of the Trinity, became fully human in history (John 1:14; 1 Tim. 3:16; Heb. 2:14–17) while no aspect of Jesus' divine being or character was diminished. Christ's full humanity qualifies Him to serve as an appropriate substitute for the sin of humankind. His full, eternal deity certifies that His sacrifice is infinite in saving value and worth.

New Age adherents use the term to denote the many gods, ascended masters, and avatars that take on human form to help lead people down the path to enlightenment or oneness with the universal spirit. They also use the term to indicate the new forms of life, whether human or nonhuman, into which a creature is reborn during the soul's progressive journey toward perfection.

*See also:* ASCENDED MASTER, AVATAR, JESUS CHRIST, REINCARNATION

## INCENSE

Aromatic spices or gum resins, such as frankincense, myrrh, and spikenard, used to produce odors when burned. In Israel's ancient worship, incense was a symbol for prayer (Ps. 141:2; Luke 1:10; Rev. 5:8; 8:3–4). Other ancient Near Eastern peoples believed that burning incense on altars placated their gods. They burned incense in rituals to call upon their gods in an expression of gratitude, happiness, or helplessness. The smoke and odor from the burning incense supposedly persuaded and seduced their gods to act.

Centuries of occultic usage have enhanced the mystical significance associated with the burning of incense. In some pagan rituals, incense burning is considered essential to the purification of the soul as it makes its journey toward enlightenment. The smoke and odor produced by the incense penetrates and cleanses the divine inner self and brings people into a conscious awareness of their godhood. In goddess cults, incense represents the element of oxygen and marks the most distant eastern corner of the universe. In witchcraft cults, the various odors produced by burning incense allegedly carry vibrations into the air, enabling adherents to control psychic space.

*See also:* OCCULTISM, POWER OBJECT, SATANISM, SYMBOLISM, WICCA, WITCHCRAFT

# INCUBUS

A demon that assumes male form in order to have sexual intercourse with women in their sleep. Some legends claim that incubi were originally the presiding priests of designated rooms within ancient pagan temples. When women came to the temples in search of enlightenment, they were seduced into the sexual service of the god. Other tales say that demon lovers gave women sexual pleasures transcending normal human experience. Still others say that incubi were invented by people as a desperate attempt to mask their sexual inadequacy. Some satanic cults believe that sexual attention from the demonic realm enhances an individual's status and power.

According to legend, an incubus is beautiful beyond expectation. It supposedly visits a virgin during the night and discharges its demonic fluids into her body. Some believe that the seed of Satan can cause phantom pregnancies. Other tales report demons taking female form, called a succubus, and then inducing nocturnal emissions from men. The evil spirit then takes male form and impregnates a woman.

*See also:* DEMON, SATANISM, SEXUALITY, SUCCUBUS

# INDIAN, AMERICAN
*See:* NATIVE AMERICANS

# INITIATION

Rite or rituals people must experience in order to become a member of a sect or society. The ceremony is to induce spiritual energies enabling the initiates to receive mystical powers, as well as an awareness of their evolutionary past. New Age cults offer hundreds of differing initiations tailored to satisfy the special interests of the individual. Experiencing these rites allegedly brings freedom from stress, spiritual answers to universal questions, and unlimited mental abilities. Each ceremony supposedly aids in the evolutionary progression to godhood and union with the universal spirit.

Most New Age initiations include some form of contact with the spirit guides of ascended masters. These entities supposedly exist in an astral dimension and come to earth to help people on their journey to enlightenment. Although some initiates report intense feelings of joy, peace, or universal oneness, initiations can also produce intense negative effects. These are often dismissed as a necessary step in spiritual growth. Because these initiatory rites produce powers and emotions that are often short-lived, initiates must go through subsequent rituals to perpetuate the experiences.

*See also:* ENLIGHTENMENT, SPIRIT GUIDES, SYMBOLISM

# INTERCONNECTION

A term denoting the oneness of all things. New Age adherents also use "interconnection" to refer to a universe in which each action, movement, or force alters the cosmic whole. They describe the universe as a fluid, ever-changing energy pattern, a living organism to which each entity in the cosmos is vitally linked. Some believe that because action affects action, compassion must be promoted to bring about interconnection. In this context, "compassion" means the ability to feel the whole so strongly that it inspires global unity.

*See also:* ATONEMENT, GLOBALISM, HOLISM

## INTERDEPENDENCE

The belief that the existence of human-kind and nature is fused, and the survival of each depends on the other. Interdependence reputedly permeates the economic, ecological, and political spheres of life. Adherents suggest that the value of all future goals should be measured, not by moral standards imposed by individuals, but by the contribution that objectives make in promoting global unity and the evolutionary transformation of the human race.

*See also:* GLOBALISM, HOLISM,
ONE-WORLD IDEAL, TRANSFORMATION

## INTUITION

The direct and immediate apprehension of a concept, proposition, or entity without conscious dependence upon reason and the senses. The types of this intuitive knowledge include simple hunches, the relationships between known facts obtained from the senses, and an immediate awareness of the truthfulness of scientific theories and mathematical propositions. Other types include experiences of realities, such as time, space, and values, as well as persons and God, apart from any deliberate forethought. Experts disagree about the origin of intuition, its exact relationship to the intellect and senses, and the legitimacy of its claims. In the West, the consensus is that, apart from empirical verification and logical analysis, knowledge gained by intuition alone is invalid. Instead, intuition is valued for the hypotheses it can generate concerning possible new relationships between intellectual concepts and data obtained from the senses.

In New Age thinking, the concept of intuition takes on a completely different meaning. The term is used to denote a highly developed extrasensory perception. New Age adherents refer to intuition as the manifestation of innate psychic abilities in the human subconsciousness. In some circles, intuition allegedly proves the existence of a universal knowledge that goes beyond the known and delves into unseen forces of insight and information. Others think the crown of the head, known as the *chakra,* is the place where psychic energies and intuitive powers exist. The central stem of the brain supposedly provides the best access to the massive bundle of nerves that connects the cerebral hemispheres, also known as the *corpus callosum.* Proponents believe that as people open themselves to higher states of consciousness, unseen universal forces give them an intuitive knowledge of the past, present, and future. They say that once the doors of paranormal awareness are opened, people can begin to develop and explore new levels of intuition through inner guides, automatic writing, and channeled entities.

*See also:* CHAKRA, EXTRASENSORY
PERCEPTION, IMAGINATION, PSYCHIC,
WHOLE BRAIN THINKING

## IRIDOLOGY

The study of the iris of the eye for indications of bodily health and disease. Holistic healers believe the eyes represent a window into the internal workings of the human body, displaying the past, present, and future conditions of systems and organs. Iridologists think everything in the universe is interrelated and interconnected through the exchange of cosmic energy. Therefore when irregularities in the human body occur, these can be detected by looking for very minute changes in the iris of the eye. Holistic healers claim iridology is an important tool for preventing and treating physical problems, as well as deterring iatrogenic, or physician-induced, illnesses. Iris diagnosis relies heavily on observation and intuition while the patient lingers in an altered state of awareness.

*See also:* ALTERED STATE, DIVINATION,
HOLISTIC HEALTH

## ISKCON
*See:* HARE KRISHNA

## JAINISM

An Indian religion with close connections to Buddhism, though there are disagreements about which is older. Claiming a membership of more than 1 million believers, the number is probably about half that in India. Jainism is one of the Eastern sects to make extensive use of the Internet, and several sites make translations of the sacred texts readily available for download in English. There is mild interest in Britain, which has had an affinity for Indian religions going back to colonial days, and a growing number of searching North Americans are being drawn to the writings. The extreme animal rights activism connected with New Age belief is connected with Jainism.

The name is derived from the ancient Indian word for "conqueror," one of the epithets popularly applied to the reputed founder of the sect. Jainism bears a striking resemblance to Buddhism in its monastic system, its teachings, sacred texts, and mythology. The two religions share indebtedness to the teachings and practices of Brahmanism.

According to Jainist tradition, the founder lived in the sixth century B.C. and was approximately contemporary to Gautama Buddha. He was the son of a local ruler, and his family name was Jnatriputra. While still a young man he felt the emptiness of a life of pleasure and gave up his home to become an ardent follower of the Brahmans. He carried the principle of self-mortification to the extent that he went about naked and unsheltered. Accepting the Brahman principle that salvation is by personal effort alone, he rejected the Vedas and the Vedic rites. Because of this, he was considered a heretic. He gathered disciples and went about preaching his doctrine of salvation, organizing converts under a monastic rule. Many accepted his teaching but not the monastic life of extreme asceticism. These lay Jainists contributed to the support of the monks.

Jainists are now divided on the propriety of going about naked, and the White-Robed Sect in northwest India is the more numerous. To this sect belong a few communities of nuns. The naked ascetics in southern India mostly go naked now only at mealtimes.

The Jainist creed consists of the "three jewels" of right belief, right knowledge, and right conduct. Right belief embraces faith in Jina as the true teacher of salvation and accepts the Jainist scriptures as authoritative. These scriptures are similar to the Buddha's writings but less extensive, laying greater stress on bodily mortification. Right conduct means embracing monastic asceticism.

The doctrine of karma is central to Jainism. Earthly existence is misery. Freedom from rebirth is the goal. But, while the pantheistic Brahman looks for absorption in Brahma and the primitive Buddhist seeks nirvana for extinction of conscious, individual existence, the Jainist believes in a final abode of bliss, where the soul enjoys a spiritual, conscious existence. Like Buddhists and Brahman, Jainists believe that the traditional gods may exist but are able to offer little help. They are not worshiped. Imposing temples are erected to Jina and other teachers, and worship centers around them. Salvation is obtained by self-purification alone. This is accomplished by twelve years of ascetic life as a Jainist monk and eight rebirths are necessary to prepare one for the Jainist heaven.

The sacredness of life has been more scrupulously observed in practice by the Jain than by Brahmans or Buddhists. Brahmans tolerate the slaughter of animals for food, for sacrifice, or to show hospitality. Buddhists will eat meat on special occasions. Jains wear veils to avoid sucking in an insect. They strain their water and sweep the ground ahead of them to avoid stepping on an insect. They feed rats and even have set up "hospitals" to care for them. A monk who has lived his twelve years and does not want to continue the ascetic lifestyle is allowed to commit suicide.

*See also:* BUDDHISM, KARMA, SALVATION

# JEHOVAH'S WITNESSES

Modern Arian sect growing out of nineteenth-century rationalistic Christianity. Jehovah's Witnesses pioneered their views through a literary empire and through personal evangelism. The group rejects Trinitarian doctrines and traditional Christian teachings about the person and work of Jesus Christ. They are highly millennarian in outlook and use an extreme literalism in interpreting the Bible.

The organization testifies to its beliefs through literature published by the Watchtower Bible and Tract Society. In the late 1870s, Charles Taze Russell (1852–1916) founded what is now the Jehovah's Witnesses. He rejected the Congregationalist theology in which he was raised, especially the teaching of eternal torment, all forms of organized religion, professional ministry, and the idea of church buildings.

In 1870, when Russell was eighteen, he organized a Bible class in Pittsburgh, Pennsylvania. In 1876, the group chose him as their pastor. From 1876 to 1878, Russell worked as an assistant editor for a monthly magazine published in Rochester, New York. When a disagreement arose over his rejection of the atonement of Christ, he resigned his position. In 1879, Russell started a magazine called *Zion's Watchtower.* By 1884, Russell had established Zion's Watchtower and Tract Society in Pittsburgh. In 1908, he moved the headquarters to Brooklyn, New York, where it has remained.

From 1886 to 1917, the organization published a series of seven books entitled *Studies in the Scriptures.* Russell penned the first six. In 1917, the year after Russell's death, the seventh volume, entitled *The Finished Mystery,* was published. This caused a schism in the organization.

Early in his career, Russell became convinced that the return and millennial reign of Christ were imminent. He censured organized religions and lauded the study of eschatology, the doctrine of last things. He concluded that Christ would invisibly return in 1874 and that in 1914 the "time of the Gentiles" would come to an end.

Russell was succeeded by Joseph Franklin Rutherford (1869–1942), under whose leadership the group became known as the "Jehovah's Witnesses," based on Isaiah 43:12. Through his prolific writing, he shaped the theology of the group, intensified their hostility toward organized religion, and refined proselytizing techniques. At the end of the century, membership was more than 3 million worldwide.

As pacifists, the Witnesses renounce all forms of secular politics. They reject blood transfusions. They believe that Jesus Christ paid a ransom to Jehovah God to remove the effects of Adam's sin. This provides a righteous foundation upon which people can save themselves by good works. When good people die, their souls sleep until the resurrection, whereas evil people are annihilated at death.

The Witnesses believe that Jesus rose from the dead as a divine spirit, that He spiritually returned to earth in 1914, that He is progressively overthrowing the worldly organization of the Devil, and that He will one day establish a divine, millennial kingdom on earth after the battle of Armageddon. God will resurrect genuine believers to a life on earth. However only a select group of 144,000 will rule with Christ in heaven (based on Rev. 7:3–8).

*See also:* ATONEMENT, HELL, JESUS CHRIST, WATCHTOWER BIBLE AND TRACT SOCIETY

# JESUS CHRIST

The name "Jesus" is derived from the Greek *'Iesous,* a transliteration of the Hebrew name *Yeshua*, which means "Yahweh saves." "Christ" is derived from the Greek word *Christos,* which is a translation of the Hebrew word *mashiach,* which means "the Anointed One." The combination of the two names indicates that Jesus Christ is the chosen one whom the Father sent to deliver people from their sins.

The Bible teaches that in His incarnation, Jesus became a man (John 1:14; 1 Tim. 3:16; Heb. 2:14–17). Therefore, He was fully human, having intellect, will, and emotions. But unlike the rest of humanity, Jesus was also fully divine.

As the Son of God, He is eternal and unchanging in His being (John 1:1–2; Heb. 13:8). He lived without sin or ability to sin (2 Cor. 5:21; Heb. 4:15; 7:26). Through His death and resurrection, He makes salvation available to all humanity (1 John 2:2). Regarding the forgiveness of sin, those who trust in Christ alone receive eternal life (John 3:16). In contrast to the Christ proclaimed in Scripture, the New Age Jesus was a man who achieved great things, or a created being who was given the status of god, or a man who is no better than the rest of humankind. He is identified as a prophet and messenger, a great moral teacher, or a mystic. The most prevalent New Age concept presents Jesus as a great avatar who, through many incarnations, achieved the wisdom necessary to lead humankind to enlightenment. Through the discovery of an energy force within himself, this Jesus was able to evolve into a higher state of divine awareness, achieving Christ-consciousness.

Some New Age adherents claim that Jesus first came to earth as the incarnate Adam. His mission was to make people aware of their personal divinity. He returned as Noah, Joshua, and various others through numerous incarnations. Jesus continued to enhance his positive karma and blazed the way for humankind's spiritual evolution to godhood. In his final incarnation, Jesus represents the first person on earth who became fully aware of his innate divinity. The crucifixion of Christ symbolizes the final step he took to unite with the universal life force known as "God."

*See also:* AVATAR, CRUCIFIXION, NEW AGE MOVEMENT, RESURRECTION, SALVATION

## JONES, JAMES (JIM) WARREN (1931–1978)

The charismatic leader of the People's Temple, a late-1970s cult remembered for the mass suicide of 914 people, including more than 240 children. Jones began his quest for power in the late 1950s when he established the Christian Assembly of God in Indianapolis, Indiana. Here he preached a message of social and racial equality to an integrated congregation. He portrayed the world as hostile and heading for destruction and depicted himself as the only one who could help his followers survive the coming ordeal. Initially, he claimed he was God's personal messenger, then the physical manifestation of Jesus Christ, and finally God Himself.

In 1965, Jones moved his church to California where his revival-style meetings increased the size of his congregation to several thousand members. At first, the community applauded his programs to help the poor, and he was appointed chairman of the San Francisco Housing Authority in 1976. In 1977, rumors surfaced of Jones gouging people for money, controlling his followers through extortion and beatings, and advocating sexual promiscuity.

Eventually the rumors about Jones were reported in the press, and this prompted him to flee with hundreds of followers to a rural commune named Jonestown in northwestern Guyana, South America (Jones had purchased the property in 1974). The cult leader was now free to demand absolute obedience from his followers. He isolated them from the outside world and used armed thugs to guard his compound. He maintained control over the group through verbally abusive tirades, food and sleep deprivation, and extremely harsh working conditions.

In November 1978, Congressman Leo Ryan from California and three journalists visited the Jonestown site to investigate charges made against Jones. On November 18, Jones ordered the deaths of Ryan and his colleagues. Jones then enforced a mass suicide on his followers by telling them to ingest a deadly potion of powdered fruit drink mixed with cyanide. Most of the followers obeyed without question, though apparently some resisted and had to be forced to comply.

# JUNG, CARL GUSTAV (1875–1961)

A Swiss psychotherapist and founder of analytical psychology. Jung, who was born in a small rural town in Switzerland, credited a large portion of his beliefs and theorizing to the influence of his parents and grandparents. His father was a Lutheran minister who doubted the validity of his faith and responded to his son's inquiries with coldness and detachment. This eventually led Jung to reject institutionalized Christianity. The parents of Jung's mother were spiritualists, and she exhibited a dual nature. Her daytime personality was sociable and loving, while her nighttime disposition was preoccupied with the supernatural and clairvoyance. Jung also believed he had a dual personality. He said the first was conscious and rational, while the second was unconscious and irrational. This latter aspect of his disposition fueled his lifelong interest in the paranormal and the occult.

Jung studied medicine at Basel University, psychiatry in Zurich, and psychopathology in Paris. He also studied philosophy and theology, including the works of Plato (an ancient Greek philosopher), Eckehart (a German mystic), and Kant, Hegel, and Nietzsche (all German philosophers). In 1909, he and Sigmund Freud began collaborating, but their once close association ended by 1914. Jung established his own theory and practice known as analytical psychology. Throughout his life, he experienced periodic visions and dreams that contained vivid religious and mythological features. These experiences motivated Jung to study myths, dreams, and the psychology of religion. He had a keen interest in world religions, and this prompted him to investigate the indigenous peoples of Africa, America, and India. He also studied Gnosticism, mythology, and medieval alchemy.

Jung's writings emphasize the deifying of self and the pyschologizing of God. He stressed that people should become aware of the conscious and the unconscious aspects of the psyche and learn to harness both. He is most famous for propagating the theory of the "collective unconscious," a dimension that holds all the symbols and memories of the entire human race. He maintained that the spiritually advanced could tap into this incredible source of knowledge. New Age adherents today use Jung's theories and writings extensively.

*See also:* ARCHETYPE; COLLECTIVE UNCONSCIOUS; FREUD, SIGMUND

# K

**KABBALAH (CABALA, KABALA)**

The Hebrew word for "tradition," *kabbalah* originally referred to the legal tradition of Judaism. It later came to signify mystical Jewish tradition, especially the system that arose during the twelfth and thirteenth centuries. Proponents emphasized Theosophy (Eastern pantheistic teachings about evolution and reincarnation), mysticism (the belief that direct knowledge about God, spiritual truth, and Ultimate Reality can be acquired through subjective experiences), and thaumaturgy (the performance of miracles).

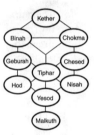

**Kabbalah—tree of life**

In northern Europe, adherents stressed the conjectural aspects of Kabbalah, while in southern Europe the practical and socio-ethical aspects were emphasized. Initially, few people were interested in Kabbalah. But following the Jews' eviction from Spain in 1492 and from Portugal in 1495, interest significantly increased.

Around 1290, a Spanish scholar, Moses de Leon, wrote the *Zohar (Book of Splendor),* which became the classic document of the Kabbalistic tradition. In 1548, Moses Cordovero wrote *Padres Rimmonim (Garden of Pomegranates),* in which he presented a more systematic treatment of the system's basic teachings. These documents, as well as other written and oral traditions, were a major influence in the rise of Hasidism. This Jewish mystical sect began in Poland around 1750 and opposed rationalism and ritual laxity. An idealist named Isaac ben Solomon Luria further developed the teachings of Kabbalah, and this influenced the development of the Sabbatean movement led by Sabbatai Zevi.

Kabbalah is supposedly based on the Hebrew Scriptures. The sect's adherents interpreted the Old Testament using a cipher method involving alpha and numeric symbols. Kabbalists came to believe that through a series of hierarchically descending radiations from the godhead, matter was created and the world was formed in intermediate stages. The sect maintains that varying aspects of the soul inspire and guide people on their religious quest. These spirit guides aid in the literal, symbolic, intuitive, and spiritual interpretation of the biblical text. Kabbalists have demonstrated an obsession with the inner life of God and its relationship to the inner life of people and the world as a whole. This mind-set has driven them to probe into the mysteries of the occult. In their efforts to reveal the secrets of the powers of God, zealots have attributed mystical powers to the letters and numbers of the Old Testament Scriptures. They believe that the mysterious, twenty-two letter Hebrew alphabet is the divine key to unlocking the secrets of the spiritual realm.

*See also:* LURIA, ISAAC BEN SOLOMON; MYSTERY; NUMEROLOGY; SPIRIT GUIDES

**KACHINA (KATCHINA)**

Deified ancestral spirit in the religion of the Hopi, Zuni, and other Pueblo tribes of present-day Arizona and New Mexico. They believe that when people die, their spirits are transformed into kachinas, that then make their home in the underworld, the place of departed souls. Kachinas or kachinam represent generalized mythical conceptions, not individual ancestors. More than 250 kachinas have been recognized, though the exact number of these departed spirits is disputed.

The Pueblo Indians believe the kachinas control the forces of nature, as well as tribal rules and laws. The deified spirits also govern the sun and rain, crops and animals. Kachinas are thought to spend half of every year in villages of the Hopi, and then return to underground abodes for the rest of the year. During agricultural ceremonies, dancers wear elaborate masks and colorful costumes to impersonate the ancestral spirits. The dancers attempt to lose their own identity, adopting the identity of the spirit so that gifts and powers of the kachina might become part of their family for future generations.

Hopi and Zuni are known for their carved-wood kachina dolls, which supposedly represent departed spirits. After a ceremonial dance, the children receive these dolls and are encouraged to identify with the ancestral spirits represented by the dolls. The kachina doll has attracted the interest of New Age adherents, who search the rituals of Native American tribes for keys to understanding the mysteries of the spiritual realm.

*See also:* NATIVE AMERICANS, SPIRITISM

# KARMA

The force generated by the sum total of a person's actions, especially religious or ritual actions, whether good or bad. Karma is the Sanskrit word for "fate," "actions," and "work." In Eastern religions, adherents believe that what people do in this life results in correspondingly positive or negative fruits, either in the present or in a future life. As such, karma is viewed as a metaphysical principle. Otherwise known as the law of karma, adherents believe people are bound to an endless cycle of birth, death, and rebirth. The force generated by a person's actions perpetuates the transmigration of the soul from this life to the next. The ethical consequences surrounding the karma predetermine the nature of a person's next existence.

According to Hindu tradition, a perfect balance existed in the beginning within the "godhead," the universal essence from which all things originate and to where all things go. Then something happened to disrupt the harmonic balance, and this set the wheels of reincarnation into motion. Because bad

karma originated with the universe itself, it is not possible to prevent its existence. Hinduism teaches that each life is on a journey to nirvana, the final state of existence in which a perfect balance exists between accumulated good and bad karma. Proponents maintain that when people reach nirvana, all traces of desire and individual consciousness will be extinguished.

The Hindu belief in karma is not characterized by a rigid and fixed uniformity. Rather, various views prevail. Some seek to accumulate good karma in hope of securing an advantageous rebirth. Others think that all forms of karma are evil and try to escape altogether from the endless cycles of rebirth. Some think that whatever happens to people is predecided by their karma. Still others believe that more influence is exerted by fate, human effort, or divine intervention. Meanwhile, some maintain that one form of karma is decided at birth and evidenced during the present life. A second form of karma remains hidden and inactive in this life, while a third form of karma, accumulated in this lifetime, manifests itself in a future life.

*See also:* DHARMA, GUILT, HINDUISM, NIRVANA, REINCARNATION, SIN

# KEMETIC ORTHODOXY

A modern, syncretistic religion that tries to recreate the traditions of ancient Egypt, which followers call "Kemet." In practice, Kemetic Orthodoxy borrows many beliefs and practices from such African diaspora religions as Ifa, Akan, and Voodoo in its worship of the god Netjer. Its spiritual leader, Tamara L. Siuda, who calls herself Sekhenet-Ma'at-Ra Hekatawy I. Siuda founded the Temple of Kemetic Religion in 1988, and was ordained into the Kemetic priesthood during the Parliament of World Religions in Chicago in 1993. In 1996 she was crowned the 196th Nisut-bityt of the Kemetic Orthodox Faith at facilities set up near the pyramids at Luxor, Egypt.

Kemetic Orthodoxy requires a commitment to preserving African heritage and calls itself a "monolatrous" religion. Monolatry tries to mediate between monotheistic worship in one god and polytheistic honoring of multiple gods, According to practitioners, monolatrous religion professes one god or divine force (Netjer or "divine power"), which interlinks with lesser beings. Those who follow Kemetic Orthodoxy believe these lesser forms of Netjer correspond to the gods and goddesses of Ancient Egypt.

The House of Netjer, the only full temple of the Kemetic Orthodox faith, is in Chicago, Illinois. Much of the organization's international work of aggressive evangelization among African-Americans is conducted over the Internet. The House of Netjer's on-line ministry includes spiritual support and counseling, chatrooms and courses in Kemetic Orthodox spirituality and religious topics. Twice each month there is an on-line worship ritual.

## KEYS, DONALD (b. 1924)

Peace advocate and consultant to the United Nations. Keys is noted for cofounding the Planetary Citizens organization in 1972. In the belief that humankind is approaching a transformation of individual and collective consciousness, he helped to establish Planetary Citizens. The organization serves as an interconnecting link for New Age networks and as a political guide to newly emerging planetary values.

*See also:* GLOBALISM, PLANETARY CITIZENS, TRANSFORMATION, UNITED NATIONS

## KHUL, DJWHAL

*See:* DJWHAL KHUL

## KI

The Japanese name given to the cosmic energy force believed to permeate all living things, instilling life, health, and well-being. Buddhists call the force ch'i, while Hindus refer to it as Prana. This life force supposedly emanates from the celestial cosmos, flows through people, and then returns to the universal essence.

*See also:* BALANCING, CH'I, COSMIC ENERGY, PRANA

## KIERKEGAARD, SØREN (1813–1855)

A Danish philosopher, theologian, and writer. His books and articles cross the conventional boundaries separating theology, philosophy, psychology, and devotional literature. He was born in Copenhagen, Denmark, the youngest of six children. While he was still an adolescent, his three sisters, mother, and a brother died. His father was a wealthy wool merchant and stern Lutheran with a gloomy, guilt-ridden temperament and vivid imagination. The father dominated Kierkegaard's life until his death in 1838. In 1840, Kierkegaard became engaged to Regine Olsen, but within a year he broke the engagement. This event was the catalyst for his intense search for authentic selfhood.

Kierkegaard lived only forty-two years, yet he laid the foundations for modern existentialism. This body of ethical thought regards human existence as ultimately beyond explanation. Kierkegaard possessed an acute analytical mind and literary talents, and he used these abilities to extract insights from his own suffering. He struggled to make the Christian faith real in his own life, and this is reflected in much of what he wrote.

Kierkegaard was troubled by the apparent "spiritlessness" of historical Christianity and the dispassionate rational analysis of idealism (this theory says reality transcends what is evident to the senses and true reality exists only in the mind). In his writings, Kierkegaard sought to help his readers develop an inward personal concern, believing this was the basis for authentic Christianity. He stressed that each person is a unique and self-aware being, not a clone devoid of individual identity. He taught that people can actualize their selfhood by exercising their freedom of choice and taking responsibility for their actions.

Kierkegaard believed the achievement of genuine selfhood involved a synthesis of dissimilar elements, such as necessity and freedom, soul and body, temporality and eternality. He taught that the exercise of genuine passions—not fleeting emotions but rather enduring concerns—brought about the synthesis necessary for self-realization. Kierkegaard held that faith is the supreme passion for Christians. He saw Christianity not as mere intellectual assent based on objective evidence, but rather a state of being in which the entire self is totally rooted in God. He stressed a "leap of faith" in which adherents make a passionate commitment to God despite the presence of uncertainty and objective reasoning. For Kierkegaard, each individual's personal encounter with God, especially through suffering and repentance amidst the chaos and conflicts of life, was at the heart of the Christian faith.

New Age philosophy uses concepts introduced by Kierkegaard. Some stress individual freedom to the point where conformity to rules and regulations is denounced. Others emphasize the subjective nature of existence to such an extent that eternal moral standards and unchanging propositional truths mean nothing. This has led to an arbitrary elevation of personal opinion over the claims of objective evidence. Still others underscore the importance of having a personal encounter with the universal essence. This means jettisoning objective reasoning, making a leap of faith, and becoming totally absorbed in the cosmic presence said to permeate all reality.

*See also:* FAITH; HEGEL, GEORG WILHELM FRIEDRICH

# KINESIOLOGY

The study of the principles of mechanics and anatomy in relation to the movement of the human body. Based on experiments from the Esalen Institute, kinesiologists maintain that both conscious and unconscious personality traits are reflected in human movement. Therefore when movement is altered, the personality will change. In this system, the answers to all problems supposedly lie within the depths of the individual, and the therapist's role is to supply the technique that will expe-

dite self-realization. Proponents believe all human movements have a meaning. The therapist gives patients the opportunity to discover this "self," and take the first step down the road to higher consciousness.

*See also:* ESALEN INSTITUTE, HOLISM, PSYCHOTHERAPY, SELF-REALIZATION

# KIRLIAN PHOTOGRAPHY

A process developed by Russian electrician Semyon Kirlian (1900–1980) in 1939 for measuring and recording the living auras believed to surround the human body. All living things reputedly produce an energy source revealing itself in varying colors and intensities relative to shifts in physiology and emotions. Through Kirlian photography, the image of this aura is thought to be captured on film.

This high voltage photographic process uses two electrodes that are energized by a high frequency electrical field. The object to be photographed and an unexposed strip of film are placed between two electrodes and charged. The result seems to register phenomena invisible to the human eye. More conventional scientists think the resulting aura is an ionization of the air from heat generated by a person's body. New Age adherents claim the aura is spiritual radiation emanating from the person's soul.

*See also:* AURA, COLOROLOGY, COSMIC ENERGY

# KISMET

A Turkish word derived from the Arabic term *qismah,* which means "portion" or "lot." This refers to the divine principle, determining cause, or will by which entities come into existence, and events are directed. This unseen power is all-encompassing and controls human destiny. Chance and Kismet differ. Chance represents the absence of laws in which events occur unpredictably without any discernible human intention or observable cause. Kismet signifies a cosmic determinism void of ultimate meaning or purpose, being mindless, senseless, impersonal, and incomprehensible. In this scheme, freedom is not absent, just thwarted and overruled.

Perhaps similar to the English word "fate," kismet can also refer to an inescapable and frequently catastrophic outcome, condition, or end. Kismet condemns the poor and disabled to suffering as a punishment for an unknown sin. In Oriental religion, kismet is viewed as a dark, sinister power that brings tragedy into the lives of people, frustrates human efforts, and makes the future precarious and uncertain. This view pervades the thinking of Hinduism and Buddhism and is spread by proponents of New Age thought.
*See also:* KARMA

## KNIGHT, J. Z. (b. 1946)

One of the most popular leaders in the New Age Movement. J. Z. Knight is best known as the channel for the ancient wisdom of Ramtha, a divine entity from the Atlantian age. Knight was born in a small town in New Mexico as Judith Darlene Hampton. In her early thirties, she went from obscurity to international fame in a relatively short period of time. Although Knight claimed to have received a traditional Christian upbringing and professed to be a Christian, she denounced the church at an early age and determined to define God on her own terms. Throughout Knight's younger life, her precognitive and past life dreams, visions, and UFO encounters, as well as demonic intrusions and various psychic phenomenas supposedly prepared her to serve as the channel for Ramtha.

By 1972, at the age of twenty-six, Knight had become a rising cable television executive. On the advice of a psychic, she moved to a small farming community in Washington state where she was told she would meet a great teacher from the spiritual dimension. Shortly after settling into her new home, Knight became severely ill. After failing to recover from her illness, she went to a church healing meeting. Upon approaching the altar, she denounced Satan and Christ, allowing the minister to heal her only in the name of God. She later claimed this "miracle" healing was a manifestation of her own power.

In 1977, Knight became involved in two life-changing relationships. First, she married Dr. Jeremy Wilder, and second, she became possessed by Ramtha. The newly married couple embraced the power of the occult. Not long afterward, Knight fell under the control of Ramtha, who claimed to be an ancient warrior who had ascended to godhood but now had returned to earth as a prophet of the coming New Age. Before long, Ramtha was channeling his thoughts and powers through Knight, preparing her for a yet unknown spiritual mission.

Knight has received ridicule from both inside and outside New Age circles. Charges stem from accusations of bogus channeling, offering self-serving investment advice, and living an outrageously extravagant lifestyle. However the message of Ramtha has been received and adopted by millions of initiates. This spirit proclaims that all life is divine, that people are their own gods, that Jesus is just one of many great moral teachers, and that Christ is simply a state of mind. Ramtha also claims that Satan and sin do not exist, that people create their own realities, and that evil is a matter of personal judgment. Death is not the end of life, but a gateway to another realm of existence. Salvation is not deliverance from personal sin, but rather becoming one with the universal essence.
*See also:* ASCENDED MASTER; ATLANTIS, LOST CONTINENT OF; DEMON; PYRAMIDOLOGY; RAMTHA; TRANCE CHANNELING

## KRISHNAMUATI, JIDDU (1895–1986)

An educated young Brahman who was handpicked and groomed by the occultic Theosophy Society to become the New Age messiah. In 1909, theosophist leader Annie Besant prophesied the coming of a great world leader. Then she and her society established new organizations to raise money to pay for the training of Jiddu (Sorbonne) Krishnamuati. Touring throughout India and Europe, he and his messages were widely accepted. Krishnamuati instructed people to discard their old theologies and beliefs and claimed he could tell them everything they needed to know about philosophy, psychology, and religion. This New Age follower spoke about god in the first person and reputedly performed many miracles.

In the mid-1920s, Krishnamuati came to America. Within a few short years, preparations were made for a great ceremony in which he would approach an altar, be possessed by the spirit of Lord Maitreya (the anticipated great and final New Age messiah), and be proclaimed as the new world leader. However when the momentous ceremony arrived, Krishnamuati threw off his robe and crown, denied he was the anticipated avatar, and returned to Europe. He spent the next fifty years writing books, traveling around the world, and telling others about his paranormal encounters with the cosmic consciousness of the divine. In 1985, members of the United States Senate honored Krishnamuati as a leader of peace.

*See also:* BESANT, ANNIE WOOD; MAITREYA, LORD; THEOSOPHY

# KRONING

Leadership training technique developed by Charles Krone. His objective is to increase business productivity through extensive mind-control methods disguised as motivational instruction. The technique is based on the occult teachings of Russian mystic Georges Guarjieff. Those trained in Kroning use New Age transformational techniques that are masked in "bafflegab." This alleged alternative language is understood only by insiders and used to introduce initiates to the concepts of universal consciousness. The seminar leaders claim that by teaching attendees to consider a purpose greater than themselves, their work productivity will be enhanced and maintained.

*See also:* COSMIC CONSCIOUSNESS, TRANSFORMATION

# KUBLER-ROSS, ELIZABETH (b. 1926)

A Swiss-American physician born in Zurich who is considered a leading authority on thanatology, the study of the phenomena of death and the psychological mechanisms people use to cope with it. Kubler-Ross studied medicine at the University of Zurich and became a naturalized United States citizen in 1958. While practicing as a psychiatrist in Chicago, she began to see the process of dying as an inseparable part of life. She has devoted her career to the care of terminally ill patients, helping them to accept and learn to cope with approaching death. For over two decades she has headed the Shantl Nilaya Growth and Health Center in Escondido, California, where she conducts research into the phenomena of near-death experiences.

In 1969, Kubler-Ross wrote a book entitled *On Death and Dying.* In it, she identified five stages of dying as denial, anger, bargaining, depression, and acceptance. The goal of this process is to urge patients to withdraw their emotional bonds with the living and to adopt a nondefensive posture of "letting go." However other investigators have not been able to confirm the findings of Kubler-Ross, bringing into question the clinical validity of her model. Many have concluded that she collected her data unscientifically and analyzed it erroneously. Overall, her work has alerted physicians and other health-care providers to the reality that their perceptions of dying and death are usually quite different from their terminally ill patients.

The book by Kubler-Ross, however, also contains theories and philosophies based on personal occult experimentation. Through conversations with her spirit guide, named Salem, and the near-death experiences of others, she concluded that a glorious afterlife follows death. She believed that upon death every person is bathed in light and love as they enter "heaven." Here they serenely await their family and friends in order to bring to completion those things left undone.

The theories of Kubler-Ross on dying and death have become so popular among New Age adherents that a large number of self-help books on the subject have been published. Almost all of them are based on a Rogerian psychological model. The underlying theory is that people are paralyzed by inhibitions and anxiety. Their anxiety about dying and death results from the inability to express themselves fully. They also have certain inhibitions that need to be overcome.

Kubler-Ross assumes that a harmony, or congruence, exists between the human organism and its psyche. Treatment includes reflecting back to the patients their own thoughts and words to obtain insight. Through this reflection, patients plumb the depths of their psyche to find answers to their own problems and use this information to change their attitude toward dying and death. Armed with a new and fresh understanding about themselves, patients are freed from anxiety and depression. As a result, death is seen as a natural process and no longer threatening.

*See also:* DEATH, NEAR-DEATH EXPERIENCE, SPIRIT GUIDES

## KUHN, THOMAS (1922–1996)

An American philosopher and scientist. Kuhn is best known in New Age circles for his theories on the historical significance of scientific revolutions. He believed these upheavals resulted from psychological and sociological forces that heavily shaped the logic and conclusions of researchers. Kuhn introduced the concept of a "paradigm shift," the evolutionary emergence of a new perspective that displaces traditional views. He theorized that as time passes, contradictory points within a given mind-set begin to build, until a crisis arises, and a new theory emerges to explain the existing problems. Kuhn maintained that this paradigm shift is always constructive, not destructive, but noted resistance always accompanies the radical change in thinking. Kuhn concluded that the following generation actually brings about the collective change of consciousness. They accept and rely upon theories previous generations were unable to embrace.

New Age adherents have adopted the idea of paradigm shift to explain the process of

drastically altering the universal consciousness of humankind. Their strategy includes incorporating their pagan views into politics, medicine, religion, and education. They encourage an "enlightened" generation of young adults to urge the following generation to accept and build upon the new paradigm. This process is to continue with each subsequent generation until they have reached the ultimate paradigm for humanity.

*See also:* CRITICAL MASS, EVOLUTION, QUANTUM LEAP

## KUNDALINI

The cosmic life force of the goddess Shakti, which lies coiled at the base of the human spine until activated, then transmits to the brain the stimulation for the enlightenment process. *Kundalini* is derived from a Sanskrit word meaning "circular" or "coiled." Proponents believe that through the practice of Hindu yogic exercises, this dormant energy is aroused, enabling people to tap into the powers of their inner self.

**Kundalini—life force of the goddess**

According to yoga philosophy, several points of physical or spiritual energy, called chakras, exist in the human body. Once Kundalini is awakened, it uncoils upward through the seven chakras of human energy. The yogic life force supposedly moves through energy channels wound in a double spiral on either side of the human spine. As Kundalini uncoils upward, energy is released in the yogi until it reaches the last chakra, or crown of the head. Here Shakti and Shiva, the Hindu gods of regeneration and destruction, meet in a psychosexual union. At this point, the yogi experiences enlightenment and is divided from Brahma, the Hindu three-in-one god, only by a thin veil.

*See also:* BRAHMA, CHAKRA, HINDUISM, SHIVA, YOGA

# L

## LAO-TZU (LAOZI, MASTER LAO)

A sixth-century-B.C. Chinese philosopher. Lao-tzu, which means "aged man," was an older peer of Confucius (551–479 B.C.). According to legend, Lao-tzu served in the imperial court as the custodian of the royal archives. Despite his teaching and instruction, Lao-tzu became disaffected by the reluctance of people around him to follow what he claimed was the way to achieve natural goodness. As a result, he traveled westward toward modern-day Tibet when he was eighty years old. Upon arriving at the Hank Pass, a guard named Yin Xi, or Yin Hsi, asked Lao-tzu to write down his teachings. Legend says he complied in a five-thousand-word document called the *Daode Jing,* or *Tao-te Ching*, which means "The Way and Its Power." However numerous scholars think the text is the collective work of many unknown authors, editors, and sources. They say the work fits the time frame from 200–100 B.C., dating the work several centuries after Lao-tzu lived.

The Chinese regard the *Daode Jing* as the foremost work of Taoism. This mystical philosophy teaches people to conform themselves to the Tao by simple, unassertive action. They believe the Tao is the guiding principle and unfathomable source of all reality. Chinese philosophy asserts that Ultimate Reality is a harmony of opposites called Tai Chai. Through richly poetic imagery, the *Daode Jing* urges people to avoid all activity and desire and to cultivate simplicity and balance in order to achieve harmony with the ebb and flow of the universal way, or Tao, as exemplified in nature. Adherents maintain equanimity by learning how to fuse the masculine force called yang with the feminine force called yin through effortless action.

New Age adherents have made extensive use of the *Daode Jing.* They claim an eternal, harmonizing, and universal force flows through all living things. New Age adherents also assert that humanity's divine unity with nature can only be understood through mystical revelations. They maintain that the future of humanity depends on everyone refocusing their attention on the teachings of the *Daode Jing* to bring greater enlightenment. This is a prerequisite to the dawning of the new age of Christ-consciousness.

*See also:* CHRIST-CONSCIOUSNESS, TAOISM, YIN/YANG

## LAST DAYS

*See:* ANTICHRIST, ARMAGEDDON, SECOND COMING OF CHRIST

## LAVEY, ANTON SZANDOR (1930–1997)

Shaping occult ideas to fit the spirit of America's emerging counterculture, Anton LaVey founded the First Church of Satan in San Francisco and wrote *The Satanic Bible.* LaVey's interest in the occult developed at an early age, as a result of hearing stories from his grandmother about vampires and witches. As a teenager, LaVey's interests drew him into the musical and metaphysical aspects of the occult. This involvement continued to grow during the years in which he worked as a circus entertainer, organ player, and police photographer. In 1966, following LaVey's portrayal of Satan in the cultic film *Rosemary's Baby,* he founded the first organized Church of Satan in California. Headquartered in an impressive three-story, Victorian home, the "church" developed the organizational structure necessary to become recognized as a tax-exempt religious organization.

LaVey promoted a self-styled form of satanic worship. He said that the Devil is nothing more than a symbol for the evil nature within humankind. Manifestations of Satan are a release of psychic energies. All people are inherently selfish and violent. If people are to survive and ultimately rule the world, they must live a brutal, selfish existence. Toward this end, *The Satanic Bible* (1969) outlines several doctrines that are the keystone of his cult. Satan represents indulgence rather than abstinence, the physical rather than the spiritual, and undefiled wisdom rather than self-deceptive hypocrisy. Satan also chooses vengeance over forgiveness, selective kindness and responsibility over absolute morality, and the evil nature of humankind over the divine.

LaVey presented his organization as a temple of glorious indulgences. His purpose was to gather like-minded people together so they could focus their energies on manipulating the dark forces of nature. He believed that people can change events by the mere exercise of their will. He also taught that people have the right to command creation to serve them and, in the process, to reveal its mysteries and powers.

*See also:* ANTICHRIST; LUCIFERIC DOCTRINE; *Satanic Bible, The;* SATANISM

## LAZARIS

*See:* PURSEL, JACK

## LEARY, TIMOTHY (1920–1996)

A psychologist and former professor of law at Harvard University. In the 1960s Timothy Leary advocated the use of LSD (*lysergic acid diethylamide,* also known as "acid"), an organic compound that produces psychotic symptoms. Leary believed human self-awareness was a chemical phenomenon that could be altered and influenced by taking certain drugs. By ingesting LSD, people could be open to unknown spiritual dimensions. Leary taught that LSD altered the human consciousness and enabled people to achieve greater enlightenment.

Upon his return from a trip to India, Leary said he saw a cosmic connection between Eastern religious practices and the psychotic effects produced by LSD. Along with the "acid" rock music of the 1960s, he promoted the use of hallucinogenic drugs. Leary popularized the slogan "turn on, tune in, and drop out" as the motto for the emerging drug culture. Drugs were presented as a way of looking inward for universal answers to the problems facing humankind. Leary was ostracized from academia after conducting numerous experiments on students using hallucinogenic drugs. He had promised them the secret of discovering the existential meaning of life.

*See also:* ALTERED STATE, COSMIC CONSCIOUSNESS, DRUG, LYSERGIC ACID DIETHYLAMIDE, ROCK MUSIC

## LEMURA

In New Age mythology, a continent that allegedly existed in the Pacific Ocean. Its inhabitants, the Lemurians, were the third of seven root racial groups on planet earth. Lemura supposedly is also the counterpart to the fabled continent of Atlantis, which legend says sank beneath the sea. The inhabitants of Lemura reputedly were as equally advanced in technology and intellect as the people of Atlantis. Folklore says the Lemurians destroyed themselves as a result of their advancements, just as did the Atlantians.

Lemura plays an important part in the New Age study of the spiritual evolution of humankind. Because of the widespread distribution of the lemur, some New Age adherents speculate that a land bridge once connected Africa, the island of Madagascar, and India, allowing the creatures to migrate from one place to another. Theosophists refer to lemurs in discussing humanity's evolutionary descent from spiritual to physical form. The Lemurians supposedly had large gelatinous bodies but took on solid form at the midpoint of their existence. These people are described as being twelve to fifteen feet tall, having no forehead, and possessing three eyes, one on each side of the head and one in the back of the head.

*See also:* ATLANTIS, LOST CONTINENT OF; EVOLUTION; NEW AGE MOVEMENT; ROOT RACE

152

# LEVITATION

The act or process of floating in air. New Age adherents believe some people have the supernatural ability to raise or float objects and people in the air, in apparent contradiction of gravity. Construction of megaliths on ancient sites, such as Stonehenge in south England and the pyramids in Egypt, is sometimes cited as evidence of levitational powers. In Eastern religions, levitation of the human body plays a vital role in the spiritual evolution of the soul. Levitation represents the rapturous love between people and the gods, a customary part of spiritualistic ceremonies and séances. Purported mediums use it to demonstrate their power over the spirit world.

During the 1960s, American youth became obsessed with Eastern religious philosophy and practice. This sparked a new interest in the development of supernatural powers. Transcendental meditation has promised to help initiates release an arsenal of innate abilities, including levitation and psychokinesis, the movement of objects through the powers of the mind apart from any physical means. Proponents tell initiates to go beyond the conscious state of objective reasoning in order to tap into the powers of the supernatural. They consider this a necessary step in becoming fully aware of the divine self.

*See also:* PYRAMIDOLOGY, SELF-REALIZATION, TRANSCENDENTAL MEDITATION

# LIFESPRING

A motivational training group founded by John Hanley in 1974. Lifespring utilizes techniques that were first developed by Werner Erhard for use in his EST (Erhard Seminar Training) program. Lifespring blends the ideas and methods of traditional psychotherapeutic disciplines and Oriental religions. The organization maintains that all people hold painful experiences that are trapped and controlled by the mind. These barriers supposedly prevent people from experiencing and expressing their innate perfection as human beings.

Hanley uses six-day seminars to free people and allow them to experience their "self." People are placed in groups and barred from talking, eating, drinking, or chewing gum, as well as smoking, using the rest room, wearing watches, or leaving the assembly. Trainers use lecture, shouts, insults, and commands to bring about a life-changing experience of "enlightenment" in the attendees. In addition to intense emotional confrontation, trainers use guided meditation and the probing of bodily sensations, emotions, and memories. The intent is to create an environment where people can deal with their own troubles and problems, expand their self-awareness, and transform their personality, replacing their existing belief system with New Age ideas. They learn about their divine inner nature and their ability to control their unlimited supernatural powers.

*See also:* ERHARD, WERNER HANS; HUMAN POTENTIAL MOVEMENT

# LIGHT

In orthodox Christianity, a metaphor used to describe God and His activities. He created light, is clothed with light, and blesses people with light (Gen. 1:3; Ps. 36:9; 104:2; Isa. 45:7). In the New Testament, "light" is used to describe the Messiah. He is portrayed as the source of moral purity, truth, and wisdom (John 1:4–8; 8:12; 9:5; 12:46). In contrast, darkness is a term used to illustrate all that is characterized by moral perversion and superstition. It describes nontruth and error (John 12:35–36; 1 John 1:5–7). Though Satan is the prince of darkness, he often masquerades as an angel of light (2 Cor. 11:14). At the end of the age, God will condemn the wicked to utter darkness and bathe His people with the light of His presence (Rev. 18:23; 21:23; 22:5).

New Age adherents use "light" to refer to Satan, psychic illumination, or something that enlightens or informs, as well as a medium through which other dimensions of reality are revealed. They also use "light" when referring to a set of occultic principles, standards, or opinions, as well as the divine goal of a spiritual journey, a noteworthy clairvoyant, or a charismatic leader. New Age adherents believe that light and darkness are simply two equal but opposite forces, like good and evil. When joined in a unified state, they complement each other.

Some New Age adherents believe Lucifer, the fallen rebel archangel or Devil, began as a white spiritual light and from this light came all other living things. Therefore all people are made up of a pure light-energy or pieces of the universal whole. New Age adherents insist that all spiritual paths have light within them and are acceptable means of reaching divine enlightenment. In some circles, Lucifer refers to the angel of light who reveals the path to Christ-consciousness. Proponents urge people to journey toward this light, discover it within themselves, and finally unite with it as one.

*See also:* CHRIST-CONSCIOUSNESS, GREAT INVOCATION, LUCIFERIC DOCTRINE

## LIGHT-BODY

A state of existence as pure ethereal energy. The ancient Greeks believed that when spiritually evolved beings journeyed to the next dimension, they were clothed in a light-body. This metamorphosis is a goal of many New Age enthusiasts. They claim that specially designed "ascension" chambers help people to achieve the transformation of consciousness deemed necessary to reach the fourth dimension, called the light-body. This light-body exists in the same realm as the light of Christ-consciousness, the great white light (brotherhood), the hierarchy of light, and the angels of light.

*See also:* COSMIC ENERGY, ETHER, FOURTH LEVEL, LIGHT

## LIGHTNING

The flashing of light caused by a natural, brief, high-current electrical discharge in the atmosphere. The discharge path is usually several miles in length. At any given moment throughout the planet, more than two thousand thunderstorms can exist. These can pro-duce flashes of lightning at the rate of one hundred per second.

Throughout history, the occurrence of lightning has fascinated people, defied their analysis, and fueled their speculation. The ancient Greeks and Romans believed lightning was a weapon of their angry gods. Some Native American tribes held that lightning brought the forbidden gifts of the divine to humanity. Other peoples conjectured that a masculine deity fell from heaven to earth on a lightning bolt as the primordial fertilization of the female Deep, Abyss, or Mother Earth, leading to the creation of all living things. New Age adherents assert that lightning symbolizes divine illumination falling from heaven to aid the human race on its spiritual journey to perfection.

*See also:* CREATION, LUCIFERIC DOCTRINE, NATIVE AMERICANS, SYMBOLISM

## LITTLE PEBBLE (OUR LADY OF THE ARK)

A breakaway Roman Catholic group centered in Australia, regarded with some fear for their similarity to other doomsday cults. William Kamm, is the leader or "seer" of The Little Pebble, that also goes by the name "Our Lady of the Ark." Kamm claims ongoing contacts with Christ, the Virgin, and other saints and angels. Most of the prophecies he reports are apocalyptic in nature and condemnatory of the state of the Roman Church. Kamm's messages exhort followers to pray continually.

A German layman, born in 1950, Kamm founded the "Marian Work of Atonement" organization in Australia in the early 1970s. He received his name, "Little Pebble," probably a reference to Peter, in one of his visions in the early 1980s. Believing Mary has suspended rules regarding adultery in his case, he has openly lived with several women. He was divorced in 1977. His prophecies frequently indicate that he will become Pope. Most followers live in an isolationistic monastic lifestyle in remote settlements scattered around Australia.

## LIVING WORD, CHURCH OF THE (THE WALK)

A "restoration movement" led by Apostle John Robert Stevens. Church of the Living Word has at least one hundred churches in the United States. The Walk publicly denies sanctioning any extrabiblical revelation, but Stevens claims apostolic privilege to impart new levels of revelation to his people. All members are to submit to those proclamations without question. The teachings are particularly intolerant of individualism, since the Christians are to lose their identity in Christ. Some teachings approach psychic and occult practices. Followers are told they must work their way to the point at which they can see and hear what is happening in the spiritual realm. Members practice such rituals as the "glory chain," by which blessing is psychically passed among members through hand gestures. Stevens also teaches that astral projection can be performed.

*See also:* ASTRAL PROJECTION

## LOCAL CHURCH

An exclusivistic church movement that loosely follows the writings of Watchman Nee, but takes them to extremes that the Chinese evangelist probably would not have appreciated. The beginnings of the Local Church occurred within Nee's Little Flock Movement in China before the communist revolution. It's leader from the beginning has been a close associate of Watchman Nee (1903–1972), Li Chang-Shou, who goes by the name "Witness Lee." The movement has grown to world status with a sizable number of congregations in the United States. Each church considers itself the only expression of Christianity in its surrounding community. Li was born in 1905 and made a profession of faith in Christ in 1925. He came under the influence of the Plymouth Brethren and became Nee's associate in 1933. From Nee, Witness Lee picked up an extreme tripartite view of the human being as body, soul, and spirit, as well as an expectation that there will be only a partial rapture of the saints when Christ returns. Only genuine overcomers are to be caught up to be with the Lord before the Tribulation. Disenchanted with divisive Western missionary programs, Watchman Nee taught that there should be only one church organization for each city. Lee has interpreted that to mean that his is the only church in those cities where the Local Church is active.

During the antidenominational backlash of 1960s Christianity, the movement achieved considerable strength in Western U.S. cities and around major universities. A strong centralized organization followed a business model, allowing little dissent or discussion of policies at the local level. Since the 1970s most growth has been on college campuses and among disaffected mainline church members.

In the late 1980s, when the Local Church seemed to have momentum and high ecumenical respect, a California church left the body after publishing a strongly worded rebuke of authoritarian controls, teachings that did not conform to Scripture, and questionable financial practices by Witness Lee and others. There also were allegations of sexual misconduct against Witness Lee's son, Philip, who was excommunicated in 1988. Despite these and later charges, the Local Church continued to grow through the 1990s.

## LOGOS

The English transliteration of a Greek term. The Greeks used *logos* to refer to both the spoken word and thought or reason. They also applied *logos* to the universe to represent the cosmic power of reason, the abstract force bringing order and harmony to the perpetual flux of all things. Jewish and Christian Scripture use *logos* to refer to God's utterances, commands, wisdom, and revelation. The Gospel of John uses *logos* to refer to Jesus. The Logos is the agent of creation, the source of temporal and eternal life, and the Ruler of the universe (John 1:1–18).

New Age adherents often deify Satan, or Lucifer, as the Logos. He is symbolized by a serpent or as the Dragon of Wisdom. Some believe the first word ever uttered was "om," which was understood as *I am*. Any entity reputedly must pass through the Logos before becoming a physical reality. New Age adherents chant the mantra "om" to contemplate Ultimate Reality, become enlightened about their inherent divinity, and release the unlimited powers of the spiritual realm.

New Age adherents maintain that the Solar Logos, or sun god, created the Word that brought the star systems into existence. They believe the Solar Logos is also the mighty "I Am" that created Mother Earth and all its life, the physical manifestation of spiritual intelligence. They claim that at the start of every new age, the Solar Logos sends a christ, or a lesser aspect of a celestial trinity, to impart the wisdom necessary to bring about a global transformation.

Other New Age adherents speak about an Earth Logos, the divine energy of god, the spiritual entity that exists within the collective soul of humankind. Some identify the Earth Logos as Sanat Kumura, the Lord of the World who resides in the spiritual kingdom of Shamballa. Others herald Lord Maitreya, the New Age christ, as the Earth Logos and the second person of a cosmic trinity. This so-called trinity also includes Sanat, the father, and the cosmic consciousness, or universal spirit.

*See also:* CREATION; MAITREYA, LORD; OM; SANAT KUMURA

## LORIAN ASSOCIATION

A New Age organization founded to promote the spiritual enlightenment and unity of the world. In 1973 David Spangler and fellow members of the Findhorn Foundation started the Lorian Association in Madison, Wisconsin. Findhorn members came from Scotland to the United States to help prepare for the release of the "Visacred" writings of noted theosophist Alice Ann Bailey. Bailey's work included nearly twenty books, each one containing an esoteric account of a New Age in which Lucifer reigns supreme. Bailey's writings supposedly were inspired by an alien spirit named Djwhal Khul. According to Bailey, the entity ordered that only "believers" would have access to her writings until 1975. At that time the world would be ready

for the enlightened teachings. The Lorian Association and other New Age organizations were to play a part in preparing the world to receive this transcendental information.

*See also:* BAILEY, ALICE ANN; DJWHAL KHUL; FINDHORN FOUNDATION; SPANGLER, DAVID

## LOTUS

Any of five species of water lilies that are often represented in Egyptian and Hindu art.

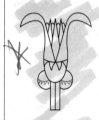

Lotus—bud, bloom, and seed

The Buddhists of India, Tibet, and China consider the flowers of the lotus as sacred. In ancient Eastern religions, the lotus was a religious symbol of the Great Mother Goddess. In ancient Babylon, the plant represented the vulva of the goddess. According to legend, the vulva became impregnated with a jewel. It then transformed into the mystical combination of masculine and feminine opposites, with the bud, bloom, and seed forming a three-in-one goddess. According to Hindu belief, the lotus represents the precreation womb of Mother Nature in which the elements were cosmically united and from which the sun god was born. These teachings echo throughout goddess cults of the New Age Movement, where rites and rituals use the lotus to help initiates search for the goddess within them.

Some Eastern traditions suggested that the halo of the lotus, or aura of glory, represents the cosmic spiritual energy surrounding the universe. Someday a thousand points of light supposedly will spring from the minds of the most enlightened, making known the universal unconscious. In Buddhist tradition, the lotus became the symbol for the quest to obtain enlightenment. The roots of the plant represent the struggles of life, the stem represents the spiritual journey, and the bloom represents cosmic awareness. These Eastern influences permeate the teachings of the New Age Movement where the lotus flower symbolizes spiritual perfection. This flower represents the divine wisdom of the indwelling self, which is seeking to realize its inherent Christ-consciousness and unite with the universal cosmic force.

*See also:* BUDDHISM, GODDESS WORSHIP, HINDUISM, MOTHER EARTH

## LOVE FAMILY
*See:* ARMAGEDDON, CHURCH OF

## LOVELOCK, JAMES E.
A British biologist who formulated the Gaia hypothesis in 1969. This theory is named after Gaea, the Greek earth goddess and mother of the titans. According to the hypothesis, the planet is a living organism, and its ability to sustain and advance life is affected by its biosphere. Lovelock maintained that all life on earth is an integrated and interdependent whole. With the help of U.S. biologist Lynn Margulis, Lovelock further refined the theory and discussed it in a book entitled *Gaia: A New Look at Life on Earth,* published in 1979. While his theory influenced studies on the ecology and environment, critics pointed out that certain aspects of the theory appeared nonscientific and cultish in nature. Consequently, Lovelock adjusted his views more closely to those held within the scientific community regarding the maintenance of equilibrium in biological systems.

New Age adherents have been quick to capitalize on the idea that the earth and its inhabitants are a single, self-supporting organism. They argue that the expansion of human civilization has upset the balance of Gaea, or Mother Earth. To regain this balance, all negative influences must be cleansed from society. Only then will humanity be able to achieve higher levels of consciousness and global unity with Gaea.

*See also:* BALANCING; GAEA; PURIFICATION; SCIENCE, NEW AGE

## LSD
*See:* LYSERGIC ACID DIETHYLAMIDE

## LUCIFERIC DOCTRINE
The New Age explanation for the origin, person, and work of Lucifer. They claim that more than 18 million years ago, the Morning Star struggled with an unjust God, who banished him to earth from Venus. Whereas God gave Lucifer the responsibility to nurture the physical nature of humankind, God gave Christ,

**Lucifer—occult symbol for the Supreme One**

Lucifer's brother, the responsibility to cultivate the spiritual nature of humankind. Filled with jealousy, Lucifer believed God preferred Christ over himself. The Light-Bearer then defiled Eve, causing him to feel separated from his godhood. In an attempt to redeem himself and humanity, Lucifer abolished Eden and sent humanity on the spiritual path toward enlightenment. Therefore New Age adherents depict Lucifer as the heroic angel of humanity's evolution. They praise him as the force that awakens humanity's desire for divinity and enables people to achieve Christ-consciousness.

Cultists say that Lucifer resides in the heavenly kingdom of Shamballa, where he reigns over a spiritual hierarchy of ascended masters. This elite group of entities reputedly have reached the highest possible level of spiritual consciousness, and have the high privilege of guiding humankind into the New Age. This hierarchy is often referred to as the Great White Brotherhood. Members are called ascended masters, spirit guides, inner guides, psychic guides, spiritual counselors, or higher selves. Supposedly Lucifer also goes by many names, such as Shiva (Hinduism), Buddali (Buddhism), and Pan (Greek mythology). New Age adherents call him Sanat Kumura, the Light of the World, and the Great Initiator, as well as the Christ Force, the Agent of God, and the Ruler of Humanity.

The plan of Lucifer is to create a powerful network of initiates, to whom he will give a significant place in the kingdom of the New Age. Initiates receive esoteric knowledge, gifts, and powers, as well as the secret of becoming personally divine. Proponents draw large numbers of people into the initiation rite, promising that their participation will lead to the global transformation of human consciousness and the revelation of cosmic realities. In turn, these devotees network throughout the world to spread the New Age promise of a global community characterized by universal peace, love, and harmony.

Cosmic spirits provided the world with the Great Invocation, a prayer that will channel enough energy to bring the New Age messiah, Lord Maitreya, to earth. At that time, the Luciferic Initiation will take place. The Morning Star will force people to make a decision. They can either choose to follow his divine light, which leads to godhood, or they can be ejected by the Shamballa force to the inner worlds for rehabilitation. This mass initiation and purification is the final step leading to the inauguration of the New Age. At that time, people will experience enlightenment and become one with the universal cosmic essence.

*See also:* ANTICHRIST; GREAT INVOCATION; GREAT WHITE BROTHERHOOD; PLAN, THE; PURIFICATION; SATANISM

## LUCIS TRUST

Another name for the Lucifer Publishing Company. Noted theosophist Alice Ann Bailey (1880–1949) originally founded the company in 1922. Despite the name change to Lucis Trust one year later, the organization still claimed Lucifer as its founding father and the coming messiah of the New Age. By printing information that was self-contradicting and cryptic, the leaders believed only the spiritually advanced would understand it. This was deemed a necessary precaution as they prepared the world for the day when Lord Maitreya would be introduced. Subjects included Eastern mystic techniques, reincarnation, and karma, as well as anti-Semitism, the divinity of humanity, and details about the coming New World Order. Lucis Trust also distributed the Great Invocation, a prayer that promises to bring a

Shamballa force of spiritual energy as final preparation for the reign of Lucifer in the New Age.

Bailey did not limit Lucis Trust merely to publishing enterprises. The organization also includes World Goodwill (a political lobby), Arcane School (an educational organization), and Triangles (an altruistic program). The nonprofit, tax-exempt organization finances its printing activities through a trust fund that holds all the copyrighted works of Alice Bailey. Each part of the organization does its part in disseminating Bailey's New Age ideals. All of Bailey's nearly twenty books were reputedly dictated to her by her spirit guide, Djwhal Khul. This Tibetan master claimed to be a spiritually evolved being who had returned with others to assist people on their journey to higher consciousness. Djwhal Khul allegedly resides in the astral kingdom of Shamballa and relays the wisdom of Lucifer, his master.

*See also:* ARCANE SCHOOL; BAILEY, ALICE ANN; DJWHAL KHUL; GREAT INVOCATION; LUCIFERIC DOCTRINE; WORLD GOODWILL

## LURIA, ISAAC BEN SOLOMON (1534–1572)

Jewish Kabbalist, surnamed Ashkenazi, called Ari [lion]. At Safed, Palestine, he led a school of mysticism that combined Messianism with older kabbalistic doctrines. Luria was concerned with the nature of, and the connection between, earthly redemption and cosmic restoration.

*See also:* KABBALAH

## LYCANTHROPY

Legendary power to shape-shift between a human and a wolf form. In European folk tales, humans assume the form and characteristics of a werewolf ("man-wolf") at night and roam in search of people to devour. Despite their appetite for human flesh, they drink no blood, tire easily, and travel on either two feet or four. The werewolf has hollow eyes, long fangs, and unruly hair. These creatures suffer from burning skin and insatiable thirst. By daybreak the werewolf must return to human form by shedding and hiding its wolf's skin. Legend says that if someone finds and destroys the animal skin, the werewolf dies. If a werewolf is merely wounded, it immediately changes back to human form, and the human body will have a similar wound.

Many ancient pagan religions believed that by venerating certain deities, their followers had the ability to transform themselves into different kinds of man-animals (such as boars, tigers, hyenas, and cats), thereby gaining access to certain supernatural powers. Some worshiped the Great She-Wolf (a pseudonym of Diana), considered queen of the goddesses. Some mythological legends tell the story of the Zeus Lycaios (the most sacred of wolf deities) turning a Greek king named Lycaon into a wolf. Werewolves reputedly carried the dead and lost their souls upon entering the Arcadian temple on Mount Lycion. Wolf worship was active as late as the seventeenth century. In some parts of the world, followers prayed for healing, guidance, and to be transformed into werewolves to protect their holdings from intruding demons.

Some occultists hold that someone can voluntarily become a werewolf by obtaining a magical salve. Overuse can supposedly cause someone to become a werewolf involuntarily. Also a malevolent witch can cast a spell, causing someone to involuntary become an werewolf by drinking water from the track of a wolf or by receiving numerous bites from a vampire. Some claim that the longer people practice werewolfism, the more difficult it becomes to distinguish the human characteristics from the animal characteristics. One story is that the sign of the cross can transform a werewolf back into its true identity.

*See also:* SYMBOLISM, WITCHCRAFT

# LYSERGIC ACID DIETHYLAMIDE (LSD)

An organic psychotropic compound that induces psychotic symptoms resembling those of schizophrenia. In 1943 a Swiss chemist named Albert Hofmann (b. 1906) discovered the effects of LSD, also known as "acid," when he accidentally ingested a small amount of the compound. By 1949 LSD had become an experimental tool in the psychiatric world. By 1960 Dr. Timothy Leary and others were touting the drug as the chemical key to unlock mystical dimensions. Although the U.S. government eventually prohibited the possession, distribution, and sale of LSD, a subculture used it anyway.

Researchers have noted that LSD increases the pulse rate, blood pressure, and temperature, and dilates the pupils of its users. People who ingest LSD lose contact with their environment, become unresponsive to stimuli, and experience hallucinations and delusions. Users progress from feelings of unreality and perceiving "magical" insights, to depression and anxiety, and finally panic and terror. Small doses of LSD are very potent, and repeated use can cause people to become psychologically dependent.

Some New Age adherents claim they experience a "good trip" when they use LSD. They report traveling through varying dimensions of consciousness, beyond the physical limitations of time and space. They remember seeing a vast array of colors and vivid hallucinations. They also say they experience heightened intellectual clarity, profound insight, and extraordinary vision. Continual use causes people to think that the illusions and hallucinations they experience are reality. They begin to crave the drug-induced mystical high, and take ever-increasing doses to achieve the same psychedelic effect.

Other users claim to experience "bad trips." In these instances, people report being confronted by frightening ideas from their unconscious. They experience terrifying auditory and visual hallucinations, as well as nausea and chills. Many report having repeated and uncontrolled "flashbacks," a reoccurrence of hallucinations weeks or even months afterward. Overdoses can lead to unconsciousness and death. New Age adherents are prone to disregard the "bad trips," claiming that LSD is a gateway to other dimensions of reality. By taking it, the user allegedly has a greater chance of becoming enlightened. The drug supposedly is the chemical "avatar" to a New Age. Proponents claim that as more people use LSD, it will aid in the cosmic transformation of the world.

*See also:* ALTERED STATE; AVATAR; DRUG; ENLIGHTENMENT; LEARY, TIMOTHY; MYSTICISM

# M

## MACLAINE, SHIRLEY
## (b. 1934)

Actress, singer, dancer, and author who espouses pantheism and reincarnation. Through her exploration of metaphysics, Shirley MacLaine has become a prominent spokesperson for the New Age. She was born on April 24, 1934, in Richmond, Virginia as Shirley MacLean Beaty. She attended a Baptist Sunday school at a young age, but later rejected what she perceived to be the rigid authority of Christianity. By the time she reached young adulthood, she was an avowed atheist.

MacLaine's first love was dancing. By the age of twenty, she had gone from chorus girl to a star on the Broadway stage. By her late thirties, MacLaine was an active feminist. By her early forties, she had set off on a spiritual quest in which she traveled around the world in search for occultic enlightenment. Over the next two decades, MacLaine's journey would take her deeper and deeper into New Age thinking. In numerous books and seminars, she recounted her "progress." MacLaine's seminars struck a responsive chord across America, and her best-selling autobiographical accounts became handbooks for New Age ideology. Today she oversees Uriel Village, a three-hundred-acre spiritual retreat in Baca, Colorado, where attendees can experience weeklong initiations into numerous occult practices.

MacLaine's first book entitled *Out on a Limb* was published in 1983 and made into a television movie in 1987. Both recount the onset of her journey into the New Age and introduce a bizarre host of characters and experiences. MacLaine describes numerous incidents that she believed validated her reluctant conversion to occultism. These include visits to South America, an encounter with a trance channeler, and traveling through altered states of consciousness into astral dimensions beyond time and space. Espousing reincarnation, MacLaine believes she was once a French aristocrat, a Buddhist monk, and a Spanish infant, as well as a Russian ballet dancer, a Brazilian witch doctor, and an Incan youth. She also claims to have been a Mongolian nomad, a grandfather, his grandson, and a citizen of Atlantis.

MacLaine's second book entitled *Dancing in the Light* was published in 1985. By this time, she was no longer a seeker but a confirmed New Age enthusiast, obediently following the guidance of her professed higher self. MacLaine asserts that human consciousness consists of visible and invisible dimensions, and the latter can only be reached through an altered, trancelike state. She says that while in this dimension, she met her higher self. MacLaine describes this entity as a seven-foot, androgynous oriental. This being claims to be the omnipotent soul that retains all knowledge throughout the cosmic cycles of reincarnation. In MacLaine's next book entitled *All in the Playing* (1988), she explores the contemporary revival of spiritual feminism, such as goddess cults and witchcraft. Another book entitled *Going Within* (1989) focuses on techniques of ascending the levels of human consciousness.

Although MacLaine's adopted philosophy is standard New Age rhetoric, she has the added benefit of her celebrity status. She holds to a pantheistic worldview in which people are the divine creators of Ultimate Reality. She teaches that people's individual souls were seduced by the beauty of physical creation; therefore they forgot their connection with the higher vibration of divine light. The fear and desperation existing in the world allegedly produce the illusion of good and evil, a problem that can be eliminated through reincarnation and the karmic laws of justice. MacLaine believes that God is an impersonal energy force. She depicts Jesus as an adept yogi who, before ascending to a higher state of existence, mastered the physical world and tried to impart the same knowledge to others. She believes the New Age is the time for people to be reintroduced to their higher selves and looks for the day of global enlightenment when people will recognize the innate divinity of eternal wisdom, collective knowledge, and unlimited human potential.

*See also:* FEMINISM, GODDESS WORSHIP, HIGHER SELF, NEW AGE MOVEMENT, OM, REINCARNATION

## MACROBIOTICS

The belief that an extremely restricted diet of chiefly whole grains promotes health and well-being. Michio Kushi is the originator of macrobiotics. His Massachusetts-based educational organization, the Kushi Institute, along with its worldwide affiliates, promotes the teaching and practice of macrobiotics. Kushi says that wholeness and happiness depend on an active interplay between universal order and everyday living. He espouses maintaining a balance between the universal opposites of reality. Macrobiotic devotees advocate a "metaphysical" dietary system of grains and vegetables, enhanced by spiritual exercises, meditative techniques, and love for nature. Through the careful selection, preparation, cooking, and consumption of foods, people can harmonize themselves with the cosmic consciousness and enhance the physical, spiritual, and intellectual evolution of humanity.

*See also:* COSMIC CONSCIOUSNESS, VEGETARIANISM

## MACROCOSM

The complex universe as a whole, including the way it is ordered and operated. In New Age thinking, each person is considered a microcosm of the universal macrocosm. Adherents believe all people share in the cosmic life force permeating the universe and are interdependent on it; therefore, the only way to maintain balance in the macrocosm is to promote harmony within each microcosm, each individual.

*See also:* COSMIC CONSCIOUSNESS, INTERDEPENDENCE

## MAGIC (MAGICK)

Use of charms, spells, or rituals to produce supernatural effects, control events in nature, influence people, and predict the future. Magic is common to most societies and cultures and is considered either "black" or "white," either evil or good respectively. Black magic, or sorcery, attempts to produce harmful results like misfortune or death through such methods as curses, spells, the destruction of dolls representing enemies, and the establishment of alliances with evil spirits. White magic tries to undo curses and spells and to use occult forces for the good of oneself and others. Practitioners try to compel a god, demon, or spirit to work for them, and they may follow a pattern of occult practices to bend psychic forces to their will.

An alternative term, "magick," refers to the ritual invocation to the powers of darkness. Magick utilizes dramatic ceremonies that include costumes and symbols, potent incense and mystical sacraments. Practitioners believe that performing magick causes reality to conform to their will and enables them to explore supernatural dimensions, that supposedly enhances the divine potential of all humanity. British occultist Aleister Crowley (1875–1947) introduced the term "magick" to distinguish the various forms of ceremonial magic from illusions created by sleight-of-hand performers.

Some New Age adherents claim that magical powers are generated, not from demonic realms, but from the universal forces that permeate all life. Others contend that magic, like all occult practices, summons its powers from entities in alternate dimensions, invoking spiritual laws to which all, including God, are subject. Contemporary witches, occultists, and spiritists believe the essence of magic lies in the establishment of an interactive bond with the divine cosmic energy. In this way, adherents can explore the hidden realities of forgotten powers existing in the human soul.

The role of magic varies from one culture to the next. In one society, magic might occupy a central position in primary rituals that involve the well-being of an entire community, such as hunting and farming. In another society, magic might be limited to minor, peripheral, or private acts. Practices can be seen in the ancient Egyptian, Greek, and Roman religions. During the Middle Ages, some churchmen asserted that magic was the key to controlling supernatural powers. A belief in witchcraft was carried to colonial America from Europe. The witch trials that occurred in Salem, Massachusetts, from March to September of 1692 were, perhaps, the most notorious episode of a witchcraft hysteria. In the centuries that followed, the prevalence of magic practitioners seemed to decrease. But during the late nineteenth and early twentieth centuries, the West began to see renewed interest in the practice of magic. By the time of the counterculture movement in the 1960s, New Age adherents had become enthusiastic supporters of magic.

Contemporary magic can be broadly categorized into two groups. One group uses sorcery, such as spells, curses, and hexes, for personal gain. The other summons occultic entities for "spiritual" reasons, such as becoming more enlightened, exploring alternate realities, or achieving immortality. In either case, words, symbols, objects, and movements are used in rituals to invoke cosmic powers.

New Age adherents consider color magic as one of the most effective methods to promote spiritual and psychic development. Homeopathic, or sympathetic, magic attempts to control people, objects, or events through charms and spells. Practitioners claim that once contact is made with a personal item of the victim, the destructive magical influence cannot be broken. Death magic is the acquisition of power through the ritual invocation of demonic entities and may include anything from astral travel to spirit materializations.

*See also:* COLOROLOGY, COSMIC ENERGY, HOMEOPATHY, INCANTATION, SATANISM, SORCERY, VOODOO, WITCHCRAFT

## MAHARAJ JI
*See:* DIVINE LIGHT MISSION

## MAHARISHI MAHESH YOGI (b. 1911)

An Indian guru who is responsible for introducing Transcendental Meditation (TM) to the West. Yogi was born in northern India in 1911 and graduated from Allahabad University in 1942 with a degree in physics. That same year he met a spiritual teacher named Guru Dev and remained his devoted disciple until Dev died in 1953. For the next two years, Yogi lived as a hermit in the Himalaya Mountains where he refined his understanding of what Dev had taught him. After arriving in Los Angeles in 1958, Yogi began spreading his brand of Hinduism which he called Transcendental Meditation.

The countercultural movement of the late 1960s was receptive to Yogi's message of love, peace, and quietness. However by the early 1970s, interest in TM began to wane, due in part to a strained relationship between the guru and the British rock group The Beatles. After a brief stint in India, Yogi returned to America. He reintroduced TM as the Science of Creative Intelligence (SCI) and replaced religious jargon with psychological terminology. By the middle of the decade, he achieved great popularity as thousands of people flocked to his expensive TM sessions. He claimed that if adequate numbers of people practiced TM, personal and global imbalances would be replaced by the universal life force. In addition, humankind would reach a critical mass, and the human race would experience a quantum leap in evolutionary progress.

In 1977, against the assertions of Yogi and his devout followers, a federal court in New Jersey ruled that SCI was a religion and therefore could not be taught in public schools. This prompted other states to take similar action. Despite these setbacks, Yogi has tens of thousands of followers throughout the United States and around the world. He controls a number of TM organizations, such as the Maharishi International University (1971) and the Maharishi Technology of the Unified Field (1982). He also maintains headquarters in North America and Europe. At his fully accredited Maharishi International University in Fairfield, Iowa, students practice "experiencing" education at their deepest intellectual levels.

*See also:* ENLIGHTENMENT, HINDUISM, MANTRA, TRANSCENDENTAL MEDITATION

## MAITREYA, LORD

The future and final manifestation of the eternal, ultimate Buddha. Legend says that Maitreya is a messianic figure who has attained a perfect state of enlightenment and lives in a celestial realm called Tushita Heaven. Buddhists believe that Maitreya will appear after a period of earthly decay and decadence, and that his presence will signal a revival of truly enlightened teaching.

A New Age leader and lecturer named Benjamin Creme (b. 1922) has perpetuated the Maitreya tradition. He claims that this individual will be the fifth incarnation of Buddha, as well as the Muslim Mahada, the Hindu Krishna, and the Christian Jesus. In Creme's work entitled *Reappearance of Christ and the Masters of Wisdom,* he asserts that Maitreya resides with the ascended masters. This group of spiritually evolved souls chose to return to earth to lead humankind into the New Age of enlightenment. Maitreya has attained a high seating in the Hierarchy of Masters, answering only to Sanat Kumura, or Lucifer, the star who was cast from Venus to Earth. Proponents teach that at the dawn of each new age, Sanat Kumura sends forth a christ to impart knowledge that will bring about the spiritual transformation of loyal adherents. Many leaders, organizations, cultists, and pseudo-religions await the appearance of Lord Maitreya as the messiah of the Aquarian Age.

Maitreya reputedly is the teacher who emerged in London in 1977, and began to "overshadow" Creme with telepathic messages about the world to come. By 1980, Creme had established the Tara Center to disseminate Maitreya prophecies and instructions. These claim that humanity is on the verge of being transformed into a race of gods. However this process will require the reorganization of old social structures, the creation of a global society, the removal of guilt and fear, and the uniting of people's minds with the spiritual knowledge of ancient mysteries. Creme says that in the meantime, Lord Maitreya quietly works to prepare world leaders for his future appearance.

*See also:* ANTICHRIST; ASCENDED MASTER; CREME, BENJAMIN; GREAT INVOCATION; SECOND COMING OF CHRIST

## MANDALA

A Hindu or Buddhist symbolic diagram of the universe that is used for ritual purposes. The mandala typically includes a group of cosmic deities, their emblems, or their magic syllables. These are arranged in one or more circles, and the circles are surrounded by a square. The square is then aligned to the points of the compass.

**Mandala— geometric symbols used in meditation**

During meditation practices, cultists try to visualize images of mandalas. They believe the kaleidoscope patterns focus the concentration of initiates and induce an altered state of consciousness that grants them access to the knowledge and powers of the spiritual realm. Meditation on the complex network of geometric symbols and rainbow colors cleanses the negative energies of learned values. Meditation reprograms the mind to accept new lessons through the mystical interpretation of the visual energy center of the third eye (on the center of the forehead).

Swiss psychologist Carl Jung (1875–1961)

considered the mandala to be an archetype, a preexistent image representing the psychic contents of humanity's collective unconsciousness, as opposed to the personal unconsciousness. The mandala is therefore an inborn image that suggests the most fundamental motifs and themes of human existence. Similar archetypes exist in people of all times and from all places and are regarded as mythological representations of the universal self. Jung taught that the Christian concept of the image of God was an archetype imprinted in the minds of every person. He urged people to make the God image dominant in their personality.

New Age adherents believe the mandala has the inherent power to inspire the harmonious balance between humanity and the universe, thereby restoring order to an otherwise chaotic existence. Some cults suggest that the foundations of cities were originally derived from the mandala ground plans of long lost civilizations, such as Atlantis. Jung suggested that the construction of cities in a particular manner represents the projection of archetypal images from within the collective human unconscious. New Age adherents encourage people to visualize images of mandalas as a way to promote enlightenment and to bring about the evolutionary advance of the human race to godhood.

*See also:* ALTERED STATE; CENTER; CIRCLE; JUNG, CARL GUSTAV; TRANSCENDENTAL MEDITATION

# MANISM

The cultic worship of ancestors. Manism is the belief that people are direct descendants of the gods. In ancient Greece and Rome, devotees regularly performed sacrificial rituals, divinations, and prayers to honor the dead.

# MANTRA

A mystical syllable or sacred formula, usually in Sanskrit, used in rituals, prayers, incantations, and meditation. Hindus and Buddhists believe mantras are an embodiment of particular deities or representations of spiritual forces. They claim that when devotees chant a mantra, they tap into the supernatural powers of a deity and invite it to enter them. The mantra allows them to escape from worldly distractions and to journey into an altered state of consciousness. By repeatedly chanting the sacred formula, advocates claim people can be delivered from the world of illusion and ultimately unite with the cosmic consciousness. New Age adherents enthusiastically promote the use of mantras. Through the use of prayers and incantations in prescribed rituals, pupils are taught to empty their minds of all thoughts.

*See also:* ALTERED STATE, HINDUISM, OM, SOUND THERAPY

# MARIJUANA

A drug preparation made from the dried leaves and flowering tops of certain hemp species. Slang terms for marijuana include "weed," "pot," "Mary Jane," "tea," "gage," and "grass," and as a cigarette, "reefer" and "joint." People have used the drug for thousands of years as an intoxicant and for medical purposes. The drug is smoked, mixed in beverages, and eaten in cakes to produce an intoxicating effect upon the cardiovascular and central nervous systems. When taken in small amounts, marijuana causes users to feel relaxed and sleepy. But larger amounts of the drug cause users to hallucinate. This distorts their senses, alters their awareness of time, causes short-term memory loss, hampers basic thought processes, and impairs eye-hand coordination. Even larger doses of marijuana produce anxiety, panic, delusions, and paranoia. Scientists believe that smoking the drug can have adverse long-term effects on the lungs.

Individual state and local laws prohibited the use of marijuana in the United States around 1900, followed by a federal ban in 1937. Despite these legal measures, the sale, possession, and usage of the drug continued to increase in the following decades, especially during the 1960s. This led various advocacy groups to lobby for the legalization of marijuana's "recreational" use. Since the heyday of the countercultural revolution, new growing techniques have increased the potency of the psychoactive component of the drug, called *tetrahydrocannabinol* or THC, at least fivefold.

New Age adherents recognize that the sensual trance induced by taking marijuana is similar to those experienced by Eastern mystics. Advocates smoke, eat, and drink marijuana to alter their state of consciousness, free them from the bonds of physical reality, and put them in touch with other dimensions of existence. Users are supposedly more receptive to the influence of ascended masters and personal spirit guides, who will lead them to greater enlightenment and unity with the cosmic life force.

*See also:* ALTERED STATE, DRUG

## MARX, KARL (1818–1883)

German philosopher, political economist, and revolutionary whose writings, especially *Das Kapital,* gave the name to the political and social theory of Marxism. This theory gives class struggle a primary role in leading society from democracy under capitalism, which reputedly is characterized by materialism and mediocrity, to a socialist society, then to communism. The ultimate goal is to establish a classless society.

Marx was born to Jewish parents in the Prussian town of Trier. His father converted to Lutheranism, primarily to retain the family's position in the face of Prussian antisemitism. Marx attended the University of Bonn and then studied at the University of Berlin. Here he was captivated by Georg Hegel's (1770–1831) philosophy and became critical of traditional religion and society. After receiving his doctorate in philosophy in 1841 from the University of Jena, Marx worked as an editor in 1842 for a liberal democratic newspaper. The publication's antigovernment stance caused Prussian officials to ban publication in 1843. Marx moved to Paris, Brussels, and finally London, at the same time refining his social and economic views.

Marx began to immerse himself in the anti-Christian writings of Ludwig Feuerbach. He asserted that God was a human invention and that religion reduced people to groveling, evil creatures. Feuerbach argued that if religion—especially as practiced by the church and sanctioned by the government—was abolished, people would be freed to overcome their alienation toward themselves. Marx applied these ideas to social and economic theory. He maintained that the private ownership of property dehumanized people, alienating them from each other and themselves. By abolishing private property, people would become less selfish and more interested in benefitting humanity as a whole.

Marx believed that human history is a succession of clashes between economically hostile groups. The main antagonists are the proletariat, or working class, and the bourgeoisie, or capitalist class. Class struggle is the catalyst for change. After a glorious battle, conflict will be eliminated, private property abolished, and political power centralized in the hands of a collective world government. This flawless society will bring perfection to humankind morally, emotionally, and socially. He justified the use of education, economic force, and violence to achieve his utopia.

According to Marx, the world is a ceaseless motion of chaotic and evolutionary forces. His theory of dialectical materialism teaches that changes in society result from a clash in historical forces. Religion is an opiate used by the rich to distract the poor from their plight. Therefore he advocated abolishing religion.

Many of the ideas advanced by Marx have found a home in New Age philosophy. Adherents agree with Marx that people are the masters of their own destiny. They agree with the goal of establishing a world government and a classless society.

*See also:* HEGEL, GEORG WILHELM FRIEDRICH; ONE-WORLD IDEAL; PURIFICATION

## MARY

The mother of Jesus; a central figure in Roman Catholic theology and worship. Church doctrine and practice encourages a filial devotion to her, invoking her name for maternal intercession, and imitating her as the outstanding role model. Second-century mystics called Mary "the new Eve," the companion of the new Adam, Christ. In A.D. 431, church leaders in Ephesus called Mary the "Mother of God," or "God-bearer" (*Theotokos*). This gave further incentive for her veneration. People dedicated sanctuaries to her and offered prayers in her name. During the Middle Ages, church leaders taught that she was sinlessly perfect and shared in the redemptive suffering of Christ. While Jesus is acknowledged in the Marian cult, He is often demoted from His role as the Mediator of salvation. Devotees have progressively exalted Mary over Christ and attribute salvation to her intercession.

For centuries, apparitions and accompanying messages from Mary have been reported. One legend from the thirteenth century says that Saint Dominic (1170–1221) received a visit from the Virgin Mary, who gave him a ring of beads, the rosary, to use when invoking her aid. In commemoration of a sixteenth-century "visitation" to the Aztec Indian Juan Diago, Mary was named the patroness of all the Americas. In 1858, fourteen-year-old Bernadette Soubirous had numerous religious visions in a grotto near Lourdes, France. Since then, other apparitions of Mary have been seen by devout Roman Catholics, such as in Fatima, Portugal, in 1917. At these and other sightings, predictions indicate that a tremendous catastrophe will occur on earth, unless humanity seeks worldwide ecumenical unity.

New Age gurus have perpetuated the image of Mary as a sinless vessel, chosen at the age of four to be a channel for the avatar named Christ. Some cults maintain that ascended masters trained Mary to tap into psychic and metaphysical realities and to foresee the future through astrology. Others say that Mary serves as an example of someone who first became enlightened to her undefiled inner self and then became united with the universal Christ-consciousness. The increasing occurrences of Marian apparitions is given as evidence of an eruption of archetypes in the psychic content of humanity's collective unconsciousness. New Age adherents believe this is preparing the way for the union of the world with the cosmic essence.

*See also:* APHRODITE, AVATAR, DIANA, GODDESS WORSHIP, JESUS CHRIST, MOTHER EARTH, ROSARY, VENUS

## MASLOW, ABRAHAM (1908–1970)

Influential humanistic psychologist and founder of the Association for Humanistic Psychology. Abraham Maslow received his Ph.D. degree from the University of Wisconsin, served as a departmental chairman at Brandeis University, and was the president of the American Psychological Association. In 1961, he founded and published the *Journal of Humanistic Psychology*. He wrote more than 150 publications over a period of thirty-eight years, ending with his final work, *The Farther Reaches of Human Nature,* published in 1971.

Maslow, along with Carl Rogers (1902–1987) and Rollo May (1909–1994), classified humanistic psychology as a "third force," an alternative to the schools of psychoanalysis and behaviorism. Maslow believed people are unique, good, and full of potential. He maintained that people's fundamental problem is a lack of awareness of their full potential. The counselor should facilitate the discovery of the patient's full potential. He believed this can be done by having them climb "the ladder" of their basic human needs. Maslow taught that people's needs on the lower end on the scale must be met before they can advance to the higher levels.

Maslow's hierarchy of needs begins with physiological deficits, such as thirst, hunger, and fatigue. The second level contains the need to avoid pain, feel secure, be free from chaos, and build structure in life. The third level contains the need for belongingness and love. The fourth level contains the need for esteem, self-respect, adequacy, and competence. The fifth and final level contains the need for self-actualization, understanding, and aesthetic pleasure. According to Maslow, self-actualized people manifest the values extolled by humanism, including self-acceptance, acknowledgment of others, as well as openness and autonomy.

New Age philosophy has adopted many of Maslow's ideas. His fascination with mysticism and altered states of consciousness, as evidenced in his book *Motivation and Personality* (1954), is affirmed by those who believe in the importance of unifying the mind, body, and soul. The Association for Humanistic Psychology is drawn by pantheistic worldview assumptions in its goal of helping people to tap into the universal source of their human potential. The Association also fits into New Age thinking in its commitment to assist people in achieving trance-like states through occultic practices.

*See also:* HUMAN POTENTIAL MOVEMENT, HUMANISTIC PSYCHOLOGY, TRANSPERSONAL PSYCHOLOGY, VALUES CLARIFICATION

# MATERIALISM

The theory that physical matter, by its movements and modifications, is the only or fundamental reality. Proponents claim the material world is uncreated, eternal, indestructible, and unalterable in its basic elements. They see force as inseparable from matter. Therefore no matter exists without force, and no force exists without matter. Since no force, or causative agent, exists independently, then matter has no creator. The universe, as it now exists, came from the gradual evolution of matter and force. All forms of life, all causes, and all effects are the direct result of physical and chemical forces at work in matter. Adherents believe that no power exists, except in association with matter. Therefore, no divine being with creative power, or any created human soul, can exist.

All sources of phenomena and activity, whether immaterial or material, are considered inseparably linked to existing matter. The causes and effects evident in all aspects of life, whether physical or mental, are due entirely to physical forces. All thought and feeling, as well as all tangible, concrete action, are due to the composition and movement of sub-atomic particles. This theory effectively invalidates any concepts of the divine and supernatural and attributes the existence of the universe to a collection of material causes and effects. The immaterial or spiritual aspects of existence are viewed as illusions. This philosophy has lead to the modern belief that the highest values or objectives in life are found only in material well-being, in the acquisition of material goods, and in the furtherance of material progress.

Materialism finds its earliest formal expression in the writings of such ancient philosophers as Leucippus (c. 400 B.C.), Democritus (460–370 B.C.), and Lucretius (96–55 B.C.). But the prevalence of Christianity caused the popularity of materialism to wane considerably, even though nature worship continued to exist in the pagan religions of Europe.

During and after the Renaissance, materialism reemerged, especially in the views of Thomas Hobbes (1588–1679) and Karl Marx (1818–1883). In modern times, the theory continues to have its adherents among Westerners. In fact, the popular idea that money, not God, keeps the world operational is a variant form of materialism.

New Age adherents have long supported key tenets of this theory. Occultists deny the existence of a supreme, personal, and self-aware God. Instead, the concept of "God" is reduced to an impersonal life force. Progressive evolution has replaced the Christian concept of a divine Creator who providentially governs his creation. Drawing upon materialistic thinking, New Age adherents say that life is void of absolutes and constants. Therefore everything is relative, changing, and chaotic, the product of random events and chance interactions. Materialists see themselves at the center of their universes, the masters of their destinies, and the makers of their own values and morals.

*See also:* ENLIGHTENMENT; MARX, KARL; SCIENCE, NEW AGE

# MATERIALIZATION

The appearance of a spiritual entity in bodily form. Materialization reputedly takes place through the supernatural powers of a medium, who acts as a bridge between alternate dimensions of existence. Some New Age adherents maintain that certain individuals possess vibratory energy, enabling them to serve as instruments of communication to ethereal dimensions, thereby converting this energy into a material shape. Others contend that spirits are nothing more than manifestations of the collective unconscious and occasionally materialize in archetypal images by psychic projection. These materializations typically occur at séances. The medium first enters a trancelike state. Then a milky-white ectoplasmic substance appears and takes the shape of a human being.

*See also:* COSMIC ENERGY, ECTOPLASM, ENTITY, GHOST, MEDIUM, SÉANCE, SPIRITISM

## MATUS, DON JUAN

A fictitious Yaqui Indian sorcerer. Proponents claim this entity instructed anthropologist Carlos Castaneda in the ways of the shaman. Don Juan described what he said was an ancient religious practice in which people used hallucinogenic drugs to cross the threshold of human consciousness and journey into the realm of the supernatural. Once initiates achieved a heightened state of awareness, they would experience a divine union with nature, acquire unlimited amounts of ancient knowledge, and meet numerous spiritual allies.

After returning to California from the Mexican border area of the Southwest, Castaneda began to publish the messages of Don Juan. These books have become popular among New Age adherents. Titles include *The Teachings of Don Juan: A Yaqui Way of Knowledge* (1968), *Journey to Ixtlan* (1972), *The Fire Within* (1984), and *The Power of Silence* (1987). A common mystical theme in these books is that people keep each other in bondage by demanding adherence to traditional thoughts and actions.

*See also:* CASTANEDA, CARLOS; DRUG; NATIVE AMERICANS; SPIRIT GUIDES

## MAYANS

A race of Native Americans who lived in southern Mexico and Central America, and whose civilization reached its height around A.D. 1000. Their descendants, the modern Mayans, live in the same regions today. Historians have applauded the Mayans for their outstanding achievements in architecture, art, and mathematics, as well as astronomy and chronology. Historians once thought the Mayans were a gentle people who resorted to war only when threatened. However contemporary findings show a gruesome side to the Mayan civilization.

Blood was the adhesive of Mayan life. Not only did the Mayans offer human sacrifices from their own tribes, they also waged war to procure additional captives for their sacrificial rituals. The Mayans believed the spilling of blood nourished the gods and goddesses and established order within the universe. The Mayans, like their New Age counterparts, justified these actions with the philosophy that human existence is merely an illusion and that genuine reality exists in union with the cosmic life force. Modern-day occultists continue to use the Mayan almanac to predict the future. They also use Mayan astrological, chronological, and numerological calculations to guide their everyday lives.

*See also:* ASTROLOGY, BLOOD SACRIFICE, ZIGGURAT

## MEDIARCHY

The formation of powerful media networks to disseminate information. The concept of mediarchy was introduced by New Age advocate Jose Argüelles. He maintained that inundating people with occultic teaching would accelerate the enlightenment process and catapult humanity into the New Age. Argüelles, who is known for organizing the Harmonic Convergence in 1987, claims that television, radio, newspapers, and magazines are already networked. He says these forms of communication will one day become a dominant world force to bring about the transformation of human consciousness.

*See also:* ARGÜELLES, JOSE

# MEDICINE, NEW AGE

Methods of treatment based on ancient metaphysical and occultic beliefs. Practitioners claim people have the innate ability to heal themselves through the manipulation of a divine energy force. By entering altered states of consciousness, patients realign their mind, body, and spirit with the universal life force that permeates human existence. This process eliminates the accumulation of unbalanced energy, the presumed cause of illness and pain, and restores mental wholeness and physical well-being. As with any holistic healing techniques, the success of New Age forms of medical treatment is often temporary. Therapists usually demand that patients continue therapy while learning the revelations of ancient pagan belief systems.

*See also:* HOLISTIC HEALTH

# MEDICINE WHEEL (CIRCLE)

Ancient gathering sites that were constructed to enable people to connect with the infinite forces of the universe. These meeting places were primarily built by Great Plains tribes of North America. The sites were constructed in the shape of a circle to symbolize the Native American concept of the universe as a huge spiral. For thousands of years, people gathered at these meeting places to pray, perform healings, and observe ceremonies.

In a typical medicine wheel, people would place thirty-six stones within a circle. Each stone represented a specific part of the universe and was laid in a certain spot in accordance with directives issued by a spirit guide. Dances, plays, or symbolic sacrifices, enhanced by chants, drums, and smoke, were acted out to reflect and honor a particular spirit that they believed would bestow gifts, powers, and blessings in return. These ancient gathering sites remain extremely popular among New Age adherents who attend ceremonies to share philosophies and channel the energies of Mother Earth. Many believe that by interchanging knowledge and prophecies, humankind will achieve an enlightened understanding of the interconnection of people with one another, their planet, and their universe.

*See also:* CIRCLE, NATIVE AMERICANS

# MEDIUM

Human channel of communication between the material and spirit worlds. Mediums have played a significant role in various spirit religions. In animistic belief systems, the shaman is a type of medium, a connection to world spirits. The more usual conception of a medium as one through whom the dead or demons speak is well attested in ancient Near Eastern sources. Egyptian references in the dynastic periods are frequent, and spiritualist mediums are ubiquitous in Indian Hinduism.

The ways in which mediums work has varied widely, from the Greek oracle priestesses to New Age trance channelers. Séance mediums have traditionally shown the presence of spirits by table levitations, speaking in a spirit's voice, automatic writing and drawing and displaying the various forms of extrasensory perception.

Use of mediums in Eastern and native American religious practice has remained relatively consistent. The West, on the other hand, has been ambivalent toward mediums, sometimes burning them at the stake in medieval and Renaissance Europe and sometimes celebrating them in high society as in the Victorian era. Following World War I, mediums enjoyed a resurgence in Europe and North America.

Since the 1960s, New Age beliefs have favored those channeling mediums whose bodies are thought to be taken over by spirits from legendary societies, souls of the recently deceased, and extraterrestrials. Some look to channelers for enlightenment wisdom from ascended masters and spirit guides. Another New Age belief is that channelers are able to tap into the deepest level of the human psyche, where the universal knowledge of the collective unconscious resides.

Those skeptical of mediums and channelers have found ample evidence of the use of illusion and fraud. Some well-known stage magic and mentalist performers have demonstrated that any apparent sign of spirit presence can be duplicated on stage.

*See also:* ASCENDED MASTER, AUTOMATIC WRITING, NECROMANCY, SPIRIT GUIDES, SPIRITISM, TRANCE CHANNELING

## MEHER BA'BA (1894–1969)

A spiritual master in western India who gained a worldwide following. From 1925 through the last forty-four years of his life, Meher Ba'ba observed total silence and did not write. He communicated through an alphabet board and gestures, dictating several books by alphabet board. He observed that he had come "not to teach but to awaken." He practiced silence because "things that are real are given and received in silence."

Merwan Sheriar Irani was born into a Zoroastrian family. While in college he met "perfect masters" who helped him find his own identity as the avatar of this age, an incarnation of God in human form. He placed himself among such figures as Zoroaster, Rama, Krishna, Gautama Buddha, Jesus, and Muhammad. He taught that the goal of life is to realize the absolute oneness of God, from whom the universe emanated as a result of the whim of unconscious divinity to know itself as conscious divinity. Each entity must go through an evolution of seven forms on the way to god-consciousness: (1) stone or metal, (2) vegetable, (3) worm, (4) fish, (5) bird, (6) animal, and (7) human. The human being then must traverse an inward spiritual path to eliminate individuality and be awakened to the "real self" as God.

Meher Baba taught a doctrine of love as a way to be conscious of the oneness of all life. He lived a life of service to the poor and sick, including cleaning the latrines of untouchables and bathing lepers. On trips through the United States and Europe, he established the Meher Spiritual Center in Myrtle Beach, South Carolina, in 1952. The drug culture of the 1960s was drawn to him for spiritual guidance, but he warned against the use of any mind-altering substances.

*See also:* AVATAR; GAUTAMA, SIDDHARTHA; ZOROASTRIANISM

## MERIDIANS

A series of twelve pathways on each side of the human body through which vital energy allegedly flows. The ancient Chinese believed the meridians channeled through the deep tissues of the body and only on occasion touched the surface. They attributed diseases to an imbalance in the energy flow of the body and concluded that curative treatment points were located where the meridians surfaced.

By inserting needles in these various points, acupuncturists claim to remove excessive pressure, break down blockages in the energy flow, and restore perfect balance throughout the body.

The Chinese originally designed the meridian system on an astrological year. Each of the 365 acupoints located along the meridians were believed to correspond directly with specific bodily functions. These include functions associated with the heart, lungs, and colon, as well as the gallbladder, liver, and other vital organs. New Age adherents regard acupuncture as a holistic form of treatment to help people maintain a harmonious balance of energy within themselves and with the cosmic life force.

*See also:* ACUPRESSURE, ACUPUNCTURE, CH'I, HOLISM

## MESCALINE

*See:* PEYOTE

## MESMER, FRANZ ANTON (1734–1815)

A German physician known primarily for his theory of animal magnetism. Mesmer was born in Iznang, Austria. He studied philosophy at a Jesuit university in Bavaria and medicine and theology at the University of Vienna. In his doctoral thesis, he investigated the idea that heavenly bodies influence health and disease. He postulated that magnetism emanated from the stars, animals, and iron. He also maintained that the human body is inherently polarized into positive and negative magnetic fields. He theorized that by connecting this polarity with the Universal Spirit, power would be created from the union and cure any illness.

Mesmer was convinced that magnets could attract and apply the celestial forces. He believed that objects somehow captured magnetic fluids from the atmosphere and revitalized the body's central nervous system. This prompted him to use iron magnets and hypnosis to treat neurotic patients. His theories and name also contributed a new word to the English language, the verb "to mesmerize."

Hypnosis, or "mesmerism," which seeks to alter a patient's conscious level of awareness, has become an accepted technique within the psychotherapeutic community. Holistic healers contend that hypnotic suggestion can produce incredible physiological results by inducing the body to release healing energy from within, thereby blocking pain and altering biological functions. Others contend that, by transcending the many levels of consciousness, patients can unblock psychic barriers, paving the way for the development of a wide range of divine powers. This leads to enlightenment and union with the cosmic life force.

*See also:* BALANCING, HYPNOSIS, POLARITY THERAPY

# METEMPSYCHOSIS
*See:* TRANSMIGRATION

# METAPHYSICS

A division of philosophy that explores the fundamental aspects of reality and existence. Metaphysics deals with the nature of life, the origin of the universe, and the way the mind operates. It seeks to determine whether perceived objects are an illusion or real, whether the external world exists apart from our consciousness, whether the universe is chaotic and incomprehensible or orderly and intelligible, and whether reality can be reduced to a single underlying substance. Concerning the latter, some think all reality is fundamentally material or physical, while others insist that it is nonmaterial or spiritual. Metaphysics also explores the argument concerning permanence and change. Idealists say every entity in the universe has a function or part of a supernatural principle or goal, which is the ultimate source and cause of all change. In contrast, materialists think that change is the result of physical entities randomly acting and reacting with one another.

In New Age metaphysics, reality is illusory, the human psyche is part of a greater collective consciousness, and reality can be reduced to a single cosmic force. All people originate from and belong to this universal life principal. Through mind-altering techniques, people can become more enlightened to their divine self, as well as their place within the cosmos. Occultists assert that when people become aware of their ability to experience truth and self in relation to the god within them, this will bring about a quantum increase in planetary consciousness. It will also serve as a catalyst to establish a new age of understanding and peace.

*See also:* COSMIC CONSCIOUSNESS; INTERCONNECTION; QUANTUM LEAP; SCIENCE, NEW AGE

# MICROCOSM

A system that is analogous to a much larger system in its development, configuration, or composition. New Age adherents believe human nature is a microcosm of the universal essence. Each person plays an interrelated and interdependent role in the macrocosm, or universal order. Adherents claim that humanity's atomic construction, physiological design, and divine nature are evidence of the constant interaction between people and their universe. The ability of people to change reality with their minds proves the existence of an intrinsic connection between the spiritual and material dimensions. New Age adherents say that through enlightenment people become aware of their place within the cosmic order and obtain access to the mysteries, magic, and powers of the universe.

*See also:* COSMIC ENERGY, MYSTERY

## MIDDLE WAY

The Buddhist path to enlightenment that seeks to avoid the extremes of both affluence and asceticism. Along this path, initiates empty their minds, accrue merit by performing rituals, and seek to obtain a greater realization of the divine nature within themselves. Devotees learn to eliminate desire by following the Eightfold Path, consisting of eight points arranged in three categories. The first category pertains to wisdom *(Panna)* and includes right understanding and right thought. The second category addresses ethical conduct *(Sila)* and includes right speech, right action, and right livelihood. The third category calls for mental discipline *(Samadhi)* and includes right effort, right awareness, and right meditation. New Age adherents assert that the Middle Way and Eightfold Path constitute the right living of the dharma, or moral law. Advocates say that those who follow these prescribed religious and ethical duties will earn merit toward higher rebirths, thereby escaping the laws of karma.

*See also:* BUDDHISM, DHARMA, EIGHTFOLD PATH, KARMA

## MIND BODY MEDICINE

Also called Ayurvedic Medicine, a New Age healing and health phenomenon of the 1990s, based on ancient Indian Hindu healing arts. This set of diet and meditation intensive therapies was made immensely popular by Indian physician-writer Deepak Chopra. Tenets draw on meditation, quantum healing, diet, and harmony among the dosha. Central to healing is self-knowledge and self-actualization. The theory is that health is a higher state of consciousness and higher states of consciousness will naturally lead to better health.

Mind body medicine maintains that for every experience in the mind there is a corresponding physiology change. Chopra believes in reducing stress through biofeedback and meditation, balanced nutrition, yoga exercise, herbal medicine, massage, sound, movement, and aromatherapy. Ayurvedic healing developed around 1500 B.C. in ancient India's Vedic period.

Its principles of preventative care relate to preparation of balanced meals and arranging a harmonious environment, as well as therapy for those who are ill. The goal is to help the individual discover a personal knowledge of living. Ayurveda holds that physiology is governed by three biological *doshas*—vata, pitta, and kapha. Vata controls nerve impulses, circulation, respiration, and elimination. Pitta controls metabolic processes. Kapha is responsible for growth and protection. Illness is caused by an imbalance among the doshas, which disrupts the flow of energy. Stress and poor nutrition contribute to disruptions and the resulting buildup of body toxins. Mind body medicine relates closely to transcendental meditation techniques.

Quantum healing or quantum medicine is essential, according to proponents, for ensuring total health. This approach is related to quantum mechanics, in which everything causes everything else. In quantum healing, the human mind, soul, and body must be examined as one entity. When one is out of balance, the entire being loses its equilibrium. Quantum healing involves a shift in the fields of energy information in the body, so as to correct an idea that has gone wrong.

Ayurvedic nutrition involves consciousness of one's interaction with food as part of the universe. That includes conscious meditation on the cook and even the farmer who grew it. Processed and canned foods are avoided since they do not provide easy access to the food's life energy. Taste also is important, as are fasting and frequent use of enemas for detoxification and purification.

*See also:* CHOPRA, DEEPAK; MEDICINE, NEW AGE

## MIRROR

A polished or reflective surface. The mirror has played an important part in religious beliefs. Ancient societies believed the mirror had the ability to capture the souls of people in its reflection. Some contemporary goddess cults see the mirror as a symbol of the love of self, the creative force of the universe, and all that thrives within it. One popular belief holds that in the beginning was the Goddess—the All—who saw her reflection in the curved mirror of space and fell in love with it. She drew forth the image and made love to herself. As ecstasy burst forth in song, worlds were conceived. The Goddess swelled with life and gave birth to spirits who filled the earth and became human beings.

Neopagan feminist cults use this creation account to teach that the mirror is an ancient representative of the Goddess and a tool for use in rituals of worship and the practice of magic. In initiation rites, the mirror may become part of a "love oneself reenactment" of the ancient goddess myth. Others may utilize the mirror's mystical powers to focus universal cosmic forces within the soul and traverse the doorway to spiritual realms. Still others use mirrors to conjure up images of the past, present, or future. Contemporary neopaganism teaches that such opposites as good and evil are simply the mirror images of universal reality and different swirls of the same energy force. New Age adherents contend that the universe itself is merely an illusory reflection of the human consciousness. Devotees must reach past the mirror's shiny surface to understand hidden truths.

*See also:* GODDESS WORSHIP, ILLUSION, VENUS

## MONISM

The view that all reality is ultimately one, not twofold (as in dualism), and not many (as in pluralism). Monism says only one unifying principle, being, or type of being exists. Because reality is an undifferentiated oneness or unity, real change and individuality are impossible. Differences in phenomena and experiences are due to different states in which a single all-encompassing principle or substance might manifest itself. Any appearance of plurality is either illusory, or in a transitory mode of operation based on the one reality. Pantheism is a religion based on monism.

New Age adherents have adopted this scheme of thinking. They assert that no distinction exists between God and creation. They teach that God is one manifestation of the all-inclusive Absolute Being, and human beings are manifestations of God or the divine substance. New Age adherents believe that since humanity is part of a unified whole, they have the power to tap into a universal energy source and manipulate animate and inanimate matter. This allegedly will help bring about the enlightenment of the world, as well as humanity's union with the cosmic life force.

*See also:* CONFLUENT EDUCATION, CONSCIOUSNESS, PANTHEISM, PRANA

## MONTESSORI

A method of instructing children that stresses the development of a child's own initiative. This approach was developed in 1907 by Maria Montessori (1870–1952), an Italian physician and educator. The core of the method consists of self-motivation and individualized learning. Advocates believe the techniques inspire children to unlock hidden mysteries within themselves, ultimately resulting in the emergence of a new type of person. Montessori foresaw a spiritual evolution in the thinking of people in which everyone would recognize the interdependence of all life. She believed it was imperative to instruct children concerning their place in the transformational process that would ultimately usher in global peace.

The Montessori method found favor with the Italian fascist premier Benito Mussolini (1883–1945), who popularized the teaching throughout Italy during the 1920s and 1930s.

While the pedagogy is frequently practiced today by educators who would not accept its original New Age message, the technique remains popular with occult Theosophy organizations and Eastern religious leaders. Montessori education has been adopted by more than three thousand public schools across the United States.

*See also:* CONFLUENT EDUCATION, TRANSPERSONAL PSYCHOLOGY

## MONTGOMERY, RUTH (b. 1912)

A noted New Age writer, Montgomery's books reputedly depict the channeled wisdom of numerous spiritual entities. Montgomery was once a highly respected syndicated columnist in Washington, D.C. At the height of her career, she was assigned to investigate the mysterious world of demonic communication. She became convinced that these spirits were the departed souls of people who reside in the astral planes of existence. She began to channel the messages of these demons to the world, which eventually earned her the title "The Herald of the New Age."

Montgomery says that when she achieves an alpha state of consciousness through meditation, unseen forces manipulate her fingers across the page. In this way, spirits of the cosmic realm unveil to her New Age lessons on the divinity of humankind, reincarnation, and the world to come. Montgomery is also known for introducing demons to the world. She calls these evil spirits "walk-ins," claiming these spirits are reincarnated souls from the astral dimension who have inhabited the bodies of unwilling human hosts who are forced to serve as occult leaders.

In her writings, Montgomery portrays Christians as ignorant, small-minded people who refuse to accept the "truth" about the teachings of Christ. She believes Christ was a New Age guru who taught that people are gods and are one with the universal life force. Montgomery claims that the self-serving religious hierarchy of the church removed important New Age teachings from the Bible in the sixth century. She holds that the church's rejection of reincarnation and necromancy is evidence of an underdeveloped consciousness. Christians are oblivious to the spiritual evolution of humankind and are therefore unfit for the coming kingdom of the Aquarian Age.

Montgomery predicts that as humanity enters the twenty-first century, the world will experience a radical positional shift in the cosmos. This momentous event will result in a period of chaos, destruction, and spiritual cleansing. Christianity will be eradicated because believers will enter another dimension of existence. Montgomery says those who survive this time of radical change will continue as Homonoeticus. This new race of people is unencumbered by physical form

and exists in harmonious cooperation with loving spirits from other dimensions. Montgomery says this future world will be characterized by joy, courage, and compassion, and the human race will have achieved enlightenment and universal peace in oneness with the cosmic life force.

*See also:* ALPHA LEVEL, CHRIST-CONSCIOUSNESS, HOMONOETICUS, REINCARNATION, WALK-IN

## MOON, SUN MYUNG (b. 1920)

Founder of the Holy Spirit Association for the Unification of World Christianity, otherwise known as the Unification Church. Moon was born in Pyungan Buk-do, North Korea. In 1945, Moon began his public ministry. In 1953, he outlined his spiritual beliefs in a book entitled *Divine Principle* and established the Unification Church in 1954.

During the Korean War, communist officials arrested him several times, but United Nations' forces eventually released him from prison. In the years that followed, he won many converts to his cult from Korea, Japan, and the United States. In 1982, a U.S. court convicted Moon of tax evasion and imprisoned him. However, a large number of religious organizations charged that the government was guilty of harassing him.

New Age adherents are quite sympathetic to Moon's beliefs. He advocates the unification of Eastern and Western religions. He claims to be on a mission from God in which he is endeavoring to finish what Christ failed to do, by bringing salvation to the spiritual *and* physical dimensions of people. Within the Unification Church, Moon is called the "Lord of the Second Advent" and the "promised Messiah."

Unificationists, or "Moonies," are instructed that they can only reach God through their "Master," Sun Myung Moon. This teaching resembles New Age ideas of communing with the universal essence through a spirit guide or ascended master.

*See also:* SALVATION, UNIFICATION CHURCH

## Mormon, The Book of

One of the sacred texts of the Church of Jesus Christ of Latter-Day Saints, or Mormons. According to their founder, Joseph Smith (1805–1844), God the Father and God the Son materialized before him in 1820, having chosen him to bring a restoration of true Christianity. In 1823, the angel Moroni allegedly appeared at Smith's bedside, repeating the divine commission to establish the restored Christian church. In 1827, the heavenly messenger presented Smith with gold plates inscribed with Egyptian hieroglyphics. Smith's "translation" of the plates continued until 1829, resulting in *The Book of Mormon* which was published in 1830.

Other standard sacred writings of the Mormons are *Doctrine and Covenants* and *The Pearl of Great Price*. According to Mormon doctrine, a group of people migrated from Jerusalem to America around 600 B.C. After Christ rose from the dead, He appeared to these people in the Western Hemisphere. *The Book of Mormon* claims divine authority for interpreting Old Testament prophecy, asserts that it is part of the new covenant to Israel, and witnesses to the truth of the Christian gospel. In his writings, Smith claimed that John the Baptist had bestowed the priesthood of Aaron upon him, authorizing him to speak and act on the Lord's behalf, thus assuring the salvation of humanity. Smith maintained that the true Christian church had ceased to exist long ago, and that he and his followers were sent to restore it to its rightful place of honor. Mormons teach that God continues to reveal His "word" to individual faith-seekers, to leaders of local Mormon churches, and especially to the President-Prophet of this Utah-based church.

New Age adherents have endorsed a number of doctrines taught in *The Book of Mormon*. Occultists claim that new revelation occurs continually today. They also assert that other faith traditions speak for "God" in addition to the Christian church. Leaders applaud the assumption that people can become gods by progressing from one spiritual state of existence to another throughout eternity. New Age adherents embrace the idea that salvation (according to their definition) depends on the performance of good works, the acquisition of wisdom, and the seeking of enlightenment.

*See also:* BIBLE, MORMONISM, URIM AND THUMMIM

## MORMONISM

The teachings and way of life advocated by Joseph Smith (1805–1844) in *The Book of Mormon* and perpetuated in the religious movement he founded. The group contains two major branches. The Church of Jesus Christ of Latter-Day Saints is headquartered in Salt Lake City, Utah, while The Reorganized Church of Jesus Christ of Latter-Day Saints makes its headquarters in Independence, Missouri. The members of the movement are often called Mormons or Latter-Day Saints. About two-thirds of their 7.7 million members live in the United States, principally in the western part of the country. The remaining one-third are scattered throughout the world, especially in Latin America.

According to Joseph Smith, God the Father and God the Son materialized before him in 1820 and revealed that they would use him to bring about a restoration of true Christianity. In 1823, the angel Moroni allegedly appeared at Smith's bedside to repeat the divine commission about establishing the restored Christian church. In 1827, the heavenly messenger supposedly gave Smith some thin metal plates, gold in appearance, inscribed in an Egyptian hieroglyphic language. Smith's "translation" of the plates continued until 1829. The resulting *Book of Mormon* was published in 1830.

Not long afterward, Smith and his associates founded The Church of Jesus Christ of Latter-Day Saints. Smith and a small group of followers settled in Kirtland, Ohio, and Jackson County, Missouri. However religious persecution forced the group to relocate first to northern Missouri and then to Nauvoo, Illinois. Mounting tensions with nearby residents climaxed when an angry mob murdered Smith in Carthage, Illinois, on June 27, 1844. The church then appointed

Brigham Young (1801–1877) as its new leader. Between 1846 and 1847, he led a group of Mormons from Nauvoo across the plains and mountains of the American West to the Great Salt Lake Basin. Here this branch of the Mormon church experienced steady growth.

The standard sacred writings of the Mormons are the Christian Bible, *The Book of Mormon, Doctrine and Covenants,* and *The Pearl of Great Price.* According to Mormon doctrine, a group of people migrated from Jerusalem to America around 600 B.C. After Christ rose from the dead, He appeared to these people in the Western Hemisphere. *The Book of Mormon* purports to be an interpretation of Old Testament prophecy, part of the new covenant to Israel, and another witness to the truth of the Christian gospel. In his writings, Smith claimed that John the Baptist had bestowed the priesthood of Aaron upon him, giving him the authority to speak and act in the name of the Lord, thereby assuring the salvation of humanity. Smith maintained that the Christian church had long ceased to exist, and it behooved him and his followers to restore it to its rightful place. Mormons teach that God continues to reveal His word to individual faith seekers, to leaders of local Mormon churches, and especially to the President-Prophet of the Utah-based church.

Latter-Day Saints believe that the entire universe is inhabited by a multitude of gods. They procreate spirit children who are clothed with bodies on different planets. Mormons teach that God was a spirit being who became a mortal named Adam and then evolved into an exalted being, or Adam-god. Mormons also believe people eternally progress from a spiritual state to mortality, and then to an afterlife where the resurrected will receive a heavenly reward. Church leaders baptize members at the age of eight or older. In fact, Mormons are encouraged to undergo numerous vicarious baptismal rites on behalf of their dead ancestors. At one time, Mormons practiced polygamy to give spirit beings the chance to become incarnate, and eventually achieve godhood. Latter-Day Saints believe that through continued good work within the church, people can obtain salvation and ascendancy to godhood.

New Age adherents have endorsed a number of Mormon doctrines. Occultists claim that new revelation occurs continually today. Occultists assert that other faith traditions, besides the Christian church, speak for "God." Cult leaders applaud the idea that people either are or can become gods, and that people eternally progress from one spiritual state of existence to another. New Age adherents embrace the idea that salvation, regardless of its definition, is linked to the performance of good works, the acquisition of wisdom, and the seeking of enlightenment.

*See also:* ANGEL; ATONEMENT; *Mormon, The Book of*

## MOTHER EARTH

From earliest times, people have venerated the earth as the creator, nourisher, and ultimate destroyer of humankind. She is also referred to as Gaea, Mother Nature, and the Mother Goddess. Ceremonies were designed to worship her greatness, appease her anger, and harness the forces of the universe.

The countercultural revolution of the 1960s revitalized interest in the worship of Mother Earth. Occult leaders promised initiates they would obtain peace, power, and wisdom if they were able to reach the essence of Mother Earth laying dormant within them. New Age organizations have arisen to protect this cosmic goddess, and devotees have invented unofficial holidays to worship her.

Advocates claim that Mother Earth has been seriously abused by the unhindered growth of human civilization. They say the increase in natural disasters is the harsh plea of the cosmic goddess who is warning people about the devastating consequences of their apathy to environmental issues. New Age adherents insist the only way to cleanse Mother Earth of these global abuses is by bringing about the enlightenment of the human race.

*See also:* ECOFEMINISM; GAEA; GODDESS WORSHIP; LOVELOCK, JAMES E.

# MUELLER, ROBERT

A New Age educator, social theorist, and author. For nearly forty years, Mueller served in administrative offices of the United Nations (U.N.). As Assistant Secretary General of the United Nations, Mueller was in charge of thirty-two specialized agencies dedicated to promoting world cooperation. In 1972, he helped found Planetary Citizens. This New Age organization focuses on examining alternative ecological lifestyles, bringing the public into planetary consciousness, and influencing global leaders to accept the idea of establishing a one-world government. Mueller spent his later years serving as chancellor at the University of Peace in Puerto Rico. In his book *New Genesis,* he delineates the steps humanity needs to take to bring about global spirituality.

When Mueller was forty-six and working in the office of the U.N. Secretary General, a Burmese Buddhist named U Thant converted him to New Age ideals. As Mueller's interests in the occult developed, he became open to the influence of Djwhal Khul, a spirit who claimed to be an ancient Tibetan bringing "wisdom" from alternate planes of existence. Mueller believes that the future of humankind depends on the transcendence of all national, economic, and religious differences. He says the time has come for people to prepare for union with the cosmic essence. As society evolves into a global community, all people must yield themselves to the universal life force. Mueller advocates establishment of a one-world religion that transcends all differences and joins all peoples with the great divine Spirit. He believes a coming messiah will unite the world in a divine government. This New Age christ supposedly will help people get in touch with their divine self and usher in the Aquarian Age of global peace, harmony, and enlightenment.

*See also:* DJWHAL KHUL, GLOBALISM, ONE-WORLD IDEAL, PLANETARY CITIZENS, UNITED NATIONS

# MUSIC, NEW AGE

The rhythms, melodies, and harmonies produced by composers and performers to alter or enhance people's state of consciousness and to aid in meditation. New Age music is characterized by uplifting themes, nonlinear song forms, harmonic consonance, and contemplative melodies. Musicians use sounds from nature, traditional ethnic songs, and acoustic, electric, and electronic instruments to create an ambient effect. New Age music originated in instrumental pieces produced in the mid-1970s. Windham Hill, which is the leading company producing New Age music, began in 1976. It typically sold its product in health food stores and occult shops. Today mainstream companies also produce synthesized vocal, instrumental, and children's records in what has proven to be a multimillion dollar industry.

New Age music is sometimes referred to as "audio valium," a stress reducer. Serious artists insist that the intent of the sound is far more important than the music itself. They say the listening experience will be enhanced by meditation and occultic practices. New Age artists have claimed that their music is the highest form of spiritual sound on earth and aids in the journey to enlightenment. They believe their ethereal music creates a bridge between the conscious and the subconscious, helping listeners to draw closer to their divine self and unite with the Universal Mind. Occultists say New Age music will play a fundamental role in the transformation of the world because it will condition people to accept occultic philosophy, achieve inner peace, and attain enlightenment.

"Inner harmony" music is most in tune with New Age philosophy. The gentle, flowing music with its repetitive, unstructured monotones is designed to create an environment in which listeners are able to focus on their meditative and relaxation techniques. Artists claim they are aligning themselves with universal energy forces to produce music devoid of tension or demands. "Progressive" music is also in tune with New Age philosophy. Its mellow rhythms are combined with high intensity electronic instruments to stimulate listeners' senses. Some think the music alters the brain's alpha waves or creates psychic vibrations. Others say it hypnotizes the analytical part of the brain and invigorates the creative part of the mind with intuitive messages from alternate dimensions of reality.

New Age music is sometimes used to help patients recover from depression, mental illness, and physical ailments. In some instances the sound is applied directly to the patient's skin in an attempt to synchronize the music with the vibrations emanating from the human body. Holistic healers say life-giving energy is released when patients hear the appropriate tones, frequencies, and beats. The New Age music harmonizes their internal biorhythms with the Universal Mind. In other instances, patients listen to music filled with subliminal messages of an occultic nature. The idea is to reprogram thinking to achieve greater self-awareness and become attuned to the truths conveyed by spirit guides.

*See also:* ALTERED STATE, OM, PEACE, SOUND THERAPY

## MYSTERY

The subjective feeling of mystery has fascinated worshipers in all religions and cults, including historic Christianity. However, the concept of mystery can take two very different forms, either of which can lead to error.

First, mystery inspires awe through the contemplation of the unknown and hidden. It prompts people to look beyond what can be understood and imagined to what is accessible only through faith. In this way, a sense of mystery relates closely to mystical experience. Christianity deals in the great mystery of a God who is transcendent as well as imminent. In the New Testament, Paul describes the gospel as a mystery God has both revealed and hidden (e.g., 1 Cor. 2:1; Col. 1:26–27). Paul also finds mystery in iniquity (2 Thess. 2:7).

Second, mystery feeds a human passion for secret knowledge. Through this secret knowledge people seek to gain access to a higher plane, to eternal life, or, through magic formulas, to the supernatural. In the Greco-Roman culture that Paul addressed more people followed mystery cults than all other forms of religion combined. Common to these

cults was a belief that life after death was attainable through secret knowledge. The Roman orator Cicero (106–43 B.C.) proclaimed that the Eleusinian mystery cults of Athens were the reason one could have joy and hope. The penalty for revealing details of cultic rituals was death, but enough details leaked out that it is known that they used dance, drama, and mime.

Secret cants, oaths, esoteric knowledge, and initiation rituals remain central to mystery-based religions and philosophies. Mystery plays a vital role in such diverse modern groups as Wicca, Satanism, Voodoo, and Santeria cults, the Ku Klux Klan, Muslim Sufism, Scientology, and Rosicrucianism. The Masonic movement has gloried in secret knowledge and rites since the days of the medieval craft guilds.

While Greco-Roman mystery cults have passed from the scene, others have proven to be incredibly durable. Among the most enduring are the Zoroastrians, Christian docetic theologies, Jewish Kabbalism, and divination and astrology rituals. Even the ancient Egyptian cult of the dead, founded about 2400 B.C., has enjoyed considerable interest during the twentieth century.

*See also:* ALTERED STATE, DECREE, MYSTICISM, POWER OBJECT, PURIFICATION, SPIRIT GUIDES, SYMBOLISM, TRANSCENDENCE

## MYSTICAL TRAVELER

A guiding spirit who assists people in their journey to enlightenment. The mystical traveler exists in the sublevels of human consciousness. Advocates believe this entity can help people reach a state of perfection, thereby avoiding the endless cycles of reincarnation. Popularizing the idea of mystical travelers is the New Age educator John Roger Hinkins, who operates out of a holistic center called Baraka in Santa Monica, California. He uses six-day insight transformational seminars to introduce people to their guiding spirit. Strict disciplinary methods and various New Age techniques help attendees meet their mystical traveler. This guide will aid them in the transcendence of their souls.

*See also:* AVATAR, ENTITY, SPIRIT GUIDES

## MYSTICISM

The view that awareness of Ultimate Reality may be gained through a heightened state of mental perception and excitement. The mystical experience is designed to take participants beyond the boundaries of reality through a succession of physical sensations, resulting in the perception of direct communication with the inner god. The goal is to become awakened to the deity within, thereby uniting with the universal life force. Sharing in this common objective are the Ultimate Reality of the New Age, the satori of Zen, the samadhi of Yoga, and the nirvana of Hinduism.

New Age mysticism gained its initial popularity during the 1960s. Eastern mystics promised their followers personal freedom, spiritual fulfillment, and a limitless array of innate abilities. Even today, proponents tell initiates they can achieve altered states of consciousness through self-discipline, diet, meditation, and the use of hallucinogenic drugs. They introduce these initiates to ascended masters who will guide them in their journey to enlightenment. New Age mystics report feelings of euphoria, peace, and universal oneness, as well as a renewal of energy and a greater appreciation for the earth's beauty. They assert that universal life forces have given them intuitive bursts of insight and creativity.

*See also:* ALTERED STATE, NEW AGE MOVEMENT, SATORI, TRANSCENDENTAL MEDITATION

## MYTHOLOGY

Symbolic folk stories and beliefs that help a people develop ultimate values and understand the cosmos. Myths concern deities, ancestors, and legendary heroes. Traditionally a myth has been thought of as a story not based in historical fact. Technically, however, facticity is irrelevant to whether a character or story is mythological. How a culture uses the story makes it myth. This modern understanding easily leads to serious misunderstanding, however. The definition sets all religious beliefs within the "myth" category. Religious "myths" are more easily dismissed as mere cultural elements.

Those who study ancient folktales have noted a similarity in themes among quite dissimilar peoples. This has been explained as a sign that all people face the same anxieties and conflicts and have similar wishes and dreams. Further, some situations, values, and concerns are common among cultures.

The New Age explanation is that myths originate in the deepest level of the human psyche the universal storehouse of wisdom residing in the collective human unconscious. If myths hold symbolic truths that leap the barriers of language and culture, people can use them to journey deep within the psyche. The stories are a way to drink from the vast wisdom of the ascended masters, and a means of bridging the cycle of life, death, and rebirth.

This also makes the myth a cosmic reservoir of archetypal images. In one theory, when a people strongly holds to a common mythology, cultural barriers will go down, the world will unite, and humanity will move toward aquarian enlightenment.

*See also:* CAMPBELL, JOSEPH; SYMBOLISM; TRANSFORMATION

# N

## NATION OF ISLAM
*See:* BLACK MUSLIMS

## NATIVE AMERICANS

Native inhabitants of the Americas, probably of Asian origin. Although the myths of Native Americans are as distinct as their cultures, they share animistic ties to the land, plants, and animals through belief in a powerful mystical essence. Tribal members thought it important to be at one with nature by opening up their minds and allowing vibrations of the world to become their own. A variety of spirits have been called upon for supernatural powers and secrets of witchcraft.

The shaman, or medicine man, was usually the tribal spiritual leader. His task was to manipulate the supernatural forces of the universe, both good and evil, and to divine the unknown. The shaman wielded great influence within his tribe. Amid a pageant of smoke, costumes, and drugs, he sometimes used psychic surgery and hand trembling to find and eliminate an offending spirit within a person. The shaman played the role of herbalist, sorcerer, and magician as he sought to reharmonize people with the universe, curing their ills.

Native Americans believed in a pantheon of spirits, including a master creator. They also believed in a heavenly afterlife that was similar to earth and reserved for skillful hunters and women. According to many traditions, religious rituals freed the mind from evil and enabled people to tap the powers of guardian spirit guides through life. In Native American folklore, the Great Spirit is a reference to a permeating energy force or sun god. Mother Earth is a reference to a cosmic and loving benefactor.

The mystical beliefs of Native Americans have resonated among New Age adherents.

Techniques used in divining and healing remain popular. These include star gazing, performing ritual sacrifices, and wearing amulets, as well as dancing and chanting. New Age adherents are particularly interested in medicine wheels, sweat lodges, and rockwalls, erected long ago as sacred sites and later abandoned. These locations reveal more information about ancient philosophies and ceremonies.

*See also:* ANIMISM, MEDICINE WHEEL, MOTHER EARTH, SHAMAN, SPIRITISM, SUN DANCE

## NATURALISM

The theory or philosophy that nature is the sum of all existence. This includes those things that are observable, predictable, and of material reality. Therefore spiritual or supernatural causes do not exist. Taken a step further, this means that neither God nor any immaterial dimension to human life exists—nor does life after death. Because the universe is only matter and energy, it operates in a deterministic fashion. This means such things as human freedom, absolute moral values, or an overall purpose for history and humanity do not exist.

Many New Age adherents would be considered naturalists in a broad sense, not a strict sense, because the true naturalist does not believe in any spiritual realm. However New Age adherents are prone to invoke the natural forces within the cosmos to achieve health, wealth, and success. In place of individuality and freedom, they emphasize oneness with the universe and the goal of losing individual identity within the great cosmic consciousness. In this scheme of thinking, objective moral standards for distinguishing good from evil do not exist. Proponents consider everything relative and subjective. New

Age adherents consider the biblical concept of an all-powerful and all-wise heavenly creator to be a myth. They believe people are continuously evolving into a higher form of life. Their ultimate goal is to achieve divine enlightenment.

*See also:* CREATION, EVIL, SIN


## NATUROPATHY

A system of treating diseases that relies exclusively on natural remedies. Naturopathy avoids the use of drugs and surgery. Adherents emphasize the use of natural agents (air, water, and sunshine), natural products (herbs and vitamins), and physical means (dieting, massages, and electrical treatments). In 1901, a German osteopath named Benedict Lust (1872–1945) introduced the concept of naturopathy. He based his system on the same holistic healing practices found today in New Age therapies, such as homeopathy, acupuncture, and reflexology. All these approaches make the same assumption that disease results from an imbalance or obstruction in the flow of the universal life force within a person. Holistic healing says that by breaking down blockages in the energy flow, perfect balance can be restored throughout the body and with the cosmic essence.

*See also:* ACUPUNCTURE, ALLOPATHY, HERBALISM, HOLISM, NATURALISM


## NAZISM

*See:* HITLER, ADOLF


## NEAR-DEATH EXPERIENCE

A phenomenon experienced by people who are clinically dead for short periods of time. Despite the variety of people who are near-death survivors, many, but not all, report having similar and extraordinary experiences. They typically remember hearing their physician pronounce them dead. These individuals report seeing themselves outside their physical body. Like bystanders, they watch as a medical team tries to resuscitate their corpse. They relate hearing a loud buzzing or ringing sound and feel as if they were moving through a dark void or tunnel.

As the near-death experience continues, the survivors recall others coming to meet and help them. They also remember seeing spirits of deceased relatives and friends, and especially a spirit who is loving, warm, and indescribably radiant. This spirit shows them an instantaneous and sweeping view of key events in their life, and somehow nonverbally asks them to appraise the way they lived.

If the near-death experience continues, the survivors report coming to a barrier that some researchers think symbolizes the boundary separating earthly life from the next life. The survivors learn this is not the time for them to die, so they return to earth. They remember not wanting to come back because of experiencing deep feelings of peace, joy, and love.

Near-death experiences were also known in antiquity but were generally dismissed as occult phenomena. Scientific opinion began to change in the early 1970s when Elizabeth Kubler-Ross and Raymond Moody conducted further research into the phenomenon. Despite continued serious study, no generally accepted theory explains what causes a near-death experience. Some label it as the result of a psychological defense mechanism. The person becomes psychologically detached, not wanting to admit imminent death. Others say drugs, such as anesthetics or hallucinogens, produce the experience. Still others think the person experiences a seizure-like neural firing pattern in the temporal lobe of the brain.

New Age adherents believe near-death episodes are related to an out-of-body experience called astral projection, an altered state of consciousness. Occultists hold that these people learn about their past lives as well as the relative nature of good and evil. As a result of encountering the great cosmic spirit, survivors supposedly have a precognitive glimpse into the future. They have undergone a rebirth of their psyche, giving them an enlightened view of their place in the universe and their union with the permeating life force.

Upon returning from their near-death experience, some people experience feelings of depression as they attempt to integrate what they have learned into traditional Christian beliefs. Some survivors confidently relate that ascended masters and extraterrestrials will benevolently guide them, reveal hidden truths, and teach them how to manipulate positive and negative energy forces. Numerous people claim they now have psychic abilities, along with an increased interest in alternate dimensions of spiritual reality. They report no longer fearing death because they regard it as a transition from one astral plane of existence to another.

*See also:* ASTRAL PROJECTION; DEATH; KUBLER-ROSS, ELIZABETH; SPIRIT GUIDES

# NECROMANCY

The practice of conjuring up spirits of the dead in order to reveal the future or influence the course of events. Necromancy, which literally means "divination of corpses," was common among ancient pagan cults. These cults believed that dead spirits could redeem themselves from sins committed in their former lives by serving the living. This belief still permeates some New Age cults. These cults use demonic rituals and techniques to summon entities that can provide omens about the future or secrets from the past.

*See also:* DIVINATION, MEDIUM, SPIRITISM

# NEUROLINGUISTICS

A psychological programming technique that uses linguistics and physiology to diagnose and modify behavior patterns. Neurolinguistic therapists believe that by observing and interpreting a patient's body language, word patterns, pitch tones, and eye movements, they can determine and treat unconscious phobias and insecurities. The behavior modification process requires patients to enter altered states of consciousness before reprogramming can begin. Advocates claim those experiencing this trancelike state meet their "higher self" and become more enlightened about their place in the universe.

*See also:* ALTERED STATE, HIGHER SELF

# NEW AGE ART
*See:* ART, NEW AGE

# NEW AGE BIBLE
*See:* BIBLE, NEW AGE

# NEW AGE MEDICINE
*See:* MEDICINE, NEW AGE

# NEW AGE MOVEMENT (NAM)

A broad coalition of various networking organizations that believe in a New World Order, a new world (pantheistic) religion, and a New Age christ. The NAM received its basic name from astrology. Proponents claim a new age of peace and harmony will replace the current world system. Various terms describe the NAM such as Aquarian Conspiracy, New World Consciousness, Cosmic Consciousness, and Cosmic Humanism. Other terms include Mystical Humanism, Human Potential Movement, and Holistic Health Movement. Many symbols represent the NAM, such as the rainbow, pyramid, triangle, eye in triangle, unicorn, and Pegasus. Others include concentric circles, rays of light, yin/yang symbol, and the third eye or all-seeing eye.

The basic belief system of the NAM includes an impersonal "god" (or force); an eternal universe; the illusory nature of matter; the cyclical nature of life; the necessity of reincarnations; the evolution of humankind; the presence of continuing revelations from beings beyond this world; a christ who is a spiritually attuned master, guru, swami, yogi, or avatar; the union of all people with "god" or the Universal Mind; the need for transcendental meditation; and such occult practices as astrology, mediums. Adherents believe in vegetarianism, one-world government, and syncretism—the unifying of all religions.

The basic goals of the NAM are to establish a one-world political and economic system (globalism); establish a one-world religion based on the guidance and thoughts of ascended masters, masters of wisdom, masters of the universe, and spirit guides; establish a world leader, teacher, and savior known in occult circles as Lord Maitreya; achieve world peace and attain godhood through self-realization techniques; indoctrinate the next generation of children with NAM beliefs; discredit Christianity as obsolete; demonstrate that Christians are a dangerous menace to society; and urge society to isolate and eliminate Christians.

New Age adherents say people have forgotten their true divine nature. Because of Christianity, people are not aware that they are fundamentally connected to "God" and have emanated from "God," the life force underlying nature. They claim people have been deluded into thinking they are separated from each other, from nature, and from the existential substance beneath all things. New Age adherents propose a paradigm shift in people's thinking as the solution. They try to convince people that everything is fundamentally divine because everything flows from the universal self or "God."

This Ultimate Reality is not a lifeless energy. but a cosmic consciousness. Such mind-expanding techniques as yoga and meditation help people experience their oneness with the universal life force. As they learn to use these techniques, their minds will actualize reality. People are on a spiritual journey to perfection. Humankind's long-term goal is to achieve enlightenment, thereby earning release from the endless cycles of reincarnation. New Age adherents encourage people to get in touch with their spirit guides, also called ascended masters, disembodied spirits, angels, and UFOs. These entities allegedly help people walk the path leading to psychic transformation, as well as uniting them with the cosmic consciousness.

*See also:* AQUARIUS, AGE OF; HUMAN POTENTIAL MOVEMENT; ONE-WORLD IDEAL; THEOSOPHY

## NEW AGE MUSIC
*See:* MUSIC, NEW AGE

## NEW AGE POLITICS
*See:* POLITICS, NEW AGE

## NEW AGE SCIENCE
*See:* SCIENCE, NEW AGE

## NEW GROUP OF WORLD SERVERS (NGWS)

An elite fraternity whose members consider themselves the custodians of The Plan, an occultic blueprint for world domination. In 1925, the spiritual entity known as Djwhal Khul told occultist Alice Bailey (1880–1949) to establish NGWS. Bailey considered the members of the NGWS as the elite guards of the coming Aquarian Age. Along with the NGWS, she established World Goodwill, the political lobbying aspect of the New Age Movement, and Lucis Trust, the publishing house that produces and distributes occultic literature.

The members of NGWS work together to prepare the world for the reappearance of Lucifer as the New Age christ. They believe that when he establishes his global kingdom, they will be corulers with him. The primary headquarters for the NGWS are found in London, New York, and Geneva. Each office complex is governed by the Hierarchy. This group of spiritual masters, whose messages are channeled through demons, believes their destiny is to replace the old Piscean Age with the new Aquarian Age.

Members of the group believe this New World Order will solve all the problems facing humanity and enable people to achieve godhood. Bailey taught that the New Age will be made up of two categories of people, the thinkers and the servers. The thinkers are represented by the average New Age follower. The servers, such as members of NGWS, are leaders from every walk of life who dutifully recruit and train the thinkers.

*See also:* BAILEY, ALICE ANN; DJWHAL

KHUL; LUCIS TRUST; PLAN, THE; WORLD GOODWILL

## NEW JERUSALEM, CHURCH OF THE
*See:* SWEDENBORGISM

## NEW THOUGHT
A metaphysical philosophy of mental healing first promoted by Warren Felt Evans (1817–1889) in the latter part of the nineteenth century. This eclectic viewpoint says that all human ailments are a result of mistaken beliefs, and people have the ability to heal themselves from within. When the human mind draws upon the body's latent divine powers, problem-solving, stress relief, and physical healing allegedly take place. This New Age approach to therapy lays at the heart of such cults as Mary Baker Eddy's Christian Science Church and Charles and Myrtle Filmore's Unity School of Christianity.

*See also:* CHRISTIAN SCIENCE, HOLISM, UNITY SCHOOL OF CHRISTIANITY

## NEW WORLD TRANSLATION
The official Bible translation for the Jehovah's Witnesses. The version is officially entitled *The New World Translation of the Hebrew Scriptures* and *The New World Translation of the Christian Greek Scriptures*. Produced in 1950, it is far from a genuine translation of the original texts. Instead, it renders the Bible into the mold of Jehovah's Witnesses theology. Though the title claims to be a translation, leaders did not disclose the names of the translators or their credentials as competent Bible scholars.

*See also:* JEHOVAH'S WITNESSES, WATCHTOWER BIBLE AND TRACT SOCIETY

## NIHILISM
The belief that established values and beliefs are baseless, and that existence is pointless and futile. The Russian novelist Ivan Turgenev (1818–1883) first popularized the concept in his book entitled *Fathers and Sons*. Nihilism came to signify the complete rejection of tradition, morality, authority, and the social order that codified them. Proponents argue that nothing exists, nothing is knowable or can be communicated. What cannot be verified by sense-experience is unintelligible. Nihilists claim that morality is the product of either social conditioning or mere feeling.

New Age adherents reflect a nihilistic view of life when they say nothing can be proven scientifically and moral absolutes do not exist. Many occultists would agree with nihilists that contemporary society exists apart from the harmony of nature and must be replaced by a New World Order. Like nihilists, New Age adherents are striving to liberate humanity and transform society. They believe existing political, social, and religious institutions, especially Christianity, must be eliminated in order to ensure the evolutionary advancement of humankind and its eventual union with the cosmic consciousness.

*See also:* DEATH, NEW AGE MOVEMENT, VALUES CLARIFICATION

## NINE, THE
Entities from Sirius, a binary star in the constellation Canis Major. Richard Price, the cofounder of the Esalen Institute, first named these spirits "The Nine." They supposedly channeled New Age messages of wisdom through an English woman named Jenny O'Connor, who lived at the Institute. Price advertised that "The Nine" were active in gestalt sessions and courses offered by his organization. Some think these entities are mere inventions of O'Connor's unconscious psyche, while others believe they are genuine spirits from the ethereal dimension. In either case, these respected "residents" of the Institute are held in high esteem and assist the organization's leadership in making management decisions.

*See also:* DEMON, ESALEN INSTITUTE, TRANCE CHANNELING

# NIRVANA

The state of being in which personal desire and individual consciousness are extinguished. Nirvana, which in Sanskrit means "act of extinguishing," is characterized by a release from the endless cycles of reincarnation and the extinction of individual consciousness. The term also refers to a place or state of oblivion to care, pain, or external reality. This condition of enlightenment and release is allegedly achieved in this life through spiritual and physical exercises, or after death. Different sects use other terms to refer to the same concept as nirvana. It is *satori* in Zen, *samadi* in yoga, and *fana* in Sufism. New Age adherents refer to nirvana as enlightenment or Cosmic Consciousness. They claim it represents the point at which people realize their personal divinity.

*See also:* BUDDHISM, HEAVEN, KARMA, REINCARNATION

# NOSTRADAMUS, MICHAEL (1503–1566)

A French physician, astrologer, and author of a collection of prophecies. Michael Nostradamus was born Michel de Nostredame, the son of Jewish merchants in Saint Remy, France. When Nostradamus was a young boy, his parents were forced to convert to Catholicism. By his mid-twenties, Nostradamus became a successful physician. A plague swept through western Europe, killing his wife and children. His patients lost faith in the medical abilities of a physician who could not save his own family. Then the church court in his area threatened a renewed inquisition because of the Protestant Reformation, so Nostradamus fled.

Nurturing a growing interest in alchemy, astrology, magic, and the occult, by 1550 Nostradamus resettled in the small village of Salon where he began to write his occultic prophecies. He completely withdrew from the medical profession and soon developed a reputation for compiling almanacs filled with timely predictions. By 1555 he had collected his predictions into a single volume entitled *Centuries,* which was said to reveal the fate of humanity some two thousand years into the future. The work consists of ten books, each containing one hundred quatrains, or four-line verses. Nostradamus deliberately made the quatrains ambiguous to protect himself from his enemies.

Nostradamus enjoyed a loyal following among the French royalty, notably Catherine de' Medici. Although Nostradamus was not known for his magical powers, legendary stories of conjured spirits and magic mirrors grew because of his advisory position to the queen. Henry II also played an important role in the growing popularity of Nostradamic predictions because the monarch's death is reputedly foretold in a quatrain of *Centuries.* Some claim the prophecies of Nostradamus foresaw the Great Fire of London in 1666, the deaths of several monarchs, obscure facts concerning the French Revolution, the rise of Napoleon and Hitler, and World War II. Though his writings are void of details about events, *Centuries* remains a classic of New Age literature.

*See also:* PRECOGNITION

# NUMBER OF THE BEAST

The number 666, appearing in Revelation 13:18. In John's vision about the end times, he saw a hideous creature emerge from the land to serve as the lieutenant of another creature that had risen from the sea (Rev. 13:1, 11). The beast from the land will force everyone to have a mark placed on their right hands or on their foreheads (Rev. 7:3). Whatever the nature of this mark, it will signify loyalty to the beast from the sea (Rev. 13:12–16).

In the apocalyptic vision, the beast from the land was seen to require that all people have this mark before they could buy or sell, which would place great economic pressure on God's chosen people to worship the beast from the sea. Refusal to do so would invite their death (Rev. 13:17). John describes the mark as the name of the first beast in numeric form. The number 666 stands for a person or possibly for fallen humanity (Rev. 13:18).

In Hebrew numerology the number of "man" is 6, leading scholars to speculate that the enigmatic number could refer to a human attempt to be like the triune God. Satan and the two beasts form Revelation's unholy trinity. In Jewish thought the number of God's perfection is 7.

Or the number could be a code name based on the numerical value of the letters, a custom in Jewish numerology that John's hearers might have understood. Some have identified the three sixes with Nero, one of Rome's most degenerate emperors.

New Age writings have sought to reinterpret the number 666 to serve their version of the apocalypse. A standard view is that the number points to the New Age christ, Lord Maitreya, who will bring about the ultimate transformation of human consciousness. Occultists claim that 666 is the sacred number of divine light, the driving force of spiritual evolution that enables individual wills to join the divine. Repetition of the number is symbolic of the perfect manifestation of nature in the mental, astral, and physical planes of existence. Neopagans say that 666 is symbolic of sexual union between the great Mother Goddess, represented by the triangle, with the universal god of forces. This results in the manifestation of evil that they claim emanates from the unenlightened prior to the dawning of the New Age.

Some claim that 666 is the mystical number that will unlock the powers of the ethereal realm so that people can reach enlightenment. New Age adherents emphasize the triangular balance of universal forces represented by 666. The number empowers them to communicate light and sound vibrations to beings of superior intelligence on this planet and to those who exist in other dimensions of reality. If enough initiates meditate on 666, the christ of the Aquarian Age will come to earth. He will enable humankind to make a quantum leap in consciousness and experience global peace.

*See also:* ANTICHRIST, BABYLON, BEAST, NUMEROLOGY, TRIANGLE

## NUMEROLOGY

The study of the occult meanings of numbers and their influence on life. Numerology is based largely on the belief that the universe is governed by numerical laws, to which all things are harmoniously related. Therefore the karmic cycles of birth and death are accompanied by exact numerological conditions that serve as hidden keys to the past, present, and future. Jewish kabbalists taught that numerological mysticism should be combined with the enigmatic power of words. This led them to devise a twenty-two letter Hebrew alphabet, which provided the keys to universal transcendence. Some contemporary occultists attach numerological significance to colors.

Every person's birthday reputedly has a particular astrological sign, as well as its corresponding number. This number symbolizes specific occultic powers and qualities. In order to obtain an individual's significant numbers, the numbers of the person's birthday are added together and combined until a single digit can be reached (for example, March 10 is $3 + 10 = 13$; $1 + 3 = 4$). After determining the numerological significance of each letter, a similar process is applied to the name of the individual (for example, John Doe is $1 + 6 + 8 + 5 + 4 + 6 + 5 = 35$; $3 + 5 = 8$). Once these numbers are determined, adherents believe they can reveal the intellectual acumen, emotional stability, and physical characteristics of the people being examined. These numbers are combined with other numbers, such as those of a date or person, to predict future events.

New Age adherents have also assigned meanings to numbers. One (1) represents ambition, forcefulness, and reason; two (2) represents quietness, modesty, and humanity; three (3) represents the unholy trinity and woman; four (4) represents justice and totality; five (5) represents marriage; six (6) represents perfection, harmonic balance, completion, and light; seven (7) represents life; eight (8) represents new beginnings; nine (9) represents fervency, impulsiveness, power, authority, and the perfected form of the unholy trinity (in other words, $6 + 6 + 6 = 18$; $1 + 8 = 9$); and ten (10) represents fruition and completeness.

Jewish linguistics assigned numbers to

letters of the alphabet, and some symbolic meaning can be attached to some numbers in Scripture as a teaching aid, not in the magical sense that became common in the Kabbalah or in New Age thinking.

*See also:* ASTROLOGY, KABBALAH, KARMA, NUMBER OF THE BEAST, SYMBOLISM

# O

## OCCULTISM

A belief in the existence of secret knowledge and supernormal powers and the possibility of bringing them under human control. The word *occult* is derived from a Latin verb meaning "to cover up" or "to conceal." Therefore the occult delves into what is mysterious, inscrutable, and beyond the realm of ordinary human comprehension. Occultists say hidden resources exist in the universe that are available only to the initiated. Through secret practices, the enlightened are able to tap into the power of the supernatural, get in touch with entities from the astral realm, and foresee and manipulate the future.

The concept of occultism dates at least as far back as ancient Babylon. A worldwide interest in its esoteric knowledge and practices continues. This is especially true among New Age adherents who believe the era of traditional Christian religion has ended, and the Aquarian Age has dawned. Occult leaders recruit and train initiates to develop powers of extrasensory perception (ESP), astral (out-of-body) travel, psychokinesis (moving material objects with the mind apart from any physical means), and levitation. Typical occult practices include sorcery, witchcraft, seances, divination, and astrology, as well as palmistry, divining with rods, pendulums, crystal balls, and other forms of clairvoyance.

*See also:* DEMON, HOLISM,
SPIRIT GUIDES, SPIRITISM,
TRANCE CHANNELING, WITCHCRAFT

## ODIC FORCE

An occultic force of supernatural power believed to produce psychic phenomena when combined with heat or light, magnets or chemical action. New Age adherents refer to the "odic force" when they talk about the human aura. They describe the aura as an energy field emanating from people. This field varies in color and intensity, depending on the condition of the mind, body, and spirit of the individual.

*See also:* AURA, COLOROLOGY,
KIRLIAN PHOTOGRAPHY, PSYCHIC

## OIL

Throughout history, people have used various types of oil as a cosmetic, food, medicine, lighting fuel, an embalming agent, and in various religious rites. Pagan religions used oil to predict the future. Diviners believed it was a bad omen for oil to slick in water, rather than to bead. They took it as a sign that someone would become gravely ill and would use all sorts of incantations to "contain" the disease within the beaded oil. In contemporary witchcraft cults, initiates consider oil as one of the three most important tools in the practice of magic. Along with candles and incense, oil supposedly works to awaken and stimulate the powers of the universe that lie within humankind. Practitioners use specific oils to anoint the body during divination sessions. They believe that by doing this, they can help people obtain wealth, protection, revenge, or power. Some occultists claim that oil is a symbol of the divine ray of understanding received by a perfected soul on a higher plane of existence.

*See also:* AROMATHERAPY, HERBALISM

## OM

A mantra consisting of the sound "om" and used to contemplate Ultimate Reality. This mantra reputedly contains all the primal vibrations of the universe and is considered the queen of all mantras. Hindus believe OM is the irreducible logos through which all existence must pass. They believe the Mother Goddess spoke the sound "om" when creating the earth.

OM is the most commonly heard mantra in Eastern meditation practices. Devotees believe it represents Brahma, the creator god. By chanting OM, they supposedly can summon the deities embodied by its sound. The cosmic vibrations associated with OM allegedly produce an altered state of consciousness within, making divine powers available to those chanting. New Age adherents chant OM to relax while they meditate. Some occultists believe this mantra is the verbal representation of innate divinity. By chanting it, initiates can achieve enlightenment and progress toward union with ultimate truth.

*See also:* GODDESS WORSHIP, HINDUISM, LOGOS, MANTRA

## OMNIPOTENCE

The state of unlimited power and absolute authority and influence. In orthodox Christian theology, only God can be described as all-powerful and able to accomplish His purposes in any realm or dimension. However, absolute power does not mean an infinite ability to act apart from the restraints of reason and morality.

God will not do those things that contradict His essential being and character. Absurdities and immoralities are not within the scope of His absolute power.

New Age adherents hold that all people have the innate ability to be all-powerful. They reason that the human race is inherently divine and has the collective potential to experience unlimited powers. New Age adherents are eager to bring about a harmonic convergence of the world, believing that only then will humanity's true greatness and power be achieved. All who are enlightened will allegedly become islands of omnipotence, possessing the ability to manipulate the fabric of space and time, as well as communicate with visitors from alien worlds.

*See also:* NEW AGE MOVEMENT

## ONE, THE

The impersonal energy or force that permeates the universe and cannot be rationally perceived. Adherents base this belief on the Hindu teaching that Ultimate Reality is an impersonal oneness that is beyond all distinctions, including those of a personal and moral nature. They see the universe as the continuation and extension of cosmic reality. Therefore people can only be in their true selves when they are united with the Universal Mind. Because their essence is identical to that of God, they are inherently divine. A spiritual entity will eventually be revealed on the physical plane of existence as a profound leader and guru.

*See also:* HINDUISM

## ONE HUNDRED FORTY-FOUR THOUSAND

The number of those "sealed" from all the tribes of Israel in Revelation 7:4. The identity of the 144,000 saints in Revelation remains a matter of debate among biblical scholars. Some say the 144,000 (calculated using twelve as a multiple of twelve) symbolizes the fullness of the people of God. Others contend this figure is a specific number of believers that God will in some way shield during a final period of distress or that they are a select group from the twelve tribes of Israel whom God will protect during the second half of the Great Tribulation.

New Age adherents hold that this number represents an army of rainbow warriors who will be the divine leaders in the emerging planetary kingdom. These warriors, after being culled by the Spiritual Hierarchy, were united in the Harmonic Convergence of 1987 and have surrendered to the universal life force. Occultists say the rainbow warriors know the identity of their leader in the coming New World Order. They have pledged allegiance to Satan, or Lucifer, and his human representative, who will eradicate all opposition, establish planetary government, and usher in heaven on earth.

*See also:* LUCIFERIC DOCTRINE, RAINBOW, SPIRITUAL HIERARCHY OF LIGHT

# ONE-WORLD IDEAL

New Age advocates teach that Ultimate Reality is the Oneness that supersedes all separation and differentiation among people. Their supreme objective is for everyone to abandon all forms of self-identity and become identified with, or merged into, the Universal Mind. The establishment of a global democratic order is considered a vital step in bringing about the evolutionary advancement of humankind.

A unified economy is central to this vision for a united humanity and evolutionary advancement. Money is at the heart of this globalist hope, both as an instrument of power and a catalyst for change. Those who control the planetary economic infrastructure will control the currencies, armies, media, and educational institutions of the world.

To promote their ideals, New Age adherents have directed world attention on widespread problems such as war, hunger, poverty, and ecological disasters. These are the tools they intend to use in justifying the reorganization of political power, the redistribution of wealth, and the assimilation of ecumenical religious beliefs.

In order for humanity to make a quantum leap in evolutionary advancement, all people also must be united around the same enlightened religious beliefs and practices. New Age thought defines salvation as acquiring a new perspective concerning the interconnectedness with all things, especially the divine Oneness. Salvation is based on human effort. People achieve perfection and enlightenment through a gradual process. The goal in this life, and in countless reincarnated lives, is to merge into the impersonal Oneness. According to New Age adherents, Jesus is not a savior, nor deliverer from sin, but an example of self-actualization. He demonstrated how to trust in the healing powers of the mind, how to open up to the universal life force, and how to reach the ultimate state of bliss known as nirvana.

The alliance of world religions, based on mutual cooperation and understanding, will eliminate remaining barriers separating people and prohibiting global peace. New Age ideals base this concept on the premise that all religions share certain universal truths that transcend perceived differences. When a sufficient number of initiates recognize the wisdom of these core "truths," a cosmic force will be released, creating a new planetary consciousness of spiritual unity. This new consciousness will replace the ignorance of traditional religion.

Christianity is regarded as a particular enemy in this process, a collection of outdated moral attitudes, no longer applicable to human spiritual needs. The negative energy of Christianity inhibits the arrival of Lord Maitreya. Supporters of the Aquarian Age christ advocate elimination of orthodox Christianity and its followers as a necessary step before their messiah can establish his global religion, in which he reveals the ancient mysteries of ascended masters.

*See also:* ANTICHRIST; ASCENDED MASTER; POLITICS, NEW AGE

# ORACLE

A person, place, or object believed to be the point of contact between the human and the divine and through which the gods reveal the past and present as well as their will for the future. In ancient Greece, an inquirer would go to the shrine of a deity. Here the priest or priestess would establish contact with the god or goddess and ask it to make its will known. The prophecy, which revealed hidden knowledge or divine purpose, was often in the form of an enigmatic statement or fable. Famous historical oracles were at Delphi and Delos.

Historians consider the most famous oracles to have greatly influenced life in ancient Greece by advising teachers, travelers, philosophers, and rulers on matters of religion, economics, and politics. Some New Age adherents believe that modern-day oracles serve as willing channels for divine entities. Others think the mind of the oracle awakens when he or she is in a trancelike state. In either case, oracles reputedly have a heightened perception of the universal intelligence, enabling them to reveal the ancient wisdom of the ethereal realm.

*See also:* DELPHIC ORACLE, DEMON, TRANCE CHANNELING

## ORGONE

A vital energy believed to permeate nature and influence health. The concept was first introduced in the 1940s by Austrian psychoanalyst Wilhelm Reich (1897–1957). He maintained that a cosmic force known as orgone energy could be measured during the expansion and contraction of the orgasmic reflex. Reich claimed that this force not only powered the movement of the stars and planets but also energized the human body's central nervous system. He viewed any blockage in this system as responsible for all psychological disorders.

In an attempt to measure and focus this cosmic force, Reich developed the orgone energy accumulator, or the orgone box. He maintained that the device, made of layered steel wool, could measure orgone deficiency, collect orgasmic energy, and redistribute it to whomever sat on the seat of the box. Reich's distribution of the instrument eventually put him in violation of federal law in the United States. He defied an injunction against selling the device and was sentenced to a federal penitentiary, where he died.

*See also:* COSMIC ENERGY, SEXUALITY

## OUIJA®

A board game that is frequently used as an occult channel to the spirit plain or an extrasensory perception aid. The word *ouija* combines the French word *oui,* which means "yes," with the German word *ja,* which also means "yes."

Players take turns asking questions about the past, present, or future, and seek answers as a pointer is moved aimlessly across a series of letters, numbers, and symbols. The pointer or message indicator is called a planchette, a three-legged, heart-shaped device with a transparent viewfinder. While each participant lightly touches the planchette, it moves to specific letters or numbers to spell out an answer.

William Fuld developed the game in the late 1890s. It is manufactured and distributed today by the Parker Brothers Company.

Some psychologists claim the game enables people to release subconscious memories as they safely experience the polaric interplay between the left and right hemispheres of the brain. It is also used, however, to attempt occult communication, the channeling of spirit entities, to develop psychic abilities, and to holistically diagnose and treat physical ailments.

*See also:* DIVINATION, SPIRITISM

## OUROBORO

The Great World Serpent that reputedly represents the never-ending cycles of life. The serpent, sometimes called the earth dragon, allegedly lives forever in the underground as the dark aspect of the sun god. The

Ouroboro— common New Age symbol for the cycle of life

ouroboro symbolizes such pagan deities as Thoth (Egypt), Hermes (Greece), and Vasuki (India). The Gnostics called the ouroboro the king of heaven and the revealer of ancient mysteries. The higher degrees of the Masonic Order revere the symbol as the great light of secret societies and the universal agent of truth. They say its life-giving principles are preserved in ancient books of sacred magic. Some contemporary goddess cults believe the ouroboro originally represented the female deities, while other cults believe its androgynous nature symbolizes universal wholeness.

*See also:* GNOSTICISM, KUNDALINI, SERPENT

## OUT-OF-BODY EXPERIENCE

A sense of separation from the physical body and of being able to view oneself and others from an external vantage point. Out-of-body experiences are usually reported in near-death experiences. New Age advocates encourage the deliberate separation of the astral body to achieve spiritual purification.

*See also:* ALTERED STATE, ASTRAL PROJECTION, NEAR-DEATH EXPERIENCE

## OVERSHADOW

A telepathic form of channeling made popular by Benjamin Creme, in which spiritual entities reputedly obtain control of the mind and sometimes the body of an individual. These entities claim they are the as-cended masters of people who have achieved enlightenment and now have returned to earth to assist humankind in its divine transformation. New Age disciples believe these spirits hold the wisdom and secrets of the universe. As initiates attempt to attain godhood, they allow themselves to become spirit-possessed. These overshadowing entities deliver messages from their spirit guides about the divinity of humanity, the imminent arrival of a cosmic christ, and the establishment of a one-world government, that are all common New Age themes.

*See also:* ASCENDED MASTER; CREME, BENJAMIN; ENTITY; TRANCE CHANNELING

# P

## PAGANISM

Literally "a country religion," referring to the religions followed by natives of a geographical area. *Paganism* was first used to denote any polytheistic religion and especially Roman polytheism. As used today, a pagan is a follower of any of a number of animistic New Age beliefs.

Paganism achieved new respectability within the drug culture of the 1960s and the rise in occultic practice in the West. The Internet allowed opportunities for better communication and recruiting among these groups, and by the end of the twentieth century a loose confederation of neopagan "denominations" had emerged: Asatru, Celtic tradition, Church of All Worlds, Druid, Mediterranean tradition, Native American, and Shamanism. Wiccans, earth mother/goddess cults, and some practitioners of white witchcraft loosely fit into one or more of these groupings. In general neopagans have been identified with sensuality and an obsession for nature rituals, shamanism, and sexual magick.

At the end of the twentieth century, there were at least fifteen thousand informational and e-business web sites and chat rooms devoted in part or exclusively to promoting pagan beliefs. Some analysts were calling animism the dominant religion of the West.

*See also:* ANIMISM

## PALMISTRY

*See:* CHIROMANCY

## PAN

The Greek god of nature identified with woods, fields, and wildlife, as well as flocks, shepherds, and hunters. Pan had a human torso with the legs, horns, ears, and beard of a goat. In folk tales, Pan would haunt isolated rural areas and strike intense fear in travelers who crossed his path—a concept from which we get the word *panic.*

Greek mythology says that in Pan's youth, he was horribly ridiculed by the immortals. He then escaped to the woods as head of the Satyrs, or the Hidden Ones. According to legend, Penelope was waiting for the return of her husband, Odysseus (king of Ithaca) from a long absence. During this time, an eager group of would-be lovers beleaguered Penelope. One of these was Pan who took the form of a he-goat in his attempt to court her. Because of Penelope's faithfulness to Odysseus, she refused to accept Pan's offer of marriage. Later Pan fell in love with another woodland nymph named Syrinx, but she was frightened and disgusted by the half-man, half-beast creature and fled from him. To end the chase, Syrinx pleaded with the gods who turned her into a patch of reeds to disguise her from the approaching Pan. In sorrow, Pan cut seven reeds of varying lengths that he used to make a musical instrument of mystical powers that bore the name of his beloved.

In ancient times Pan worshipers would deck altars, sing praises, and celebrate festivals in his honor throughout Greece, Asia Minor, Egypt, and even Africa. Many believed Pan's horns signified the exalted thoughts of the divine and that his music could stir the mystical powers of nature. New Age adherents extol Pan as the alter ego of Satan, the incarnate symbol of the higher self that emanates from the supreme energy force. As a representative of the natural person, they believe Pan, or Lucifer, brings the desires and feelings of the unconscious mind into awareness. He serves as a perfect instrument through which people can realize the christ-consciousness, or divine nature, of their souls.

Various aspects of the horned god play a significant role in the satanic rituals of some New Age cults. Witches believe the sun represents Pan, whereas the moon represents the Great Mother Goddess. Each year Pan dies and is brought back to life in a ceremony called "drawing down the sun." (The parallel ceremony for the Mother Goddess is called "drawing down the moon.") In this ritual, the high priestess of a coven, or local assembly of witches, will call Pan's name as she invokes the god aspect of the high priest.

*See also:* DIANA, MYTHOLOGY

## PANPSYCHISM

A philosophical theory that everything in the universe has some degree of consciousness. From the Greek *pan* ("all") and *psyche* ("soul"), the concept is practically synonymous with the pantheistic Platonism of hylozoism, a central influence in New Age philosophy.

The modern school of panpsychism developed in England in the later 1800s as the Romantic Movement tried to find a place for itself in the scientific and theological revolution that accompanied Charles Darwin's (1809–1882) books on naturalistic evolution.

Panpsychists argued that evolutionary development was possible because everything is animated. The universe consists entirely of "mind stuff." The earth is a living mother.

*See also:* ANIMISM, DEEP ECOLOGY, ECOFEMINISM, HYLOZOISM, MONISM, MOTHER EARTH

## PANTHEISM

A system of thought that teaches that the supreme being is neutral, impersonal, and one with the material world. All power, activity, and life reputedly are the power, activity, and life of the Universal Mind. This concept identifies God with creation by insisting that God is the world, and the world is God. He is the substance of that the universe is the tangible evidence. People are not distinct, consciously existing personalities, but rather are a moment in the life of the Universal Mind. People are merely a mode of God's existence, and all their actions are a brief, passing display of God's activity.

Pantheists believe that people are blended back into God when they die. The absorption of the finite into the infinite supposedly is the highest destiny that can be acknowledged for people. In the Hindu religion, this destiny can only be attained for the vast majority of people after a long, repeated process of reincarnation. This process may stretch through millions of years. If people are faithful and consistent in their religious observances, they will come back into the world in a higher or superior state of existence. But people will be reborn into a lower life form if they are unfaithful and inconsistent in the performance of their religious duties.

In pantheism, everything God does is an absolute and necessary outworking of His nature. Therefore people have no true freedom of will. Instead, whatever decisions they make are an impersonal expression of the Universal Mind. Even creation itself is an eternal, necessary, and continuous evolution of the Infinite Being. History is merely the self-expression and self-evolution of God. One idea or phase of the Infinite Being is exhibited by one period in human history, whereas a different idea is expressed by another period. Pantheists consider all these things as the necessary outworking of the Infinite Being's cosmic evolution.

Evil becomes only a limitation of existence, an imperfection, and an undeveloped good. Anything finite is considered a negation of the infinite. Therefore evil is what is finite, limiting, or undeveloped. Some Pantheists teach people that their duty is to seek their own gratification and to satisfy the impulses of their own nature. To hinder or restrict such cravings and desires is to limit the self-expression and evolutionary development of the Infinite Being. This way of thinking leads to self-deification. The immaterial part of a person's being, his soul or conscious state, is the highest expression of God's existence. The human race is an incarnation of God. People are to seek personal superiority because this is a disclosure of the divine essence. Proponents claim the highest step of evolutionary development is achieved when people reach the awareness of their identity with God. The foremost goal is the recognition of absorption into the Universal Mind. Furthermore, evil is deified. Pantheists view evil as they view goodness, a tangible display of God. Both are necessary and good. Wickedness and corruption represent only one form of the activity of God.

The pantheistic concept of an abstract, amoral God is popular among New Age adherents because it supports much of their ideology. If all that exists constitutes God, then all people are gods. By becoming aware of their innate divinity, people supposedly can discern the wisdom and secrets, knowledge and powers of the Universal Mind. And finally, because humans and nature are tangible expressions of the impersonal cosmic essence, people allegedly have the power to create their own realities and control their destiny.

*See also:* GOD, GODDESS WORSHIP, HINDUISM, KARMA, REINCARNATION

## PARADIGM SHIFT
*See:* KUHN, THOMAS

## PARAPSYCHOLOGY
The study of paranormal psychological phenomena such as telepathy, clairvoyance, and psychokinesis, which cannot be explained by known scientific laws, principles, or energies. Telepathy refers to the ability to read another person's thoughts. Clairvoyance refers to the ability to discern something about inanimate objects or events without the use of the known senses. Psychokinesis refers to the ability to move and control an inanimate object or event apart from known physical energies. The field of parapsychology includes the study of *psi* communications, which deal with energy forces believed to mediate psychic phenomena. Therefore *psi* communications are personal or behavioral interactions with the environment that are not dependent on the senses or muscles.

Numerous phenomena are related to parapsychology. Five of the more pertinent manifestations are noted here. Psychic auras are emanations of the mind or spirit, apart from any physical means and detectable only by mediums. Automatic writing refers to the phenomena in which a spirit or entity from another dimension uses a person in the present space and time to act as a mechanical instrument for written communication. Out-of-body experiences (also known as astral body projections) are phenomena in which the mind or soul leaves the body, travels independently to other locations (unhindered by space or time), and then returns to the body. Poltergeists are ghosts or apparitions that display their presence in strange ways, including spontaneous and unexplainable rapping noises in a house, dishes crashing to the floor, and flying pots and pans. Reincarnation is the phenomena in which a soul leaves a corpse and occupies a new body. This supposedly explains how people, when under hypnotically induced regression, are able to provide information about other people who lived long ago.

New Age adherents say these and other phenomena still occur in everyday life. Occultists relate innumerable stories of precognitive dreams, eerie premonitions, and near-death visions. Encountering people who claim the ability to levitate objects through the air or off shelves is becoming more common. Holistic healers assert they can remove malignant tissue from patients using psychic powers. Dowsers maintain they can use mystic powers to discover the underground location of water. Gurus assert they can walk across fiery beds of coals and stones without being burned. And stage performers allege they have the cosmic ability to bend keys, spoons, and other metal objects.

Adherents relate that through direct personal experience and objective scientific methods, psychic abilities that supposedly lay dormant in all people can be brought to a conscious level of awareness for exploration and use. They offer a variety of occult explanations for these paranormal abilities.

Some say the human brain emits massive particle clouds, while others postulate the emission of electronic or gravitational fields. One group believes that latent powers within the human psyche act in response to unconscious commands. Others think the human mind is capable of tapping into a collective source of knowledge to obtain power. The most popular New Age explanation is that when people manifest psychic phenomena, they are in contact with spirits from other dimensions. These entities supposedly leave the astral plane, enter the material plane, and indwell a human host. These spirit guides reputedly assist humanity in evolving to a state of perfection.

*See also:* ETHER, EXTRASENSORY PERCEPTION, GHOST, TELEPATHY

## PAST LIVES THERAPY

The attempt to interpret the current life patterns of people based on the assumption that they have undergone hundreds or even thousands of past incarnations. Therapists sometimes use hypnotic regression to explore the depths of a patient's mind, and to retrieve repressed memories. Patients under hypnosis sometimes speak of detailed excursions into past lives and shared in the thoughts and feelings of entities living on alien worlds. In addition to hypnosis, therapists might also collect data from dreams, meditations, and visions. They also believe a patient's imagination provides a viable source of insight into how past lives influence present experiences.

Therapists believe some problems are caused by the release of unresolved negative emotions suppressed in the unconscious memory of an individual's past lives. Initiates find past lives therapy inviting because of promises to unleash their innate abilities, to awaken their forgotten powers, and to reunite them with the universal essence. They learn that personal growth can be achieved by cleansing these memories from the mind and reprogramming the body to ignore their lingering influence. Proponents claim that past lives therapy will bring a positive change in the current lives of patients by helping them

to understand their unresolved problems, as well as by enhancing their personal evolutionary development.

*See also:* EVOLUTION, KARMA, PSYCHOTHERAPY, REINCARNATION

## PEACE

New Age gurus often refer to peace as the blissful union between the lower and higher self, the harmony between nature and circumstance, or the attainment of divine awareness. Obtaining personal peace is but a stepping stone on the New Age agenda. They suggest that only enlightened humanity, after being taught to rely on their divine inner potential, can transform the consciousness of the planet, thereby ushering in the Aquarian Age of peace, love, and harmony. Occultists say that universal brotherhood, ecumenical harmony, and a one-world government will solve the planet's economic, social, and environmental problems. In their quest for world peace, they call for the eradication of all "negative" forces, such as Christianity.

*See also:* UNITY IN DIVERSITY COUNCIL

## PEACE SYMBOL

An inverted and skewed cross contained within a circle. It became a popular symbol of the anti-Vietnam War protest and Peace Movement of the late 1960s. According to church tradition, the Roman government crucified the apostle Peter upside down. In the centuries that followed, the inverted cross became the symbol for an intense hatred of Christianity. In 1099, Muslims displayed this symbol as they warred against Christians in the Crusades. The inverted cross was later used to symbolize the satanic ritual known as the "black mass." This rite mocks the Roman Catholic Mass by desecrating the host, by repeating the Lord's Prayer backward, by sacrificing animals and people on an altar, by mixing the blood from the sacrificial

**Peace symbol—the Cross, inverted and broken**

victim with wine, then drinking the mixture in homage to Satan. Anton LaVey (1930–1997), the founder of the First Church of Satan in San Francisco and the author of *The Satanic Bible,* used the inverted cross in the ceremonies he performed.

*See also:* CIRCLE, CROSS, SYMBOLISM

## PEAK EXPERIENCES

The climax of a person's self-actualization process. The concept of peak experiences was first developed by the humanistic psychologist Abraham Maslow (1908–1970). In the 1950s and 1960s, he conducted a number of experiments on psychologically "healthy" people. Compared to the norm, these subjects appeared more accepting of themselves and others, more creative, more independent, more focused, and less bound by time and space. He surmised that these exceptionally mature individuals gave psychologists a more complete understanding of self-actualized human nature.

Maslow taught that peak experiences represent an altered state of consciousness that is vital to spiritual growth and development. During a peak experience, people transcend the usual limitations of their identity to understand the world as it genuinely exists. They come to see life as an integrated and unified whole, full of beauty, truth, and goodness. Inhibitions, fears, and anxieties are replaced by a sense of awe and ecstasy. Adherents see peak events as powerfully moving events, defying explanation and leaving people feeling more positive about life as a whole. People allegedly have a better self-concept, as well as more spontaneity and expressiveness.

New Age adherents claim that peak experiences signify a religious or mystical encounter with the Universal Mind. People become enraptured with the cosmic consciousness and have a sense of profound understanding, ineffability, and transiency. During these episodes, people can regress back to previous lives or establish contact with entities from the astral plane. Advocates claim that after peak experiences, people

have a greater awareness of their innate divinity. They are more receptive to the wisdom and guidance of ascended masters. They learn from their mystical encounters that evil simply does not exist, only illusory variations of the great cosmic force that permeates life.

*See also:* DRUG; HUMAN POTENTIAL MOVEMENT; MASLOW, ABRAHAM; SELF-ACTUALIZATION

## PENDULUM

A weight suspended from or affixed to a low friction support, allowing it to swing back and forth freely under the influence of gravity alone. A pendulum forms the active part of a metronome, a device used by musicians to display a constant tempo.

Some occultists use a simple string and weight pendulum to practice radiesthesia, the attempt to discover the location of hidden objects through the use of divination techniques. Others use the pendulum to detect biological radiations, predict future events, develop psychic abilities, and diagnose illnesses. Some think the pendulum is reacting to distortions in the earth's electromagnetic field, while others attribute the pendulum swing to the unconscious movement of the diviner. A popular belief among diviners is that the pendulum reacts to vibrational energy that emanates from all matter. In the diagnosis of the human psychophysical condition, the radiation of positive energy supposedly is indicated by a clockwise circle, whereas negative energy is indicated by a counterclockwise circle of a suspended pendulum. Some New Age adherents claim people who use pendulums are able to enter altered states of consciousness, gain access to the Universal Mind, and receive "wisdom" from spirit guides.

*See also:* DIVINATION, HOLISM, POWER OBJECT, RADIESTHESIA

## PENTACLE

A type of five-pointed star or pentagram, often found within a circle. A pentacle is distinguished from the more commonly seen

198

occult pentagrams in that it points upward rather than downward. The pentacle was popularized at the end of the twentieth century among Wiccans and other neopagans who sought to distance themselves from the evil, goat's head, black magic Satanism normally associated with the pentagram. In animistic conception, the pentagram or pentacle represents the interconnection of the earth elements, spirit, water, fire, earth, and air. The diagram is drawn so that spirit (always shown at the top) connects with fire and earth. Water connects with air and earth. Fire connects with spirit and air. Earth connects with water and spirit. Air connects with water and fire.

*See also:* PENTAGRAM, SYMBOLISM

## PENTAGRAM

A five-pointed star, usually made with alternate points connected by a continuous line appearing within a circle. The pentagram is universally associated with many practices of the New Age, including Satanism, witchcraft, and paganism. For centuries, occultists have revered the pentagram above all other occult symbols because they consider it the most powerful tool in the invocation of spirit entities.

Witchcraft cults, in the belief that invoked forces cannot leave the pentagram without permission, conjure from outside the circle.

In contrast, Satanists welcome demonic possession and therefore summon forces from within the pentagram. The symbol allegedly signifies the reemergence of the serpent, which they

**Pentagram**

say is the universal agent of truth. Contemporary pagan cults believe the pentagram is the star of knowledge, as well as a symbolic representation of Mother Earth. Other New Age adherents claim the pentagram is a symbol of divine good and the supernatural power of humanity's innate energy force. Still others believe the circle represents the endless cycle of the divine manifestations of the human soul. However others say the circle symbolizes the feminine aspect of humanity. When the feminine circle is merged with the masculine star, it supposedly creates a powerful lens that can be used to invoke the earth's energy force.

The five points of each pentagram have occultic significance. The points may symbolize the four elements of nature and the human spirit, as well as the five stages of life, the five senses, or the essence of existence. Often a human being is sketched in the pentagram with arms stretching upward. This, along with the points of the star, symbolizes the human body. It indicates either the balancing of self or the five areas of spiritual evolution.

In contemporary witchcraft, a pentagram drawn clockwise banishes the spirits, whereas a counterclockwise pentagram invokes energy forces. The pentagram may have three points up, symbolizing the divine power of humanity over the universe. When three points are down, it represents bestiality and darkness or signifies humanity's victory over Christ. The reversed pentagram, within which the horned god (or Mendes goat) is depicted, serves as the universal symbol of satanic worship, rituals, and cults. Practitioners claim that using the pentagram will enable them to communicate with their divine inner self and ascended masters.

*See also:* GOAT OF MENDES, SATANISM, SYMBOLISM, WITCHCRAFT

## PERENNIAL PHILOSOPHY

The idea that all religious beliefs come from one truth and are separated only by insignificant doctrinal concepts. Perennial philosophy was first introduced by the English novelist and essayist Aldous Leonard Huxley (1894–1963). New Age adherents have used this viewpoint to their advantage as they attempt to establish a worldwide religion. For years, gurus and swamis have entered into altered states of consciousness to affirm the "truthfulness" of perennial philosophy and to urge their followers to bring about the uniting of all religions under the lordship of the Aquarian Age messiah.

*See also:* GOD, ONE-WORLD IDEAL

# PEYOTE

A desert cactus, scientifically known as *Lophophora williamsii,* native to central Mexico and the southwestern United States. People use the tubercles of this cactus to produce an alkaloid drug called mescaline, which causes hallucinations and other psychedelic effects. When ingested, the drug stimulates the body's autonomic nervous system. Users report seeing brilliant colors and vivid designs and remember having a distorted perception of space and time. They may also experience anxiety, nausea, vomiting, and rapid heartbeat.

Members of the Native American Church use the crowns of the peyote, otherwise known as mescal buttons, as part of their religious rituals. They believe mescaline is a source of spiritual power. Those who eat these crowns experience a mind-altering trance that reputedly allows them to commune with the great universal spirit.

Mescaline usage gained considerable popularity within the drug culture of the 1960s. New Age adherents claim that taking mescaline, along with other hallucinogenics, opens up pathways to alternate dimensions in which reality becomes illusion and illusion becomes reality.

*See also:* ALTERED STATE, DRUG, NATIVE AMERICANS

# PHRENOLOGY

The theory that certain mental capacities can be understood by interpreting the shape and bumps of the skull. Phrenology, which literally means the "science of the mind," originated in the early 1800s through the writings and lectures of Franz Josef Gall (1758–1828) and Johannes Kaspar Spurzheim (1776–1832). These two men held that the human anatomy directly influences such mental behavior as self-esteem, conscientiousness, and spirituality. They postulated that personality and character traits are centered in the brain, and that highly developed abilities can be detected by enlarged brain areas. These supposedly were evident by the location and size of bumps in the skull.

Therefore Gall and Spurzheim set out to create phrenology "maps" of the cranium to show the places where specific abilities were located. These maps were then used in hospitals where clinicians would find the region of a patient's brain that was responsible for an illness. They would then examine the corresponding bumps on the skull of a client. The problem would be treated with techniques such as cutting off the blood supply, resting, eating good food, and exercising.

Although phrenology was later discredited as unscientific, New Age adherents continue to affirm the theories and techniques associated with it. Occultists will examine people's skulls, the location and shapes of bumps, to determine their character and predict the future. This may be combined with trances, hypnosis, and seances to indoctrinate initiates into thinking they can get in touch with their divine self, explore the mysteries of the cosmos, and become one with the Universal Mind.

*See also:* DIVINATION, TRANSPERSONAL PSYCHOLOGY

# PISCEAN AGE

The age of the human race that is coming to a close, giving way to the Aquarian age of enlightenment. This New Age understanding of history is based on the astrological hypothesis that humanity experiences an evolutionary transformation at the end of every two-thousand-year cycle. Each cycle is characterized by one of the twelve signs of the zodiac. At the dawn of each new age, the sun enters a new cycle. Astrologers believe the sun entered the Piscean constellation about the time of the rise of the Roman empire. Almost two thousand years have elapsed, and occultists say that the sun is about to enter the Aquarian constellation and usher in the New Age of enlightenment, peace, and cosmic consciousness. They have no regrets about seeing the end of the Piscean Age, which they regard as characterized by darkness, ignorance, and violence.

*See also:* AQUARIUS, AGE OF; ASTROLOGY; NEW AGE MOVEMENT

# PLACEBO

An inert or innocuous substance that is prescribed for the mental relief of the patient rather than its actual medicinal effect on a disorder. In most cases, the active drug is replaced by an inactive compound such as sugar. A "placebo effect" occurs when psychological and physiological improvements take place based solely on the expected therapeutic value of the placebo."

Holistic healers claim that people have forgotten their innate, divine powers to heal themselves. Various techniques, such as the placebo effect, supposedly can be used to help patients achieve new levels of awareness concerning their psychic abilities to heal themselves. The placebo effect is said to prove a direct connection between the human psyche and the body's inherent therapeutic powers.

*See also:* AWARENESS, HOLISM, MYSTICISM

# PLAN, THE

An organized agenda for the establishment of the New World Order that will be controlled by the Aquarian Age christ. The Plan is said to have been revealed first to Alice Bailey (1880–1949) in the 1930s. She was instructed to keep it hidden until 1975, some thirty years after her death. She obtained these mysteries from channeled spirits who proclaimed that this was when the world would be ready to hear the message. The Spiritual Hierarchy of Masters, an exalted group of divine spirits, has allegedly also revealed aspects of The Plan.

The Plan calls for people to be taught their oneness with the impersonal, universal God. The first step is to convince young adults about these teachings. The next step is for them to pass this "knowledge" to their children. As more people come to realize their innate divinity a critical mass will be reached, bringing about a worldwide transformation in consciousness. When this is achieved, the New Age christ will begin purging the earth of all "negative influences" in accordance with The Plan. Those who oppose the global transformation will be sent to an alternate dimension until they have spiritually evolved enough to return to earth.

Lord Maitreya will establish a one-world religion, a one-world government, and a one-world economy. Through a quantum leap in the spiritual evolution of humanity, the world will become a paradise characterized by peace, love, and unity.

*See also:* ANTICHRIST; BAILEY, ALICE ANN; NEW AGE MOVEMENT; ONE-WORLD IDEAL; PURIFICATION

# PLANETARY CITIZENS

A global organization dedicated to the establishment of a federated world government. Planetary Citizens was originally founded in 1972 by New Age activist Robert Mueller, editor Norman Cousins, and peace advocate Donald Keys. The organization, headquartered in the United Nations' plaza, boasts an impressive membership roster that takes responsibility for innovative economic, ecological, and ecumenical research. Planetary Citizens serves as an activist group committed to global transformation through political action. Members believe the first step in achieving planetary consciousness is to expand every person's mind-set from local to global. The second step is to force national leaders to join a planetary government. In 1982, Planetary Citizens gave birth to Planetary Initiative, a networking organization responsible for the worldwide propagation of the organization's message.

*See also:* GLOBALISM; KEYS, DONALD; MUELLER, ROBERT; ONE-WORLD IDEAL; POLITICS, NEW AGE; TRANSFORMATION

# PLANETARY COMMISSION FOR GLOBAL HEALING

*See:* PRICE, JOHN RANDOLPH

# PLANETARY INITIATIVE FOR THE WORLD WE CHOOSE

A political partnership of sponsoring organizations that promotes globalization in the belief that humanity's only hope for peace is globalization. Founded in 1982, Planetary Initiative makes use of a powerful information network to help establish a one-world system of government, economy, and religion. Through its publication *The Initiator,* the organization disseminates its teachings to a worldwide audience. Along with Planetary Citizens, Planetary Initiative seeks to assist the New Group of World Servers, an organization founded by noted theosophist Alice Ann Bailey (1880–1949). Planetary Initiative board member David Spangler was an avid student of Bailey. From Bailey he learned that Lucifer is the necessary energy force overseeing the transformation of humankind into a unified world of divine souls.

*See also:* BAILEY, ALICE ANN; GLOBALISM; NEW GROUP OF WORLD SERVERS; SPANGLER, DAVID

## PLANETARY PENTECOST

A manifestation of psychic abilities and cosmic awareness initiated by global mind-link events. These planetary meditation sessions supposedly will bring energy waves to earth from the ethereal realm, unleashing abundant supernatural powers. During the Planetary Pentecost, ascended masters will help participants understand and implement the message and mission of Lord Maitreya. Their work will not be completed until people become enlightened, united with themselves, united with the Universal Mind, and united under the rule of the coming New Age christ.

*See also:* ASCENDED MASTER, NEW AGE MOVEMENT, TRANSCENDENTAL MEDITATION

## PLEIADEIANS

According to the Unarius Academy of Science, a UFO and psychic research cult, the Pleiadeians are a species of intergalactic missionaries from a planet in a star system from the constellation Pleiades who will bring the knowledge needed to achieve harmony and peace. The Pleiadeians will invite Earth to join the Interplanetary Confedera-

tion of Planets, an alliance of thirty-three planets. In 1984, Unarius founder Ruth Norman (1904–1971) (who called herself Uriel) announced that she had received a message from Alta, the scientific leader of the planet Vixall. Alta supposedly informed her that, in 2001, a delegation from the planet Myton would come to earth and land on a submerged Atlantis somewhere in the Bermuda Triangle. Over the next nine years, thirty-one other craft would follow, each bearing one thousand "Space Brothers." Unarius has purchased land where the space craft will interlock to form an educational center.

*See also:* ASCENDED MASTER, UNARIUS ACADEMY OF SCIENCE

## POLARITY

The condition in which opposing forces allegedly conduct a cosmic energy flow through all existing life forms. Although these forces supposedly manifest contrasting properties and are exerted in opposite directions, they work together to create a balance of energy that holds the universe intact. Proponents say polarity directs the movement of the stars, the change of seasons on earth, and the spiritual evolution of humankind. Polarity maintains the cosmic balance between such opposites as male and female, good and evil, and life and death.

New Age adherents contend that the cosmic life force constantly flows into and through the human body, then out into the universe. To achieve oneness with the cosmos and experience enlightenment, people must first recognize and accept the polarity of forces that makes them whole. The practice of occult rituals and meditation techniques reputedly helps people tap into the life force that gives them health and happiness. Some sects teach that these opposing forces represent the innate god and goddess-like qualities within all people. Through the ascension of human consciousness, initiates can supposedly access these divine powers.

*See also:* CH'I, POLARITY THERAPY, TRANSCENDENTAL MEDITATION

## POLARITY THERAPY

A holistic healing practice. Polarity therapy operates on the premise that a cosmic energy flow forms the basis for all of life. This energy flow is characterized by a polarity of forces exerting pressure in opposite directions. Through their interaction, this life force is conducted through every person before it returns to the ethereal realm. Polaric therapists maintain that a blockage or imbalance in the life force can result in mental, physical, or spiritual infirmities. Advocates claim this condition is alleviated by rebalancing the energy flow within the patient.

Polarity therapy was first suggested by an osteopath named Randolph Stone (1890–1981). An avid enthusiast of Eastern religious philosophy and practice, Stone believed the cosmic force of opposites in the universe radiates from an astral dimension. He suggested that the head and the feet acted as the positive and negative poles of a weblike network of energy currents throughout the body. By the gentle massage of polar reflex points, the therapist manipulates the energy currents, releasing harmful blockages while rebalancing the cosmic flow.

*See also:* ACUPRESSURE, BALANCING, HOLISM, YIN/YANG

## POLITICS, NEW AGE

A powerful movement for achieving New Age goals by participating in the political apparatus of Western countries. New Age political advocates claim the future of humankind depends on the eradication of social barriers and the redetermination of values and objectives. This supposedly will foster a transformational burst of human consciousness and permit a New World Order to arise from the ashes of the old. Since the late 1960s, New Age advocates have successfully established a powerful political base of like-minded organizations and governmental leaders to promote their agenda and bring about global transformation. Occultists try to focus the public's attention on such problems as war, hunger, environmental concerns, and social injus-

tice. By doing this, they believe they can justify the reorganization of political power, the redistribution of wealth, and the homogenization of philosophical belief.

*See also:* GLOBALISM; ONE-WORLD IDEAL; PLAN, THE

## POLTERGEIST

Ghosts or apparitions that manifest themselves in strange ways, including spontaneous and unexplainable rapping noises in a house, dishes crashing to the floor, or pots and pans flying through the air. "Poltergeist" is derived from the German verb *poltern* meaning "to knock," and the noun *geist* meaning "spirit." Some think the manifestation of poltergeists results from the soul or spirit of the deceased trying to communicate with the living. However, others say the phenomena is the unconscious projection of psychic energy or a manifestation of humankind's collective unconscious. In some cases the activities of a poltergeist are linked to an adolescent living nearby. Supposedly the child is beginning to learn how to control his or her telekinetic powers.

*See also:* GHOST, SPIRITISM

## POWER ANIMAL

A spiritual being who has taken the form of an animal to enhance the wisdom and powers of a particular individual. Primitive societies believed animals were highly developed spiritual beings or deities who channeled their knowledge through a chosen tribal member. Those who acquired a power animal were among the most respected of spiritual leaders because their affinity with the animals they hunted assured tribal subsistence. Shamans, or occult priests or priestesses, reputedly could control their tribe's power animal because they were attuned to the pulsating rhythm of the life-giving energy force of the universe. When power animals met, they supposedly would fight to the death, taking their human counterpart with them. The spiritual being that proved the stronger of the two would grant a greater life expectancy to the shaman and the tribe.

New Age adherents regard the power animal as the protector, servant, force, and even the alter ego of the sorcerer. Adherents considered some of these entities as benevolent companions while others were regarded as malevolent beings. They supposedly give sorcerers the ability to do harm and create other power animals who will carry out their evil demands. Practitioners enter into an altered state of consciousness to consult and journey with their power animals and heal others. They rely on these entities to obtain esoteric wisdom, knowledge, and abilities believed necessary to manipulate people and exploit their world.

*See also:* SHAMAN, SPIRIT GUIDES

## POWER OBJECT

An object that supposedly can be used to summon and control supernatural forces. The history of power objects is long and diverse, encompassing every form of occult garb and accessory. This includes the talisman and

**Athame— power object**

feathers of the shaman, the wand and chalice of the witch, the skull and dagger of the Satanist, as well as the crystals and pyramids of the New Age follower. Advocates claim that power objects are extensions of the human body that can channel the energy of the soul. Power objects supposedly can manipulate the vast psychic forces of the Universal Mind, as well as disclose the mysteries of the astral dimension. New Age adherents welcome the use of power objects, believing they are one more tool to bring about the cosmic consciousness of the human race and the establishment of the Aquarian Age of enlightenment and peace.

*See also:* CHALICE, COSMIC ENERGY, FEATHER, PYRAMIDOLOGY, QUARTZ CRYSTAL, TALISMAN, WITCHCRAFT

## PRANA

The Hindu name for the cosmic force believed to permeate all living things, instilling life, health, and well-being. Other names for the breath of life include ch'i (Buddhists) and ki (Japanese). Advocates teach that the body is energized by five vital fluids, or pranas. They believe this omnipresent spiritual energy emanates continuously from a universal source, flows through every person, and then returns to the cosmos. Any imbalance in the prana supposedly leads to negativity in the body, manifesting itself in disease, sickness, and eventually death. Some holistic healers claim they can channel prana by using psychic injections that give the necessary energy for patients to realign themselves with the flow of universal forces. Hindu yogis advise deep breathing exercises to absorb prana, which fills practitioners with life, health, and unlimited psychic powers. New Age adherents regard prana as humanity's physical link with the divine. They claim this life force identifies the purpose of humanity's existence, making them the masters of their fate.

*See also:* CH'I, COSMIC ENERGY, GOD, HINDUISM, HOLOTROPHIC BREATHING, KI

## PRECOGNITION

The prediction of a future event that cannot be inferred from present knowledge. Proponents claim enhanced psychic abilities cause this phenomenon. New Age advocates believe that, like other extrasensory perceptions, precognitive powers are available to anyone who wants to learn how to use them. Anyone can access these abilities while in a trancelike, hypnotic state. Psychics display precognitive abilities without the restrictions of time and distance. Some say this is because the past, present, and future of humankind exists on a single dimensional plane, accessible at will through the manipulation of consciousness. Others believe psychic powers emanate from a spiritual dimension where the communicatory skills of supernatural entities manifest themselves in human channels.

Some New Age adherents suggest that those with precognitive abilities can only forecast one of many alternate futures. They base this idea not only on the premise that reality is timeless, but also on the idea that future events can affect past events and vice versa. The extent to which a past event can be altered by psychic means from the future depends on the characteristics of the event itself. Others postulate that psychic powers, such as the psychokinetic ability to manipulate matter, can influence the outcome of the precognition. In either scenario, New Age initiates are taught that they can tamper with time, journey to parallel universes, and eventually merge their consciousness with the Universal Mind.

*See also:* CLAIRVOYANCE, PSYCHIC, TRANCE CHANNELING

## PRICE, JOHN RANDOLPH (b. 1932)

New Age author and theoretician. John Randolph Price says that he receives his prophetic material from Asher, his spiritual guide. Price founded and serves as president of two organizations. One is the Quartus Foundation, dedicated to spiritual research. The other is the Planetary Commission. Price has written a number of New Age works, including *Practical Spirituality, The Planetary Commission,* and *Superbeings.*

Price believes everything in the cosmos is a vital part of the universal whole, and that individual actions invariably affect everything else. He maintains that if 1 percent of the earth's population can simultaneously send thought-messages of peace to the Universal Mind, this will result in a quantum leap in cosmic consciousness. Many New Age organizations agree with Price. Therefore they are at work to increase the number of enlightened people by encouraging initiates to practice meditation, as well as establish contact with their ascended masters. On December 31, 1986, Price made the first attempt to unite scattered New Age factions in a synchronized moment of global harmony. He claimed that this event, which he called the

World Healing Event, marked the end of the old human race of the Piscean Age, and brought about the emergence of a new race of god-beings for the Aquarian Age.

*See also:* CRITICAL MASS; PLAN, THE; POLITICS, NEW AGE; PURIFICATION; WORLD HEALING EVENT

## PROPHET, ELIZABETH CLARE
*See:* UNIVERSAL AND TRIUMPHANT, CHURCH

## PSI PHENOMENA

The general descriptive term of the late 1900s for any event that cannot be accounted for by natural law or by knowledge gained with usual sensory abilities. The discipline concerned with investigating such phenomena is called parapsychology. Extrasensory perception phenomena (ESP) include clairvoyance (discerning something about inanimate objects or events without the use of known senses), telepathy (reading another person's thoughts), precognition (predicting a future event, the occurrence of which cannot be inferred from present knowledge), or retrocognition (knowing about past events apart from having any access to information about those events). In these areas someone is believed to have acquired knowledge of facts, thoughts of others, or information of future events without the aid of the physical senses. Psychokinetic (PK) phenomena are physical in character, such as changing the shape of an object, levitating it, or manipulating how a die will fall or what card will be played.

The study of psychic phenomena began amid the spiritualistic occultism of the late 1800s. Much of this study was aimed at debunking the frauds who were preying on gullible believers, but since believers have gravitated toward the research, such groups have tended to be apologists for the occult. The first such group, the Society for Psychical Research was founded in London in 1882. Media interest and the movement away from rationalism to postmodernism at the end of the twentieth century has made study of psi phenomena as intense an interest as ever.

*See also:* CLAIRVOYANCE, EXTRASENSORY PERCEPTION, PSYCHIC, PSYCHOKINESIS, TELEPATHY

## PSYCHE

The totality of all the extrasensory processes, both conscious and unconscious, including the cognitive, conative, and affective dimensions. Derived from a Greek word meaning "breath," "life," or "soul," psyche can refer to the human mind, personality, or true self. According to the Austrian neurologist Sigmund Freud (1856–1939), the psyche is made up of the id (the unconscious source of vital energy), ego (the conscious mediator between a person and reality), and superego (the internalization of the parental conscience and the rules of society). In contrast, the Swiss psychologist Carl Jung (1875–1961) said the psyche is made up of the ego (the center of personal consciousness), shadow (the personal unconscious), persona (the facade toward the outside world), and animus (the inner disposition or governing spirit).

New Age adherents claim the psyche is the locus of human existence, holding secret powers and wisdom. Echoing Jung, they believe in the existence of a "collective unconscious," a dimension of reality containing the symbols and memories of the entire human race. The spiritually advanced supposedly can tap into this incredible source of knowledge. As a result, New Age adherents give high priority to the exploration of the human psyche, believing it holds the key to the spiritual evolution of humankind.

*See also:* COLLECTIVE UNCONSCIOUS; JUNG, CARL GUSTAV; TRANSPERSONAL PSYCHOLOGY

## PSYCHEDELIC

The name given to a class of consciousness-altering drugs and plants. When ingested, these substances can produce abnormal psychic effects, such as hallucinations or psychic states resembling mental illness. The more powerful psychedelics are LSD, psilocybin, and mescaline. Marijuana is a milder psychedelic drug, used more widely than the other three. Although federal, state, and local laws in the United States prohibit or restrict the ingestion of these substances, people continue to use them for recreational purposes.

Psychedelic drugs tend to dilate the user's eye pupils as well as increase pulse rate, blood pressure, and temperature. Users tend to lose contact with their environment, act and respond abnormally, and experience hallucinations or delusions. Users start out with feelings of unreality and perceiving "magical" insights, and move toward feelings of depression and anxiety, followed by panic and terror. Repeated use of these substances can cause psychological dependence in users.

Some New Age adherents advocate the use of psychedelic drugs to enable people to tap their innate divine powers and communicate with entities from the astral plane. By taking psychedelics, people supposedly can achieve higher or deeper levels of awareness, discover repressed memories from past lives, unite with the cosmic forces of nature, and thereby achieve enlightenment. Proponents assert that as more people use psychedelics, it will aid in the evolutionary transformation of the world.

*See also:* ALTERED STATE; DRUG; LEARY, TIMOTHY; LYSERGIC ACID DIETHYLAMIDE

## PSYCHIC

A person who allegedly has the ability to perceive objects, thoughts, or events without the mediation of the known human senses. New Age adherents actively propagate the concept that every person innately possesses an untapped reservoir of cosmic energy. When people enter into an altered state of consciousness, their spirit guide supposedly enables them to use this supernatural force. By doing so, they increase the awareness of their divinity, heighten their extrasensory abilities, and open themselves to the knowledge and wisdom found in union with the Universal Mind.

Some occultists say psychic energy is commonly demonstrated by human intuition, imagination, and dreams. But advocates contend that strong forces within people tend to deny innate creative forces. Therefore innovative methods must be employed to transcend the levels of normal consciousness, thereby reestablishing communication with the astral plane. Only when people are able to gain access to the divine force, through meditation exercises or by ingesting hallucinogenic drugs, can they experience psychic phenomena. Only then are they able to know the true peace, love, and joy of enlightenment. By getting a critical mass of people to tap into their psychic powers, New Age adherents believe human beings will experience an evolutionary transformation, unite with the collective unconscious, and achieve godhood.

*See also:* ALTERED STATE, COLLECTIVE UNCONSCIOUS, INTUITION, TRANSCENDENCE

## PSYCHIC SURGERY

Use of nonsensory states of consciousness and paranormal powers to initiate physical healing. Occultists teach that reality knows no boundaries because all things flow together. They see the apparent distinctions between the mental and physical as mere illusions. Even people, normally presumed to be separate entities, are a part of the infinite whole, like drops of water in a ocean. Advocates maintain that through meditative techniques and psychedelic drugs, people can tap into the vast forces of the universe and perform psychic surgeries.

Psychic surgeons claim they can remove diseased tissue, bone fragments, and malignant organs without the use of medical instruments or anesthetics—and without causing blood loss or scarring to their patients. Psychic surgeons claim that the presence of spiritual entities endows them with this ability. These entities diagnose the problem of their human host, then perform the operation on the patient. Psychic surgeons say they are not bound by conventional rules and restrictions. They assert that they can visualize the evil presence within their patient (usually manifested as a physical ailment), reach into the cavity of the body, and perform the excision.

*See also:* HOLISTIC HEALTH, PSYCHIC, TRANCE CHANNELING

## PSYCHOANALYSIS

A method of treating emotional disorders and analyzing psychic phenomena. This approach originated in the 1890s with the Austrian neurologist Sigmund Freud (1856–1939), and then was developed further by his students and others. This process involves three related activities. The first involves researching the human mind, especially the inner experiences such as emotions, feelings, and thoughts, as well as dreams and fantasies. The second involves gathering information in an orderly way about the mind and how it works. The third involves developing different methods for treating disorders of an emotional or psychological nature.

Freud made the assumption that people are self-gratifying animals. He taught that through the evolutionary process, people have developed two basic drives—eros and thanatos. Eros, from the Greek word for sexual love, represents the sum of life-preserving instincts. These are manifested as impulses to gratify basic needs as subliminated impulses, or as impulses to protect and preserve the body and mind. Thanatos, from the Greek word for death, represents an innate and unconscious tendency toward self-destruction. Thanatos is the underlying cause for aggressive and destructive behavior.

In Freudian theory, the two basic drives of eros and thanatos make up the id and ultimately push humankind toward becoming self-gratifying. In Freudian psychoanalytic theory, the id is one of the three divisions of the psyche. (The other two divisions are the ego and superego.) The id lies completely in the unconscious and serves as the source of psychic energy. Psychic energy is derived from instinctual needs and drives. The ego serves as the conscious mediator between the person and reality, especially by functioning both in the perception and adaptation of reality. The superego is only partly conscious and represents the internalization of the parental conscience and the rules of society. The superego functions to reward and punish through a system of moral attitudes, conscience, and a sense of guilt resulting from the inner drives of eros and thanatos in conflict with each other. The constant stress and strain between these two entities of the id impel people to self-gratification. Because of the conflict between the people's impulses and the world in which they live, anxiety is created.

Freud taught that guilt is the result of the superego—with its socially imposed standards—suppressing the ego from experiencing what the id is driving it to express. Therefore, people feel guilty because their behavior violates the rules imposed by the superego. The way to resolve this anxiety supposedly is by experiencing self-gratifying behavior in a socially acceptable way.

According to Freud, therapists are explorers who go back into the patient's past to probe their inner psyche. Therapists investigate conflicts that have taken place within the id. They bring this unconscious conflict to the surface and help the patient resolve it.

New Age adherents agree with Freud's teachings that the human race is evolving and that psychic energy exists within people. They see the inner drives of eros and thanatos as evidence of harmonic imbalance between people and the cosmic life force. They affirm the idea of exploring the psyche through a variety of techniques, such as free association and dream analysis to gain insight for tapping into unlimited human potential.

*See also:* CONSCIOUSNESS; FREUD, SIGMUND; JUNG, CARL GUSTAV; UNCONSCIOUS, THE

## PSYCHOENERGY

Extrasensory energy believed to exist within the human mind beyond the confines of physical matter. When the human consciousness manipulates psychoenergy, it produces paranormal phenomena. Just as the five senses respond to external stimuli, adherents believe psychoenergies respond to vibrational impulses that are scientifically undetectable. These cosmic forces emanate from a fourth dimension of existence and are the key to unlocking the mysteries of the mind. New Age advocates propose that by transcending the levels of human consciousness (objective reasoning), people will be able to recognize their divine place in a universe of interacting spiritual energies.

*See also:* CONSCIOUSNESS, EXTRASENSORY PERCEPTION, FOURTH LEVEL, TRANSCENDENCE

## PSYCHOKINESIS (TELEKINESIS)

In parapsychology, the action of mind on matter through which objects are caused to move or change as a result of mental concentration upon them. Psychokinesis (PK) and extrasensory perception (ESP) are the two major types of psi phenomena. The most violent PK phenomena studied are the supposed actions of disembodied spirits. These phenomena are called poltergeists.

*See also:* COSMIC ENERGY, EXTRASENSORY PERCEPTION, PARAPSYCHOLOGY, PSYCHIC

## PSYCHOMETRY

The psychic ability to divine information about an object or its owner by coming in contact with the object or in close proximity to it. Practitioners claim they can foretell a person's future by interpreting the vibrational energy given off by an object belonging to that person. Some claim that psychometry has proven useful in finding lost children by handling a toy belonging to the child. They claim that vital mineral deposits can be discovered by touching a map of a specific area.

*See also:* DIVINATION, OCCULTISM, PARAPSYCHOLOGY, PSYCHIC

## PSYCHOTECHNOLOGY

An assortment of paranormal techniques used to induce altered states of human consciousness. Advocates claim that transformational methods can free people from conventional dependencies and increase their innate human potential. Contemporary psychotechnology originated from ancient pagan religions in which the ritualistic manipulation of human thought played an important part in initiatory transformation. Such occult practices have found a new audience in the youth of the West. Old and new methods alike lure initiates with promises of spiritual enlightenment, unlimited human potential, and psychic powers of healing and insight. Advocates say that when practitioners enter an altered state of consciousness, they are able to bypass analytical thinking and tap into the brain's intuitive powers. This allegedly allows devotees to experience an enlightened awareness of their multidimensional self. This includes their divine potential, their unity with all humankind, and their mystical connection to the cosmic force.

*See also:* ALTERED STATE; INTUITION; SCIENCE, NEW AGE; THOUGHT ADJUSTERS; TRANSFORMATION

## PSYCHOTHERAPY

The use of psychological means to treat mental, emotional, or nervous disorders. Any situation involving therapy assumes that at least two parties are interacting—the party requiring remedial treatment and the party providing the treatment. Research in psychotherapy indicates that several variables affect the outcome of the treatment. Client variables are most important. These include such factors as the severity of the condition, the onset of the problem, and the duration of the presenting symptoms, as well as the support systems in the environment, the inner fortitude of the individual, and the motivation for change. Therapist variables also are important, including personal styles, attitudes, and genuineness. Finally, therapy techniques affect results when measuring the outcome of the treatment.

New Age psychotherapists operate with the belief that they can modify the behavior of patients by manipulating their conscious and subconscious processes. Occult healers have derived many of their theories and practices from pagan Eastern religions. They assume that people are innately divine. Therefore one therapeutic goal is to urge people to recognize their inherent godhood. Another belief is that the mind, body, and spirit are an interconnected triad that should be diagnosed and treated as a comprehensive "whole." These psychotherapists see illness and pain as an accumulation of unbalanced energy that is easily corrected by realigning the vibrational forces of the mind, body, and spirit. They operate on the premise that psychic powers are obtained while in an altered state of consciousness. New Age psychotherapists may urge their patients to enter a trancelike state through meditation exercises. They urge patients to tap into the universal life force that supposedly permeates human existence, and thereby experience physiological healing. This is to help patients resolve their problems by trusting in their divine sense of inherent goodness and infinite human potential.

*See also:* FREUD, SIGMUND; JUNG, CARL GUSTAV; PSYCHOTECHNOLOGY

## PURIFICATION

The process by which New Age adherents intend to eliminate negative influences and the presumed hindrance in transforming the world. According to New Age doctrine, the Christian belief in a separate, almighty God was necessary in the old Piscean Age because of humanity's diminished spiritual capacities. Human consciousness has now allegedly regained the psychic energy necessary to recognize its inherent divinity. New Age adherents see those who oppose this evolutionary advancement and enlightenment of the world as evil forces, deserving of expulsion. In preparation for the coming Aquarian Age, these negative influences will be purged from society, allowing for the cleansing and beautification of Mother Earth for her consort, Lord Maitreya. Those who refuse to transcend the lower consciousness will be banished to alternate dimensions of existence until they become spiritually enlightened. Only then will they be allowed to return to Mother Earth. The New Age christ will preside over this purification process.

*See also:* ONE-WORLD IDEAL; PLAN, THE; TRANSFORMATION

## PURSEL, JACK

A California businessman who claims he is the channel for a spirit from the ethereal realm named Lazaris. This entity waits at the edge of reality to show people how to make the journey to the astral dimension. Lazaris helps his initiates activate the forces of the cosmos and become one with the Universal Mind. Lazaris is exceptionally bright, articulate, funny, and possesses the ability to instill a deeper sense of spirituality within his followers. Unlike other channeled entities, the disembodied Lazaris claims no previous incarnations and claims no particular age, for time and space do not exist in the ethereal realm.

Pursel travels across the United States to hold transcendental weekends. The meetings begin with a spiritual discourse in which Lazaris teaches that traditional Christianity is responsible for the separation, denigration, and abasement of all humankind. He teaches disciples how to recognize and appreciate their so-called divine self.

Pursel's discussions with Lazaris are interwoven with guided meditative exercises in which he leads attendees to the Causal Plane. This is the inner dimension in which the thoughts and feelings of people are allegedly transformed into light or physical reality. The initiation process also includes "blending," an occult technique in which Lazaris combines his energy with that of his students to instill a synergic understanding of transcendental love. Finally, Lazaris teaches use of power objects to summon and control supernatural forces. The entity claims that the power objects are extensions of the human body that can channel the energy of the soul. Initiates learn to use power objects

to manipulate the vast psychic forces of the Universal Mind and disclose the mysteries of the astral dimension.

*See also:* GUIDED IMAGERY, LIGHT, POWER OBJECT, TRANSFORMATION

## PYRAMIDOLOGY

The belief that the pyramid, an occult symbol, can enable people to perform psychic feats such as telepathy, clairvoyance, and psychokinesis. The pyramid played a significant role in the mystery religions of ancient civilizations. Because the number four was considered the symbol of the male deity and the number three was the symbol of the female deity, the pyramid represented the perfect hierarchical ordering of society. Divine power supposedly emanated from the apex of the pyramid, then down onto the rest of creation.

New Age adherents believe pyramids have universal secrets built into their dimensions. These objects supposedly serve as receptacles for cosmic energy that, when harnessed by people, can give them untold psychic powers. Holistic healers laud the ability of the pyramid to restore a person's harmonious balance with the universe. They say the pyramid is a gateway to the Universal Mind and enables its users to discover the secrets to the past, present, and future of humankind. Some use the pyramid as a meditative tool in the belief that the energy it radiates can heighten their awareness, amplify their thoughts, and raise their vibrational levels. As more people use pyramids in this way, a critical mass supposedly will be reached, bringing about a worldwide transformation in consciousness that will usher in the New Age of enlightenment, peace, and cosmic consciousness.

*See also:* EYE OF HORUS, GOD, MYSTERY, QUARTZ CRYSTAL, TRIANGLE

## PYTHAGOREAN

One who holds to the doctrines and theories of Pythagoras (c. 580–500 B.C.). He was a Greek philosopher, religious leader, and mathematician who was born on the island of Samos, located in the Aegean Sea off the coast of Turkey. After extensive travels in the East, Pythagoras settled in Crotona, Italy, where he established a secret fraternity of aristocrats. This society maintained that the soul is immortal and separable from the body, and that the soul is reincarnated in different animal forms until it completes its transmigratory journey. Because of this belief, Pythagoreans tended to be vegetarians. They reasoned that leading a pure life would enable them to set their soul free from their body.

Pythagoreans believed in the mystical significance of numbers and that all relations can be reduced to number relations. The number one represented reason; two represented man; three represented woman; four represented justice (since it is the product of equals); five represented the union of man and woman (the numbers two and three); and six represented perfection. The number ten held sacred significance. Its pyramidal structure allegedly represented the totality of human reason and justice, as well as the cosmic creation through the four universal elements of earth, air, water, and fire.

Even the movement of the heavenly bodies had some cosmic numerical significance to Pythagoreans. They assigned the feminine qualities of the earth to even numbers and gave the masculine qualities of the celestial spheres to odd numbers. They also linked odd and even numbers, in tables of opposites, as well as with good and bad. Pythagoreans noticed that the vibrating strings of musical instruments produced melodious tones, especially when the ratios of the lengths of the strings were whole numbers. From this observation they concluded that music had an inherent mathematical structure and mystical power. Daily sessions of singing could transform the emotions of people, relieve their fears, and dissipate their worries.

New Age adherents have taken bits and pieces of what Pythagoreans believed and mixed in their own occult views of reality. They say the universe is governed by numerical laws to which all things are harmoniously related. They also believe the karmic cycles of birth and death are accompanied by exact numerological conditions that serve as hidden keys to the past, present, and future of people. Every person's birth has a particular astrological sign and its corresponding number. This number represents specific occult powers and qualities. Some contemporary occultists attach numerological significance to colors, adding new dimensions to the analyzation process.

*See also:* MUSIC, NEW AGE; NUMEROLOGY; SCIENCE, NEW AGE; VEGETARIANISM

# Q

## QUANTUM LEAP

The New Age belief that humankind is gradually progressing toward worldwide enlightenment. While humanity's spiritual evolution has occurred throughout the centuries, proponents say the pace has quickened with the dawning of the Aquarian Age. They propose that a quantum leap is necessary for humanity to achieve a burst of insight and cosmic consciousness.

*See also:* EVOLUTION; KUHN, THOMAS; TRANSFORMATION

## QUANTUM PHYSICS

A theory based on the premise that all perceptions of reality are the result of the action and interaction of indivisible particles and elemental forces. Quantum physics studies laws and processes of nature, such as electricity, gravity, and subatomic particles.

The work of quantum physicists has left researchers with unanswered questions about such astronomical phenomena as neutron stars, black holes, and gravitational waves. New Age adherents offer their own explanations for the mysteries of the universe. Some claim that our perception of reality is an illusion created by the energy impulses of the brain. These impulses work together in codes, creating experiences that have personal meaning. By entering into altered states of consciousness, people can transform pure thought into matter. If people can channel and enhance the vibrational patterns pulsing in and out of existence, then they can alter reality.

*See also:* METAPHYSICS, MYSTICISM

## QUARTUS FOUNDATION FOR SPIRITUAL RESEARCH

*See:* PRICE, JOHN RANDOLPH

## QUARTZ CRYSTAL

A hard, crystalline, and glassy-looking mineral consisting of silicone dioxide. Found throughout the world, this mineral exists as a component of sandstone and granite or as pure crystals in such rocks as agate, chalcedony, flint, and opal. Scientists have even found the mineral in some meteorites and lunar rocks. Quartz is used for a variety of industrial purposes such as an abrasive or as a key component in the manufacture of glass, ceramics, cements, and mortars.

Crystalogy, or the belief in the supernatural powers of the quartz crystal, has its origins in the ancient cultures of Greece, Egypt, Babylonia, and India. The ancient Greeks considered the mineral an enduring gift from the gods and used it to deter thirst and to enhance their ritual sacrifices. The Hindus of India believed quartz crystals functioned as an astrological door to the past and the future. Other pagan Oriental religions believed the light, which was reflected and refracted by the substance, illumined their minds and connected them with the great cosmic consciousness. Some held that crystals allowed people to make contact with spiritual beings, while others thought these spirits existed within the crystals themselves.

The quartz crystal plays a key role in New Age thought and practice. Some occultists claim that the quartz in the crust of the planet represents the sacred bones of Mother Nature, making it an essential substance to all life forms. Others maintain they can use quartz to summon and control supernatural forces. As with other power objects, the quartz crystal is an extension of the human body that can channel the energy of the soul. Crystal meditation enables people to connect their inner self with a universal energy force, allowing them to access unlimited mental powers.

Some enthusiasts place the mineral in their refrigerators to keep food fresh, under their pillows to assure good dreams, in their gardens to guarantee healthy plants, or in their barnyards to keep flies off cows. Crystals reputedly can induce pregnancy, cure loneliness, reduce stress, and heal ailments such as arthritis and blindness through psychic means. The substance has the power to amplify, realign, and balance energy patterns within the human body, resulting in the complete harmony of mind, body, and spirit. In some cases, adherents place crystals directly on specific areas of the body believing they will transmit continuous vibrations until healing occurs.

Clairvoyants and diviners employ "crystal gazing" to enter into a trancelike state so they can view future events. New Age adherents encourage the worldwide distribution and use of quartz crystals. They believe these objects are one more tool for achieving the cosmic consciousness of the human race and establishing the Aquarian Age of enlightenment and peace. If more people use crystals, the substance will act as a catalyst to cleanse humanity of all negative vibrations, thereby purifying the world for the coming age under the rule of Lord Maitreya.

*See also:* COLOROLOGY, COSMIC ENERGY, CRYSTAL, GOD, HOLISM,

# QUIMBY, PHINEAS PARKHURST (1802–1866)

A nineteenth-century metaphysical healer from Portland, Maine. Quimby believed physical ailments were manifestations of mental, emotional, and psychological aberrations. He believed he could "cure" patients by enabling them to reveal and correct their troubled mind-set. Quimby contended he could perceive the feelings of his patients simply by rendering them receptive to suggestion. With a soothing stroke of the head and gentle imagery, he could lead them from the "disease" caused by their erroneous beliefs into a state of truth and well-being. Quimby claimed that Christ used this technique to heal people through psychic means,

a process that Jesus wanted all people to use for good.

While many believed Quimby was a charlatan, few could question his dedication to his patients nor the financial success of his practice. A key incident occurred in 1862 when Quimby treated a new patient for "spinal inflammation." This patient initially placed her complete faith in Quimby's methods. One month after Quimby's death in January 1866, disciple Mary Baker Eddy (1821–1910) claimed to have taken a fatal fall. She supposedly was miraculously delivered from the injury and was subsequently endowed with the sacred writings of a new religion that she called Christian Science.

Quimby's ideas, such as all sickness being mental rather than physical, are easily recognizable in Eddy's book entitled *Science and Health* (1875). Ironically, Eddy not only denied Quimby's influence on her written work, but also derided him as an "unlearned" man. Nevertheless, his writings would play an influential role in the development of the New Thought movement, which stresses the power of the mind to heal disease and to improve life.

*See also:* CHRISTIAN SCIENCE; EDDY, MARY BAKER; NEW THOUGHT

# QUR'AN

The sacred writings of Islam. *Qur'an* is derived from an Arabic verb that means "to read." According to Muslim belief, Allah gave revelations to Muhammad through the angel Gabriel. The prophet then repeated these divine disclosures to copyists. His followers also committed the revelations to memory. A few years after Muhammad's death in 632, his followers compiled his proclamations into the book of Qur'an. In the early 650s, a group of Arabic scholars under the guidance of Uthman ibn Affan produced an authorized version of the Islamic scriptures. Numerous commentaries explain the Qur'an. In Tripoli, Libya, a library reputedly has more than twenty thousand commentaries on the book.

Muslims believe the Qur'an is the miraculous declaration of Allah. They also think the book is above human criticism and too sacred for analysis by pagans. Out of extreme reverence for the Qur'an, Muslims never hold the book below the belt. They refuse to touch it without first purifying themselves. The Qur'an is written in Arabic prose and is the earliest known work of the Islamic faith. The book is divided into 114 chapters of varying length. They contain Islamic legal, social, and civil, as well as military, commercial, and religious codes that Muslims are expected to observe. Throughout the book, the tone is dogmatic, authoritative, and stern. Muslims often will use excerpts from the Qur'an to decorate their weapons, banners, and buildings.

The main beliefs in the Qur'an teach the existence of only one God (Allah) and only one true religion (Islam). Everyone will experience a final judgment, and the wicked will be punished while the righteous will enjoy eternal bliss. The Qur'an also teaches that when humankind strayed from the path of truth and virtue, God sent prophets to show them the way back, and the greatest of the prophets were Moses, Jesus Christ, and Muhammad. The Qur'an uses graphic imagery in the form of stories to describe the rewards and punishments people will experience. Many of these accounts are also found in the sacred writings of Jews and Christians, as well as the Apocrypha. The Qur'an's admonitions, directives, and laws likewise resemble those found in the Jewish Scriptures.

Some New Age mystics claim the writings depict the evolution of the soul, while others say it describes the path for reuniting with the cosmic consciousness. Still others regard the Qur'an as a symbol of divine universal knowledge buried deep within the psyche of every person that can be tapped through enlightenment.

*See also:* BIBLE; BIBLE, NEW AGE; EVOLUTION; HADITH; JESUS CHRIST; SALVATION

# R

## RADIANCE TECHNIQUE (REIKI)

A therapeutic touch designed to tap into the healing energies that allegedly exist in the human body. Japanese scholar Mikao Usui rediscovered the radiance technique in ancient Sanskrit texts. Reiki has since undergone a resurgence of interest among those in the holistic health movement. Proponents claim physical, psychological, and spiritual ailments are simply the product of improper thinking. These symptoms result from an imbalance of energy that is easily corrected by transcending to a level of consciousness where divine awareness can be utilized.

Practitioners claim that by using a surrogate patient, healing energies can be transmitted to distant locations. Therapists claim that by laying hands on people, they can tap into the universal energy force and project its healing qualities to another location through psychic means. As Reiki students advance through seven degrees of "attunement," they learn to locate and manipulate the psychic energy centers that exist in the human body.

Reiki looks to the future when the enlightened of the world will readily understand and accept its divine powers of energy and light.

*See also:* COSMIC ENERGY, HOLISM

## RADIESTHESIA

The practice of seeking to discover the location of hidden objects through the use of divination techniques. A key tool used by practitioners is the pendulum. The device supposedly reacts to the vibrational energy that emanates from all matter. Advocates typically will hold a pendulum in a suspended position beneath the palm of their hand and over the object or question chart to be divined. The degree and direction of the pendulum swing indicates the intensity of positive and negative radiations, thereby allowing for the correction of imbalances. Some think the pendulum reacts to distortions in the earth's electromagnetic field, while others attribute the pendulum swing to unconscious movement of the diviner. Practitioners claim to develop sensitivity to the object's "powers" through personal occult practice, ancestral occult practice, or the transference of powers gained through the occult practice of another. They say the object enables them to enter an altered state of consciousness, receive wisdom from spirit guides, and attain enlightenment.

*See also:* COSMIC ENERGY, DIVINATION, PENDULUM, VIBRATIONS

## RAINBOW

The ancient Greeks believed the rainbow was the mistress of all perceptible reality. In Jewish Kabbalah, the rainbow symbolizes a sexual ritual in which the male sky god descends into the womb of the earth goddess. The Aborigines believe the Rainbow Serpent Mother made the world and gave birth to all humankind.

In New Age thinking, the rainbow is a divine symbol of the great white light. This entity supposedly divided into a spiritual trinity of red, blue, and yellow—colors appearing in the rainbow. Occultists say that the brilliant spectrum of hues represents the evolutionary progression of life throughout the different periods of history. They believe the rainbow symbolizes every individual's personal journey to enlightenment. Rainbow colors play a major role in hypnosis, witchcraft, and chakras, as well as crystals and in many other occult practices of the New Age.

*See also:* COLOROLOGY

# RAINBOW BRIDGE
*See:* ANTAHKARANA

# RAJNEESH, BHAGWAN SHREE (1931–1990)

A prominent Indian guru whose Eastern mysticism, combined with Western therapeutics, gained him considerable popularity during the human potential movement of the 1980s. He was born in Kuchwara, India, as Rajneesh Chandra Mohan, the eldest of twelve children. His parents raised him, along with his five sisters and six brothers, in Jainism, which is an offshoot of Hinduism. He studied philosophy at Jabalrur University, graduated in 1957, and then taught at Madhya State University. At some point, he claimed to have realized his innate divinity and oneness with the universe. This led him to leave the university in 1966, at which time he become a guru.

Rajneesh traveled throughout India, claiming his call to help humankind discover its need for enlightenment. Although his popularity in his native country was not substantial, he did gain a sizeable following throughout the world, especially in the United States. Rajneesh established his headquarters at Mount Abu in Rajasthan from 1969–1974. In 1974, he founded his first ashram, a Hindu religious retreat center, in a city south of Bombay called Poona. His orange-to-red clad disciples quickly increased in numbers. During the ashram's seven years of operation, about fifty thousand Americans flocked to learn from Rajneesh. These youth soaked up his promises of a new world governed by love and sexual freedom. This led to his reputation as India's "sex guru."

In 1981 Rajneesh's multimillion dollar organization ran into problems with the Indian government concerning income tax evasion. He subsequently relocated to the United States where he purchased a large ranch in Antelope, Oregon. He renamed the site Rajneeshpuram, and it became the focal point of his operation. However his troubles with the law continued, forcing Rajneesh to relocate to Charlotte, North Carolina. Federal agents eventually arrested him, and a court found him guilty of violating U.S. immigration laws. The judge gave him a suspended sentence, fined him $400,000, and deported him. Subsequently, Rajneesh flew back to New Delhi where he remained until his death in Poona in 1990.

Rajneesh, whose name means either "God Sir" or "Sir God," promoted a number of radical teachings. He condemned the powers of reason and intellect, claiming these were often in error. Instead, he advocated that people should reach beyond the physical world to achieve a quantum leap in cosmic consciousness. He promoted the complete dismantling of the family, the practice of open sex, and the abolition of all culturally imposed restrictions on personal freedoms. In fact, he taught that through love/sex meditation, people could attain higher levels of consciousness and eventually reach enlightenment. Rajneesh defined God as the divine resident within every person. He also claimed that every person was united with the cosmic essence and that death was nothing more than merging back into the universal force.

Although Rajneesh died in 1990, his strong influence continues in the New Age Movement. One of Rajneesh's converts is Richard Price, the founder of the Esalen Institute and a leader in the human potential movement.

*See also:* ASHRAM, GURU, JAINISM, SEXUALITY

# RAMTHA

An alleged spirit manifestation claiming to be "The Enlightened One." This entity says he is a thirty-five-thousand-year-old apparition who has returned to earth to aid people on their spiritual journey into the New Age. He is channeled by J. Z. Knight who describes Ramtha as a beautiful spirit of light. She says that when he manifests himself to her, he has bronze skin, ebony eyes, a chiseled nose, a broad jawline, and a winsome smile. Knight claims that Ramtha wears a purple robe over his mighty eight-foot frame. The entity radiates a dazzling display of color and light, giving his countenance a look of innocence, peace, and holiness.

Knight says that Ramtha was the mightiest of warriors long ago. He dressed in woolen robes and furs and lived on the march with his multitude of noble soldiers. At some point, one of Ramtha's colleagues betrayed him and severely wounded him with a sword. As he lay bleeding on the floor, he heard the voice of an unknown god of the ancient peoples telling him to stand. During his recovery, Ramtha claims he was stripped of his pride and hatred, and forced to contemplate all he had done in the name of human freedom. After seven years of contemplation and searching, Ramtha allegedly discovered that this god who saved his life was the innate divinity within all humanity. At sixty-three years of age, Ramtha completed his reali-zation of godhood and ascended into the heavens.

According to Knight, this entity has now returned to earth to reintroduce human beings to their divine nature. Ramtha predicts the soon dawning of a New Age in which humanity will know that psychic thought is the creative and supportive element of life—the only authority to which mankind is accountable. Ramtha teaches that people are inherently divine and the sole determiners of what they should be and do. "God" supposedly is the divine energy residing within every person, while Jesus is one of many enlightened individuals who realized their christhood and ascended to a higher plane of existence.

*See also:* DEMON; KNIGHT, J. Z.; LEMURA; SIN; TRANCE CHANNELING

# RAPTURE

In evangelical Christian theology, the term *rapture* (based on the Latin translation of the Greek verb translated "to snatch up") signifies the meeting of living and resurrected believers with Jesus Christ "in the air." Christians usually associate the rapture with the beginning of the tribulation period (John 14:1–3; 1 Thess. 1:10; 4:13–18; 5:9).

In New Age thought, the term signifies a quantum leap forward in the attainment of insight and cosmic consciousness. Jesus sup-

posedly is the prime example of transcending death and evolving into spiritual light by crossing from the physical to the astral dimensions of existence.

Occultists claim that as civilizations reach and maintain sufficient frequency levels of evolutionary vibrations, they transcend the barriers between life and universal existence. Therefore they appear invisible to the world from which they came. The mysterious disappearance of certain cultures, such as the Atlantians or Mayans, can be explained by the wondrous rapture of spiritual evolution. Some advocates contend that a similar rapture must take place before the dawning of the Aquarian Age. At that time, the negative energies of the planet will be eliminated, permitting the world to achieve harmonic balance.

*See also:* HEAVEN, PURIFICATION, TRANSCENDENCE, VIBRATIONS

# RASTAFARIANISM

A West Indian, racially-based religion that condemns all members of the white race as evil and proclaims the divinity of the former emperor of Ethiopia Ras Tafari (Haile Selassie I). The movement was begun by Marcus Garvey (1887–1940) in the 1920s as the first organized black nationalist movement. Modern Rastafarians avoid calling themselves a religion. They regard themselves as a way of life that honors the black race and seeks through the social sciences to address poverty and oppression. They speak of the authority of the Christian Bible, but consider it tainted by the whites who worked on it. Selassie is the true Messiah. Ethiopia is the true heaven. Black people are reincarnated Israelites and will one day rule the world. Civil marriage is forbidden among most Rastas as a white cultural tradition.

In contrast to Rastafarian doctrine, Selassie was not a Rastafarian, never spoke of himself in Messianic or divine terms, and considered himself a devout Christian. When the emperor died, many Rastas considered the announcement a trick by the media to undermine their faith. They now teach that, since Selassie's atoms are part of the world, his life is never-ending. Rastafarians also believe that Scripture teaches the necessity of using "ganja" (marijuana) in worship.

## REAPPEARANCE OF CHRIST AND THE MASTERS OF WISDOM, THE

A popular New Age work written by Scottish lecturer Benjamin Creme. This document depicts Lord Maitreya as the physical manifestation of the second coming of Christ. Creme's book was published in 1980 by the Tara Center, an organization designed to disseminate prophetic information that supposedly has been telepathically channeled by Maitreya. The book declares that Maitreya is the leader of an ethereal band of advanced souls who have returned to earth to assist humankind on their evolutionary transformation to godhood. Although Creme has yet to produce his cosmic christ, Lord Maitreya and the Masters of Wisdom have a popular following among New Age enthusiasts.

*See also:* AVATAR; COSMIC CHRIST; CREME, BENJAMIN; MAITREYA, LORD; TARA CENTER

## REBIRTHING

A popular New Age therapeutic practice developed by Leonard Orr. Rebirthing is designed to release people from unconscious, yet traumatic, memories of their physical birth. Orr believes that infants experience fear and anxiety during the birthing process that adversely affects the remainder of their lives. He claims that when the physician cuts the umbilical cord, infants are forced to establish new breathing patterns that rob them of access to their divine inner self.

The therapeutic process begins by teaching people the breathing cycles they supposedly lost at birth. Through the rhythmic pattern of inhaling and exhaling, participants enter an altered state of consciousness and reach the core of their inner being. Getting into contact with the true self frees the universal life force and cleanses the soul of the

distress and anxieties of physical birth. Practitioners learn to repeat these rebirthing exercises until they are adept at achieving an altered state of consciousness. With realization of this link to the cosmic mind and their innate divinity, they can create their own realities by tapping into the unlimited psychic powers of the universe.

*See also:* ALTERED STATE, HINDUISM, HOLOTROPHIC BREATHING

## REFLEXOLOGY

The holistic belief that the soles of the feet can enable people to understand the internal workings of the human body. Practitioners contend that the nerve endings in certain areas of the sole correspond with psychic pathways and connections that lead to specific systems and organs throughout the body. By applying pressure to the nerve endings in the foot, therapists seek to redirect the balance of healing energies in corresponding parts of the body, thereby relieving pain, strain, and stress.

Reflexologists assert that the foot symbolizes the upright human form. The big toe represents the head, the ball of the foot represents the heart and lungs, and the lower arch represents the liver and colon. The success of reflexology is often temporary and usually demands that patients continue therapy while learning the teachings of ancient pagan belief systems.

*See also:* CHIROMANCY, HOLISM, IRIDOLOGY

## REICH, WILHELM

*See:* ORGONE

## REIKI

*See:* RADIANCE TECHNIQUE

## REINCARNATION

A belief in the successive rebirth of souls into new bodies, as the soul progresses toward perfection. Proponents base their beliefs on the idea of karma, the Hindu concept of the force generated by the sum total of an individual's actions, especially religious or ritual actions both good and bad. Hinduism teaches that the lives of people are an accumulation of both good and bad karma. The imbalance of this accumulation determines the circumstances for the next reincarnated life. The rebirthing cycle continues until a balance of karma is reached. At this point, the individual rejoins the Universal Mind and enters the state of absolute oneness called nirvana.

Hindu tradition maintains that, in the beginning, a perfect balance existed within the "godhead," or the universal essence from which all things originate and to where all things go. Then something happened to disrupt the harmonic balance, which set the wheels of reincarnation into motion. Because bad karma originated with the universe itself, its existence is inevitable. Hinduism teaches that each life is on a journey to nirvana. When an individual reaches nirvana, all traces of desire and individual consciousness will be extinguished.

New Age adherents claim that the concept of reincarnation has been scientifically verified by research into past life memories. They maintain that déjà vu, or the feeling of having experienced something before, is an intuitive memory of past lives. Spontaneous recall supposedly occurs in young children who insist that they have lived before, while psychic recall takes place when people get in touch with memories of their past lives. This is usually accomplished through hypnotic regression. Practitioners enter altered states of consciousness and journey past the creative edge of the imagination into the realms of psychic awareness. This theory holds that every person possesses incarnational memories deep within their psyche that can be reached through hypnosis.

Some acclaim the therapeutic value of recalling past reincarnations by asserting that it has alleviated their personality disorders, eliminated their phobias, and cured their physical ailments.

*See also:* DEATH, HINDUISM, PAST LIVES THERAPY, SIN, TRANSMIGRATION

## RELATIVITY

The theory advanced by German-American physicist Albert Einstein (1879–1955), that views all motion in the universe as relative instead of absolute.

New Age adherents have philosophically used Einstein's theory of relativity to justify their claim that the world contains no moral constants. Gurus teach that everything is contingent on the individual. Since every person is innately divine and united to the cosmic mind, they are solely responsible for determining what is ethically right and wrong for them. This way of thinking lies at the heart of relativism, which rules out the existence of universal absolutes of any kind. All "truth" is dependent upon, and limited to, the individual and to the time or place in which he or she acts.

*See also:* SCIENCE, NEW AGE; TRANSFORMATION

## REMOTE VIEWING

The telepathic reception or transmittal of psychic information about distant locations and occurrences. In a unique blend of extrasensory powers, practitioners claim they can perceive past, present, and future events through clairvoyance from remote locations involving absolutely no physical contact with the subject in question. They base this assertion on the idea that psychic phenomena operates beyond the restrictions of physical laws. They say the past, present, and future of humankind exists on its own dimensional plane. Therefore, people can use the powers of remote viewing to alter the past by transmitting a precognitive image back in time.

In order to master this technique, initiates enter an altered state of consciousness in which they block out the mental noises caused by their memories and imaginations, thereby enabling them to exercise their psychic abilities. Adherents claim this will allow people to discover their union with the cosmic Mind and tap into the divine powers dormant within them. As more people take this evolutionary step, the consciousness of humankind will reach a critical mass, and be transformed.

See also: CLAIRVOYANCE, EXTRASENSORY PERCEPTION, PSYCHIC, TELEPATHY

## RESEARCH AND ENLIGHTENMENT, ASSOCIATION FOR (ARE)

A New Age organization founded in 1931 by physic healer Edgar Cayce (1877–1945). The Association for Research and Enlightenment (ARE) is dedicated to the combined study of religion, science, and philosophy, as well as psychoanalytics and parapsychology. ARE is located in Virginia Beach, Virginia, and promotes the teachings of Cayce on the subjects of reincarnation, past lives, prophecy, and psychic phenomena. In addition, ARE offers workshops and seminars in self-hypnosis, visualization, symbology, auras, numerology, and a variety of other occult studies.

Because Cayce is a forerunner of the New Age Movement, his reputation adds a level of credibility to their "research." By the time of Cayce's death in 1945, ARE had more than thirty thousand of his psychic readings on file. Today the organization continues to preserve the readings and to make Cayce's views available upon request.

See also: CAYCE, EDGAR; TRANCE CHANNELING

## RESTORATION OF THE TEN COMMANDMENTS OF GOD

Ugandan doomsday cult in which hundreds of followers committed suicide or were murdered in early 2000. Begun by Credonia Mwerinde and Joseph Kibwetere, the cult was one of several groups to predict that the world would end on December 31, 1999. Mwerinde, a former banana beer vender, was known as "the Programmer" by followers. He and Kibwetere collected a group of disaffected Roman Catholics, including two defrocked priests, Joseph Kasapurari and Dominic Kataribabo, into the movement's leadership circle. Those who joined Restoration gave all of their property to the organization, and after predictions of apocalypse proved false, many tried to leave, demanding the return of what they had given. After a fire at the cult chapel, authorities found that 530 people had died inside the building, some of whom had been stabbed or strangled. Mass graves in nearby villages turned up 394 more corpses. Most of the group's leaders were thought to have survived the mass murder-suicide.

See also: JONES, JAMES (JIM) WARREN

## RESURRECTION

A keystone belief of Christianity that, because Jesus was God, he had authority over death and was raised on the third day after his crucifixion. Christians further believe that the soul of every human being will be raised by God, either to eternal life in Christ or to everlasting punishment for sin.

Such a personal and final concept of resurrection is utterly incompatible with the animistic or pantheistic worldview of New Age beliefs. Resurrection becomes successive reincarnations or a spiritual melding with the world spirit.

Several theories have been framed to answer the obvious power and influence of the story of Christ's resurrection at a particular point in history. First, the event did not occur at all and was only given mythological or metaphorical importance by the early disciples. Second, members of an Essene sect were able to remove the body of Jesus from the cross before he was completely dead. A variation is that he was entombed while still alive and later returned to consciousness. Third, the man Jesus died, but the presence of the Christ left his body while he was on the cross and lived on. Fourth, there never was a human Jesus of Nazareth. The divine Christ only took an illusionary human form, which could not suffer or know death. Fifth, the spiritual emanation of the Christ lived on after the death of Jesus and appeared to the disciples while they were in a meditative trance, so that they encountered the Christ through trance channeling. Sixth, the Lord

Maitreya, the New Age christ, entered the dead body of Jesus and returned him to life.

*See also:* ATONEMENT, MYTHOLOGY, REINCARNATION, SALVATION

## RHINE, J. B. (1895–1980)

An American psychologist who did pioneering work in the field of parapsychology. In 1927, while at Duke University in Durham, North Carolina, Rhine began to use statistical methods to research parapsychology. In 1935, he and a colleague named William McDougall established the parapsychological laboratory, and in 1937 Rhine started the *Journal of Parapsychology*. His sophisticated and rigorous methods led to the development of parapsychology as a recognized field for quantitative research. Most of Rhine's early investigations were concentrated on three basic types of extrasensory perception—clairvoyance, precognition, and telepathy. Clairvoyance is the ability to discern something about inanimate objects or events without the use of the known senses. Precognition is the ability to predict a future event without inferring it from present knowledge. Telepathy is the ability to read another person's thoughts.

New Age adherents say that these and other phenomena occur in everyday life. Through direct personal experience and objective scientific methods, psychic abilities that supposedly lay dormant in all people can be brought to a conscious level of awareness for exploration and use. When people manifest psychic phenomena, they reputedly are in contact with spirits from other dimensions. These entities leave the astral plane, enter the material plane, and indwell a human host. Advocates claim these spirit guides assist humanity in evolving to a state of perfection.

*See also:* CLAIRVOYANCE, EXTRASENSORY PERCEPTION, PARAPSYCHOLOGY, PRECOGNITION, TELEPATHY

## RI-ME

Nonsectarian Tibetan Buddhist movement that combines various teachings without rivalry and embraces the beliefs of all schools of Buddhism. It is influential in New Age philosophy, particularly through the interest of United States film celebrities of the 1990s.

*See also:* DALAI LAMA

## RING OF STONES

Ancient, artificially designed monumental arrangements of stones. These are most commonly found throughout Europe and especially in England, Scotland, and Ireland. Most formations follow a careful arrangement with obvious seasonal or astronomical significance. Stone rings were likely constructed by pre-Celtic European tribes who worshiped the sun. They were adopted by the Celts for use in their religions.

*See also:* CIRCLE, SOLSTICE

## RINPOCHE, CHOGYAM TRUNGPA

*See:* SHAMBHALA TRAINING INTERNATIONAL

## *ROAD LESS TRAVELED, THE*

A self-help book written by psychiatrist M. Scott Peck. *The Road Less Traveled* (1980) claims to present a new psychology of love, traditional values, and spiritual growth. The author maintains that by confronting and resolving their problems, people can reach a higher level of self-understanding. He bases his argument on the premise that no fundamental distinction separates the mind and the spirit. Spiritual growth and mental growth are one and the same. Peck argues that self-understanding, self-effort, and self-discipline are the keys to achieving mental and spiritual well-being. By understanding and consistently applying the right principles and truths culled from different scientific and religious disciplines, people can achieve self-actualization.

New Age adherents identify with this approach because it fits well with their views about life. They would agree with Peck that the human mind holds the key to divine reality. By getting in touch with the inner self, people can travel the road leading to enlightenment and godhood. In this way of thinking, "god" is an impersonal reservoir of humankind's collective wisdom and experience. New Age adherents agree that the ultimate goal is for people to become an equal, interrelated part of the universal essence. They say the human race is in the process of making an evolutionary leap in cosmic consciousness that will eventually usher in the Aquarian Age of peace, harmony, and love under the rule of Lord Maitreya.

*See also:* EVOLUTION; JUNG, CARL GUSTAV; SELF-ACTUALIZATION

## ROBERTS, JANE (1929–1984)

A noted New Age author and channel for a spirit guide named Seth. This entity claims to be one of a host of ascended masters who have returned to earth from the astral dimension to assist people in achieving a transformation of consciousness. Roberts wrote twenty books "dictated" by Seth. She also disseminated Seth's messages to thousands through public appearances and seminars. One of the key teachings of Seth is that people are innately divine and have the inherent ability to create their own realities. Another assertion is that sin and guilt are merely antiquated religious notions taught by those who want to prevent people from achieving godhood. Seth maintains that a "greater self" resides within each person, the total of all the lives of all people who have ever lived throughout time. This greater self is the only authority to whom people must answer and from whom they must take their directions.

*See also:* SPIRIT GUIDES, TRANCE CHANNELING

## ROCK MUSIC

A form of popular entertainment that combined the elements of rhythm and blues with country and western in the 1950s. Since then, it has fragmented into numerous styles ranging from traditional rock and roll to heavy metal music, grunge or alternative rock, and "soft" rock.

While numerous artists and musical styles influenced early rock music, Elvis Presley is generally considered to be the first widely-accepted performer to introduce elements of overt sexuality. While much of Presley's music would be considered tame by today's standards, he had an electrifying impact on the emerging youth culture of the 1950s. Following Presley, the Beatles are the best-known early rock group. Throughout the 1960s, they experimented with different types of lyrical forms and permanently reshaped the public's view of rock music. Their later sometimes complex and sophisticated pieces were a blend of Eastern mysticism, American rhythms, and English lyrics. In contrast, groups such as the Rolling Stones and Blood, Sweat, and Tears gave rock music the image of sensuality, brashness, and alienation.

With the rise of the 1960s drug culture, such groups as the Grateful Dead and Jefferson Airplane began to produce psychedelic acid rock. By the time of the Woodstock Festival in August 1969, the theme of "turning on, tuning in, and dropping out" prevailed in the lyrics of rock music. Throughout the rest of the century, various rock groups continued to focus on themes of rebellion and immorality.

Popular rock themes such as hedonism and anarchy are affirmed by occultists. Advocates approve the widespread distribution and use of hallucinogenic drugs that they believe will help people enter other dimensions of reality and achieve enlightenment. Satanists applaud the deranged messages of some contemporary rock groups that extol murder, suicide, and rape, as well as child abuse and sadomasochism.

*See also:* DRUG; MUSIC, NEW AGE; SEXUALITY

## ROLFING (STRUCTURAL INTEGRATION)

A massage technique designed in the 1930s by biochemist Ida Rolf (1896–1979). Rolfing supposedly realigns an individual's energy pattern with that of the universal life force, leading to the enhancement of physical, psychological, and emotional characteristics. Rolf therapists receive training at the Institute of Structural Integration in Boulder, Colorado. Treatments involve ten sixty-minute sessions, each devoted to a specific part of the body. Rolfing enthusiasts believe the physical effects of aging can be reversed through the manipulation of connective tissue. The technique allegedly increases personal insight, produces bursts of intuition, and causes an array of psychic phenomena.

*See also:* ACUPUNCTURE, BALANCING, COSMIC ENERGY

## ROOT RACE

A term used to denote the origins of modern humanity. The most popular New Age theory traces the human race back to Atlantis, which, according to legend, sank beneath the sea. The theory is that seven root races originated from this continent. These include the Toltecs, Rmoahals, Tlavatli, and Turanians, as well as the Akkadians, Mongols, and Aryans—the last of which they consider the master race. According to folklore, the destruction of Atlantis brought about the scattering of these races. Those in a more highly developed state of consciousness migrated to Iran, India, and throughout Europe. The Aryans carried with them the secrets necessary for humanity's ascension to godhood. According to some, only two root races are of any consequence—those on the verge of realizing their godlike status, and those hindering the final transformation of humanity. When the Aquarian Age dawns, the latter supposedly will be banished to another dimension of existence.

*See also:* ARYAN RACE; ATLANTIS, LOST CONTINENT OF; NEW AGE MOVEMENT

## ROSARY

A circular string of beads constructed of wood, metal, or stone. In the West they are used mainly by Roman Catholics to aid in devotions. The rosary used in the West has five sets of ten beads, called decades, for the recitation of the *Ave Maria,* or "Hail Mary." Each set is separated by a single bead for the repeating of the *Paternoster,* or Lord's Prayer. When users finish with an entire decade of beads, they ordinarily recite the *Gloria Patri,* or "Glory Be to the Father." While the various prayers are repeated, worshipers are instructed to meditate on the joys, sorrows, and ineffable mysteries surrounding the lives of Mary and Jesus.

Prayer beads are also used by Muslims, Hindus, and Buddhists. Among certain New Age adherents, the worship of Mary is combined with the veneration of the Mother Goddess, or Queen of Heaven, of pagan religions. Initiates use the prayer beads to display a filial devotion to the Mother Goddess, to invoke her name for maternal intercession, and to imitate her as the outstanding role model for enlightened existence. Some gurus claim that by using the rosary to meditate on the Queen of Heaven, people can tap into metaphysical realities and foresee the future. Other occultists claim that, in using the prayer beads to channel thoughts on the Mother Goddess, users will become more aware of their divine inner self and achieve greater union with the cosmic mind.

*See also:* GODDESS WORSHIP, MANDALA, MARY

## ROSICRUCIANS

Members of an international fraternity devoted to esoteric wisdom and psychic enlightenment. Christian Rosenkreutz (1378–1484) is

Rosicrucian
Rose Cross

thought to have founded this secret society in fifteenth-century Europe. *Rosicrucian* comes from the medieval Latin *Rosae Crucis* and also from the translation of the German name for a friar. The official emblem of the Rosicrucians combines a rose and a cross.

Some historians trace the origins of the fraternity to the writings of English philosopher Francis Bacon (1561–1626). Others point to the work of a Lutheran pastor named

Johan Valentin Andrea (1586–1654). In 1614, he supposedly wrote *Fama Fraternitatis,* or *Account of the Brotherhood.* A year later, this was followed by a publication named *Confessio Fraternitatis,* or *Confession of the Brotherhood.* Regardless of the exact origin of these documents, these writings clearly contain the foundation for Rosicrucian thought. These books document the spiritual journey of Christian Rosenkreutz and his initiation into the mysteries of ancient Egyptian and other Eastern religions.

According to legend, Rosenkreutz was rejected by his contemporaries, which caused him to form a secret society. By the eighteenth century, this organization had spread throughout Germany, Poland, and Russia. It reached the shores of America as early as the 1700s. Today several orders of Rosicrucianism exist, with each maintaining a system of lodges to assist members in reaching their highest divine potential and cultivating their paranormal abilities.

The beliefs of the Rosicrucians combine ideas and superstitions from a number of sources. The fraternity views God as an impersonal and detached entity who is one with the creation. They view Jesus as an enlightened human being with the Christ-spirit. He serves as a role model, showing all people how to attain godhood.

Rosicrucians maintain that human history is characterized by evolutionary progress, and that all knowledge regarding the human race is available to those who choose to find it. They claim to have discovered information about Atlantis and Lemuria, two lost, ancient, human civilizations. The society makes a sharp distinction between the physical and spiritual realms, teaching that people can learn the cosmic blueprint for truth and enlightenment by experiencing suffering and meditation through innumerable reincarnations. Many New Age adherents have adopted these beliefs, either in whole or in part. Some think Rosicrucianism is the forerunner of modern occultism.

*See also:* CROSS, FREEMASONRY, MYSTICISM, PANTHEISM

## ROSWELL INCIDENT

Identified by UFOlogists as the site of a July 4, 1947, crash of an alien space craft. An entire mythology has arisen around the reports of the crash and the U.S. government cover-up. Debris from the craft, and the aliens found in the wreckage, are usually thought to have been taken to a mysterious Area 51 facility on a military base near Roswell, New Mexico. The actual place identified as a crash site is seventy-five miles north. Roswell now hosts an annual July 4 UFO and New Age festival. The usual explanation for the "Roswell incident" is that the wreckage was the result of problems with high-altitude balloons.

*See also:* AREA 51, UNIDENTIFIED FLYING OBJECT, UNIDENTIFIED FLYING OBJECT EXPERIENCE

## RUNE

Ancient alphabet characters of northern European peoples, often thought to have magical significance. Rune alphabets included the thirty-two-letter Anglo-Saxon, the sixteen-letter Scandinavian, and the twenty-four-letter Teutonic. Runic characters tend to be made mostly of straight lines, which

**Runes**

are easier to carve into wood or stone. These alphabets were in use at the time of Christ and did not fall into extinction until the end of the Middle Ages.

*Rune* probably means "mysterious writing." The various alphabets associated with it were used for charms and other secret inscriptions on bone, wood, metal, and stone. An important word was associated with each letter, and combinations of letters were used to convey esoteric messages of past, present, and future events.

Scandinavian mythology attributes the creation of runic letters to the Mother Goddess. She anointed women as the keepers of divine secrets throughout the ages. The legend contends that only through great sacrifice was the supreme god Odin allowed access to the secrets, which then granted him miraculous powers to interpret the past, control the present, and predict the future. In the ancient divination practice called rune casting, dice or stones inscribed with magical characters were thrown or laid in front of those searching for esoteric knowledge. Mystical answers emerged from the depths of the seeker.

New Age adherents have continued these ancient pagan practices, claiming they can awaken innate psychic powers within people. Through rune casting, occultists try to interpret the significance of different combinations of letters and symbols in hope of unlocking the mysteries of the universe.

At least one factor in the modern interest was the renaissance in Teutonic mythology stimulated by the German Nazis of the 1930s. Nazis were strongly influenced by the occult and experimented with Teutonic runes in search of secrets to an inherent power in the original Germanic peoples. The Scandinavian and Druidic peoples used runes to foretell the future. Characters would be carved into pieces of wood or stone, pulled from a bag at random and thrown down on the ground. Combinations of letters helped the user make decisions.

Modern fantasy writers have been known to draw on the Scandinavian myths, so that runic magic figures prominently in their stories. This does not mean these writers have a pantheistic worldview or a New Age orientation. For instance, J. R. R. Tolkien, a fervent Roman Catholic, included runic magic in the plots of his fantasy stories *The Hobbit* and *The Lord of the Rings* trilogy.

*See also:* DIVINATION, MAGIC

## RUSSELL, CHARLES TAZE
*See:* JEHOVAH'S WITNESSES

## RYERSON, KEVIN

A New Age channeler and seminar leader, Kevin Ryerson has promoted reincarnation, futurism, and New Age nutritional principles in books and on television. He became well known through his association with Shirley MacLaine and figured prominently in her autobiographical books as a channel for spirits that have come to help the human race on their journey to enlightenment. He is on the board of directors of the Intuition Network and teaches trance channeling and other subjects frequently in "intensives," retreats and seminars that are held around the world. He leads tours to lecture on the esoteric power of the Egyptian and Central American pyramids.

During Ryerson's adolescence, he immersed himself in the writings of the clairvoyant Edgar Cayce (1877–1945) and became fascinated with trance channeling. By Ryerson's early twenties, he was an avid student of parapsychology and psychic research. His active involvement with Eastern meditative practices led to his first encounter with spirit guides.

One popular entity channeled by Ryerson is named John. He supposedly is an Essene (with an Elizabethan accent) who lived at the time of Christ. Another popular entity is named Tom McPherson, who Ryerson portrays as an Irish pickpocket with a mischievous sense of humor. Ryerson advertises that, for a fee, his entities can tap into the collective unconscious of humankind to reveal insights from the past, present, or future. The entity named John portrays Jesus as a pristine example of one who attained enlightenment through an intensive study and application of Eastern mysticism. Satan symbolizes the human race's struggle to regain a knowledge of their inherent divinity, whereas the human soul is a metaphor for God or the Universal Mind.

*See also:* CAYCE, EDGAR; MACLAINE, SHIRLEY; TRANCE CHANNELING

# S

## SABBAT (SABBATH)

A holiday for Satanists, Wiccans, and other occultists to gather to renew their allegiance to Satan, the Mother Goddess, or nature. The *sabbat*, which is the Latin and French spelling for Sabbath, is characterized by mystic rights and orgies. Some contemporary witches maintain the sabbat is merely a social gathering at which participants celebrate the changing face of the Earth Mother who is forever pursued by the Sky Father. The ceremony supposedly reveals the times when the cycles of inner humanity and cosmic events connect, resulting in the emanation of intense rhythmic energies.

Witches typically observe eight seasonal festivals, or sabbats. These include Imbolg (or Candlemas on February 2), Spring Equinox (March 21), Beltane (or May Day on April 30), Midsummer Solstice (June 22), Lugnasad (or Lammas on July 31), Autumn Equinox (September 21), Samhain (or Halloween on October 31), and Winter Solstice (or Yule on December 22). The greater sabbats include Imbolg, Beltane, Lugnasad, and Samhain, while the lesser sabbats include the Spring Equinox, Summer Solstice, Autumn Equinox, and Winter Solstice. Witches believe the Winter Solstice marks the birth of the Sun Child, while Imbolg commemorates his growth. The Spring Equinox marks the meeting of God and the maiden Goddess, while Beltane commemorates their union in matrimony. The Summer Solstice marks the consummation of their union, while Lugnasad marks the death of God. The Autumn Solstice commemorates the return of the Sun Child to the womb of the Mother Goddess. The seasonal festivals culminate at Samhain, which is also considered the witches' New Year.

The sabbat celebrations begin at midnight and often continue until dawn. Once a revered stone is cast and the energy of Satan is invoked, the assembly of priests and priestesses lead members in ceremonial rituals, business discussions, and the exchange of knowledge, herbs, and spells. The group then finishes the nighttime observance with eating, drinking, dancing, and sometimes sexual encounters.

*See also:* BLACK SABBATH, EVIL, SATANISM, WITCHCRAFT

## SALVATION

Deliverance, rescue, or preservation. In evangelical Christian theology, salvation refers to eternal deliverance from the penalty of sin and the obtaining of new life in Jesus Christ through faith.

New Age salvation is achieved by gaining a new perspective in which people realize their interconnectedness with all things, including themselves and the divine oneness. Since people have forgotten their true divine nature, they require a paradigm shift in thinking. This occurs when people are convinced that everything is fundamentally divine because everything flows from the universal self. By breaking down psychological barriers, developing psychic powers, and achieving higher awareness, New Age adherents believe people can realize their godhood. The long-term goal is to achieve enlightenment, thereby finding release from the endless cycles of reincarnation.

*See also:* BLOOD OF CHRIST, SIN

## SAMHAIN

*See:* HALLOWEEN

## SANAT KUMURA

A spirit guide revered by New Age adherents. Occultists rank Sanat Kumura below and

226

answerable to the Solar Logos. Legend holds that after a war erupted in the heavens, Sanat Kumura was banished from the planet Venus. This entity then came to earth to link spirit guides with human hosts who would channel their messages to the rest of the planet. At the beginning of every new epoch, Sanat Kumura dispatches a christ who imparts the knowledge needed by the world to experience a shift in universal consciousness. New Age adherents say the next christ is Lord Maitreya who will usher in a time of unparalleled harmony, love, and wisdom. Under the direction of Sanat Kumura, this christ of the Aquarian Age will purify the earth of all negative elements obstructing world peace.

*See also:* ANTICHRIST, LUCIFERIC DOCTRINE, VENUS

## SANGHA

An ideal Buddhist community inhabited by those more advanced in their spiritual development than the average Buddhist. Sangha comes from a Sanskrit word meaning "association." Communal living in the Sangha can be either temporary or permanent. Monks act as leaders in the community, and live a regimented life of meditation and study of sacred texts. Lay members of the community spend most of their time worshiping Buddha, supporting the monks, or observing dharma, the moral law. Those who follow their prescribed religious and ethical duties supposedly will earn merit toward higher rebirths and escape the laws of karma.

The communal living associated with the Sangha is prevalent among New Age sects. New Age advocates believe that the more people they can get to support and participate in communal living, the closer they will come to achieving their utopian dream of ushering in an Aquarian Age of enlightenment.

*See also:* BUDDHISM, DHARMA, PEACE

## SANSKRIT

An ancient language of India and the classical language of Hinduism and its sacred writings, the Vedas. To mark such distinctions as case, number, gender, and tense, as well as person, mood, or voice, Sanskrit highly inflects its words. Elaborate derivations and compounding of its nouns, adjectives, and verbs also characterize this language. According to legend, Sanskrit was the magical language created by the Mother Goddess, Kali. The fifty letters of the alphabet *(matrika)* were considered symbols of Logos power because the creation of the world allegedly occurred through these letters. Kali supposedly attached sounds to each letter *(namtametruka)*. When each one was voiced, it brought a different aspect of the universe into existence. The goddess is often depicted with the elements as her primal mantras, which are Lam (Earth), Vam (Water), Yam (Air), and Ram (Fire). Artwork often shows the deity with a necklace of skulls depicting the letters of the Sanskrit alphabet.

Many New Age cults regard Sanskrit as a magical language. Initiates use combinations of letters and words in the superstitious belief that they possess mystical power. Some advocates claim that by chanting the letters of the mantra OM, people can summon the deities embodied by its sound. This and other mantras based on the letters of the Sanskrit alphabet are also used to achieve altered states of consciousness. Some occultists assert that certain mantras are the verbal representation of an individual's innate divinity. Therefore by chanting a special dirge, devotees reputedly can achieve enlightenment and union with ultimate Truth.

*See also:* HINDUISM, MANTRA, MOTHER EARTH, OM

## SATAN

In the Bible, Satan is portrayed as a personal and supernatural being who is exceedingly intelligent and powerful. Satan rules over a fallen hierarchy of angels. He once served in the presence of God as a specially appointed cherub (Ezek. 28:14). He was created with magnificent splendor but succumbed to pride (Isa. 14:3–17).

Satan works with his demonic cohorts (2 Peter 2:4; Jude 1:6) to perpetuate his original rebellion against God. Though he is a created, finite being, the Devil has tremendous supernatural power and sinister schemes. Because of Christ's atoning sacrifice, Satan awaits certain doom and will be forced to bow to the lordship of Christ.

New Age adherents reject the biblical teaching concerning Satan. Few occultists (other than those who identify themselves as Satanists) worship the Devil as a fallen angel whom God cast from heaven. A few sects identify Lucifer as the benevolent brother of Christ, the one who has come to aid people on their journey to enlightenment. In some cases, Satan is venerated as the symbolic representation of a permeating energy force or as the personification of the collective unconscious. In other instances, the Devil represents dark forces within the nature of humanity.

*See also:* FALL OF HUMANITY, THE; SATANISM

## SATAN, CHURCH OF

A San Francisco based cult founded in 1966 by Satanist Anton LaVey (1930–1997). He and his church entered into pop culture history in the 1970s with the Eagles' rendition of the song entitled "Hotel California." The album cover pictured High Priest LaVey himself. The Internal Revenue Service legally recognized the Church of Satan as a tax-exempt religious organization. Membership in the cult reportedly reached the tens of thousands at one time. A large percentage of that is attributable to contacts made through an international mail-order program. The more devoted and disciplined members gather in grottos, or fellowship groups, that exist around the world.

LaVey promoted a self-styled cult in which the Devil is not worshiped *per se,* but rather is held as a symbolic representation of the dark forces of power within people. He bases church doctrine on the belief that humanity is inherently selfish and violent. If people are to survive and ultimately rule, they must rely on their sinister nature to command the magical forces of the world to do their bidding.

Cult members are expected to adhere to nine satanic statements, as recorded in *The Satanic Bible,* written by LaVey in 1969. According to these declarations, Satan represents the indulgent pathway to the carnal, yet divine, nature of humankind. This explains why the Church of Satan places an emphasis upon indulgence by encouraging free sex and the use of hallucinogenic drugs. The purpose is to gather together the individual energies of like-minded members in an overwhelming force of psychic power. Church members also recite nineteen mystical incantations in an ancient occult tongue called Enochian, which LaVey claims to have translated himself. The quality and meaning of the words, when chanted in ritualistic oration, reputedly create a magical pattern of sounds that can alter reality.

*See also:* LAVEY, ANTON SZANDOR; ROCK MUSIC; *Satanic Bible, The*

## *SATANIC BIBLE, The*

An occult document written by Anton LaVey (1930–1997) in 1969. This book outlines several demonic doctrines that are the keystone of LaVey's San Francisco-based organization, the First Church of Satan. The document has a pentagram, or five-pointed star, embossed on its cover, and an inverted cross appears above the infinity symbol throughout the book. For centuries the pentagram has been the most widely revered of all occult symbols because occultists consider it the most powerful tool in the invocation of spirit entities. The inverted cross has long-served as an occult symbol for unholiness. The inverted cross atop the infinity sign possibly represents the son of Satan ruling with the Devil for eternity.

Materialism and hedonism are the two basic themes advocated by LaVey in *The Satanic Bible*. The document rejects the biblical teaching about the Devil. The book says that Satan represents indulgence, not abstinence; the physical, not the spiritual; undefiled wisdom, not self-deceptive hypocrisies; vengeance, not forgiveness; selective kindness and responsibility; as well as the divine and evil natures of humankind. New Age cults reflect the teachings of LaVey by stressing the rights of people to satisfy their carnal desires, which it claims should not be suppressed.

*The Satanic Bible* teaches that all people are inherently selfish and violent. If they wish to survive and ultimately rule the world, they must live a brutal, self-serving existence. To achieve this goal, occultists urge people to draw on the dark powers of Satan. To assist them, LaVey filled his book with lessons on the use of charms, spells, and rituals in order to produce supernatural effects, to control events in nature, to influence people, and to predict the future. *The Satanic Bible* contains information on how people can free their alleged psychic powers, learn the mysteries of the universe, and discover how to alter reality. In the 1960s and 1970s LaVey's teachings found their way into a variety of cults, as well as the rock-drug subculture. Hollywood producers hired LaVey to give them expert advice on accurately portraying satanic themes in movies.

*See also:* CROSS; LAVEY, ANTON SZANDOR; PENTAGRAM; SATAN, CHURCH OF; SATANISM

## SATANISM

The worship of Satan, either openly or secretly through a variety of ritualistic and

**Il Cornuto— sign of the Devil**

occultic practices. These might include the use of pentagrams, swastikas, inverted crosses, and other pagan symbols. Satanism can involve animal and human sacrifices, the use of hallucinogenic drugs, the consumption of blood, self-mutilation, sexual assaults, and torture.

The worship of Satan stands in direct opposition to orthodox Christianity, both philosophically and practically. It promotes the over-gratification of selfish desires, the violent abuse of others, civil chaos, and spiritual confusion among its followers. Satanism advocates a twisted view of current reality and a distorted concept of eternity. It ultimately sanctions corruption and crime, as well as rebellion against all forms of moral and religious authority.

The roots of Satanism can be found in the snake cults of ancient pagan religions. Adherents believed the symbolic representation of the Devil as a serpent held the key to salvation, defined as the evolutionary development of the human soul. In many snake cults, initiates believed divine wisdom and power were accessible to those who chose to give themselves over to Satan in bondage.

By the fourteenth century, satanic cults began to establish themselves as psuedo-religious organizations. By the nineteenth century, the modern form of Satanism was firmly established in America. It was advanced by the writings of occultist Aleister Crowley (1875–1947). The demonic rituals, such as the Black Mass, were often performed by satanic groups to parody the Christian worship service. Some rites, such as digging up graves to extract bones or body parts, were done partly to desecrate what most Christians regarded as sacred. The ceremonial sexual rites and sacrificial blood rituals practiced by some sects remain an integral part of satanic ceremonies.

The United States boasts some of the fastest growing and most highly organized networks of satanic religious organizations among the industrialized nations. Angry and disillusioned teens are often drawn into Satanism through illicit sex, drugs, and heavy-metal rock music or through occult activities. Advocates teach that the self is the highest authority, that they have the ability to alter reality, and that they can invoke spiritual entities from astral realms of existence. Initiates tend to express an intense hatred toward followers of Christ.

Many contemporary Satanists practice the Law of Reversal, the redefining of evil as good, darkness as light, vice as virtue, and Satan as God. Christian symbols are transformed to coincide with satanic doctrine. The communion service is debased. Christian prayers and Scriptures are perverted into curses against God. Affirmations of the Devil as the almighty savior of humankind abound. The ultimate blasphemy is the blood sacrifice. This ritual seeks to release the life force of an executed victim (animal or human), which is then absorbed by the participants.

Satanists believe that when humanity becomes aware of the pagan forces inhabiting the earth, they will regain control of the world. Their combined mental energy will serve as a catalyst, forcing the world to a chaotic point of no return. When this occurs, those who hinder the evolutionary advancement of the human race will be eradicated from society. Satan will overcome all vestiges of Christianity and God, thereby reclaiming heaven's throne. Satanists teach that the Devil will leave his followers on earth to share the fruits of eternal power with spiritual forces from the ethereal realm.

*See also:* BLOOD SACRIFICE; CROWLEY, ALEISTER; LAVEY, ANTON SZANDOR; PENTAGRAM; SATAN, CHURCH OF; *Satanic Bible, The;* WITCHCRAFT

# SATORI

A state of spiritual enlightenment and intuitive illumination sought in Zen Buddhism. Satori, which is the Japanese word for "insight," represents the state achieved through meditation where all thought ceases. Adherents say satori occurs at the moment a person comes into complete harmony with the absolute Oneness of the universe. New Age adherents compare satori to the realization of cosmic consciousness in which initiates comprehend their innate divinity and union with the world force.

*See also:* HEAVEN, HINDUISM, NIRVANA, ZEN BUDDHISM

# SCHUCMAN, HELEN

A Columbia University psychologist noted for channeling messages of an entity named "Jesus" at least two or three times a day over a seven-year period (1965–1973). Schucman recorded these "revelations" in a massive three-volume set entitled *A Course in Miracles.* This twelve-hundred-page tome,

first published in 1976, is filled with religious terms and phrases. Although faint echoes of Christianity are scattered throughout the work, its philosophical framework is thoroughly occultic. Since its introduction, Schucman's work has become a best-seller among New Age advocates.

*See also: COURSE IN MIRACLES, A;* TRANCE CHANNELING

# SCIENCE, NEW AGE

A system of knowledge uniting Eastern mysticism with the theories, findings, and conclusions of modern science. New Age science is sometimes referred to as religious science or scientific occultism.

Advocates claim that both mysticism and science arose from the need of people to understand and control the enigmatic forces of nature. They further argue that mysticism and science share a common worldview, as well as a universe of inseparable, interacting, and ever-evolving components. Defenders of this idea claim that mysticism and science reject the existence of a personal, self-aware, and supreme being, the God of the Bible.

By combining teachings from the East with theories from the West, New Age scientists hope to free people from the fear of God and transport them to a higher state of cosmic consciousness.

A change in thinking has occurred in the scientific community in the West. The French mathematician and philosopher René Descartes (1596–1650) took an analytical approach to science by separating problems into component parts and arranging the parts in logical order. The English mathematician and physicist Isaac Newton (1642–1727) used an analytical approach to formulate his theories about gravity, motion, space, and time.

Albert Einstein (1879–1955) used an analytical approach to devise his theory of relativity. His theory states that energy and matter are different manifestations of the same phenomenon and can be transformed into each other in terms of the relationship $E = mc2$. Einstein discovered that no absolute motion exists in the universe, only relative motion. This has revolutionized the way scientists view the universe and the way it began.

The work of subsequent scientists has left researchers with many unanswered questions about bizarre astronomical phenomena, such as neutron stars, black holes, and gravitational waves. New Age scientists have seized the opportunity by claiming that in order for humankind to survive, science must merge with Eastern mysticism. Occultists argue that universal vibrations emanate from a cosmic dimension, and these can be interpreted and controlled by the human brain. They also claim that by having mysticism and science work together, people will be able to accurately predict the future and examine similar concepts about the oneness of all existence.

New Age scientists say that, once people discover their union with the cosmic Mind, they will be able to tap the divine powers dormant within them. As more take this evolutionary step, the consciousness of humankind will be transformed.

A plethora of New Age organizations, universities, and research facilities now exist to provide a forum for scientists and occultists to share their findings on various subjects. These include telepathy, biofeedback, and holism, as well as imagery, meditation, and various other practices designed to help people get in touch with their higher self.

*See also:* CRITICAL MASS, MYSTICISM, QUANTUM LEAP, TRANSFORMATION

## SCIENTOLOGY

A New Age cult based on the writings and teachings of L. Ron Hubbard (1911–1986). Scientology mixes Eastern mysticism, psychotherapy, and science fiction. Initiates pay large sums of money to attend therapy sessions to have the chance of experiencing past life regressions and relocating the divine self.

In 1950, Hubbard wrote a book entitled *Dianetics: The Modern Science of Mental Health*, which presented a unique form of counseling. He claimed that people are plagued by the harmful influence of engrams,

the excruciating memories of past experiences. These engrams confuse people's reactive or unconscious mind. Trained counselors called auditors work with patients to subdue the engrams and increase the power of people's analytical, or conscious mind. This "cures" the patients of their psychosomatic and emotional illnesses, leading to a dramatic improvement in their quality of life.

In 1951, Hubbard published *Science of Survival,* in which he outlined the religious basis for Scientology. This paved the way for the founding of the Church of Scientology in 1954. Scientology holds that the universe is filled with gods, and Jesus is one of these innumerable deities. People are godlike, immortal souls called thetans. Every thetan allegedly has painful experiences from the past that must be audited. Counselors use a device called an E-meter to measure electrical impulses flowing from a patient's body and to detect the precise problem areas within the spiritual psyche.

By going through this mental extraction process, patients are freed from negative forces, paving the way for them to tap into the latent deity within them. Those who are cleared experience a quantum leap in their spiritual powers and awareness. Proponents deny the existence of sin and evil and believe that the concept of hell is a cruel hoax. Scientologists say the biblical concept of heaven is mere myth. They say bliss exists when people fully realize and experience their deified self.

*See also:* ENGRAM; HUBBARD, L. RON; PAST LIVES THERAPY

## SÉANCE

A meeting in which participants try to communicate with the spirit world or souls of the deceased through the use of a medium or channel. The medium acts as a bridge between the physical and spiritual realms. Years ago, séances were held in dimly lit rooms to keep participants from discovering the trickery of the spiritist. However séances now take place in open, well-lit rooms.

Participants are usually seated at a table

and told to focus their combined mental energies on an object such as a crystal ball. The medium enters a trancelike state to establish contact with the spirit world. After the participants have meditated, the medium invites the group to ask questions and receive answers from the entity. The spirit might have the medium say or write what it wants communicated, or it may give its message through an occult device such as an Ouija® board or tarot cards. Participants have reported feeling the séance table tilt or seeing an ectoplasmic substance appear, which supposedly means that a spirit wants to materialize.

*See also:* CRYSTAL BALL, LEVITATION, MATERIALIZATION, TAROT CARDS, TRUMPET MEDIUM

## SECOND COMING OF CHRIST

The Christian belief that at the end of the age Jesus will return to earth with His saints to defeat His enemies and establish His kingdom. Christ's return will be personal, bodily, visible, and unmistakable to the entire world.

New Age adherents reject the biblical teaching about the second coming of Christ. They view Jesus as a prime example of those throughout history who have realized their godlike potential. He shows everyone how to become aware of their divine self and activate the cosmic energy within. Occultists redefine the second coming as that moment in time when the human race achieves a final and lasting state of harmonic convergence. A global cosmic consciousness supposedly will prevail, making it possible for the New Age christ, Lord Maitreya, to appear. Through his leadership, all negative influences will be eliminated from the world, paving the way for an unprecedented time of universal peace, enlightenment, and prosperity.

*See also:* CREME, BENJAMIN; MAITREYA, LORD

## *SECRET DOCTRINE, THE*

A two-volume New Age work written by Helena Petrovna Blavatsky (1831–1891) in 1888. This occult publication articulates the basic beliefs of the Theosophical Society. This organization believes a universal philosophy unites all the world's religions. All the sacred texts of these religions contain an outer, or exoteric, meaning and an inner, or esoteric, meaning. The deep devotion of the Theosophists was to unveil the hidden meaning of these texts so that all people might come to realize their innate divinity and union with the cosmic mind.

Blavatsky claimed that spirits from the astral dimension told her what to write in *The Secret Doctrine*. The book glorifies Lucifer as the Light Bearer and the Morning Star. His lifeline is traced from the serpent in the Garden of Eden to the New Age christ. The book depicts Satan as the dragon of wisdom who connects the esoteric truths of all ancient religions except Christianity. *The Secret Doctrine* promotes the Aryan Race theory, the extermination of all conflicting forces, and the practice of lewd acts. The book also demonstrates an intense hatred of Christianity, depicting it as the only religious system that will not conform to the unified religion of the New Age.

*See also:* ARYAN RACE; BLAVATSKY, HELENA PETROVNA; THEOSOPHY

## SELF-ACTUALIZATION

The realization of an individual's full human potential. Kurt Goldstein (1878–1965) first coined the term in the 1940s while working in New York. He maintained that all people have an intrinsic principle, or motivational force, that drives them to achieve a sense of completeness. This desire is characterized by self-acceptance, acknowledgment of others, openness, and autonomy. Abraham Maslow (1908–1970) popularized the concept of self-actualization by teaching that it was an ongoing process in which people sought to become fully functional. He said that those who were self-actualized have a clear insight into life, as well as a deep appreciation for it. They accept themselves and others, demonstrate increased creativity and intuition, do not easily conform to the decrees of society, and have a greater desire for deeper relationships.

Maslow taught that the self-actualization process culminates in "peak experiences." These represent an altered state of consciousness, which is vital to spiritual growth and development. Examples of peak experiences include falling in love, gaining inspirational insight, or appreciating a piece of music. During these times, people mystically transcend the usual limitations of their identity to understand the world as it genuinely exists. They come to see life as an integrated and unified whole, full of beauty, truth, and goodness. Inhibition, fear, and anxiety are replaced by awe and ecstasy. Peak experiences are powerfully moving events that defy explanation and leave people feeling more positive about life as a whole. Self-actualized people have a better self-concept and more spontaneity and expressiveness.

New Age adherents have used the concept of self-actualization to promote their claim that people are innately divine but have forgotten their godlike status. Through the use of mind-altering techniques, they can achieve greater self-awareness. Through peak experiences, they transcend the natural realm, establish contact with spiritual guides from the astral dimension, and become one with the Universal Mind. At this point, people are supposedly self-actualized, the goal for which the entire human race must strive.

*See also:* MASLOW, ABRAHAM; PEAK EXPERIENCES

## SELF-HYPNOSIS

A psychotherapeutic practice that uses subliminal "tapes," directed visualization, and meditative techniques to alter the consciousness and reprogram the mind. The practice is sometimes referred to as autogenic or synthetic hypnosis. This practice requires patients to enter a trancelike state. Suggestions are fed into their unconscious minds. Initiates believe that self-hypnosis can enhance their human potential. By linking their psyche with the Universal Mind, they can gain new knowledge, experience holistic healing, and achieve enlightenment.

*See also:* ALTERED STATE, TRANSCENDENTAL MEDITATION, VISUALIZATION

## SELF-REALIZATION

The state in which people become aware of their innate divinity and oneness with the universe. Such enlightenment supposedly is achieved through spiritual and physical exercises. Those who have attained self-realization begin to see humanity as good; evil is a mere illusion. Once people become aware of their divine self, they can create their own realities. Occultists assert that when a critical mass of people achieve this state, it will inaugurate the Aquarian Age.

*See also:* EVIL, HINDUISM

## SELF-REALIZATION FELLOWSHIP (SRF)

*See:* YOGANANDA, PARAMAHANSA

## SENSORY DEPRIVATION

The reduction or elimination of normal sensory input. Sensory deprivation can lead to a distortion in thinking and perception and can also produce an increase in persuadability, altered mental activity, and hallucinations. Two types of hallucinations have been reported. One involves bright lights, meaningless sounds, and vague forms, such as lattice work, cobwebs, and spirals. The other involves lights and sounds that are organized, complex, and meaningful, and can include voices, music, and intricate scenes. These often appear to be three-dimensional, vivid, and surreal.

Some religious cults use sensory deprivation to manipulate and indoctrinate unsuspecting initiates. By reducing or eliminating normal sensory input, initiates are led to believe they can transcend the conscious realm and enter an altered state of awareness. While in this condition, they supposedly have the ability to use their innate psychic powers, manipulate reality, and bend time. Some practitioners claim that sensory deprivation leaves them feeling rested and more enlightened. However others have noted that the experience leaves them feeling emotionally troubled, to the point of becoming mentally unbalanced.

*See also:* ALTERED STATE, AWARENESS

# SERPENT

One of the oldest symbols of occult power. Ancient civilizations believed that the serpent embodied the wisdom and secrets of life. In India, the serpent was most prominent as the Kundalini. This cosmic life force reputedly lies coiled at the base of the human spine until it is activated and transmitted to the brain, thereby stimulating the enlightenment process. In Egypt, the serpent is depicted by the Ouroboro, a beautiful dragon or serpent that supposedly represents the never-ending cycles of life. In Syria, a Gnostic sect known as the Ophites based their worship in the second and third centuries A.D. on the image of the serpent. They believed that humanity continued to exist beyond death in an unending cycle of evolutionary development.

Contemporary cults teach that the serpent represents Lucifer, whom they say is the supreme victor over life and death. The serpent is also associated with the feminine principle. Proponents personify the Mother Goddess as Eve, from whom all people allegedly can obtain the key to esoteric knowledge. Matriarchal cults worship Mother Earth, or Gaea, as the one who inspired the first serpent priestess to use her benevolent powers to create humanity. The serpent is the light of truth residing within the soul of humanity that can awaken people to their divine self. New Age psychologists use serpent imagery to help patients enter a trancelike state and discover their innate psychic potential. Some occult leaders claim that the serpent symbol can help people shatter the illusion of separation between themselves and the Universal Mind, enabling them to achieve enlightenment. In this state of altered consciousness, people seek to experience the merging of good and evil, sickness and health, mortality and immortality, and light and darkness.

*See also:* DRAGON, EVIL, KUNDALINI, SATAN, SYMBOLISM

# SET, TEMPLE OF

A schismatic sect that withdrew from the Church of Satan in 1975. Michael A. Aquino (b. 1949) left the organized religion, claiming that founder Anton LaVey (1930–1997) was exploiting the Church of Satan for personal gain. Aquino and a group of his followers, The Council of Nine, organized the Temple of Set to keep the ideals of Satanism "pure." Aquino's book *Coming Forth by Night* expresses specific teachings on which the Temple of Set is based. The Temple has about 2000 members. Like the Church of Satan, the Temple of Set stresses individual self-improvement and self-worship as the highest being. The adherents look for guidance to the original priesthood of Set in Egypt, teaching that the pure, pre-satanic deity was later recast as an evil principle. Set is often portrayed as a man with the head of an animal, typically a hyena. Members of the Temple desire to evolve towards personal divinity through deliberate exercise of the intelligence and will. Therefore, the organization condemns use of mind-numbing drugs, entertainment, and even mystical worship experiences. Setians pursue a wide variety of secular interests in order to fully develop as individuals.

*See also:* AQUINO, MICHAEL; SATAN, CHURCH OF; SATANISM

# SETH

*See:* ROBERTS, JANE

# SEXUALITY

The New Age Movement is preoccupied with issues surrounding sexuality. Many New Age adherents promote open sex and complete freedom from moral inhibitions and absolutes. Some also advocate the complete dismantling of the family as a threat to individual evolution. They claim that people can attain enlightenment more quickly through sexual activities, especially when expressed in a trancelike state. Through sexual encounters, people supposedly become one with themselves, each other, and the universal life force. Occult leaders believe that if they can get more people to embrace their views of love/sex meditation, a critical mass will eventually be reached and usher in the Aquarian Age of joy, harmony, and self-awareness.

In this way of thinking, right or wrong behavior simply does not exist. New Age adherents see people as gods who determine for themselves what is proper or improper. As people get in touch with their divine self, they decide for themselves the validity of such activities as adultery, homosexuality, or abortion. Sexual experimentation is encouraged to help people connect with their inner psyche and align them with the Universal Mind. Sexual perversions are viewed as unfinished transitions from one dimension of existence to another. Violent crimes such as rape, incest, or the sexual abuse of children are explained away in terms as "the fulfillment of karmic laws."

*See also:* ABORTION, KARMA

## SHADOWS, THE BOOK OF (GRIMORE)

A personal journal kept by an individual witch or coven. The Book of Shadows documents the continuous record of satanic practices for future use. A witch's grimore might include a personal account of dreams, poems, and stories, as well as incantations, astral journeys, and transformations. A coven's grimore might also include historical accounts of various meetings, detailed instructions for conducting ritual sacrifices, and a diverse collection of magical spells for distribution among coven members. Traditionally, each witch hand-copied her grimore, and passed down the legacy of magical secrets to others before her death. Modern-day witches believe a personal journal gives a unique perspective on an individual's transformational process, and provides insight into the psychic realm beyond what is knowable through the rites practiced by the coven.

*See also:* BLACK MAGIC, MAGIC, SATANISM, WICCA, WITCHCRAFT

## SHAMAN

A priest or priestess who uses occult practices to cure the sick, divine the unknown, and control events. Shamans operate in the unseen world of gods, demons, and ancestral spirits. These entities can be summoned or heard through inspired mediums. In more primitive cultures, shamans are involved in spotting and attracting animals, birds, and fish for their tribe. They also manipulate the weather, drive away evil spirits, counter the effects of taboos and spells, cure the sick, and escort the souls of the deceased to the underworld.

Shamanism teaches that the soul is a precarious psychic unit that is prone to leave the body, making it easy prey for sorcerers and demons. Illness and death are examples of losing the soul due to the malevolent work of these entities. To prevent this evil from happening, shamans use their esoteric knowledge to enter altered states of consciousness and journey to other dimensions of reality. Their goal is to locate the patient's soul, capture it, and return it safely to its physical body. The soul can have gone to any of several places. The shaman can easily retrieve the soul if it is in a relatively safe place, such as the village. However the shaman must work with a spirit guide, sometimes associated with a particular animal, if the soul is in to a dangerous place, such as the bottom of the sea or the realm of the dead.

In the New Age Movement, the shaman can be a satanic priest or priestess, a witch or witch doctor, medicine man, sorcerer, magician, or guru. In each case, the shaman enters an altered state of consciousness and searches the realms of illusion to find ancient lost knowledge, acquire unlimited power, and obtain personal guidance from ascended masters. Some elements of shamanism are evident in the holistic health movement. Practitioners claim that the mind, body, and spirit are an interconnected triad that should be diagnosed and treated as a comprehensive "whole." They believe illness and pain are an accumulation of unbalanced energy. People correct these imbalances by journeying to the ethereal realm and realigning the vibrational forces of the mind, body, and spirit with the cosmic consciousness.

*See also:* SPIRIT GUIDES, SPIRITISM

## SHAMBALLA

A mythical haven in the Tibetan mountains inhabited by a superior race of beings who await the dawn of the New Age. As the time draws near, the souls of this race will leave their bodies and journey to other parts of the world to help people achieve higher levels of consciousness. Occultists claim that these ascended masters, such as Alice Bailey's Djwhal Khul, communicate with the world through human hosts who have voluntarily allowed themselves to be possessed.

New Age adherents assert that the kingdom of Shamballa exists in the astral plane. It is governed by a hierarchy of ascended masters who are overseen by Lord Maitreya, the New Age christ. In order to usher in the Shamballa force of the Aquarian era, all people around the world must chant together an occult prayer called the Great Invocation. This will cause the Luciferic Initiation to take place. The Morning Star will then force people to make a decision. They can either choose to follow his divine light, leading to godhood, or they can be ejected by the Shamballa force into the inner worlds for rehabilitation.

This mass initiation and purification is the final step leading to the inauguration of the New Age. When this happens, people will experience enlightenment and become one with the universal cosmic essence.

*See also:* ANTICHRIST; BAILEY, ALICE ANN; DJWHAL KHUL; GREAT INVOCATION; MAITREYA, LORD; PURIFICATION

## SHAMBHALA TRAINING INTERNATIONAL

A Buddhist organization systematizing the teachings of Tibetan mystic Chogyam Trungpa Rinpoche (1939–1987), founded by his son, Sakyong Mipham Rinpoche (b. 1962), in 1992. Chogyam Trungpa founded such organizations as Vajradhatu, Shambhala Training, and Nalanda. His son Sakyong Mipham Rinpoche organized all of these into one group, Shambhala Training International. Shambhala is an ancient philosophy of enlightenment by which individuals are to live meaningful lives and actualize their potential through qualities of dignity, fearlessness, and gentleness. Shambhala Training International is an umbrella organization to unify all organizations promoting this philosophy.

Chogyam Trungpa Rinpoche was born in Eastern Tibet and was appointed by the Dalai Lama to be spiritual advisor to the monks who fled to India after the invasion of Tibet by China. He also took a fellowship at Oxford University in 1964. Rinpoche founded the Samye Ling Meditation Center in Dumfriesshire, Scotland, in 1968, the first center for Tibetan Buddhist practice in the Western world. In 1969, after a spiritual turning point, Rinpoche demitted his monastic ordination and married an English woman.

He wrote and established meditation centers in North America, the first designed to allow Westerners to seek out Eastern teachings without traveling to Tibet and other monastic centers. He founded the Naropa Institute in Boulder, Colorado, the first accredited Buddhist University in the West.

Shambhala had approximately six thousand followers worldwide in 1999.

## *SHARE INTERNATIONAL*

A New Age magazine published by the Tara Center. This organization was established by occult leader and lecturer Benjamin Creme (b. 1922) who claims to be the telepathic channel for Lord Maitreya, the New Age christ. Not only does Share International publish the latest messages from Maitreya, but it also promotes the social, political, and economic globalization of humanity. This magazine is part of a massive network of people, services, and organizations. Advocates believe this complex web of communication will generate a metaphysical power that will one day bring fragmented psychic clusters together and trigger a paradigm shift in human consciousness. This will lead to a global transformation and usher in the Aquarian Age of peace, joy, and enlightenment under the rule of Lord Maitreya.

*See also:* CREME, BENJAMIN; GLOBALISM; MAITREYA, LORD; TARA CENTER

## SHINREIKYO

An eclectic pantheistic religion founded in 1947 and growing in part from a pacifistic movement in Japan before and during World War II. Kanichi Otsuka (Kyosama) was born in 1891 on the Island of Shikoku. He later claimed that he had been born with extraordinary abilities, caused by his special unity with the universe.

Shinreikyo believers claim that Kyosama understood the mechanism of everything on earth and even the world that exists beyond time and space. On Mount Koya he studied Buddhism, though he did not admit that anything was new to him. In 1912 Otsuka departed for a journey through Korea, Manchuria, and Mongolia. Wherever he went, Kyosama cured the sick, helped those in trouble, and repaired machinery. He then married Kunie Miyashita, who became his coleader. While he worked as an electrical engineer and inventor, the couple petitioned their government to follow a course toward peace. Members of the religion now regard the fact that the two were not imprisoned or killed as proof of their divine power. Kyosama also conducted a healing ministry similar to that of Pentecostals he had seen.

After the war, with the encouragement of former admiral Eisuke Yamamoto, Kyosama began holding meetings in Tokyo, from which the religion grew. *The Divine Teachings of Kyosama* are never read by anyone outside the faith, though a summary volume is available to the uninitiated. There are about one hundred thousand adherents. The beliefs are pantheistic and influenced by Taoism's quest for the ultimate and Buddhism's teaching that everything emanates from, and is connected to, one source. There also are Christian and Shinto elements. Its practical "power for living" focus has made Shinreikyo one of the more successful postwar religions. Adherents seek the Divine Power and divinity that was possessed by Kyosama, who is God made flesh and brings the way, the truth, and the life.

## SHIVA (SIVA)

The second god of the Hindu triad of deities. The other two are Brahma and Vishnu, the gods of creation and preservation respectively. As the Destroyer, Shiva is responsible for the eradication of the old to make way for the new. Shiva and its representative gods allegedly play a prominent part in the purification process that will precede the global transformation leading into the New Age. Occult leaders assert that Shiva represents the eternal existence of the mind, soul, and energy of the universe. This deity is the source of all happiness, as seen in the joy it brings to those who exercise creativity. Many New Age adherents participate in the Dance of Shiva in hope of discovering their divine self, obtaining a more intimate understanding of life's mysteries, and becoming one with the Universal Mind.

*See also:* BRAHMA, HINDUISM, VISHNU

## SIBYL

Legendary Greek and Roman prophetesses whose divination powers were thought to come from the god Apollo. The first mention of these women comes from the late second millennium B.C. when a sibyl is said to have predicted the Trojan War. The sibyls lived in caves or near streams and prophesied in frenzied trances. Their methods and possible use of hallucinogenic drugs is strikingly like that described among prophetesses at the Delphi oracle and also those involved in some forms of modern divination.

*See also:* DELPHIC ORACLE,
DIVINATION

## SIKHISM

A monotheistic religious sect founded in the Punjab of northwest India by Guru Nanak (1469–1539) in the sixteenth century. Nanak spent most of his childhood in the company of Hindu and Muslim holy men and was preoccupied with religious questions. After many years of meditative prayer, Nanak claimed that Lord Brahma, the Hindu creator deity, appeared to him and granted him the divine power to perform miracles. This included the raising of the dead and the controlling of the forces of nature.

Sikhism is a mixture of the common elements of Hinduism and Islam. The sect affirms the unity of God, the kinship of humanity, and the futility of idol worship. Sikhism also believes that people can escape the cycle of death and rebirth *(samsara)* and come to know God through the practice of meditation. The sect also rejects the ceremonial and ritualistic tenets of Hinduism and repudiates the caste system of India.

Sikh followers vow not to cut their hair, drink alcoholic beverages, or smoke. They are easily recognizable by the turbans they wear. Like Islam, Sikhs reserve sacred times for prayer—usually in the morning. The *Granth Sahib,* or *Adi Granth,* is the holy book of Sikhism and contains chants of Sikh gurus, as well as hymns written by Hindus and Muslims.

An offshoot of Sikhism, called Sikh Dharma, led by a man named Yogi Bhajan, has exposed people in the West to the monotheistic religious sect. His main group is the Healthy, Happy, and Holy Organization (or 3HO), which he founded in 1969. Cult members use a vegetarian diet and various New Age meditative techniques, including the chanting of holy music taken from ancient Sanskrit. In an attempt to attune to the forces of change in religious consciousness, 3HO members seek spiritual enlightenment through communal living. The cult boasts that their several thousand members will be ready for the transition from the Piscean to the Aquarian Age, from the material to the spiritual, and from the individual to the universal consciousness.

*See also:* BRAHMA; HEALTHY, HAPPY, HOLY ORGANIZATION; HINDUISM; REINCARNATION

## SIN

In orthodox Christianity, sin is defined as any lack of conformity to, or transgression of, God's moral standards and commands (Gen. 3:1–7; 6:1–8; Ps. 51:4; Isa. 59:2; Rom. 3:9–23; 5:12–21; Eph. 2:3; 1 John 3:4–15).

New Age adherents define sin as any denial of the union with the cosmic consciousness. To find this unity, occultists say people must enter into a trancelike state, get in touch with the Universal Mind, and recognize the divine self within them. Those who reject their innate divinity and union with the Great Spirit are considered guilty of "cosmic treason."

New Age adherents assert that the tangible world is an illusion. Therefore no moral absolutes exist, nor do any rules or standards apply. No distinctions exist between good and evil, right and wrong, or God and Satan. The biblical concept of sin is the religious superstition of a bygone era, totally out of step with the more enlightened views of the Aquarian Age. The denial of sin will remove false "guilt," alter perceptions, and allow the human race to achieve its full cosmic potential. Each person is part of the universal life force, able to create reality and subconsciously alter space and time to enhance psychic development.

New Age adherents claim that the spiritual evolution of humanity relies on releasing people from the shackles of moral restraints.

*See also:* EVIL, GOD, GUILT, KARMA

## SMITH, JOSEPH

*See: Mormon, The Book of;*
MORMONISM

# SOKA GAKKAI

A philosophical and political reform movement that was begun in 1930 as an association of the Nichiren Shoshu strain of Buddhism. Makiguchi Tsunesaburo (1871–1944) and Toda Josei (1900–1958) first called their organization Soka Kyoiku Gakkai ("Association for the Creation of Values") and founded a journal that was popular and controversial during the intense nationalistic period of prewar Japan. In 1937 the movement separated into the Soka Gakkai religious sect.

Makiguchi, the movement's philosopher, denied that the three great traditional values of Japanese life (what is good, what is true, and what is beautiful) are inherently valuable at all. He argued that truth may lead to intense suffering as easily as it leads to happiness. Therefore, the only true value is happiness.

As a religion, Soka Gakkai became a voice of dissent against the government of Japan during the 1930s, and the leaders resisted government attempts to merge all Japanese religions into a single nationalist force. As a result, Makiguchi died in prison. Toda came out of prison with a more intense appreciation for the spiritual, which characterized the organization when it was reestablished in 1947. It remained highly political and is foundational to the Komeito, the "party of clean government."

Soka Gakkai has grown to several million members, who regard their belief system as the only true form of Buddhism, because their form is contextualized for the modern world. A strict sectarianism reached its height in the 1970s and then became more moderate. Members have sometimes been accused of forcing the conversion of family members.

Large bodies of believers live in France and the United States. The religion is almost entirely an urban phenomenon.

*See also:* BUDDHISM

# SOLOVIEV, VLADIMIR (1853–1900)

Russian philosopher and theologian who sought to combine Christianity and Hegelian pantheism. After opposing Roman Catholicism, Vladimir Soloviev joined the church to promote his views that there should be a single Christian church.

# SOLSTICE

Twice-yearly solar holiday on the calendars of nature religions, the New Age movement, and witchcraft. In scientific terms the solstices occur on about December 22 and June 22, when the sun is directly overhead at its most southern and northern reaches on the globe. By watching shadows and then carefully engineering rock formations to cast shadows at precise marks, ancient civilizations have usually been able to mark the solstice with accuracy.

Some peoples have viewed the solstices as marking the midpoint in seasons; in the Western calendar it came to be viewed as the beginning of a new season. The December solstice marks the beginning of winter in the northern hemisphere and summer in the southern hemisphere; June's solstice marks the start of summer north of the equator and winter to the south. Originally this conception came from the zodiac, in which the summer solstice introduces the sign of Cancer and the winter solstice the sign of Capricorn.

Nature and sun-worshiping religions have always attached importance to these changes in the sun, setting them aside as feast days and special observances—sometimes marked by human sacrifice and sexual fertility rituals. Winter solstice or Yule was particularly important in northern climates, since the people had no firm assurance until the sun changed its path that the spring would ever return. In some more southern cultures, among native Central Americans for example, the summer solstice was more dramatic and heralded. Modern New Age religions tend to regard the summer solstice as a time of particular harmonic convergence and great psychic power. The winter solstice is more carefully observed by neopagans, with its connection to life and death in the earth energy cycle.

*See also:* CELTIC PAGANISM, RING OF STONES, STONEHENGE, ZODIAC

# SOMA

Intoxicating and hallucinogenic plant juice used for ritual purposes. Although soma has never been positively identified, many think it is a leafless vine of the milkweed family found in India. For centuries, Indian worshipers would offer the plant to their gods and goddesses and drink its juice, known as "moon-blood," in the belief that it would give them health and immortality. New Age adherents have mythologized soma to mean the immortal life force within people that can only be released through meditation exercises. By sitting in different yogic positions and repeating Hindu mantras, worshipers supposedly can liberate their soma and experience unlimited divine wisdom and powers.

*See also:* MANTRA, TRANSCENDENTAL MEDITATION, YOGA

# SOPHIA MOVEMENT

In late twentieth-century Christianity, a radical feminist occultism that invaded mainline churches. The Sophia concept appears frequently in goddess worship or Wiccan connections, and the movement within Christian churches connected the Earth Mother symbol with the laudatory statements addressed to wisdom in the biblical book of Proverbs. The writer of Proverbs chapters 1–9 frequently personifies wisdom as a woman (Gk. *sophia*). The Sophia movement's leaders sought to make that personification a reference to God as female. In Scripture liturgy, they tried to change all references to deity to the feminine form.

This movement reached its height at the 1993 Re-imagining Conference, an ecumenical conference of feminists primarily drawing from the Presbyterian Church in the USA, The United Methodist Church, and the Evangelical Lutheran Church in America (ELCA).

Participants prayed to "Our Maker Sophia" and called for Sophia's aid in replacing traditional Christianity. Much of the liturgical imagery was highly charged with intimate references to female anatomy and sexuality.

Cult watchers identified the theology of the Sophia movement as primarily Gnosticism. In Gnostic religion Sophia is venerated as "Mother Wisdom," the fallen creator of earth, wind, fire, air, and water and mother of the evil demiurge who was the God of Israel.

*See also:* ECOFEMINISM, FEMINISM, GODDESS WORSHIP, MOTHER EARTH

# SORCERY

The ability to manipulate supernatural powers and control others through the use of evil spirits. By using black magic, the sorcerer attempts to harm others through curses, spells, and the establishment of alliances with wicked entities. Contemporary sorcerers believe that the essence of their power lies in the establishment of an interactive bond with the divine cosmic energy. Once this bond is created, they can explore the hidden realities of forgotten abilities existing in the human soul. Although each method of sorcery appears to produce successful results, the powers sought are difficult to control and can lead to the mental, physical, and spiritual deterioration of the practitioner.

*See also:* DEMON, MAGIC, SATANISM, WITCHCRAFT

# SOUND THERAPY

An occult healing practice designed to promote wellness and wholeness through the use of chanting, singing of hymns, and listening to music. Proponents base sound therapy on the belief that sound has the power to release psychic healing energies. Ancient pagan religions claimed that such power was first demonstrated in the creative utterances of the Great Goddess who spoke the world into existence. Today holistic healers use the constant repetition of certain notes to restore harmonic balance within their patients. Some occult leaders assert that the ethereal vibrations of certain sounds bring subliminal messages of wisdom and love to humankind. These tonal pulsations allegedly can only be received while in a trancelike state.

Some sects claim that the Universal Mind

radiates eighty-one healing sounds through psychic means. Others say the twelve notes of the diatonic scale, including semitones, contain their own cosmic healing qualities. Adherents believe each note correlates to one of the twelve astrological signs, which also equates with a specific area of the human body. Sound therapists prescribe music or tones that they believe will facilitate a person's natural healing process. They will place speakers directly on specific areas of the patient's body where they will transmit continuous vibrations until healing is achieved. Therapists use major chords for physical ailments and minor chords for mental ailments.

In audiochromopathy, therapists combine sound with various colors and lights to activate psychic energy centers known as chakras. They believe that practicing Hindu yogic exercises will cause this dormant energy to arouse, enabling people to tap into the powers of their inner self. The yogic life force supposedly moves through energy channels wound in a double spiral on either side of the human spine, bringing about a state of cosmic bliss and enlightenment.

*See also:* CHAKRA, COLOROLOGY, LIGHT, VIBRATIONS

## SPANGLER, DAVID

The acknowledged architect of the New Age Movement, Spangler was born into a devout Christian home. He claims to have had numerous childhood experiences involving psychic and mystical phenomena. While attending college in California, Spangler decided to devote himself to the spread of New Age doctrine and practices. His early speeches were heavily influenced by the works of theosophist Alice Ann Bailey and focused on the esoteric philosophy of occult doctrines. After he began channeling his own spirits, he prophesied that Lucifer is the energy force that will oversee the transformation of humankind into a unified world of divine souls.

Spangler initially served as the educational director of the Findhorn Foundation, a New Age organization dedicated to the establishment of global peace and enlightenment. In 1973, Spangler and fellow Findhorn Foundation members started the Lorian Association in Madison, Wisconsin. Findhorn members came from Scotland to the United States to help prepare for the release of the occult writings of Bailey and to promote the spiritual enlightenment and unity of the world. In 1981, Spangler helped found a political partnership of sponsoring organizations called Planetary Initiative. The organization's goal was to promote economic, political, and religious globalization, believing this to be humanity's only hope for peace.

Spangler has written a number of books, including *Revelation: Birth of a New Age* (1976). He claims this book was dictated to him by a cosmic entity named "Limitless Love and Truth," surnamed "John." Spangler's *Revelation* is a New Age reading of the end-time prophecies recorded in the Bible, especially the book of Revelation. Spangler discusses "The Plan," which he says is a blueprint for the establishment of the New World Order under the rule of the Aquarian Age christ. The world is heading toward a mass initiation ceremony in which the enlightened will be marked to enter the New Age, whereas the unenlightened will be sent to "inner worlds" for rehabilitation.

In 1977 Spangler wrote *Reflections of the Christ*. The author proclaims Lucifer as the christ-force within all humankind and the impulse that will enable people to reach their divine selves, or Christ-consciousness. Spangler describes Lucifer as an agent of God's love, the Deva of the New Age, the Light of the world, and the Great Initiator. All the enlightened of the earth will simultaneously chant the Great Invocation, a New Age prayer. This will bring the Light to earth to oversee a great Luciferic Initiation. This will set the stage for Lord Maitreya to establish a one-world religion, a one-world government, and a one-world economy.

*See also:* FINDHORN FOUNDATION; GREAT INVOCATION; LORIAN ASSOCIATION; PLAN, THE; PLANETARY INITIATIVE FOR THE WORLD WE CHOOSE

## SPIRIT GUIDES

Entities believed to be from ethereal dimensions of existence, to whom mediums go for wisdom and guidance. Some entities reputedly have existed for thousands of years, successfully acquiring the wisdom of the ages. These beings call themselves "ascended masters" or "spiritual teachers" and claim to have come to help people through a particularly difficult time in their psychic evolution. Ascended masters usually communicate through a trance channeler who acts as an intermediary between the physical world of illusion and the cosmic world of reality.

Common New Age Teaching states that everyone has a personal spirit guide with whom to establish contact. These personal entities are thought by some to be manifestations of the repressed divine self. By entering a trancelike state, people can communicate with their spirit guides and tap into the collective unconscious.

It has been charged that some experimental creativity enhancing curricula actually were teaching children to try to establish contact with their spirit guides. In one controversial curriculum, elementary students were encouraged to take an imaginary journey to a mystical place. They were to take an imaginary friend to guide them, who could be a real person, an animal, or a cartoon character. The teacher was then to encourage the children to make this imaginary guide a constant friend and helper through life.

*See also:* ASCENDED MASTER, DEMON, ENTITY, GUIDED IMAGERY, TRANCE CHANNELING

## SPIRITISM (SPIRITUALISM)

The belief that spirits of the dead can communicate with the living, usually through a medium. Spiritism was practiced by the ancient peoples of Egypt, Babylon, Persia, and India. However in 1843, modern spiritism was revived by Andrew Jackson Davis (1826–1910), a New York shoemaker.

Interest in spirits reached almost epidemic proportions in Western Europe and the United States in the second half of the nine-

teenth century. It drew some impetus from transcendentalism and the romantic philosophy that was highly influential in the early Victorian era. Philosophically, spiritists are related to Unitarianism. Its most vigorous center of influence was northern New York State, which in the mid-1800s produced a variety of religious and philosophical movements. The event that touched off enthusiasm occurred in 1848, when three sisters, Margaret, Kate, and Leah Fox, claimed to receive answers to questions from spirit "rappings" in their parents' farmhouse in Hydesville, New York. The entity was the departed soul of a man named Mr. Splitfoot, who had been murdered years earlier in the home. After moving to Rochester, New York, the Fox sisters drew greater attention to their claims in America and Europe.

In 1852 a convention for spiritists met in Cleveland, Ohio. By the mid-1850s, spiritism was thriving on both sides of the Atlantic. By the early twentieth century, people had established spiritist churches and organizations. The oldest of these, the Universal Church of the Master (UCM), was founded in 1908 and incorporated in 1918. The popularity of spiritism skyrocketed during the countercultural movement of the 1960s. No longer did mediums, or channelers, merely establish contact with departed spirits. They now communicated with extraterrestrials from other galaxies and entities from ancient lost civilizations such as Atlantis. Some modern spiritists claim to levitate objects, predict the future, and mentally control physical objects. They try to heal the sick through psychic means and use extrasensory perception to "read" thoughts.

Spiritists tend to have a common core of beliefs. They affirm the parenthood of "God" over a human brotherhood and sisterhood, while rejecting all historic Christian teachings. The "Golden Rule" is the essence of morality. Those who love truth and goodness can achieve perfection by living according to this ethical principle. The spiritist's universe is an integrated psychic system of divine wisdom. Physical and spiritual phenomena show God's infinite intelligence. People are divine, and their conscious identities and existence continue after death. Living people need only reach into the ethereal realm to communicate with the departed.

*See also:* DEMON, MEDIUM, SÉANCE, TRANCE CHANNELING

## SPIRITUAL EMERGENCY NETWORK (SEN)

An organization established to deal with the negative effects associated with occult mind-altering techniques. Consciousness researchers Stanislav and Christine Grof founded SEN in 1980. They initially established the headquarters of the organization at the Esalen Institute, a center for humanistic psychology in Big Sur, California. SEN later relocated its main offices to the California Institute of Transpersonal Psychology. SEN reportedly has more than fifteen hundred members stationed in forty-two regional centers throughout the world.

Over the years, numerous reports of negative effects associated with trying to transcend the human consciousness have come to light. Transpersonal psychologists encourage clients to resume their mind-altering practices, bolstered by the hope that they will eventually overcome the negative effects and reach a blissful state of union with the cosmic consciousness.

*See also:* ESALEN INSTITUTE, TRANSPERSONAL PSYCHOLOGY

## SPIRITUAL HIERARCHY OF LIGHT

The highest level of enlightenment. This universal hierarchy is sometimes referred to as the Great White Brotherhood, the Luciferian Brotherhood, and the Great White Lodge, as well as the Masters of Wisdom and the Brotherhood of Spirits. The hierarchy reputedly includes ascended masters, spirit guides, angels, and other astral beings. When channeled, these entities claim to be spiritually evolved beings who have come to earth from the ethereal dimension to lead humankind to a higher consciousness of Light. They use human hosts to reveal and channel teachings. The Spiritual Hierarchy of Light says that Lucifer is an angel who destroyed Eden to allow humanity to achieve godhood.

*See also:* ASCENDED MASTER, GREAT WHITE BROTHERHOOD, LUCIFERIC DOCTRINE

## SPLIT-BRAIN RESEARCH

The neurological study of the human brain based on the theory that the left and right hemispheres have individual yet interacting purposes. Through split-brain research, scientists hope to discover how the brain learns, stores, and evaluates information, acquires knowledge, and increases its understanding. Behavioral scientists believe the left side of the brain is the analytical hemisphere, which takes in new data, systematically sorts it, and categorizes it for future use. By applying reason and logic to this information, the left side of the brain draws conclusions and makes inferences. The right side of the brain is the creative hemisphere characterized by intuition, artistic ability, and musical talent. It can step back from the mass of detail and visualize the global aspects of a problem or plan.

Although split-brain researchers recognize that each hemisphere of the brain performs certain unique functions, they are careful to stress that this organ of thought and neural coordination operates as an integrated unit. If one side of the brain is not functioning properly, it adversely affects the ability of the other side to operate normally. By working together, every aspect of the brain enables people to receive stimuli from sense organs, to interpret and correlate the data to formulate motor impulses, to send information to receptors on the body surface, and so on.

New Age theory has incorporated the language of split-brain research in occult teaching. The hemispheres of the brain, it is said, are able to operate in alternate dimensions of reality. The analytical centers are actually taking information from a physical reality

*See also:* INTUITION, TRANSPERSONAL PSYCHOLOGY, WHOLE BRAIN THINKING

# STARSEED

Crystals that New Age mystics believe were deliberately placed in the rocks of the earth by entities from the astral dimension. These starseeds are the Light-Body intelligence of spiritually advanced extraterrestrial beings who originated from cosmic realms and give off pure energy emissions. By using these starseeds, New Age adherents claim they can channel messages from interplanetary sources in neighboring galaxies. Occult leaders encourage the worldwide distribution and use of starseeds, saying these objects serve to bring about the cosmic consciousness of the human race and the establishment of the Aquarian Age of enlightenment and peace. If more people used starseeds, the substance supposedly will act as a catalyst to cleanse humanity of all negative vibrations and purify the world for the coming rule of Lord Maitreya.

*See also:* EXTRATERRESTRIAL INTELLIGENCE, LIGHT, NEW AGE MOVEMENT, QUARTZ CRYSTAL, VENUS

# STEINER, RUDOLF

*See:* ANTHROPOSOPHY

# STIGMATA

Bodily marks, sores, or pains that correspond to or resemble the crucifixion wounds of Christ. Stigmata supposedly appear on the body of people when they are in a state of religious ecstasy or hysteria. Some devout Roman Catholics claim to have received stigmata on their heads, shoulders, hands, and feet, as well as near their hearts. Although some make claims of having perpetual stigmata, most say they experience this phenomena during traditional Catholic holy days that commemorate the crucifixion of Christ. This includes the Lenten season and Good Friday.

New Age mystics say they experience stigmata while in altered states of consciousness. They assert that these bodily marks show evidence of their psychic connection with the universal christ-consciousness. They encourage others to pursue the same mystical experience and establish direct communication with their inner selves. Their goal is to become awakened to the deity within, thereby uniting with the cosmic life force.

*See also:* BLOOD OF CHRIST, CHRIST-CONSCIOUSNESS

# STONEHENGE

A prehistoric ceremonial ruin of megaliths, or gigantic upright stone slabs, on the Salisbury Plain in Wiltshire, England. Archaeologists believe that prehistoric people built the circular formation of megaliths over a period of many centuries in four successive stages. During the first phase (c. 2800 B.C.), an earthen wall was constructed around a circular trench six feet deep and 320 feet in diameter. The ditch had an entrance on the northeast side. Outside of it was a wooden gate and a large, upright boulder. Inside the entrance they constructed a loop of more than fifty underground burial chambers for cremated bodies.

During the second phase (c. 2100 B.C.), a dirt road led to the entrance. Within the center of Stonehenge, the native people constructed a double ring of huge, rough, upright stones. These and The Avenue faced the direction in which the summer solstice sunrise occurred. During the third phase (c. 2000 B.C.), thirty stones were arranged in a circle in the center of Stonehenge. On top of these, builders placed an unbroken series of horizontal stone lintels. Within this ring were five twenty-two-foot-high trilithons, or structures made of two upright stones and capped by a lintel. Around 1550 B.C. these were used to make two horseshoe-shaped formations, with one inside the other. During the fourth phase (c. 1100 B.C.), the builders extended the road from Stonehenge to the River Avon, about one and one-quarter miles.

The accuracy and ability of these prehistoric peoples in arranging and fitting the megaliths at the site is amazing but not uncommon in ancient cultures. Historians and archaeologists continue to debate why Stonehenge was built. Some have conjectured that it was a

Druid temple. However these Celtic priests and wise men did not reach the British Isles until 550–450 B.C., long after Stonehenge was built. The most promising view holds that the site was used as an astronomical observatory. Such a lookout post would have been important to a prehistoric pagan religion. Some have speculated that each megalith is aligned with varying positions of the sun, moon, and stars. This supposedly enabled ancient astrologers to calculate the length of seasons and when eclipses would occur.

Occult groups have altogether different theories about the significance of Stonehenge. One story suggests that giants were in the process of bringing the megaliths from Africa to Ireland, but Merlin of King Arthur fame intercepted and magically transported the huge stones to the Salisbury Plain. Some New Age adherents insist the ancients used psychokinesis to levitate the fifty-ton boulders into place. (Psychokinesis, or PK, is the ability to move material objects by mental power alone, apart from any physical energy.) Others claim that Stonehenge was created and left by extraterrestrials from a distant galaxy. Still others assert that technologically advanced people from Atlantis built the amazing site. These claims and counterclaims appear to be based on conjecture, lacking in scientific fact.

*See also:* ASTROLOGY, CIRCLE, DRUIDS, MYTHOLOGY, SOLSTICE

## SUBCONSCIOUS

The portion of the mind that is thought to hold psychic memories not immediately available to the conscious. It is also called the preconscious, co-conscious, paraconscious, and unconscious. The subconscious supposedly is responsible for the retention of memory (subliminal and conscious), the generating of new ideas and insights, the discerning of patterns, and the control of bodily reactions. In altered states such as dreams, trances, or visions, the subconscious allegedly becomes the dominant and accessible gateway for others in reprogramming the mind. New Age adherents claim that people must tap into their subcon-

scious before they can achieve oneness with the Universal Mind. This is accomplished by entering a trancelike state, either through meditation or hallucinogenic drugs, and allowing spirit entities to guide initiates to the astral plane.

*See also:* ALPHA LEVEL, ALTERED STATE

## SUCCUBUS

A demon that assumes female form to have sexual intercourse with men in their sleep. According to legend, demons take female form and then induce nocturnal emissions from men. Then the evil spirit takes male form, called an incubus, and impregnates a woman with the semen. Such visitations reputedly cause nightmares, mental instability, and even death.

*See also:* DEMON, INCUBUS

## SUFISM

A mystic sect of Islam dating back to the eighth century A.D. that developed mainly in Persia, or modern-day Iran. Sufism is derived from the Arabic word *sufiy,* which means "man of wool." This derivation arose because in ancient Islamic cultures, ascetics typically wore garments made of wool. Sufism represented a reaction by pious Muslims against the formalism, legalism, worldliness, and loose morals that prevailed at the time. Proponents claimed that people could obtain a spiritual knowledge of Allah and an understanding of truth through personal experience. The study of the Qur'an, the sacred writings of Islam, was de-emphasized while the cultivation of a mystical encounter with God was stressed.

Sufi leaders, called Shaykhs, asserted that followers could gain direct contact and oneness with "God" through intense meditation, fasting, celibacy, and long prayer vigils. Mystical singing and twirling dance motions, called whirling dervishes, supposedly enabled people to achieve a spiritual awakening, predict future events, and contact spirit guides.

In 1910 a Shaykh named Haerat Pir-O-Murshid Inayat Kahn (1881–1927) introduced Sufism to the United States. Under the leadership of his son, Pir Vilayat Inayat Kahn, Sufism experienced considerable growth. In keeping with typical New Age teaching and practice, he claimed that people must open their minds to alternate dimensions of reality in order to achieve oneness with God.

## SUICIDE

The act of self-inflicted, self-intentioned death. In orthodox Christian thought all human life has intrinsic value or worth because God views it as precious (Gen. 1:26–28; 5:1; 9:6; Exod. 20:13). This implies that all human life belongs to Him and that He alone has the right to take it or command when it should be taken. In addition, it means that each individual has divinely ordained, inviolable rights and responsibilities to maintain and preserve life.

These concepts are rejected by many advocates of the New Age. They claim that suicide is a morally neutral choice which enables a person to leave the physical realm temporarily until the cosmic forces call for a more favorable return. "Spiritual emergencies," the New Age euphemism for depression, self-mutilation, or suicidal tendencies, reputedly are common obstacles in attaining enlightenment. These emergencies are also the natural by-products of ascending the various levels of human consciousness. Some authoritarian occult leaders indoctrinate naive followers into thinking that committing suicide is sometimes necessary to achieve union with the cosmic consciousness.

*See also:* DEATH

## SUMMIT LIGHTHOUSE

*See:* UNIVERSAL AND TRIUMPHANT, CHURCH

## SUN DANCE

A ritual performed by the Plains Indians

of North America either individually or in groups, to commemorate the summer solstice. Historically the Native American participants danced around a central pole for as long as four days and nights. During this time, they fasted and inflicted wounds on various parts of their bodies. The initiates abused themselves in order to experience sacred dreams, visions, and psychic powers. Some tribal members played drums and sang, while the rest watched. Though not now so violently, Native American religionists still perform the sun dance to give thanks to the Great Spirit, or sun god, and to request abundant provisions for the coming year. The ritual symbolizes both the separation and unity of humanity and the powers of nature. It also represents encounter with the divine forces that flow through all living things.

Many New Age adherents celebrate a modernized version of the sun dance. Part of the ritual includes a mystery circle, which symbolizes the eternal essence of all creation. The circle encompasses a center pole, and at the top of the pole they place an object that represents the Great Spirit or sun god. The circle is divided into four quadrants to correspond with the four points of the compass. The west (rain) symbolizes the good things to come; the north (winter) represents health and guidance; the east (morning star and sun) symbolizes wisdom; and the south (spring) represents the birth and rebirth of life after death. Dancers believe the powers of the spirit world are unlimited at the center of the circle.

*See also:* CIRCLE, NATIVE AMERICANS, SOLSTICE

## SUPERCONSCIOUSNESS

A heightened state of awareness that allegedly is the second level of the unconscious mind. The superconscious is sometimes called the collective unconscious, the higher self, or the New Age heaven. Proponents believe it contains the accumulated memories of all humankind. Occultists say the superconscious operates as an objective, impersonal observer of everything that takes place around the world. It reputedly is the focal point of the divine self and a silent witness to the Akashic Records, the thoughts, words, and events of all human life contained within the Universal Mind.

New Age adherents claim people can use a wide range of techniques to access their superconsciousness. As initiates enter a trancelike state, they supposedly journey through lower levels of the unconscious mind and obtain new insights into reality. Once people make it to their superconsciousness, they allegedly have reached an enlightened condition. By activating this heightened state of awareness, advocates claim they can tap into their unlimited divine potential, control reality, and alter the future. They unite with the Universal Mind and are freed from the world of illusion. New Age adherents maintain that if enough people succeed in accessing their superconsciousness, a critical mass will be reached to bring about psychic purification, of the world.

*See also:* AKASHIC RECORDS, COLLECTIVE UNCONSCIOUS, HIGHER SELF, HUMAN POTENTIAL MOVEMENT, TRANSFORMATION

## SUPERSTRING THEORY

A New Age distortion of a similarly named hypothesis appearing in theoretical physics. Some scientists have proposed mathematical models called superstring theories to explain the forces and elements of the cosmos. Some have conjectured that the fundamental particles of the universe are radically minute in size, and that each of them exists as a one-dimensional string. They theorize that groups of these strings exist in more than the traditional four dimensions, which are the three dimensions of space plus the dimension of time. Recent scientific discoveries have fueled speculation that the equivalent of at least eleven dimensions exist.

These groups of strings supposedly can combine, separate, rotate, and curve, hence the name "superstring" theory. Some physicists have postulated that after the Big Bang (a cosmic explosion that supposedly marked the beginning of the universe), seven of the eleven dimensions retracted into nonspace. They say that the superstrings existing in these other dimensions emit different frequencies in a variety of combinations. The frequencies emitted by superstrings in the traditional four dimensions supposedly are responsible for the presence of energy and matter. And the superstrings that exist in the other seven dimensions create the vibrations responsible for time and space.

Superstring theories are supposed by some to offer proof that every component of the universe, such as human beings, holds within itself the knowledge of the entire cosmos. And the superstring theories proposed by physicists allegedly "validate" their claim that people can journey to other dimensions of reality by entering altered states of consciousness. These assertions resemble what ancient pagan religions professed centuries ago. This is seen in Hindu folklore, which teaches that tiny cosmic threads called sutras exist throughout the universe and emit sounds. The first intonation that broke the cosmic silence reputedly is represented by the mantra "om." Adherents say that the Mother Goddess spoke the sound "om" when she created the earth. According to the legend, as "om" divided into subsounds, matter and energy were created. The cosmic vibrations associated with "om" produce an altered state of consciousness, whereby devotees are able to gain access to divine powers.

*See also:* CREATION; OM; SCIENCE, NEW AGE

## SUZUKI, DAISETSU TEITARO (1870–1966)

Japanese scholar whose writings on Zen Buddhism became widely read in the West. Suzuki first came to prominence when he translated Immanuel Swedenborg's *Heaven and Hell* (1910). Through his studies he became an expert on Western thought and so was able to translate the ideas of Eastern Buddhism for a Western audience. He travelled widely in the West and in 1921 married an American.

*See also:* SWEDENBORGISM

# SUZUKI, DAVID T. (b. 1942)

Environmentalist, broadcaster, speaker, and prolific author with a world wide audience. By academic discipline, the Vancouver, British Columbia, scientist is a geneticist, but he has become famous for his popular application of the principles and ethics of Mahayana Buddhism to ecology and personal views of reality in general.

Suzuki's radio program for the Canadian Broadcasting Company, *The Nature of Things* has been syndicated internationally, and he lectures for such environmentalist groups as the Canadian Parks and Wilderness Society. He has established a foundation to promote his environmental strategy of pacifism and negotiation for ecological change. Suzuki works to convince industry and government leaders, as well as the general public that humankind must take its rightful place as just one component in a balanced world ecosystem.

Suzuki's many books include: *The Sacred Balance: Rediscovering Our Place in Nature*, *From Naked Ape to Super Species: A Personal Perspective on Humanity and the Global Ecocrisis*, and *Earth Time*. He also has written on Japanese religion and his Buddhist faith.

*See also:* BUDDHISM, ECOTHEOLOGY, *Ectopia*, ENVIRONMENTALISM

# SWEDENBORGISM

The occult theology invented by the Swedish scientist and philosopher Emmanuel Swedenborg (1688–1772) and continued by the Church of the New Jerusalem. Swedenborg was born in Stockholm, Sweden, and reared in a prestigious family. His father was a Lutheran pastor and court chaplain to the king of Sweden. Emmanuel Swedenborg studied and taught at the University of Uppsala. He had a keen interest in cosmology, the study of the origin, processes, structure, and space-time relationships of the universe. This fueled his study of physics, mathematics, and mechanics. During his long career, he demonstrated formidable talent as a mathematician, natural scientist, mining expert, engineer, and inventor.

Swedenborg studied physiology, psychology, metaphysics, and theology. In 1743, he claimed to have had a mystical flash of enlightenment in which he saw the spiritual world underlying the physical realm. Many of his theosophical beliefs, which he claimed were divinely revealed interpretations of Scripture, are based in part on that experience. He asserted that in his subsequent visions and dreams, he debated theology with Cicero, the apostle Paul, Augustine, Luther, Calvin, and others. Swedenborg claimed that spirit guides channeled their thoughts through him. His contemporaries dubbed him a "seer of divine wisdom."

Swedenborg rejected the orthodox view of the Trinity. He said that God is a single being with three manifestations—love, wisdom, and activity. Swedenborg asserted that redemption was God overcoming the ever-increasing powers of hell. Jesus is a finite Trinity of soul, body, and power who came to earth, lived a sinless life, and overcame the world's evil. In this theosophical system, reality consists of three spheres. These include the divine mind (represented by love), the spiritual world (represented by wisdom), and the natural world (represented by activity, its cause, effect, and end). When people devote themselves to the practice of love, the acquisition of wisdom, and enlightened use of the natural world, they become one with "God" and the rest of humankind. Swedenborg taught that unifying the creator with the creation is the destiny or goal of every person, thereby representing salvation. Christ embodied this ideal.

The heavenly world corresponds to the physical one. Earthly marriages supposedly have heavenly counterparts. Swedenborg maintained that people are inherently good and fully able to choose the path of good. When people die, they journey to the ethereal realm and become angels if they ascend to heaven or demons if they descend to hell. Swedenborg claimed to have had a vision of the last judgment and return of Christ. Based on this vision, he asserted that God was bringing about the advent of the New Church.

Swedenborg did not intend to start a new religious movement. But references to a "new Jerusalem" in his writings prompted his followers to establish the Church of the New Jerusalem in 1788. Since its modest beginnings, the cult has established a noteworthy presence in Great Britain, the Scandanavian countries, and the United States. The Church of the New Jerusalem claims that Swedenborg's writings came from God and are therefore divinely inspired. Much of the sect's teachings, operation, and activities are based on Swedenborg's Bible commentaries. New Age adherents perpetuate his doctrines.

*See also:* ANGEL, DEMON, ESOTERIC PHILOSOPHY

# SYMBOLISM

The nonverbal language of the New Age Movement in which the abstract ideas, feelings, and philosophies of the human psyche are united and reflected in the images and actions of reality. Occultists teach that this world is an illusion, an archetype of the ethereal realm. Proponents believe New Age symbols such as the rainbow, pyramid, yin/yang, and pentagram are the visible images of the collective unconscious, a universal repository for all the wisdom of humankind. These symbols serve as beacons for seekers as they travel down the path to enlightenment. The letters, gestures, sounds, and motions associated with these symbols present a window into the unconscious mind and represent the key for experiencing a quantum shift in thinking.

Although occult symbols may appear irrelevant to the uninformed, they convey a wide range of meanings to those familiar with New Age ideology and practices. An intimate understanding of symbolism supposedly is the key for discovering the divine self. Occultists teach that within each symbol lies a secret, within each secret lies a force, and within each force lies the power to change the past, transform the present, and alter the future. Symbols are the lenses through which psychic energy is channeled and materialized. People can use these symbols as a gateway to the astral realm. New Age adherents tell initiates that these symbols can help them transcend reality, establish contact with spirit guides, and manipulate alternate dimensions of existence.

*See also:* MYSTERY, PENTAGRAM

# SYMPATHETIC MAGIC

The casting of a spell or curse on an object in the belief that the person or entity the object represents will be affected. Practitioners of sympathetic magic assert that vibrational impulses permeate the universe and that psychic pulsations in an object can be used to the detriment of corresponding pulsations in a person or entity. A voodoo priest or priestess might stick pins in a doll to harm the person it symbolizes. Or a witch might obtain a lock of hair or a piece of clothing from someone to cast an evil spell on him or her. New Age adherents claim they are only interested in the positive aspects of sympathetic magic. Some occultists use quartz crystals to vicariously heal people from a distance. Others use gemstone elixirs, made from powdered stones, or water dipped with a stone implement, to induce psychic healings in patients far removed from the practitioner.

*See also:* MAGIC, QUARTZ CRYSTAL, VOODOO, WITCHCRAFT

# SYNANON

A self-help treatment center founded in 1958 by Charles Dederich, initially to offer therapeutic aid to heroin users. The California-based organization advocated the use of group encounter therapy and other occult practices to free addicts from their addiction to drugs. As New Age ideologies overran Synanon, it succeeded in winning legal recognition as a religious movement. In later years, the cult faced charges of inflicting verbal and physical abuse on its members (especially children), employing brainwashing techniques, and depriving some initiates of food and sleep.

*See also:* DRUG

# SYNCHRONICITY

The simultaneous and coincidental occurrence of two meaningful but not casually connected events. Swiss psychotherapist Carl Jung (1875–1961) believed that synchronicity occurred in psychic events, such as when two people separated by a wide distance have similar thoughts or when someone experiences a mental image of an event before it happens. Though such occurrences appear to be related, they cannot be explained by conventional theories of causality.

Jung stressed that people should become aware of both the conscious and unconscious aspects of the psyche and learn how to harness them. As people become spiritually advanced, they can tap into the collective unconscious, a dimension holding all the symbols and memories of the entire human race. For Jung, this key unlocks the understanding of how synchronicity occurs. He urged people to become more acquainted with their inner self by listening to its voice. As people do this, they allegedly will understand themselves better, as well as the collective unconscious, thereby learning how to create new realities.

*See also:* ARCHETYPE; COLLECTIVE UNCONSCIOUS; JUNG, CARL GUSTAV

# SYNCRETISM

The attempt or tendency to combine different forms of belief or practice into one religion. This occurs when elements of one religion might be assimilated by another, or when two or more opposite beliefs might join together to form an entirely new belief.

Syncretism is at the heart of the New Age Movement in blending Eastern mysticism, Christianity, humanism, neopaganism, and the occult. New Age adherents assert that all reality is an illusion. Therefore different and sometimes contradictory belief systems can be mixed to arrive at "truth." A set of core beliefs supposedly is common to all systems of thought, and these are found in the ideas and practices advocated by New Age adherents. In their way of thinking, all paths lead to "God," the divine energy that permeates all life. They teach initiates that the syncre-

tistic beliefs of the New Age can assist them in their efforts to discover their divine self and become one with the Universal Mind.

*See also:* GOD, JESUS CHRIST, ONE-WORLD IDEAL

# SYNECTICS

An occult mental exercise introduced by William J. J. Gordon, on the premise that the mind learns better when it can relate new knowledge to what it already knows. Synecticists believe that metaphors of reality can build symbolic bridges between the left and the right hemispheres of the brain. This enables people to recognize new information by comparing it to previously known and understood information. New Age educators say that innovative methods of "whole brain" learning are necessary to induce a paradigm shift in the thinking of humankind. They see this as a vital step in the evolutionary development of humanity and the establishment of an Aquarian Age of peace and enlightenment.

*See also:* CONFLUENT EDUCATION; KUHN, THOMAS; WHOLE BRAIN THINKING

# SYNERGY

The combined action or operation of different entities or conditions whereby the result of the total effect is greater than the sum of the individual effects. Humanistic psychologist Abraham Maslow (1908–1970) first used the term "synergy," which literally means "working together." He was referring to the increase of creative energy that is emitted when natural systems work together in mutual cooperation. New Age adherents believe that synergy is one key to the peaceful existence and evolutionary advancement of humankind. They advocate communal living, cooperative trade, and a return to nature as a means of fostering universal peace. Their ultimate goal is the "synergy" of all governments, religions, and economies of the world.

*See also:* COSMIC ENERGY; MASLOW, ABRAHAM; ONE-WORLD IDEAL; PEACE

# SYNTROPY

The belief that nature is inwardly driven to perfect itself. This concept, first introduced by biochemist Albert Szent-Györgyi, is the opposite of entropy, which says that every system in the universe tends to move in the direction of disorder and degradation. New Age adherents use the idea of syntropy to support their claim that an inherent life force exists in the universe. This force inspires humanity to develop an increasingly evolved network of communication, cooperation, association, and awareness.

Syntropy represents the collective need of the human race to induce a quantum leap toward a perfected universal order through telepathic means.

*See also:* EVOLUTION, QUANTUM LEAP, TRANSFORMATION

# TALISMAN

An occult object used either to protect against harm or to promote good fortune. Users believe that when the talisman is subjected to magical incantations, it can change the flow of cosmic energy. The talisman is often made out of metal or stone and is usually marked with magical signs such as a picture or a character believed to control supernatural powers. The talisman is similar to an amulet or charm. However, the talisman is usually carried instead of worn, and it supposedly harnesses greater powers. In earlier centuries, the talisman figured prominently in alchemy, witchcraft, sorcery, and shamanism. Today the object is popular among New Age advocates.

*See also:* AMULET, CHARM, COLOROLOGY, NUMEROLOGY, SYMBOLISM

# TANTRA

A group of late Hindu or Buddhist sacred texts that deal with mysticism, magic techniques, meditative rituals, and sexual practices. These religious writings originated in the sixth century A.D. and are attributed to the Hindu destroyer god Shiva or his wife Shakti. She is otherwise known as the Great Mother Goddess and the feminine principle of all deities. The tantras are based on the Buddhist belief that the world is an illusion, full of contradictions whereby evil coincides with good and immorality coincides with morality. Advocates teach that every person has dormant psychophysical powers that can be developed through ritual techniques and meditative exercises.

In addition to making symbolic gestures and chanting mantras, devotees learn to use sexual forces and icons to develop their extrasensory abilities. They supposedly can experience a sexual union with Shakti. By this means, adherents can supposedly arouse the cosmic life force known as Kundalini, thereby harnessing the powers of the divine self.

*See also:* HINDUISM, KUNDALINI, SHIVA, TRANSCENDENTAL MEDITATION

# TAO OF PHYSICS, THE
*See:* CAPRA, FRITJOF

# TAOISM (DAOISM)

The chief philosophy and system of religion existing in traditional China. According to legend, Taoism was founded by the sixth-century B.C. Chinese philosopher Lao-tzu. The word "Tao" means "the way," which devotees believe is the guiding principle and unfathomable source of all reality. The key sacred text of Taoism is the *Daode Jing,* or *Tao-te Ching,* meaning "The Way and Its Power."

Taoism maintains that "God" is an impersonal force, the existence of which is beyond understanding or differentiation. Taoists believe that nature is eternal, not created, and say it represents impersonal principles that cause inescapable outcomes. According to Taoism, Ultimate Reality is a harmony of opposites called Tai Chai. These opposites include female and male, darkness and light, death and life, and contraction and expansion—all of which they consider as mutually interdependent dualities. In this way of thinking, good and evil are coequal and interdependent. The feminine force called yin and the masculine force called yang maintain a duality that counterbalances evil and good.

Taoism claims real moral distinctions do not exist. The presence of chaos in society, in general and in individual lives, is due to people not aligning themselves with Tao, the universal way, which flows through nature. The remedy to social chaos is not found in externally imposed rules and regulations. People are naturally inclined to rebel against all forms of moral authority. The only way order and harmony in society can be achieved and maintained is through the principle of *wu-wei,* or purposeful inactivity. Realignment with the way restores order and harmony.

In order to achieve harmony with the ebb and flow of the universal way exemplified in nature, Taoism urges people to cultivate simplicity and balance. By yielding to the movement of Tao in their lives, people experience an inner transformation and eternal peace. They maintain equanimity by learning how to fuse yin with yang through effortless action. An important part of this process is the concept of ch'i, the breath or vital energy within a person. By nurturing and enhancing this cosmic energy, people supposedly can achieve inner tranquillity and promote societal harmony.

Taoism teaches that individual consciousness ceases to exist upon death, but a person's life force is recycled through endless reincarnations. Devotees do not see death as a loss because they consider nonexistence as more ultimate than existence.

*See also:* BUDDHISM, *I CHING,* LAO-TZU, TRANSCENDENTAL MEDITATION, YIN/YANG, YOGA

## TARA CENTER

A nonprofit organization founded in 1980 by New Age leader and lecturer Benjamin Creme (b. 1922). The Tara Center exists for the purpose of disseminating the prophecy and instruction channeled telepathically by a spirit named Lord Maitreya. Creme originally established the occult organization in Los Angeles. Today the Tara Center also has branches in New York, Amsterdam, and London. In addition to spreading New Age ideology and recruiting followers, the Tara Center exalts Lord Maitreya. They see this entity as the cosmic christ, the representative of the fifth incarnation of Buddha, the Muslim Mahada, the Hindu Krishna, and the Christian Jesus. In 1982 the Tara Center financed a campaign in which twenty major newspapers carried a full page ad introducing Lord Maitreya to the world. Creme alleges he channels divine revelation from Maitreya who works quietly behind the scenes to prepare world leaders for the coming New Age.

*See also:* COSMIC CHRIST; CREME, BENJAMIN; MAITREYA, LORD

## TAROT CARDS

A set of seventy-eight playing cards, including twenty-two picture cards, used in fortune telling and as a trump in tarok games. The inventors of tarot cards remain unknown. Gypsies or Crusaders presumably introduced tarot cards to Italy in the fourteenth century.

The tarot deck consists of two distinct groups. The Minor Arcana (or Minor Secrets) consists of fifty-six cards divided into four suits called wands, cups, pentacles, and swords. Each suit contains fourteen cards. The numbered cards range from ace to ten. The remaining court cards are unnumbered and contain the face of a king, queen, knight, and page (or knave), symbolizing the spirit, soul, vitality, and body respectively. The Major Arcana (or Greater Secrets) are twenty-two cards imprinted with a picture and title. The picture cards contain a fool (or joker) plus twenty-one cards depicting elemental forces (such as life and death), vices, and virtues. Depictions of the Moon, Judgment, Death, the High Priestess, the Hanged Man, and the Wheel of Fortune may represent Hindu mythological tales, Egyptian hieroglyphics, or the Hebrew alphabet.

Some New Age adherents claim the pictures on the cards are archetypal symbols depicting the secrets of humanity and the universe. Others say the cards represent the universal elements of life. When the tarot cards are dealt to players, the different combinations of cards allegedly are open to interpretation and manipulation. Occultists maintain that the tarot serve as a psychic point of contact between participants and the astral realm. The cards are thought to have the ability to awaken extrasensory powers of perception that control Ultimate Reality, contact extra-terrestrials, and revisit lost civilizations, such as Atlantis.

*See also:* ARCHETYPE, DIVINATION, SYMBOLISM, ZENAR CARDS

## TASSEOGRAPHY (TEA-LEAF READING)

A form of divination in which the shape and relative position of tea leaves in the bottom of a cup are interpreted to reveal hidden truths concerning a person's past, present, and future. Tasseographists will often perform a ritual and then enter a trancelike state before they examine the leaves from every angle. Some suggest the tea leaves represent the astrological configuration of the stars, while others say that the leaves depict the innate energy patterns of the client.

Mediums assert they have the psychic ability to interpret the significance of the tea leaves, whereby they make amazing predictions for their clients. For example, a triangular cluster suggests the presence of jealousy. The reading of tea leaves is popular among occultists who claim that discerning the patterns and shapes of the petals will enable them to tap into the cosmic energy of the divine.

*See also:* DIVINATION, MEDIUM

## TEILHARD DE CHARDIN, PIERRE (1881–1955)

A French Roman Catholic priest and paleontologist, Pierre Teilhard de Chardin was born at the Sarcenat in the French province of Auvergne and was ordained to the Jesuit priesthood in 1911. At the Sorbonne in Paris, he studied geology and paleontology, the science of early forms of life as recorded in the fossil records. He received his doctorate in 1922. The next year he was appointed to the chair of geology at the Institute Catholique of Paris but was expelled four years later because of his deviant views regarding cosmic evolution. He spent most of the rest of his life doing paleontological research in the Far East, primarily China. He was also involved in writing and lecturing in Europe and America.

In 1938, Teilhard wrote a massive work entitled *The Phenomenon of Man.* In the book he claimed that the entire material creation began as elemental particles and is proceeding along a fixed, evolutionary process. The creation supposedly will pass through a series of spheres and culminate in the Omega point, a transpersonal collective or universal consciousness. Teilhard meant the world will one day become unified in an organic self called "God."

In this scheme of thinking, God is a wholly immanent being who is in the process of change like nature itself. This expectation of perfect unity is a form of pantheism, a view that says that the universe is god. Teilhard saw Christ at the center of this whole evolutionary process. Christ is the converging point where all nature will unite with the cosmic divinity. Christ allegedly is motivated by love to gather together and transform everything.

Teilhard defined love as an affinity of one being, or entity, with another. He asserted that the cross is a symbol of the pain and toil associated with evolution, not the place where the God-man atoned for the sin of humanity.

Teilhard's theories about cosmic evolution and world unification are popular among New Age adherents. They claim that the human race is undergoing an evolutionary process of change. Vastly different human cultures supposedly are now converging on the Omega point. When convergence is finally accomplished, they say, the human race will achieve a new unity and cosmic consciousness. This will bring about a hyperawareness to transcend the universe. New Age adherents assert that the cultivation of love is crucial in bringing about this world transformation and creating a collective human thought.

*See also:* COSMIC ENERGY, EVOLUTION, GLOBALISM, NEW AGE MOVEMENT, ONE-WORLD IDEAL, TRANSFORMATION

## TELEKINESIS
*See:* PSYCHOKINESIS

## TELEPATHY

The ability to read another person's thoughts or mental state apart from the help of the known human senses. Telepathy is one of four categories of extrasensory perception, or ESP. The other three are precognition (the prediction of a future event that cannot be inferred from present knowledge), retrocognition (the knowledge about past events apart from having any information about those events), and clairvoyance (the extrasensory perception of inanimate objects or events). New Age adherents refer to all these phenomena as parapsychological psychic powers or *psi communications. Psi* refers to energy forces believed to mediate psychic phenomena. Since such phenomena cannot be explained by science, claims for their occurrence remain controversial.

Occultists claim that telepathic communication emanates from extra-dimensional cosmic energies. It cannot be bound by the physical restrictions of time or space. Some mediums assert that when they enter a trance-like state, they can receive communication from entities in other realms of existence apart from verbal exchange or other physical means of interaction. Others assert that by transcending the levels of consciousness, they can unblock psychic barriers, paving the way for the development of a wide range of telepathic powers. This leads to enlightenment and union with the cosmic life force. New Age adherents claim that, as more people learn telepathy, humankind will take a quantum leap in evolutionary advance toward the Aquarian Age.

*See also:* EXTRASENSORY PERCEPTION, PSYCHIC

## TEMPLE OF SET

*See:* SET, TEMPLE OF

## TENRIKYO

A Japanese religion of about 2.3 million members and fifteen thousand worship centers. Tenrikyo was founded in 1838 by Nakayama Miki (c. 1798–1887). Its beliefs contain elements of Christianity and Buddhism, though adherents disavow any connections. The woman who founded the sect said she had received a vision from "God the Parent" showing that she would become the "Shrine of God," a mediator between God and humans. She gave her possessions to the poor and performed faith healings. She was persecuted and spent some years in prison before her death in 1887.

Tenri City, population 50,000, is built around the Jiba, or place where the earth was created, according to Miki. Followers believe Miki will one day return to lead all humanity to this sacred sanctuary. Priests serve three hot meals and draw a hot bath for her each day. A sacred poem written by Miki is recited each morning and evening at places of worship. There is some disagreement about whether Tenrikyo is a polytheistic or monotheistic religion, and Miki's sacred writings can be used to argue either. There is a triune quality to this godhead, with the titles of Kami (creator), Oya (parent), and Tsu-Hi (moon-sun). Salvation means deliverance from troubles, and there is little discussion of what happens after death.

## TETRAGRAMMATON

The four Hebrew letters usually transliterated YHWH and used to refer to "Yahweh," the covenant name for the God of Israel. Tetragrammaton comes from the word *tetra,* which means "four," and *grammatia,* which means "letters." Because the ancient Jews considered the name of God too sacred to pronounce, they replaced the vowels appearing with YHWH for those of *Adonai,* usually rendered "Lord." The result is the familiar rendering *Jehovah,* which appears in the Authorized Version (KJV) and other translations of the English Bible.

The proper noun *Yahweh* is most likely a derivative of the Hebrew root *hayah,* that means "to be" or "to become." Exodus 3:13–14 reveals that the One the Israelites served is the living God. He eternally existed without beginning or end, and He is both the

Source and Sustainer of life. The name "Yahweh" is a revelation of God's dynamic, or effective, existence. His being, or essence, is not abstract and static in nature but is present and powerfully active in the history and affairs of humankind. The character of God and the nature of His promises are also revealed in His dynamic involvement as Yahweh in the lives of His people.

Jewish mystics believed the Tetragrammaton symbolized the androgynous nature of the Creator. To them, God was *both* the Mother and Father of all living things. Ancient pagan mystery religions believed the Tetragrammaton was so esoteric and sacred that it could only be pronounced once a year, and only by the high priest or priestess.

Occultists assumed the Tetragrammaton had great magical powers. Therefore they depicted it within the goddess symbol and engraved it on amulets, charms, and tools of divination. By the seventeenth century, the Tetragrammaton was regarded as the embodiment of the divine spirit and was believed to protect witches and warlocks against the demons of the underworld. The Tetragrammaton remains a popular occult symbol.

*See also:* ANDROGYNY, GOD, MYSTERY, SYMBOLISM

# THEALOGY

Study of the historical and psychological significance of a matriarchal system of worship. "Thealogy" was coined by Naomi Goldenberg and is derived from the Greek word *thea,* which means "goddess." This system of thought emphasizes the nature of the so-called Mother Goddess and her relationship with the world.

Thealogy is especially popular among certain feminist New Age groups. They believe people have forgotten the feminine powers of their divine self that exist deep within the recesses of individual and collective human consciousness.

*See also:* ECOFEMINISM, GAEA, GODDESS WORSHIP, MOTHER EARTH

# THEOSOPHY

An occult organization founded by Madame Helena Petrovna Blavatsky, the former Helen Hahn (1831–1891), and her husband Henry Steel Olcott (1832–1907). In 1872, Blavatsky arrived in the United States where she met and married Olcott. In 1875, they established the Theosophical Society in New York. At first, their organization met with lackluster interest in America. This prompted the couple to leave the U.S. in 1879 and travel to India. In 1882, they relocated the headquarters of the Theosophical Society to Adyar where the international branch for the movement has remained ever since. As the organization grew in popularity, Blavatsky began to travel to Europe and Great Britain. She eventually left India and settled in London where she remained for the rest of her life.

Meanwhile, Olcott remained in India and continued to lead the organization. One of the Society's most promising converts was an Irish-American named William Q. Judge (1851–1896). Through his efforts, Theosophy experienced a surge of popularity in America. However in 1895, a feud between Judge and Olcott caused the movement in the U.S. to split from the India-based group. Judge was succeeded by Katherine Tingley (1847–1929). During her tenure, she moved the headquarters of the American branch of the Society to Point Loma, California. When Olcott died, he was succeeded by Annie Besant (1847–1933) as leader of the Society in India. Upon Besant's death, the group was led by George Arundale and C. Jinara Jodosa. Since then, Theosophy has experienced considerable growth in Europe and the United States.

The name "Theosophy" is derived from the Greek words *theos* and *sophia,* which mean "god" and "wisdom" respectively. Theosophy claims to teach wisdom about God. Theosophy portrays itself as the great unifier and peacemaker in religion and supposedly embraces all of the best in the world's creeds, philosophies, and sciences. Theosophy is a homogenized universal fraternity where all people can unite, regardless of their race, gender, ethnicity, or faith. These ideas are heralded in three of Blavatsky's most prominent works: *Isis Unveiled* (1877), *The Secret Doctrine* (1888), and *Key to Theosophy* (1889). She wrote that a universal philosophy unites all the world's religions. All the sacred texts of these religions supposedly contain an outer, or exoteric, meaning and an inner, or esoteric, meaning. Theosophists devote themselves to the unveiling of hidden meanings in these texts so all people might come to realize their innate divinity and union with the cosmic mind.

Although Theosophy is a relatively recent movement, its origins can be traced to ancient Gnosticism, Buddhism, and Hinduism. Theosophists teach that one eternal, unchanging, and all-pervading principle beyond human understanding lies at the heart of all life. This principle, infinite in potentiality, is the basis for unchanging reality. Theosophists maintain a cyclical view of life. Just as each day begins, proceeds, and ends in a repetitive and uniform manner, so does a person's birth, life, and death repeat itself in an endless succession of rebirths. The actions of a person generate a force that perpetuates the transmigration of the soul to the next life. The ethical consequences surrounding one's karma determines their next existence.

Theosophy says that God is a universal presence or Over-Soul. The souls of all people supposedly are individualized fragments of the divine life and emanations of it. God and humanity are two phases of the one eternal life and consciousness that pervades the universe. This makes the unity of the human race an inherent part of nature. Theosophists teach that everyone has the potential within to acquire all the attributes and powers of God. Human beings allegedly are on an evolutionary journey leading to perfection. Proponents believe people have a physical body, a mental body, and an astral body. People advance through these different phases of existence through hard work and its resulting merit.

Advocates believe that through the process of reincarnation, people can become universal beings. They eventually reach Devachan, or "heaven," in which individual personality is absorbed into God's and consciousness is extinguished. Devotees regard historic figures such as Buddha and Jesus as members of a great fraternity of "masters" or "mahatmas." These perfected individuals have reached the pinnacle of evolutionary advancement and allegedly live in the remote regions of Tibet.

*See also:* BAILEY, ALICE ANN; BESANT, ANNIE WOOD; BLAVATSKY, HELENA PETROVNA; KRISHNAMUATI, JIDDU

## THERAPEUTIC TOUCH

A New Age version of ancient pagan healing techniques. Therapeutic Touch (TT) is based on the Eastern religious belief in a universal source of energy. This life force travels throughout the body and instills health, vitality, and well-being. Pain and illness result when the flow of cosmic energy is obstructed or imbalanced. TT healers contend they have the ability to visualize a cure and pass it on to a patient. By touching a person in the right spot, healers seek to realign the body's energy patterns with those of the universal force.

TT healers begin by entering a trancelike state, claiming this is necessary to invoke psychic powers. Then they pass their hands lightly over their patient's body in circular motions. This allegedly enables the healers to "scan" the body's energy flow and find areas where it has accumulated energy obstructions and imbalances. Through visualization techniques, healers assert they can eliminate these. Some claim that the patient's energy is drawn to the hands of the healer, allowing the healer to manipulate the flow at will.

Others say TT operates from the same power source as all cosmic phenomena, and it depends on the healer's ability to inject energy into his patient through psychic means. The success of TT is often temporary and usually demands that the patient continue therapy while learning the revelations of ancient pagan belief systems.

*See also:* BALANCING, COSMIC ENERGY, GOD, HOLISM, KI, MERIDIANS, PRANA

## THETANS

Godlike race of immortal souls from which humanity is reincarnated in the beliefs of Scientology. L. Ron Hubbard (1911–1986), founder of Scientology, taught that about 75 million years ago a cruel interglactic ruler named Xenu banished the Thetans to earth. Excruciating recollections of the past, called engrams by Hubbard, plague the mind by blocking the true memories of the long-ago Thetan existence.

Scientologist counselors, called auditors, are trained to help clients subdue the engrams, releasing Thetan memory power of analysis. Through this mental extraction process, disciples seek freedom from negative forces that stand in the way of the deity that exists within.

*See also:* DIANETICS; ENGRAM; EXTRATERRESTRIAL INTELLIGENCE; HUBBARD, L. RON

## THIRD EYE

The center of spiritual vision allegedly existing between the two physical eyes at the center of the forehead. This concept is based on an ancient Egyptian symbol that depicts an imaginary eye in the middle of the forehead of Horus, the pagan deity of light, goodness, and the sky. Some think the symbol

denotes the life of the soul during periods of deathlike sleep. Others say the symbol represents the all-seeing eye of Horus and its Hindu counter-

**Utchat—Egyptian symbol for the sacred, all-seeing eye**

part Shiva, the god of destruction and cosmic dissolution. Still others say that the third eye is the location of the sixth chakra, a psychic energy center. Through the practice of Hindu yogic exercises, advocates claim this dormant energy is aroused, enabling people to tap into the powers of their inner self.

New Age adherents claim that all people have dormant psychic abilities that must be recognized and brought to the awareness of the conscious mind. To help initiates achieve

this goal, a skilled practitioner will place thumb and third finger on each temple of an initiate. The practitioner then presses an index finger onto the forehead of the initiate, causing the optic nerve to be pinched and a light to flash. By meditating on the third eye, people reputedly gain insight into the Universal Mind and become enlightened. Occult textbooks describe the cosmic light of the Divine Father as being projected into the third eye of the initiate, thereby beginning the transformational process that leads to divinity.

*See also:* CHAKRA, EYE OF HORUS, LIGHT, LUCIFERIC DOCTRINE, SHIVA

## THOUGHT ADJUSTERS

Spirit guides of the Urantia Society. In 1934, seven spirit beings supposedly visited Bill Sadler (1875–1969) to reveal 2,097 pages of exhaustive cosmic truth. He wrote what they dictated in *The Urantia Book,* published by the Society in 1955, so that people on earth (Urantia) could benefit from the wisdom of these highly intelligent space creatures. Members of the Society allow thought adjusters to take control of their minds. This supposedly enables the higher self to experience the direct presence of the divine, free from the fear and confusion of normal consciousness. Once invited, the spirit beings remain with practitioners through successive reincarnations until their souls have attained unification with the cosmic consciousness.

*See also:* AVATAR; REINCARNATION; SPIRIT GUIDES; URANTIA SOCIETY, THE

## THOUGHT TRANSFERENCE

Telepathic transmission of words, sounds, or images from one mind to another. Thought transference reputedly contains subliminal messages that only the unconscious mind can interpret. Some claim this phenomenon is caused by the radiation of intense amounts of psychic energy that, when amplified by the emotions, projects images into a receptive mind. These telepathic abilities are said to lay dormant in the minds of all people and are accessed through manipulation of the human consciousness. By transcending the levels of consciousness, people can unblock psychic barriers, which paves the way for the development of a wide range of telepathic abilities.

*See also:* EXTRASENSORY PERCEPTION, PSYCHIC, TELEPATHY

## THREE REALMS

In Celtic thought, sky, sea and land are a magical trinity of harmony. The idea is similar to that of the ancient Greeks, with their four elements (earth, air, fire, and water). The number three frequently appears in Celtic literature, and the three realms can be found in Irish blessings. The Three Realms are an integral part of the Celtic idea of the world. Modern Celtic pagans set up their altars facing North, and have their circle touch the three corners of the north, the southeast, and the southwest. Modern Druids use the Greek system of corners/directions.

*See also:* CELTIC PAGANISM, DRUIDS

## TIBETAN MASTER

An alias sometimes used in reference to Djwhal Khul, the so-called spirit guide of Alice Ann Bailey (1880–1949), a noted theosophist. Some claim a superior race of beings reside in a haven in the Tibetan Mountains while they await the dawning of the New Age. Along with Djwhal Khul, these entities have come to earth to help people achieve higher levels of consciousness and usher in the Shamballa force of the Aquarian era. The Tibetan Master reputedly inspired Bailey to write nearly twenty books and establish a number of influential organizations to promote New Age beliefs and practices.

*See also:* BAILEY, ALICE ANN; DJWHAL KHUL; SHAMBALLA; THEOSOPHY

## TONGUES

In orthodox Christian tradition, speaking in "tongues" is a special ability given by the Holy Spirit. Most Protestant and Catholic traditions hold that the gift was recognizable, human languages and dialects that were unknown to the original speaker. Pentecostal and charismatic groups hold that the gift of tongues consists in the expression of estatic speech and that it is an ongoing manifestation of the Spirit. Christians generally agree that the gift in the New Testament served as a sign, or convincing proof, to unbelievers to authenticate what was spoken by the believer (Acts 2:1–47; 10:43–48; 19:1–7; 1 Cor. 12:8; 14).

New Age adherents claim that speaking in tongues is a manifestation of spirit guides from the astral plane communicating divine truth through human hosts. By entering a trance-like state, people can supposedly unleash the ability to speak in tongues, enter into the mind of the cosmic consciousness, and gain divine wisdom. People are encouraged to do this both as a way of obtaining personal enlightenment and as a way of transforming the human race. Devotees claim that in order to usher in the New Age, all people around the world must collectively speak in tongues. At that time, people supposedly will become one with the Universal Mind.

*See also:* ALTERED STATE

## TRANCE CHANNELING

The communication of information by a spirit entity through a human host. This occurs when practitioners enter an altered state of consciousness, reach deep within the subconscious levels of their mind, and establish contact with beings from the astral plane. Some think these entities are extraterrestrials from neighboring planets, while others say they are manifestations of the collective unconscious. Still others assert that they are evolving beings who have not yet completed their karmic cycle. However the most popular understanding is that these entities are ascended masters who have come from another dimension to help people on their journey to enlightenment. These spirits claim to possess the wisdom of the ages, that they will reveal to willing initiates. Through trance channeling, people allegedly can tap into the force of the cosmic consciousness and obtain unlimited powers that they can then use to create their own realities.

*See also:* ALTERED STATE, ASCENDED MASTER, DEMON, MEDIUM, NEW AGE MOVEMENT, SPIRITISM

## TRANSCENDENCE

The peak experience of self-actualization. According to psychologist Abraham Maslow (1908–1970), transcendence represents an altered state of consciousness vital to spiritual growth and development. During a peak experience, people transcend the limitations of their ability to understand the world as it genuinely exists. New Age adherents have adopted the idea of transcendence to support their teaching that people can rise above their mundane existence and become one with Universal Reality. Occultists say this peak experience is a vital part of the education, evolution, and survival of humanity and the world.

*See also:* MASLOW, ABRAHAM; PEAK EXPERIENCES; SELF-ACTUALIZATION; TRANSPERSONAL PSYCHOLOGY

## TRANSCENDENTAL MEDITATION (TM)

A religious discipline in which practitioners focus their minds on a single point of reference, visualize the deity within them, and chant a mantra, or sacred sound. The intent is to attain conscious union with the divine or the impersonal creative principle. This fosters calmness, creativity, peace of mind, and spiritual well-being.

Forms of transcendental meditation have existed for thousands of years among the religions of the world. In the 1960s and 1970s, TM was popularized in the West by the Indian guru Maharishi Mahesh Yogi (b. 1911). He taught that human beings live at a low level of conscious experience. By cultivating a mental state emptied of all thoughts or perceptions, they seek elevated levels of conscious experience, the key to enlightenment. Yogi advocated mind-altering meditative practices that include concentrating on a meaningless phrase, gazing at an object, and focusing on breathing. He claimed that those who do not regularly practice TM fail to grasp the immaterial essence of the universe and the cosmic consciousness that permeates reality.

When the Maharishi introduced TM to the West as the Science of Creative Intelligence, he tried to divest the practice of its Eastern religious embellishments. He declared that anyone could practice TM because this harmless exercise creates inner peace and an expanded mental awareness. The chanting of certain mantras supposedly enables initiates to tap the pure energy field buried deep within their subconscious. This energy is said to be linked to the unlimited creative intelligence of the universe. Once the cosmic mind is accessed, practitioners experience a dramatic reduction in stress, seen as the ultimate source of human problems. By entering into an altered state of consciousness regularly, people reputedly can achieve their full human potential, learn to screen out unwanted incoming sensory information, and realize the greater realities of the universe.

The Maharishi believes that the world is at the threshold of a New Age. He claims that as more and more people practice TM, it will eliminate personal and global imbalances with the universal life force, help reach a critical mass, and cause the human race to experience a quantum leap in evolutionary progress. Yogi maintains that TM is the solution to the world's problems and the key to attaining personal success, power, freedom, and health. The Indian guru does not mention that mantras are Sanskrit names of Hindu gods, and that their repeated recitation is a form of Hindu religious practice.

*See also:* ALTERED STATE, HINDUISM, MAHARISHI MAHESH YOGI, SANSKRIT

## TRANSCENDENTALISM

The belief that knowledge of reality can be obtained from intuitive sources rather than from objective experience. German philosopher Immanuel Kant (1724–1804) held that some concepts cannot be perceived directly through sense experience or pure reason. These include concepts dealing with space and time and with categories of judgment, otherwise known as transcendental thought. Individuals must experience states of existence that go beyond the mundane. This system of thought emphasizes the superiority of the spiritual and the transcendental over the material and empirical.

In the first half of the nineteenth century, a fresh form of transcendentalism arose in New England. Noteworthy leaders included essayist and poet Ralph Waldo Emerson (1803–1882), Unitarian minister and author William Ellery Channing (1780–1842), and Unitarian minister and abolitionist leader Theodore Parker (1810–1860). These men and others met in the Massachusetts home of literary critic and socialist George Ripley (1802–1880). They formed the Transcendental Club, which promoted their ideals. They rejected what they perceived as dogmaticism and authoritarianism in orthodox Christianity. They also stressed the immanence of God, the divinity of both humans and nature, and the supremacy of intuition over reason. These ideals have been adopted by the New Age Movement.

*See also:* NEW THOUGHT

## TRANSFORMATION

To experience a major change in form, nature, or function. In New Age literature, transformation refers to a psychic metamorphosis induced by paranormal entities. The process of change begins when practitioners induce altered states of consciousness through techniques such as sensory deprivation, biofeedback, and hallucinogenic drugs. As the process continues, indoctrination leads initiates to believe they are innately divine and have the ability to maximize their human potential. By manipulating their thoughts, they have the power to change reality.

As initiates enter altered states of consciousness, they encounter spirits claiming to be ascended masters or manifestations of the divine self. Once these entities gain control over devotees, the spirits convince them to jettison all forms of morality and to create their own rules of right and wrong. Occult leaders make every effort to recruit new followers by promoting these claims about personal transformation. They tell initiates that once enough people have gone through a psychic metamorphosis, then a quantum leap in the evolutionary development of humanity will result. This will usher in the Aquarian Age of universal peace, love, and unity.

*See also:* ALTERED STATE, GLOBALISM, HIGHER SELF, ONE-WORLD IDEAL

## TRANSFORMATION TECHNOLOGIES INCORPORATED (TTI)

A management consulting firm designed to sell New Age business training seminars to large corporations. In 1984, Werner Hans Erhard (b. 1935) developed TTI as an offshoot to EST (Erhard Seminars Training), otherwise known as The Forum. TTI is divided into approximately fifty franchises designed to cater to the needs of individual corporations.

TTI uses a variety of techniques to promote a unified vision among the employees of client companies. They use transcendental meditation, hypnosis, visualization, and positive thinking to encourage participants to become one with their company. Students also learn that by linking up with the collective consciousness of their associates, they can tap a universal source of creativity and potential. Participants are exposed to a mixture of beliefs from Zen Buddhism, Scientology, and Hinduism.

*See also:* ERHARD, WERNER HANS; HUMANISTIC PSYCHOLOGY; MYSTICISM; TRANSFORMATION

## TRANSLOCATION

Instantaneous movement from one location to another. According to legend, the universe is made up of extra dimensions of space and time. By altering the body's vibrational frequency rate, people supposedly can operate in these extra dimensions and move rapidly to different locations. They also can pass through physical barriers without damaging either themselves or the obstructions. New Age adherents claim these abilities are available to all who would transcend their subconscious and tap into the powers of the divine self. Translocators say that occult mind-altering techniques enable them to alter reality and remain totally conscious as they exist in two or more remote locations at the same time. They assert that by using translocation techniques, they can also move objects almost immediately.

*See also:* ASTRAL PROJECTION, COSMIC ENERGY, PSYCHIC

# TRANSMIGRATION (METEMPSYCHOSIS)

The movement of the soul from one body or being to another at death. The newly inhabited entity can either be human or animal, animate or inanimate. Transmigration is based on the Hindu belief that human souls are emanations of the divine spirit permeating the universe. They teach that people are born and die innumerable times. The newly acquired state in each cycle of life allegedly is determined by what was done in previous lives. Hinduism teaches that each life is on a journey to nirvana, the final state of existence that perfectly balances an individual's good and bad karma. When people reach nirvana, they supposedly will be reabsorbed into the divine essence of the universe where all traces of desire and individual consciousness will be extinguished. Transmigration is a popular teaching within the New Age Movement.

*See also:* ANIMISM, HINDUISM, INCARNATION, REINCARNATION

# TRANSPERSONAL PSYCHOLOGY

An approach to psychological and spiritual well-being concerned with esoteric mental experiences, such as mysticism and altered states of consciousness. Otherwise known as the fourth force, transpersonal psychology is regarded as paranormal, metaphysical, or suprarational in nature. This realm of "actuality" lies beyond rational, concrete, scientific, or revelatory examination. It can only be described and experienced.

This psychological approach represents a broad integration of beliefs and practices from Eastern religions, mystical Christianity, Jungian analysis, Gestalt and existential therapies, as well as music, dance, art therapies, and LSD-assisted therapy. Proponents stress the immanence of God, rather than the transcendence. The divine reputedly is an all-pervasive reality that people can encounter through mind-altering techniques. The ultimate goal allegedly is to transcend to the highest level of consciousness and become one with the Universal Mind. When self-transcendence is achieved, people supposedly experience a mystical awareness or insight.

Self-transcendence is regarded as vital to the evolutionary development and survival of humanity. Transpersonal programs usually require students to participate in emotional training, meditation, yoga, and other occult activities. They also study dreams, psychic phenomena, and parapsychology. Advocates claim that transpersonal psychology can help people become more creative, develop their fullest human potential, and achieve self-realization. They promote the widespread practice of psychic dreams, imagery, hypnosis, and autogenic experiences, as well as precognition, out-of-body travel, and drug-altered states of consciousness. These practices encourage reaching a critical mass, to transform society and establish a new era of enlightenment.

*See also:* ALTERED STATE; EVOLUTION; HUMANISTIC PSYCHOLOGY; MASLOW, ABRAHAM; TRANSCENDENCE

# TRANSPERSONAL PSYCHOLOGY, ASSOCIATION FOR (ATP)

An international organization dedicated to the exploration of the spiritual aspects of human nature. ATP produces newsletters and reference lists, as well as transpersonal psychology graduate programs that emphasize holistic healing and psychic phenomena. The psychological approach advocated by ATP represents a broad integration of beliefs and practices from Eastern religions, mystical Christianity, Jungian analysis, Gestalt and existential therapies, as well as music, dance, art therapies, and LSD-assisted therapy. They stress the immanence, rather than the transcendence, of God. ATP teaches that the divine is an all-pervasive reality that people can encounter through mind-altering techniques. The ultimate goal allegedly is to transcend to the highest level of consciousness and become one with the Universal Mind. When self-transcendence is achieved, people experience a mystical awareness or insight. New Age adherents assert that self-transcendence is vital to the evolutionary development and survival of humanity.

*See also:* TRANSPERSONAL PSYCHOLOGY

## TREE

The primary symbol of Druidism, based on the view that trees are bridges between the realms of Land and Sky, and they communicate Water (Sea) between these realms. Many gods and goddesses in Celtic mythology lived in trees or sacred groves. Trees were not themselves worshiped, but they were thought to have magical, sacred properties. This sacred tree motif has found its way into New Age ecological thought.

*See also:* DRUIDS, ECOTHEOLOGY, THREE REALMS

## TRIANGLE

Throughout history, the triangle has been used as an occult symbol. The triangle, represented by the Greek letter Delta ($\Delta$), signified the door of birth, a euphemism for female genitalia. In Egyptian lore, the triangle symbolized the female principle, as well as the trinity of Father God (Osiris), Mother Goddess (Isis), and Son (Horus). In India, the Hindu religion used the triangle to represent various deities. One triangle represented the Mother Goddess giving birth to the pantheon of deities. Two triangles atop one another in an hourglass form symbol-

ized creation and infinity. Three triangles represented the female trinity of fate. And a multitude of intertwined triangles symbolized the sexual union of the Hindu gods and goddesses. History is replete with examples of occult practices associated with the triangle. The aborigines of Australia danced in a triangular shape called *yoni yantra,* symbolizing the pubic area of the Mother Goddess. In a similar fashion, the Babylonians performed sexual rituals.

The triangle remains a powerful symbol. Cults throughout the world meditate on the geometrical figure to invoke the promised powers of Love and Light. They believe the apex of the triangle represents the hierarchy of spiritual guides who have come to earth from the astral realm to lead humanity to greater enlightenment. The world is accordingly said to be permeated with a triangular-shaped energy field. Through meditative techniques people enter a trancelike state to unite with this universal life force. If enough people simultaneously perform this meditative exercise, a triangular channel will open to the hierarchy of ascended masters and convince them that the world is ready for the messiah of the Aquarian era.

*See also:* BABYLON, GODDESS WORSHIP, PYRAMIDOLOGY, SEXUALITY, SYMBOLISM

## TRILATERAL COMMISSION

A nongovernmental advisory organization established by David Rockefeller (b. 1915) in 1973 to help various economic markets peacefully transition to a global economy. The Commission includes three hundred prominent delegates from three industrialized and economic regions of the world. These include North America (the United States and Canada), the European Union, and Japan. For the most part, delegates work in government, academia, and private enterprise. They meet every year in one of the three regions to discuss a wide range of issues, such as agricultural policy, arms control, and debt to the Third World. The international organization's aim is to establish and manage a global economy that lays the foundation for a new world order. Some critics have charged that the Commission has a New Age agenda and that many of its members belong to secret fraternal organizations with ties to the occult.

*See also:* GLOBALISM, ILLUMINATI, ONE-WORLD IDEAL, PEACE

## TRUMPET MEDIUM

A popular item used during séances that supposedly provides communication with the spirits of departed souls. The meetings are often conducted in darkness to hide the manipulative apparatus that enables the trumpet to "float" around the room, swing back and forth, bounce off the ceiling, or even rest in the hands of participants. Eerie voices emanating from the trumpet reputedly are those of spirits. The medium will invite the group to ask questions and receive answers from one of the entities.

*See also:* MEDIUM, SÉANCE, SPIRITISM

## TWELVE TRIBES MISSION (MESSIANIC COMMUNITIES)

A group that began in the 1970s in Tennessee and grew rapidly into a world movement but became infamous during the 1990s because of allegations of child abuse. Twelve Tribes Mission or the Messianic Communities promoted a lifestyle of simplicity, without the stresses of modern life, and became attractive to teenagers and young adults. The cult is based on strict Old Testament teach-

ings and is led by Elbert Eugene Spriggs (b. 1937), a former American school counselor. He goes by the name "Yoneq." Spriggs proclaimed the Christian church had died in the first century and there was no true church until he came on the scene in 1972. It was his task to replant the twelve tribes of Israel on Earth so that Christ could return. By the end of the 1990s, there were twenty-eight communities in Australia, Brazil, Canada, France, Germany, Argentina, Great Britain, Spain, and the United States.

Reports began to surface after several years of children as young as two years old being stripped and beaten almost to the point of death with canes. There were reports of child neglect and poor education at the community schools. Children are not allowed to play with toys. The community lifestyle in general is austere. Television, newspapers, radio, magazines, caffeine, alcohol, and tobacco are banned. Births are at home, and followers avoid medication and hospitals. They attend prayer meetings morning and night, sing and dance, and eat organic food. New members must sell all of their possessions and give the money to the community. Cottage industries also raise funds for the group. Followers strictly obey elders and women strictly obey men. But they are all free to lie to nonbelievers because they are not "obligated to tell the devil the truth."

## TWITCHELL, PAUL
*See:* ECKANKAR

# U

## UNARIUS ACADEMY OF SCIENCE

A psychic and UFOlogy related cult founded in 1954 in Los Angeles by Ernest L. Norman (1904–1971), who called himself Archangel Raphiel, and Ruth E. Norman (1900–1993), who took the name Archangel Uriel. Unarius stands for "Universal Articulate Interdimensional Understanding of Science." Based in El Cajon, California, the group claims about 500,000 members. Unarius followers frequently air the group's videos over public access television. After Raphiel's death in 1971, Uriel created the Center for New World Teaching as a clearing house for books and videos about interdimensional knowledge she had received from higher beings. Unarius centers exist or are planned in the United States, Canada, England, New Zealand, Nigeria, Poland, Spain, Italy, Romania, and the Czech Republic. Charles Spiegel (Antares) succeeded Uriel as director. Among his many books is an autobiography of his past life as Napoleon Bonaparte.

Unarius is a primary source for teachings about the superhuman extraterrestrials, the Pleiadeians, who they believe will found a new era of peace on earth. At this writing, their arrival is set for the year 2001. Unarius teaches that human society originally was on a quest for self-understanding and higher consciousness, but has regressed for hundreds of thousands of years. In particular the human spiritual evolution has been forgotten, the result being wars and social problems. This regression was to end in 2001, when the Pleiadeians inaugurated a spiritual rebirth of humanity.

*See:* EXTRATERRESTRIAL INTELLIGENCE, PLEIADEIANS, UNIDENTIFIED FLYING OBJECT

## UNCONSCIOUS, THE

That part of the mind or psyche containing thoughts, feelings, or other mental processes that have faded from consciousness or have never been conscious. According to the psychoanalytical theory first developed by Sigmund Freud (1856–1939), three dimensions characterize the mind—the preconscious, the conscious, and the unconscious. The thoughts and feelings of the preconscious, such as the name of a friend or the address of a relative, are not in a person's immediate awareness. However they can be recalled by focusing attention on them. The thoughts and feelings of the conscious are what people most immediately remember at any given moment.

The unconscious reputedly is made up of the id, psychic energy obtained from instinctual needs and drives. Although the thoughts and feelings of the id were once conscious, these components have been repressed in order to avoid the anxiety, guilt, or distress associated with them. Though they are unconscious, they affect the behavior of people in an adverse manner. The unconscious is seen as an irrational mixture of contradictory ideas and feelings. Access can be gained to this part of the mind or psyche only through much effort, since recalling repressed memories brings to the surface tremendous pain and sorrow. Through insight-oriented therapy, patients learn to overcome the barriers they have erected to block out these agonizing feelings, thoughts, or wishes.

New Age adherents have mixed these views with ideas from Eastern mysticism. The unconscious is the locus of both spiritual and demonic forces. It holds the past memories of actions and thoughts in this and previous lives of individuals, whereas the "collective unconscious" serves as a reservoir of the symbols and memories of all humanity. By entering into a trancelike state, people can break through their psychological barriers and tap into the unconscious, whether their own or that of the entire human race. Occult practices provide the means for entering these alternate dimensions of existence and establishing contact with entities from parallel universes. This includes such things as yoga, transcendental meditation, hypnosis, free association, dream analysis, and taking psychedelic drugs. In addition, these techniques might be used to tap into the powers of the divine self. Proponents claim that by exploring the unconscious realm, people can obtain esoteric wisdom from ascended masters, manipulate reality, and control the future.

*See also:* ALTERED STATE, COLLECTIVE UNCONSCIOUS, CONSCIOUSNESS, SUPERCONSCIOUSNESS

# UNICORN

A mythical creature having the head and torso of a horse, the hind legs of an adult male deer, the tail of a lion, the beard of a goat, and a single spiraled horn projecting from the middle of the forehead. Some legends say the unicorn was once native to India and existed throughout the world. Other tales say the animal has magical powers that can bring prosperity and luck to the owner. For protection from diseases and poisoning, people supposedly drank from the creature's horn. In central Asia, people believe the unicorn's horn can cure sexual dysfunction.

New Age adherents have perpetuated many of the myths associated with the unicorn. The horn represents the focal point of the creature's occult powers. Advocates identify the horn with the all-seeing third eye of Horus, the Egyptian god of light, goodness, and the sky. Because the unicorn is pure white in color, they often use the unicorn as a symbol for virginity. Legend says that only a virgin can capture the animal, suggesting that spiritual love is more powerful than cruelty and violence. The unicorn is also identified with the Virgin Mary and Jesus in some religious artifacts.

*See also:* EYE OF HORUS, GOAT OF MENDES, POWER ANIMAL, SYMBOLISM

# UNIDENTIFIED FLYING OBJECT (UFO)

Optical and light phenomena in the sky whose appearance, flight path, and behavior defy logical conventional explanation. People have reported seeing UFOs shaped like hats, balls, rings, triangles, squares, and cigars. These individuals come from a wide spectrum of economic, ethnic, and educational backgrounds, and many claim these flying objects are extraterrestrial in origin. However, many scientific experts believe UFOs are simply phenomena created by natural forces or aircraft. These might include the reflection of sunlight off airplanes and weather balloons, or celestial formations resulting from meteorological activity. Nevertheless, some sightings continue to defy explanation.

Some New Age adherents assert that UFOs are visitations of extraterrestrial intelligence (ETI) who bring esoteric wisdom from distant galaxies and warnings about the future. Others say UFOs are a manifestation of humanity's collective unconscious. Still others claim the mysterious flying objects are spirit guides who have taken amorphous, shape-changing forms to make themselves known to the world. Despite these different conjectures, the message reputedly proclaimed by the entities shows remarkable sameness. Through the use of human hosts, they teach that reality is made up of many parallel universes emanating from the cosmic consciousness. Proponents say people are a part of this all-encompassing life force. What people do individually and collectively affects the rhythm and flow of the universe.

These entities declare that the world is in the process of transition from one age to the next. In order for the changeover to occur successfully, a critical mass of people must voluntarily enter altered states of consciousness. Despite the environmental disasters and societal traumas this will cause, the human race is urged to press on in the quest for a quantum leap in evolutionary advancement. They say that in the not too distant future, a UFO will bring Lord Maitreya to earth so that he can personally guide the human race into the New Age. Under his leadership, all life forms emitting negative vibrations supposedly will be transported to other dimensions of space and time, leaving the enlightened to populate the earth. This will lead to a long era of peace, harmony, and joy.

See also: EXTRATERRESTRIAL INTELLIGENCE, PURIFICATION, UNIDENTIFIED FLYING OBJECT EXPERIENCE

## UNIDENTIFIED FLYING OBJECT EXPERIENCE (UFOE)

An alleged encounter with extraterrestrial (ET) entities. With the increased number of reported UFOEs, a New Age pseudo-science has arisen to explore the implications of encountering aliens from other galaxies and parallel dimensions of time and space. Reports commonly describe these creatures as about three feet tall, with oversized triangularly shaped heads, and large black eyes. Some people say that ETs have telepathically communicated with them. Others claim they were abducted by aliens, taken to a spacecraft, operated on, and then returned to earth. These sorts of assertions have been "verified" by occult mediums who contend they can talk to ETs intergalactically through telepathy, the Ouija® board, transcendental meditation, automatic writing, or various other means.

People who claim they have had a UFOE remember entering a trancelike state, observing paranormal phenomena, and receiving esoteric knowledge from aliens. These entities often claim they are spiritually evolved beings who have come to warn humankind of impending disaster, and offer salvation through personal and global transformation. The ETs deny the existence of a personal god and claim that people have latent divine powers waiting to be developed. The alien messengers predict the soon-coming world leader who will establish his rule over earth. He will also cleanse the planet of all who have not achieved a higher,

more evolved state of consciousness.

Some experts claim that repeated contact with ETs can cause terrifying physical manifestations. Abductees report feeling drained and confused from the eradication of their long-held beliefs. When a UFOE occurs, they describe a meshing of mind and matter, reality and illusion, light and darkness, masculine and feminine, and good and evil. New Age adherents claim these alien encounters are necessary for people to experience unprecedented spiritual growth and moral freedom from outdated and restrictive values.

See also: DEMON, EXPERIENCE, EXTRATERRESTRIAL INTELLIGENCE, UNIDENTIFIED FLYING OBJECT

## UNIFICATION CHURCH (HOLY SPIRIT ASSOCIATION FOR THE UNIFICATION OF WORLD CHRISTIANITY)

A cult founded in 1954 by Sun Myung Moon (b. 1920). The Unification Church has founded or purchased a number of religious and public policy institutions, such as the Washington Institute for Values in Public Policy and the International One World Crusade. They also sponsor political organizations, such as the American Freedom Coalition and the International Federation for Victory Over Communism. Their business enterprises include New World Communication and Free Press International. The church has grown to more than 3 million members worldwide, with more than thirty thousand followers in the U.S.

Critics of the Unification Church have made various charges of impropriety to increase the organization's power and influence. In 1982 a U.S. federal court convicted Moon of tax evasion. There also were charges that Moon and his followers used brainwashing tactics to obtain converts, mainly among college-age young people. Because this is a lonely and insecure age, college students are prime candidates for proselytizing.

Members of the cult have used weekend "retreats" to shower seekers with affection and times of intimate worship designed to

267

win their trust. Physical exertion, sleep deprivation, and peer pressure have also been reportedly used as tactics to mold the minds of recruits.

Unificationists speak of preferring "vertical love" to "horizontal love." Vertical love is unquestioning obedience to and affection for superiors and teachers within the Unification Church. Initiates learn to see life through the eyes of their leaders. They are taught not to question their commands, even subconsciously. Moonies define horizontal love as affection for peers or friends, which fosters independent thinking and rebellion. Just as Eve led Adam into sin, so horizontal love leads to a multiplication of sin. Members are indoctrinated to watch one another to ensure that everyone is obeying their superiors.

In his book *Divine Principle* (1957), Moon rejected the concept that God has self awareness. Instead, he said, the divine is pure, unbounded, and self-generating energy. Inherent in this was repudiation of the triune nature of God's existence. Moon maintains that God is a bipolar entity that pervades the universe. This means that God is the peaceful coexistence of masculinity and femininity, the positive aspect represented by the Father and the negative side represented by the Spirit. Likewise, human beings exist as emanations and incarnations of the divine and live in a balanced harmony of positive and negative life forces.

Moon claimed to be on a mission from God to finish the saving work of Christ. He maintains that Jesus accomplished only the spiritual redemption of humanity because His work was cut short by his arrest and crucifixion. Christ's death prevented Him from finding the perfect mate and procreating a perfect race of human beings. God subsequently chose Moon to complete the physical redemption of humankind. Within the Unification Church, devotees call Moon the "Lord of the Second Advent," the "third Adam," and the "promised Messiah." Unificationists believe they can reach God only through Moon. For this reason he maintains absolute control over his followers, even dictating whom they marry. The mass weddings Moon has performed have brought him considerable notoriety.

According to Moon, three epochs characterize human history. The first encompassed Old Testament times, the second covered the New Testament era, and the third is the "Completed Age." This last stage of salvation history is when Moon will bring about full and final redemption of the human race. When this occurs, a perfect man (Jesus) will return with a perfect woman to become the spiritual parents of all humanity. Those who accept and follow them will inherit the divine kingdom.

To help achieve the goals of the Unification Church, Moonies hold crusades. The ultimate goal is to unite churches of all beliefs and faith traditions into a single world religious organization. The purpose of the International One World Crusade is to promote this reality.

*See also:* CRUCIFIXION; MOON, SUN MYUNG; ONE-WORLD IDEAL

## UNIFIED FIELD THEORY (GRAND UNIFIED THEORY, GUT)

A set of postulates designed to explain the relationship between the known basic forces existing in nature. Proponents think four of these exist. Gravitation and electromagnetism reputedly are long-range forces. Short-range forces operate only at the subatomic particle level. These include weak interaction, or weak nuclear force, and strong interaction, or strong nuclear force. Since the days of Albert Einstein, scientists have made numerous attempts to find a GUT. Although several look promising, they are unable to verify the existence of any. However by using particle accelerators, supercomputers, and ground-based and space-based telescopes, theoretical physicists may eventually succeed in finding a GUT.

New Age adherents have used the general findings about GUTs to validate their occult beliefs. The theory of special relativity says that matter and energy are interchangeable under certain conditions, whereas the theory of general relativity states that space and time are interchangeable under certain conditions. Likewise, New Age adherents claim that all reality is unified and interchangeable. They believe "God" is a cosmic essence that exists in a multitude of interlocking space-time dimensions, and that people are emanations of this all-pervasive life force. By entering a trancelike state, they supposedly can get in touch with their divine self and learn to alter reality. Proponents say people also have the ability to transcend the traditional three dimensional universe, link with other parallel dimensions of existence, and experience a grand unification with the ethereal consciousness. They teach that if enough people do this, this will achieve a connected field of existence and pave the way for global peace and stability.

*See also:* ELECTROMAGNETIC HEALING; GOD; SCIENCE, NEW AGE

## UNITARIANISM

A humanistic religion that denies the doctrine of the Trinity and asserts that God exists in only one person. This solitary being allegedly has revealed Himself through a number of different people, Buddha, Confucius, Christ, Muhammad, and so on, as well as through sacred texts, such as the Bible, Vedas, and Upanishads. Unitarians declare that none of these sources of revelation are perfect; yet they serve as repositories of truth to help people in their religious growth and development. Unitarianism denies the orthodox Christian concept of salvation by faith in Christ. Devotees see salvation as progressively earned through developing character, nurturing the human spirit, and performing good works. Unitarianism also rejects key biblical doctrines such as the deity of Christ, His immaculate conception and birth, the depravity of humankind, the atoning sacrifice of Christ, and the judgment of God against the wicked.

New Age adherents generally agree with the tenets espoused by Unitarianism. They affirm the unity of the divine, though they reject the concept that God is a unique, self-aware person. They also affirm that innumerable paths lead to salvation, and that many people and sacred texts have enlightened humankind. Christ is merely a human being, one of many who used His wisdom and love for the good of the world. They espouse the Unitarian belief that the divine is pure love and that God would never send people to eternal punishment. The way to salvation is through good works and proper moral and spiritual development. Unitarians and New Age theologians work together for unity among the world's religious faiths.

*See also:* GOD, JESUS CHRIST, ONE-WORLD IDEAL

## UNITED NATIONS (UN)

International organization of national governments founded by the Allied Powers at the end of World War II. The UN exists to promote and preserve global peace and security; to foster cooperation among nations; and to solve humanitarian, social, cultural, and economic problems. This world body is comprised of six principal divisions. These include the General Assembly (the main deliberative body), the Security Council (the peacemaking arm), the Economic and Social Council, the Trusteeship Council (the group that oversees non-self-governing territories), the International Court of Justice (the arbitrators of disputes between nations, violations of international law, as well as the breaking of international treaties), and the Secretariat (the administrative division). The UN also has chartered a number of specialized agencies to perform tasks related to the organization's agenda. Some of these agencies include the World Health Organization, the International Monetary Fund, the International Atomic Energy Agency, and the International Telecommunication Union.

New Age adherents favor the existence of the UN because of their commitment to a globalism. In keeping with the overall philosophy of the UN, New Age adherents seek to establish a one-world government, one-world economy, and one-world religion. They strive to set the stage for world peace under the rule of one international leader named Lord

Maitreya. They regard the UN as a catalyst for global transformation and a vital link between the emergence and the enforcement of a new planetary value system. New Age adherents think the UN can help bring about the synergistic collaboration of people, services, and organizations across a worldwide network. This interplanetary web will enable people to provide support, feedback, and shared information on spiritual experiences. They say this is a vital component for the achievement of human consciousness, personal transformation, and global enlightenment. New Age adherents support making the UN the gatekeeper of wealth, power, and religious beliefs. This world body supposedly will unite the disparate peoples of the planet and foster global peace, harmony, and love.

*See also:* GLOBALISM, ONE-WORLD IDEAL

## UNITY IN DIVERSITY COUNCIL (UDC)

An agency established by the UN in 1965. UDC is dedicated to the peaceful evolution of an enlightened society and the emergence of a new civilization characterized by global cooperation and interdependence. The Council represents a mega-network of New Age organizations whose members believe that the diverseness of individual ideologies spurs the creative development of humanity. UDC oversees the festival activities associated with the International Cooperative Year and publishes the quarterly newsletter *Spectrum,* as well as the comprehensive *Directory for a New Age.* The Directory, which appears on an annual basis, lists some of the most influential occult leaders. These include prominent figures such as Marilyn Ferguson (b. 1938) and Benjamin Creme (b. 1922), as well as such organizations as the Tara Center and the Findhorn Foundation.

UDC affirms the oneness of all reality and the union of humanity in fellowship, love, and trust. The Council attempts to integrate reason and faith, as well as science and religion. Members profess an equal respect for all forms of prophecy, divination, sorcery,

and spirituality. They believe in the divine power of the individual psyche and the existence of alternate dimensions of reality which are mutually interactive and interdependent. UDC claims that achieving global unity is the only way humanity can survive. With this in mind, the UDC encourages the educational systems of the world to align themselves in a planetary network. Doing so supposedly will bring about the evolutionary transformation of humankind and usher in the Aquarian Age of enlightenment.

*See also:* GLOBALISM; ONE-WORLD IDEAL; POLITICS, NEW AGE

## UNITY SCHOOL OF CHRISTIANITY (USC)

A religious organization with beliefs mixing Eastern religion and Christian Science. Unity School of Christianity's (USC) international headquarters is based outside of Kansas City in Unity City, Missouri. Since its founding by Charles (1854–1948) and Myrtle Filmore (1845–1931) in 1889, USC has retained wide acceptance and popularity, even among orthodox Christians who often have only a vague idea of its actual doctrines. At the end of the twentieth century, the organization claimed more than 2 million members worldwide. Since Unity does not consider itself a sectarian group, most of those with some level of involvement in the organization usually remain in another religious affiliation.

USC has been effective in subtly disseminating its beliefs in mass market devotional materials. More explicit materials progressively teach the initiated. There is a vast mail order business, an extensive radio, television, and tape "ministry," and at least a dozen publications, including those targeted to children.

Converts can retain membership in other religious organizations because USC considers itself to be an eclectic blend of the best ideas and practices among the world's faith traditions. USC teaches that God is a supreme and infinitely all-pervasive essence. People are divine emanations of the Infinitude and are capable of unlimited possibilities. This potential can be unleashed through the creative power of the subconscious mind. The spiritual realm is superior to the material realm and one sins by falling prey to this illusory world.

As in Christian Science, sickness and disease are unreal maladies created by the mind and can be eliminated by right thinking. By tapping into the cosmic consciousness, people supposedly can achieve health, inspiration, and prosperity. Through a succession of reincarnations, they can journey to higher planes of existence and eventually replace their physical body with a spiritual one.

According to USC, the quest for knowledge and understanding about the spiritual realm is a never-ending process. There is no distinction between God and the earth. Therefore inspired truth exists both in the world's sacred writings and in nature. Truth particularly can be found in the creative genius of people. By looking into the psyche, people can find and know God. Christ is the archetype of those who discover God and truth within themselves. Because He is joined to the Universal Mind, He can show people how to become aware of their divine self.

*See also:* CHRISTIAN SCIENCE; FILMORE, CHARLES/FILMORE, MYRTLE; NEW THOUGHT

# UNIVERSAL AND TRIUMPHANT, CHURCH (THE "I AM" ASCENDED MASTERS, SUMMIT LIGHTHOUSE)

A New Age cult founded in 1958 by Theosophist Mark L. Prophet (1918–1973). The group, named Summit Lighthouse originally, experienced considerable growth under the leadership of Elizabeth Clare Prophet (b. 1939) following her husband's death. Eclectic and syncretistic in her teachings, Prophet wove together Eastern religious practices with Western traditions. Cult doctrine centers around the teachings of the ascended masters of the Great White Brotherhood, a group that proclaimed the coming of a New Age of higher consciousness.

The typical Church Universal and Trium-

phant (CUT) worship service is structured according to Western tradition and laced with Christian terminology. The service may begin with the reading and interpretation of the Bible. Prophet usually delivers the sermon herself, and claims she is the reincarnation of Martha, the only medium of truth in the New Age. Known as "Guru Ma" to her followers, Prophet asserts to channel messages from Sanat Kumura, the christ of the spirit world who has traveled from Venus to help humankind usher in the New Age. She claims other revelations come from Jesus, Buddha, and Saint Germaine, as well as Pope John XXIII, Mark Prophet, and even K-17, the head of the cosmic secret service. Among other messages, the ascended masters declared that Prophet and her church would hold special authority in the coming revolution preceding the dawn of the New Age. According to Prophet, the ascended masters also taught that God did not require the blood sacrifice of Christ to redeem humankind—the crucifixion was merely a pagan ritual.

After hearing the message, members solemnly draw their fingers across their chest in the sign of the cross. After completing this gesture, the decreeing begins. The decree is a high speed chant in which participants affirm the deity of the inner self. Each decree supposedly surrounds each devotee in the Violet Consuming Flame through which their karma is purified. Special spiritual significance is attached to both color and sound, as these are the standard tools used to induce altered states of consciousness.

The leadership of CUT holds preparation for the day of Armageddon with utmost respect. This explains why cult members have hoarded guns and constructed numerous bomb shelters at the cult's international headquarters in Montana. Officials of CUT have been accused of extortion, fraud, and involuntary servitude. But despite negative publicity, the cult boasts a membership of one hundred thousand with estimated assets at $50 million.

*See also:* ASCENDED MASTER, GREAT WHITE BROTHERHOOD, JESUS CHRIST, SANAT KUMURA

# UNIVERSAL MIND

A cosmic, shared consciousness through which all things exist. All creation is said to exist within the realm of a Universal Mind. This cosmic consciousness is divided into sections that permit initiates to explore the creative potential of different experiences at varying levels of existence. The mutual interaction of all animate and inanimate entities supposedly proves that all reality, including humanity, shares a common purpose. Advocates teach that all things are progressing toward perfection through reincarnation and will eventually rejoin the Universal Mind from which they originated. By entering a trancelike state, people reputedly can establish contact with the cosmic consciousness, rediscover their divine self, convert pure thought into matter, and manipulate all forms of reality.

*See also:* CREATION; EVOLUTION; INTERCONNECTION; ONE, THE; REINCARNATION

# UPANISHADS

The final section of the Vedas, the sacred texts of Hinduism. The Upanishads are thought by some to have been written between 800 and 300 B.C. and are also called the Vedanta, meaning "the end, or conclusion, of the Vedas." Of the 108 Upanishads, Hindus consider the Bhagavad Gita as the most important of them all. Like all Vedic literature, the Upanishads are written in Sanskrit, an ancient language of India and the classical language of Hinduism.

The text of the Upanishads is a mixture of mysticism and speculation and affirms the Hindu belief that a single underlying reality is embodied in the absolute self called Brahman. This impersonal, monistic force embodies all gods and goddesses. The universe allegedly continues and extends from the being of Brahman. Even the individual selves or souls of people, called *atmans,* extend from, are united with, and are identical to the essence of Brahman. The Upanishads teach that the highest goal for people is to achieve enlightenment through at least three possible avenues. The first is the way of action and ritual called *karma marga.* The second is the way of knowledge and meditation called *jnana marga.* And the third is the way of devotion called *bhakti marga.* Those who achieve enlightenment supposedly lose their personal identity in the universal self.

*See also:* BHAGAVAD GITA, BIBLE, BRAHMA, HINDUISM, SANSKRIT, VEDA

# URANTIA SOCIETY, THE

An occult organization started by Bill Sadler (1875–1969). Sadler said that in 1934 seven spirit beings revealed to him 2,097 pages of exhaustive cosmic truth. The dictation he took resulted in *The Urantia Book,* published by the Society in 1955. The book's purpose is to show people on earth (Urantia) how to benefit from the wisdom of these entities. The Society claims that this document serves as humanity's ultimate guide to truth, wisdom, and faith. It allegedly provides answers to all universal questions and supersedes all the other outdated religions of the world, including Christianity.

The Society claims that Urantia is one of trillions of inhabitable planets throughout the universe and that these are teeming with intelligent life. These worlds supposedly emanate from the divine essence permeating the cosmos. The Society also teaches that Adam came to Urantia about thirty-eight thousand years ago to help people achieve their ultimate goal, the discovery of their preexistent godhood. Initiates learn that they are aided in their quest by thought adjusters, highly intelligent space beings. Members allow these entities to take control of their minds. This frees them from the fear and confusion of normal consciousness, and allows their higher self to experience the presence of the divine. Once invited, the spirit guides supposedly remain with practitioners through successive reincarnations until their souls have attained unification with the cosmic consciousness. The Society promises that if initiates progress far enough on their evolutionary journey, they will inherit and rule over their own Urantia-like planet.

*See also:* AUTOMATIC WRITING; BIBLE, NEW AGE; FALL OF HUMANITY, THE; THOUGHT ADJUSTERS; TRANCE CHANNELING

## URIM AND THUMMIM

Possibly small flat or round objects that were cast as lots by Israel's high priest to discover God's will on particular matters (Exod. 28:30; Lev. 8:8; Num. 27:21; Deut. 33:8; 1 Sam. 28:6; Ezra 2:63; Neh. 7:65). Alternate meanings for these terms are suggested as "the lights and perfections" or "the curses and the perfections." This possibly means that if Urim, or curses, dominated when the lots were cast, then the answer was "no." If Thummim, or perfections, dominated, then "yes" was the answer. The high priest stored the Urim and Thummim in his breastplate, which was fastened to a closely fitting sleeveless vest known as an ephod.

In Mormon folklore, the Urim and Thummim take on a completely different meaning. In 1820, Joseph Smith alleges that God the Father and God the Son materialized before him and revealed that they would use him to bring about a restoration of true Christianity. In 1823, the angel Moroni supposedly appeared at Smith's bedside to repeat the divine commission to establish the restored Christian church. In 1827, the heavenly messenger gave Smith some thin metal plates that were gold in appearance and inscribed in an Egyptian hieroglyphic language. Moroni also gave him a pair of magical spectacles called Urim and Thummim to decode the mysterious lettering inscribed on the plates. Smith's "translation" of the plates continued until 1829, resulting in *The Book of Mormon* (1830).

*See also:* ANGEL; *Mormon, The Book of;* MORMONISM

# V

## VAISAKHI
*See:* BAISAKHI

## VALUES CLARIFICATION
Moral education philosophy and pedagogy developed by Louis Raths, Sidney B. Simon, and Howard Kirschenbaum in the mid-1960s. This approach is based on conceptual ideas advanced by John Dewey (1859–1952) and Carl Rogers (1902–1987). Advocates claim that within the complex society of the West, people make innumerable value-weighted decisions. Proponents state that their desire is to provide a framework for moral education that will equip people to handle ethical issues. However they do not want this approach to force a partisan or sectarian viewpoint.

Values are moral and ethical standards adopted as a result of worldview and are ultimately based upon the nature and attributes of whatever an individual places in the role of God. Those who have developed values clarification curricula redefine values as drawn from personal life experiences alone, rather than from any transcendent being. In effect, these life experiences take the place of any absolute standard of ethics and give divine authority to each individual. Inherent in this philosophy is humanistic relativism, the denial of the existence of absolute ethical standards, at least in theory.

Values clarification education assumes that, since individuals alter their values with spiritual and emotional growth and changes in conception of God, the guidelines are built on nothing outside the human mind. As needs change during maturation, these guidelines can be modified, discarded, or replaced with no thought to transcendent rules for living. In fact, propositional statements that purport to be absolute and unchanging are the true absolute evil and must be unlearned before they can be imposed upon others.

Values clarification, then, is attitude reshaping. The base attitude is that the actual *content* of values is irrelevant, except for pragmatic needs current to the individual's life at the moment. Therefore, what is taught is a process by which these pragmatic and timely values can emerge. *What* one believes is not so important as *how* one came to believe it. Students are encouraged to consider both consequences and desires in developing value guidelines by which to live. Above all, the student is to see values as a personal, autonomous choice that should not be imposed by parents, Scripture, or anything else. Nor can the student try to impose his or her values on any other person.

In teaching method, teachers place themselves in the role of morally neutral agents. They use nondirective means to help students discover and clarify the ethical guidelines they want to adopt. The goal is to create an open learning environment that is nonjudgmental of others. Critics have charged that this values-free learning environment allows no moral growth and is a reason for increasingly violent and undisciplined children. It gives students the impression that they can do whatever they want, as long as it feels good. Right and wrong simply do not exist.

Values clarification has been charged further with undermining the authority of parents and communities. Values clarification and New Age philosophy come from the same historical processes and have a similar agenda.

*See also:* CAMPBELL, JOSEPH; EVIL; GUILT; INTUITION; SIN

# VAMPIRE

According to legend and modern cinema convention, an evil spirit that refuses to enter the realm of the dead, but instead takes possession of a corpse and reanimates it. Vampires reputedly cause a cadaver to leave its grave at night, and suck blood from a sleeping person. Vampires supposedly are unnaturally pale with full red lips, canine teeth, hairy palms, and yellow fingernails. They have the ability to transform themselves into a mist, a bat, or a rodent. Folklore says that vampires prefer darkness and the color black, and that they fear crosses, church bells, mustard seed, garlic, holy water, and Eucharist bread. Traditionally, one can ward off a vampire with charms and kill the creature by driving a wooden stake through its heart.

These superstitions find their roots in the pagan belief that the dead require blood to restore them to life. Ancient cults taught that blood held the essence of all living things and that it was the medium through which reincarnated souls obtained life. Heathen worshipers used blood sacrifices to invoke the powers of their gods and goddesses, whom they thought needed blood for rejuvenation. Such pagan ideas and practices are kept alive by many satanic groups. Former members of these cults report of participants entering into a pact with dark powers before torturing their victims, draining their blood, and drinking it in ritualistic worship.

The upsurge of contemporary Gothic clubs have helped to romanticize the vampire's existence among today's young people. From readily available vampire literature, music, and movies, the "goths" adopt their style of black clothes and makeup as well as an antisocial mind-set.

*See also:* BLOOD SACRIFICE

# VEDA

The oldest sacred texts of Hinduism. Veda is the Sanskrit word for "knowledge." It reflects the Hindu belief that these documents represent the essential truths of life. The Vedas were compiled between 1000 and 500 B.C. and consist of four types of literature. The first consists of prayers, hymns, and magic spells called the *Samhita*. This entire collection is attributed to seers and poets who were considered inspired. The second contains prose explanations of the sacrifice called the *Brahmanas*. Hindus believe that the sacrifice is the fundamental agency of creation. The third is composed of instructions for meditation called *Aranykas,* and these are performed during the offering of the sacrifice. The fourth include mystical and speculative texts called the *Upanishads*. Hindus believe that a single underlying reality is embodied in the absolute self called Brahman.

*See also:* HARE KRISHNA, HINDUISM, SANSKRIT, UPANISHADS

# VEGETARIANISM

The ethic and practice of eating only fruits, vegetables, cereal grains, nuts, and seeds and refusing to eat any meat, fish, or fowl, which often includes eggs and dairy products. Some vegetarians claim that meat clouds the body's spiritual energy, while vegetables focus and enhance a person's creativity. Others maintain that because people and animals are living creatures, they should live in harmony with one another. They view the slaughter of animals for food as morally reprehensible and the exploitation and murder of innocent creatures. Still others assert with Hinduism that animals are reincarnated souls and that eating them amounts to cannibalism. With these differences of opinion, vegetarianism remains a widely accepted theory and practice in the New Age Movement.

*See also:* CREATION

# VENUS

The Roman goddess of vegetation, which by the third century B.C. became identified with Aphrodite, the Greek goddess of love and beauty. Many imperialists, such as Julius Caesar, worshiped the deity as Venus Genetrix, the wife of Anchises and the mother of Aeneas, the Trojan hero whose descendants allegedly founded Rome. The goddess was also venerated as Venus Felix (who brings good fortune), Venus Victrix (who brings victory), Venus Verticordia (who protects a woman's chastity), and Venus Libentina (the patroness of sensual pleasure).

Occult groups continue to worship Venus as the creative force from which all life exists. They perform sexual rituals in honor of the deity as the goddess of love. A few of her titles include the Queen of Heaven, the Mother Goddess, Mother Earth, Gaea, and Wicca. She is also called the Morning Star, a name also attributed to her male counterpart, Lucifer, in pagan religions. Various legends tell of an unjust God defeating Lucifer and banishing him from heaven to Venus. Other tales say that Lucifer came to Earth from Venus eighteen million years ago to attend to the physical needs of the human race. Satanists portray Lucifer as the hero who makes people aware of their innate godhood, tells them how to tap into the powers of the divine self, and describes the coming world in which they will be free to express their fullest human potential.

*See also:* GAEA; GODDESS WORSHIP; LUCIFERIC DOCTRINE; MOTHER EARTH; PLAN, THE

## VIBRATIONS

In New Age scientific theory, a complex series of vibrational patterns radiate from every thought and action of every creature, place, and object. These vibrations continuously reverberate across the universe. Attuned people can blend with the vibrational energy around them to manipulate reality and radiate high frequency "soul energy." Soul energy enables people to enter altered states of consciousness and achieve spiritual enlightenment. According to this theory, the neurobiological activity in the brain creates resonation that others can receive and understand. The body is a universal antenna that has the innate ability to register and assimilate psychic vibrations.

Proponents teach people to develop and channel this power by focusing on their receptor areas, such as the third eye, the hands, or the abdomen. These vibrations are eternal and never-ending. When people attune themselves to the harmonic oscillations of the universe, they can fathom the past, present, and future. The god of this worldview is an all-pervasive energy force, so the sending and receiving of vibrations is a way to communicate with the Universal Mind.

*See also:* COSMIC ENERGY; SCIENCE, NEW AGE

## VISHNU

One of three manifestations of Brahman, the eternal Trimutri, or three-in-one god, of Hinduism. The great triad of Hindu gods is composed of Brahma, Shiva, and Vishnu. Hindus believe Brahma is the creator of all things. Because creation is complete, this god is rarely worshiped. Shiva represents the destroyer and is worshiped for its power in eradicating the old to make way for the new. Shiva and its representative gods play a prominent part in the purification process that will precede the global transformation into the New Age. The final and most popular aspect of the Hindu triad is Vishnu, the preserver. This deity is sometimes referred to as the god of love or the savior of humanity.

Hindus believe Vishnu is Brahman incarnated into avatars who come to earth to aid people on their spiritual journey. The forms of these avatars include animals, such as fish, boars, and tortoises, as well as people, such as Buddha, Rama, and Krishna. Christ is a physical manifestation of the impersonal Brahman, so Jesus points to one way for attaining enlightenment over a period of innumerable lifetimes. Hinduism teaches that at different periods throughout the endless cycle of history, avatars are needed to show people how to become perfected. When the avatar dies, Brahma reabsorbs it back into himself. The next great avatar reputedly will be Lord Maitreya, the New Age christ.

*See also:* ANTICHRIST, BHAGAVAD GITA, BRAHMA, HINDUISM, SHIVA

## VISION QUEST

A Native American spiritual exercise in which seekers remove themselves from worldly attachments and travel deep into the wilderness for an indefinite period of solitude. Through fasting, meditation, chanting, and occasionally ingesting psychedelic drugs, seekers attempt to gain power from the spirits of their ancestors or the Great Spirit that pervades the universe. This visitation, which takes the form of a vision, dream, or sign, provides spiritual guidance, and abilities sought by the worshiper. New Age adherents have adopted the vision quest. They instruct practitioners to go through this spiritual exercise in order to contact their spirit guides and communicate with the cosmic consciousness.

*See also:* NATIVE AMERICANS

## VISUALIZATION

The process of conjuring up images in the imagination with the help of a psychic guide. Visualization is based on the idea that all people have the innate ability to create and manipulate their own reality. Advocates claim that by tapping into this divine power, people can discover the secrets of the universe and solve the riddles of life. New Age adherents derive their beliefs and practices associated with visualization from the Hindu concept of maya. This idea presents the visible world as an illusion that prevents people from realizing that all reality is absolute oneness. New Age adherents claim that through visualization, as well as other mind-altering techniques, people can rediscover their union with the cosmic consciousness and the existence of the divine self.

Many state governments have initiated visualization programs in which elementary school teachers tell children how to establish contact with their spirit guides. They tell students that they are going on an imaginary journey to a mystical place, and they will be accompanied by a "friend." This guide can be anyone or anything that the children choose, such as a man, a woman, an animal, or even a cartoon character. The teacher encourages them to make this entity their constant companion for life, and to look to it for answers when they are angry, sad, confused, or hurt.

The "adventure" usually begins with breathing exercises designed to relax the children's bodies and minds. Teachers tell them to pretend they are walking through a beautiful area, such as an open field, woods, or beach. The instructor encourages the children to visualize as many details of the scene as possible so that it becomes real to them. The teacher then leads them to a magical place, such as a garden, cave, or castle. The children are encouraged to fill this place with vivid colors, spectacular sounds, and amazing objects and creatures. They learn to think of this place as a haven where they can run for protection when life seems scary, and for answers when life seems confusing.

The teacher has the children imagine that someone "special" will always be waiting for them when they visit their magical place. They are told to think of this entity as their personal guide who will walk with them through life. The children are allowed to create this guide in any form they desire. As the visualization experience continues, the teacher has the children imagine they are in unbearable situations. They are told to handle their dilemma by looking within themselves and by talking to their spirit guides. The children supposedly can trust this entity to teach them what they need to know and how they should think and act in any given situation.

These visualization techniques are called guided imagery, minute vacations, magic adventures, and creative thinking. Regardless of the label, it represents occult practices in the guise of educational creativity.

*See also:* BRAHMA; GUIDED IMAGERY; HINDUISM; PLAN, THE; SPIRIT GUIDES; TRANSPERSONAL PSYCHOLOGY

## VOODOO (VODUN)

A pagan religion of West African origin but with Roman Catholic and Western Indian elements mixed in. Voodoo is practiced in the Western Hemisphere, chiefly by people in Haiti. "Voodoo" is derived from a West African term that means "spirit." The principle deity of this religion is called *Bon Dieu,* but there are other spirits called *loa* which adherents recognize and often associate with deceased Catholic saints, princes, priests, or warriors. Some loa reputedly are good entities known as *rada,* while other loa are malicious entities known as *petro.*

Voodoo is characterized by sorcery and rituals in which participants enter an ecstatic, trancelike state and communicate with ancestors, saints, and animal-like deities. Voodoo can also refer to those who deal in charms, fetishes, spells, or curses, which they believe hold magical power. Moreover Voodooism includes a belief in zombies. According to one popular version of this superstition, a priest, or *bocar,* causes a primitive spirit to inhabit and reanimate a corpse. Another popular version says a bocar places a living person under his control by using mind-altering drugs or poison. In either case, the entity can then be used for a variety of purposes, including the provision of free labor in the sugarcane fields.

**Voodoo— representation of Bon Dieu**

This superstition has wide appeal in a country that is poor, densely populated, and characterized by intensive, backbreaking labor.

A voodoo ceremony is usually held at night and officiated at a shrine by priests, called *hougans,* or priestesses, called *mambos.* A sacred pillar called a *poteau-mitan* is located in the center of the temple and designates where most of the pagan activities occur. Ornate floor drawings called *vevers* surround the pillar where participants perform their rituals, rhythmic dancing, sexual perversions, and sacrifices. A vever is assigned to an individual loa. During a ritual, participants allow themselves to be possessed by loa, causing them to do all sorts of bizarre acts. Animal and child sacrifices, cannibalism, and necromancy might also take place. The latter refers to the conjuring up of the spirits of the dead and communing with them in order to reveal the future or influence the course of events.

A wide variety of voodoo cults exist. In some rituals, a rhythmic drum beat compels devotees to enter an altered state of consciousness and allows a loa to displace their own souls. Their souls then journey to distant realms to receive knowledge and wisdom from deceased ancestors. Rituals might involve use of herbal incantations, candles, food, chanting, and blood sacrifices to summon deities. Participants use charms and fetishes to protect themselves from the demonic powers they are invoking.

Voodoo cults also use sympathetic magic. This involves casting a spell or curse on an object in the belief that the person or entity represented by the object will be adversely affected. Practitioners of sympathetic magic assert that vibrational impulses permeate the universe and that psychic pulsations in an object can be used to the detriment of corresponding pulsations in a person or entity.

*See also:* BLOOD SACRIFICE, MAGIC, SATANISM, SORCERY

## VORTEX

A mass of gases or fluids, such as air and water, that moves in a rapid, circular fashion, producing a depression in the center of the whirlpool, and drawing objects into the resulting cavity or vacuum. Intergalactic vortexes are said to be responsible for the creation of alternate dimensions of space and time. They also maintain that psychic energy vortexes exist in scattered power zones around the world. By entering a trancelike state, people can use these cosmic countercurrents as bridges to parallel universes and alien worlds. By getting in touch with the vibrations of energy flowing through these vortexes, people can enhance their psychic powers.

*See also:* COSMIC ENERGY, PSYCHIC, VIBRATIONS

# W

## WALK, THE
*See:* LIVING WORD, CHURCH OF THE

## WALK-IN
A reincarnated New Age disciple from the astral plane who, under certain circumstances, is permitted to take over the unwanted body of a living person. This concept was introduced to psychic author Ruth Montgomery (b. 1912) by the spirits she channeled. This concept says that a person's unenlightened soul is displaced by a more enlightened one, a walk-in, or herald of the impending New World Order. Occult leaders claim ten thousand of these entities now reside throughout the planet, and their purpose is to help the human race experience a quantum leap in evolutionary development. Walk-ins will reputedly supervise the cleansing process that must precede the Aquarian era. This includes the removal of people whose underdeveloped consciousness generates a negative force that prevents the establishment of the long-awaited millennium of peace.
*See also:* MONTGOMERY, RUTH; PURIFICATION; REINCARNATION; TRANCE CHANNELING

## WARLOCK
*See:* WITCHCRAFT

## WATCHTOWER BIBLE AND TRACT SOCIETY
The corporate headquarters for the Jehovah's Witnesses, a cult founded in the late 1870s by Charles Taze Russell (1852–1916). In 1879, Russell started a magazine called *Zion's Watchtower*. From an initial print run of six thousand, the magazine is now known as *The Watchtower* and currently sells in the tens of millions. By 1884, Russell had established Zion's Watch Tower and Tract Society in Pittsburgh, Pennsylvania. In 1908, Russell moved the headquarters of the sect to its current location in Brooklyn, New York. Today the organization is the major disseminator of information for the Jehovah's Witnesses. This includes the publication and distribution of New World Translation bibles, books, pamphlets, tracts, and magazines. The organization is also known for its extensive missionary work. Through a worldwide network of local churches, disciples go door-to-door to win followers to the group.
*See also:* BIBLE, JEHOVAH'S WITNESSES

## WATER WITCHING
*See:* DOWSING

## WAY INTERNATIONAL, THE
A cult founded in 1958 by Victor Paul Wierwille (1916–1985). He was born in New Knoxville, Ohio, and grew up in a Protestant home. In 1940, Wierwille obtained a bachelor of divinity (B.D.) degree from Mission House College in Plymouth, Wisconsin. In 1941, he received a master of divinity (M.Div.) from Princeton Theological Seminary. That same year he was ordained into the Evangelical and Reformed Church, a denomination that merged with the United Church of Christ in 1963.

During his first pastorate in Payne, Ohio, Wierwille claimed that God began to speak audibly to him about spiritual truths. He claimed that traditional churches—Protestant, Catholic, and Orthodox—had distorted the actual teachings of Scripture, and God would use him to lead people back to the truth. The seeds of his unorthodox teachings first appeared in a course entitled *Power for Abundant Living,* that he began to produce and sell in 1953. In 1955, he traveled to India as a missionary. His words and actions caused so much turmoil within his denomination that he was forced to resign his ordination in 1957.

In 1958 Wierwille established The Way International in New Knoxville, Ohio. He disseminated the cult's beliefs through the popular *Power for Abundant Living* course and film series. During the countercultural movement of the 1960s and 1970s, the organization recruited large numbers of people. To spread its message further, the organization established a number of other organizations. These include Word over the World (a foreign outreach enterprise), The Way College (an educational institution in Emporia, Kansas), Way Productions (a music company), Total Fitness Institute (a health spa), *The Way Magazine,* television and radio productions, and the American Christian Press (a publishing company). Through Wierwille's numerous books, tapes, brochures, and other publications, he succeeded in establishing an organization with tens of thousands of members spanning the world.

Those who complete the initial course entitled *Power for Abundant Living* and become members obtain further training on the group's beliefs and practices. Critics allege that converts are discouraged from thinking for themselves and are controlled through mind manipulation, sleep and food deprivation, and intensive tape seminars where questions are not allowed. Initiates are indoctrinated to believe that entertaining any critical thoughts about the organization is a sign of demon possession. Initiates are constantly pressured to remain loyal to the cult. Leaders teach members that they are twigs on the branches of a gigantic spiritual tree known as The Way. Limbs, branches, and the trunk would be the various city, state, and national organizations respectively, and Wierwille is depicted as the root of the entire system.

The Way rejects the orthodox Christian teaching that God is triune in His existence, asserting that this is a pagan notion. The group also spurns Christ's divinity, claiming that He was just a sinless human being who had a perfect soul-life. In contrast to the teaching of Scripture, The Way declares that the Holy Spirit is one of God's many attributes, an impersonal force that permeates the universe. They say that all people are entities with a body and soul, but having no spirit. The Way states that at the dawn of time, God gave Adam and Eve a choice of learning either with their senses or with direct knowledge through spiritual communication with Him. Satan allegedly tricked them into deciding on the former, and this led to their fall. Christ supposedly came to earth to restore people's choice in learning about their heavenly Father. God allegedly gives a portion of His spiritual essence, or elemental power, to His true followers. They teach that those who are genuinely saved will confess their faith publicly and speak in tongues. They can then become members of The Way International, which reputedly is the only true church of God. Members consider all other churches as apostate.

## WEISHAUPT, ADAM (1748–1830)

A Bavarian professor who, in 1776, founded an elite international organization of wealthy people known as the Order of the Illuminati. Some think this group is responsible for a massive conspiracy designed to result in world domination. Weishaupt believed that through the manipulation of the government, the economy, and religion, a select group of people could be elevated into positions of global leadership. He also believed that if all segments of the occult were brought under the control of a single organization, they could generate the power necessary to dominate the world.

Once established, the Illuminati quickly garnered support from the aristocracy who believed they came from superior bloodlines. By obtaining their support, Weishaupt assured himself of funds necessary to keep his organization operational. To avoid public detection and enhance membership, the Illuminati infiltrated the well-established and respected Continental Order of Freemasons in 1782. This created what Weishaupt termed "Illuminated Freemasonry," and enabled Weishaupt to place many members in top European governmental positions. But an overwhelming defeat in the French Revolution seemed to bring the Illuminist dream of a New World Order to an end. However the Illuminati sufficiently recovered. Less than a century later, its principles and practices resurfaced in various secret societies.

*See also:* FREEMASONRY, ILLUMINATI, ONE-WORLD IDEAL

## WEREWOLF
*See:* LYCANTHROPY

## WHITE MAGIC

The belief that occult powers can be used to undo curses and spells and to counteract the evil intentions and deeds of malicious gods, demons, and spirits. By using charms, spells, and rituals associated with white magic, practitioners allegedly can bend psychic forces to do their will. These "white witches" also reputedly control beneficial events in nature, positively influence people, and predict the future for the good of humankind.

White witches argue that by using magic in an unselfish manner for the benefit of others, practitioners can escape the control and influence of demons. Magic supposedly is an abstract set of techniques and not subject to any particular philosophy. Proponents claim this occult art is not the "truth," but rather a means of reaching and utilizing the truth. Magic gains its individual character, whether good or bad, from the practitioner. The essence of white magic lies in establishing an interactive bond with the divine cosmic energy, thereby revealing hidden realities of forgotten powers existing in the human soul. Some white witches claim they can only use their powers for benevolent purposes, while others contend that they invoke only Christian deities for their magical performances, although Scripture clearly condemns all forms of occult practice.

*See also:* MAGIC, WICCA, WITCHCRAFT

## WHITEHEAD, ALFRED NORTH (1861–1947)

English philosopher, theologian, and mathematician who was highly influential in twentieth-century religion for his relativistic metaphysical philosophy and view of God, known as "process theology." Whitehead believed that, although God exists from eternity, He is in the process of becoming, like everything in creation. Whatever happens in the universe becomes part of his being. In addition to hypothesizing a very limited God, Whitehead's ideas broke down traditional Western barriers between God and everything else, offering a back door approach to pantheism—a charge Whitehead denied.

Process theology was highly popular in the 1950s and 1960s Western church, went out of fashion, then returned at the end of the century in the similar "open theology" view of God.

*See also:* PANTHEISM

## WHOLE BRAIN THINKING (SYNCHRONY)

The ability to use the left and right hemispheres of the brain in unison. Spilt-brain research suggests that the left side of the cranium forms the analytical hemisphere, whereas the right hemisphere performs the creative functions. Nevertheless, sufficient data indicates that the human organ of thought and neural coordination operates as an integrated unit. Both hemispheres work together to enable people to receive stimuli from sense organs, to interpret and correlate the data to formulate motor impulses, to send information to receptors on the body surface, and so on.

New Age adherents have used the scientific terms and theories of split-brain research to support their claims of how the mind operates. Through whole brain thinking, a person's psychic potential, mental dexterity, and natural instincts supposedly are enhanced dramatically. Synchrony allegedly can be achieved and maintained by entering a trancelike state. They encourage devotees to set aside their logical thinking processes and let their psychic intuition take control of them. New Age adherents entice many into believing that this is the only way they can perceive what is real, recognize the divine self, and attain enlightenment.

*See also:* COLLECTIVE UNCONSCIOUS, FAITH, INTUITION, SPLIT-BRAIN RESEARCH, SYNCHRONICITY

# WICCA

A modern witchcraft group that uses magic, sorcery, and other rituals associated with pre-Christian Celtic practices. Some say the title "wicca" means "the religion of the wise," while others say it is related to the old English word *wiccian*, meaning "the practice of magical arts." Still others think "wicca" is derived from an Anglo-Saxon verb that means "to bend" or "to shape." This verb allegedly referred to those who knew how to harness and control the unseen forces of nature through psychic means.

Wiccan members claim that their practices do not involve black magic, which produces misfortune or death on its victims. Instead, they practice white magic, which uses occult arts for their good and the good of others. They teach that, while black magic violates the karmic laws of reincarnation, white magic helps to preserve and restore those laws.

Legend says that at the dawn of time, the Earth Goddess was the primordial deity of the universe and the earth was governed by a matriarchal society. The worship of the Mother Goddess of Life and the Horned God of Death maintained an atmosphere of peace, love, and harmony between people and nature. Priestesses had the innate ability to harness the psychic energy that pulsated throughout the cosmos, and this created a oneness between the earth and the divine life force. At the beginning of the Bronze Age between 4000 and 3000 B.C., folklore says that Indo-European warriors invaded the known world and disrupted the perfect harmony between humankind and nature. As a result, the Sky Father displaced the rule of the Earth Mother, thereby establishing a patriarchal rule.

According to legend, barbarians destroyed the existing civilization and the knowledge they had acquired. Nevertheless, the secret wisdom and powers associated with Earth Mother were preserved in the rites and beliefs of the druids. This priestly upper class of ancient Celtic peoples worshiped a pantheon of nature deities. They passed their esoteric knowledge down to succeeding generations. This world system will continue until the Mother Goddess is reawakened, at which time she will reestablish harmony between humanity and nature.

Wiccans contend that for five thousand years, organized religion has ignored the spiritual needs of women. They have had to defer to the spiritual interpretations of male-oriented institutions. The revival of the ancient worship of the Earth Goddess supposedly will enable women to find their roots and rediscover their divine potential. It also means they will reclaim their rightful place as leaders of a matriarchal society that is at peace with nature and united with the universal life force. Wiccans fully intend to dethrone the Sky Father and reestablish the rule of the Earth Mother over the world.

Members of the cult often gather in covens, groups of about twelve to fifteen witches, believing they can increase their psychic powers by banding together. Some covens follow traditional Wiccan rituals while others practice ceremonies that are unique to the group. The ceremonies center around the times when the cycles of inner humanity and cosmic events connect, resulting in the emanation of intense rhythmic energies. The sabbat is one popular ceremony observed by many Wiccans who gather together to renew their allegiance to the Mother Goddess.

Wiccans typically observe eight seasonal festivals, or sabbats. Halloween, or Samhain, is the most revered of all. They believe the veil between the physical and spiritual worlds is lifted on October 31. Contemporary Wiccan groups deny any demonic connotations but do celebrate Halloween as the time when the Great Horned God rises to rule during the darkness of winter. The goal of this and other sabbats is to awaken the divine consciousness of humankind. This allegedly will bring about a global transformation and reestablish a harmonious balance between earth and the universal life force.

*See also:* DRUIDS, EVIL, FEMINISM, GAEA, GODDESS WORSHIP, MOTHER EARTH, SABBAT, WITCHCRAFT

## WIERWILLE, VICTOR PAUL
*See:* WAY INTERNATIONAL, THE

## WINDHAM HILL

A production company for New Age music, Windham Hill was founded in Palo Alto, California, in 1976 by two young college students named Will Ackerman and Anne Robinson. The two invested three hundred dollars into the business. Their first production consisted of three hundred copies of a guitar solo entitled "In Search of the Turtle's Navel." In 1980, the company produced an album entitled "December" by George Winston, the first New Age record to sell more than 1 million copies. As interest in the occult grew in the West, so did the public demand for New Age music. Windham Hill was soon joined by other companies in the production of ethereal-sounding selections. Despite increased competition over the years, Windham Hill remains an industry leader.

Windham Hill offers a wide variety of vocal, instrumental, electronic, and acoustic music ranging from jazz to rock. The company sells music videos for teens and young adults, as well as a selection of products that appeal to children. They offer nonvocal recordings for enhancing the listeners' meditative, psychic, and sexual experiences. Artists who record on the Windham Hill label generally share the company's philosophical worldview. They believe that their music will help listeners attain a higher level of consciousness, discover the divine self, and fathom the depths of the Universal Mind.

*See also:* MUSIC, NEW AGE; TRANSFORMATION

## WITCH
*See:* WICCA, WITCHCRAFT

## WITCHCRAFT

An ancient form of nature religion that manipulates supernatural forces and psychic powers by using fertility rituals and occult arts, such as magic and sorcery. The beliefs and practices of witchcraft have existed for thousands of years. The occult arts were evident in ancient Egypt, Babylon, Greece, and Rome. Various forms of witchcraft existed in medieval Europe where witches were persecuted from the fourteenth to the eighteenth centuries. In 1427, a major witch-hunt took place in Switzerland. And during the Spanish Inquisition, about one hundred witches were burned at the stake because of their beliefs. Witchcraft was practiced to a limited extent in early colonial America, mainly through slaved religions.

During the 1920s, the writings of leading occult advocates in Europe and America encouraged the revival of witchcraft, sometimes referred to as the Old Religion, The Craft, or Neopaganism. Anthropologist Margaret Murray (1863–1963) wrote numerous articles and books on witchcraft. Likewise, archaeologist Gerald Gardner (1884–1964) played a major role in seeing the contemporary rebirth of witchcraft in the West. Some modern-day witches claim that organized religion has ignored the spiritual needs of women by perpetuating a male-dominated patriarchal society. This explains women's dominance in the resurgence and practice of contemporary forms of witchcraft. Nevertheless, in preindustrial pagan cultures women did not particularly dominate in the practices.

Witches tend to organize themselves locally in covens of about twelve to fifteen members. At the end of the twentieth century, estimates in the United States indicate membership of about thirty thousand. All covens, whether independent or affiliated with other similar groups, are led by a high priestess or high priest.

Some people allege that they have been reincarnated as a witch. However most practitioners go through a well-established process to become a witch. In the first stage or degree, initiates learn the beliefs and practices of witchcraft. They become skilled in the use of occult arts, such as clairvoyance, divination, astral projection, using magic, and casting spells. Once they become skilled in witchcraft, they are permitted to join the coven. In the second stage or degree, members demonstrate their ability to lead in a variety of different situations and prove themselves as future leaders. In the third stage or degree, those who ascend to the highest ranks of leadership become high priestesses and high priests. They are required to participate in a pagan ceremony called the Great Rite, which may include ritualistic sex and other occult practices.

At the heart of witchcraft is the belief that the universe is comprised of separate but equal forces of good and evil. The cosmos is a genderless, primal, eternal life force. Divinity exists within nature, as well as within people. Sin is a lack of awareness of full human potential and godhood. Some practitioners claim their goal is to reestablish a harmony between people and the universal principle. Other witches say they use occult arts to develop the collective unconscious of the human race, thereby helping people to reestablish contact with the spirit world. Many witchcraft practitioners have a deep reverence for nature, as shown in the use of holistic techniques to help people draw upon the supposed natural healing powers of Mother Earth.

The use of group magic to heal others is also a common practice of witchcraft. Practitioners claim that they use both black magic and white magic to achieve their goals. Black magic, or sorcery, attempts to produce harmful results, like misfortune or death. This involves curses, spells, the destruction of models of enemies, and the establishment of alliances with evil spirits. White magic tries to undo curses and spells, and to use occult forces for the good of others and the good of self. Witches try to compel a god, demon, or spirit to do their work for them.

Witchcraft is commonly characterized by the veneration of a fertility deity named the Great Mother Goddess, represented by the moon, and the worship of her consort Pan, the horned fertility god represented by the sun. Each year Pan dies and is brought back to life in a ceremony called "drawing down the sun." In this ritual, the high priestess of a coven will call the name of Pan as she invokes the god aspect of the high priest. The parallel ceremony for the Mother Goddess is called "drawing down the moon," and it entails invoking the goddess aspect of the high priestess.

Witchcraft cults are known to observe eight seasonal festivals called sabbats in which witches gather together to renew their allegiance to the Mother Goddess, nature, and so on. The sabbat is characterized by mystic rights and orgies. Some contemporary witches maintain that the sabbat is merely a social gathering in which participants celebrate the changing face of the Earth Mother who is perpetually pursued by the Sky Father. This transformation reputedly is a portrayal of the mythological wheel of the year. The ceremony is to reveal times when the cycles of inner humanity and cosmic events connect, resulting in the emanation of intense rhythmic energies.

*See also:* BLACK SABBATH; FAMILIAR; GODDESS WORSHIP; HALLOWEEN, SABBAT, SATANISM, WICCA

## WOLF
*See:* LYCANTHROPY

## WORLD COUNCIL OF CHURCHES (WCC)

An international and interdenominational fellowship of churches established in Amsterdam, Netherlands, in 1948. Today the Council is comprised of 335 member churches from Protestant and Orthodox groups in more than one hundred countries. And since the Second Vatican Council of 1962–1965, officials from the Roman Catholic Church have increasingly involved themselves in WCC affairs. The organization, with headquarters in Geneva, Switzerland, has no legislative authority over individual churches. However the Council gives congregations the opportunity to cooperate in areas of common interest. The organization primarily exists to foster a unity of Christian doctrine, polity, and practice, and to address worldwide social, economic, and spiritual problems from a Christian perspective.

New Age leaders favor many of the general goals of the WCC because they fit the globalist agenda of establishing a one-world religion. If this occurs, it supposedly will allow people to transcend their spiritual barriers and establish a fraternal bond of peace and love. This will foster a greater cosmic consciousness and lead to social justice, political freedom, and economic empowerment. The one-world religion advocated by New Age adherents is based on the guidance and thoughts of ascended masters, masters of wisdom, masters of the universe, and spirit guides. This orientation fits with the WCC, which has allowed Hindu and Buddhist representatives to play an ever-widening role in shaping policies and direction of the organization. Some critics of the WCC say the beliefs and practices of biblical Christianity are either ignored or rejected altogether.

*See also:* GLOBALISM, NEW AGE MOVEMENT, ONE-WORLD IDEAL

## WORLD GOODWILL

A political lobbying group that promotes the establishment of global unity as a key element to building a New World Order. World Goodwill was founded by theosophist Alice Ann Bailey (1880–1949), and the headquarters for the organization are at the United Nations Plaza. Members affirm the New Age philosophy of Bailey's spirit guide, Djwhal Khul, who claimed to be an ancient Tibetan master. As part of their globalist agenda, World Goodwill favors indoctrinating the next generation of children with occult beliefs through television, radio, education, and music. Advocates believe that by winning the minds of the next generation, they will be able to bring about a paradigm shift

in human consciousness. This will lead to a global transformation and usher in the Aquarian Age of peace, joy, and enlightenment under the rule of Lord Maitreya.

*See also:* BAILEY, ALICE ANN; DJWHAL KHUL; GLOBALISM; ONE-WORLD IDEAL; PLAN, THE; POLITICS, NEW AGE

## WORLD HEALING EVENT (WHE)

A New Age gathering of occult leaders, mediums, and holistic "physicians." The event, otherwise known as World Instant of Cooperation, World Peace Meditation, and World Healing Meditation, occurred on December 31, 1986. The memory of this event remains one of the most potent rallying forces in the New Age Movement. Hundreds of occult organizations and millions of individuals from sixty countries joined in a display of New Age ecumenism. The mystical writings of John Randolph Price (b. 1932), especially his *Practical Spirituality,* served as the catalyst for WHE. He claimed that a spiritual entity named Asher revealed to him that enlightened people of earth would one day gather together for a "Planetary Pentecost" experience of cosmic proportions.

The philosophical basis for WHE is humanity's interconnectedness with all things, especially the Universal Mind. The goal is to merge the consciousness of humanity into this impersonal Oneness. Globalists believe a minimum amount of human voltage is needed to generate enough energy to establish the infrastructure of a New World Order and to transform the entire human race. They hope to gather 1 percent of the earth's population to focus their thoughts on the concept of global peace. This supposedly will reach a critical mass of psychic energy and cause a quantum leap in cosmic consciousness, thereby sending an energy wave into the ethereal dimension. When this happens, it allegedly will summon the New Age christ to come to earth and establish world peace.

*See also:* COSMIC CONSCIOUSNESS; PEACE; PLANETARY PENTECOST; PRICE, JOHN RANDOLPH

## WORLDWIDE CHURCH OF GOD (ARMSTRONGISM)

Former salesman Herbert W. Armstrong (1892–1986) used marketing strategies to launch the Worldwide Church of God in 1933, with its sophisticated free publication, *Plain Truth*. He capitalized on radio and a generally isolationist and racist mood in the United States, to which his doctrines based on British Israelism appealed. Armstrong had left the Seventh Day Church of God under discipline for financial improprieties and doctrinal deviation. In 1947 he started Ambassador College in Pasadena, California, as an institution to train his own ministers. He developed a theology with pieces taken from Jehovah's Witnesses, Latter-Day Saints, Pentecostals, Adventists, and even Druidic writings. These he packaged around a hard-sell communications program as the original Christian teachings, which had been lost to the world after the first century.

The message lost its appeal by the 1970s, and sexual scandals tarnished the image of the church. Ministers rebelled against the totalitarian rule and fear tactics used to control the membership. Several Armstrong prophecies did not come true. The organization went into bankruptcy, though the church remained highly involved in world politics, with representatives who promoted a one-world agenda among Arab, third-world, and communist leaders. In the 1980s the church was closely watched by cult analysts as an authoritarian, mind-control cult, which exploited its members through psychological manipulation. Reports of sexual abuse of members by those in authority were frequent. A public relations team was hired to reformulate the church and its strategy.

In 1995 the entire doctrinal position of the movement changed, much to the confusion of longtime members. An extension group called the United Church of God was put into place. Those upset with abuses in the Worldwide Church of God were funneled into the new church organization. Church properties were liquidated, and the image projected was middle-of-the-road evangelical Christian. Some analysts remained skeptical that the foundational doctrinal teachings denying the deity of Christ, heaven, and hell had changed.

*See also:* BRITISH ISRAELISM

## WUNDT, WILLIAM (1832–1900)

German philosopher and physiologist. Wundt founded the study of psychology as an academic discipline. He argued for the importance of mental and psychic medicine as a treatment form often more important than physical medicine. He opposed the rationalism of science and especially medicine, stressing the intuitive and subjective. His influence gave psychology a strongly antirationalism bent that opened the door to a variety of Eastern mysticism and parapsychological influences.

As a theologian, Wundt tried to build a theology of theistic evolution that would be acceptable to orthodox faith. He was also a founder of the comparative religions movement, which seeks common origins, development, and themes in all the world religions.

# Y

## YAHWEH
*See:* TETRAGRAMMATON

## YANTRA

A geometric diagram used as a mystical symbol in Eastern meditative practices. The yantra consists of concentric shapes that are intended to convey spiritual doctrines, philosophical concepts, and personal insights to those who contemplate its form. Hindus and Buddhists believe that yantras embody particular deities or representations of spiritual forces. When devotees gaze at a yantra, they try to tap into the supernatural powers of a deity and invite it to enter their bodies. The yantra allows them to escape from worldly distractions and journey into an altered state of consciousness. By remaining transfixed on the sacred symbol, advocates claim that people can be delivered from the world of illusion and ultimately unite with the cosmic mind. New Age adherents have enthusiastically promoted the use of yantras. Instructors of transcendental meditation teach initiates to empty their minds of all thoughts as they contemplate a yantra. Cult leaders have been known to use the yantra as a mind-control technique to manipulate and coerce their followers.

**Yantra—diagram used in meditation**

*See also:* HYPNOSIS, MANTRA, TRANSCENDENTAL MEDITATION

## YIN/YANG

The opposite but complementary forces or principles that are thought in Eastern religion to exist throughout the universe. Yin refers to the passive, negative, female cosmic element, whereas yang refers to the active, positive, masculine cosmic element. While yin is the breath that continuously forms, changes, and renews the earth, yang is the light that shines forth and comprises the heavens.

Chinese dualistic philosophy says that Tao, or "The Way," produced the impersonal force or existence called the One. The One produced the two opposite but balancing forces called yin and yang. These bipolar forces then produced the three, or the yin, yang, and ch'i. The "ch'i" literally means "breath" and refers to the vital energy that permeates the universe and is a part of every living entity. From these three, ten thousand things have emerged, referring to the world. This way of thinking sees no distinction between good and evil. Both are considered coequal and mutually interdependent. Yin and yang maintain a duality that counterbalances evil and good. The symbol for yin and yang, a circle with black and white halves that twist into each other, illustrates this relationship of interdependence and interactivity.

**Yin/Yang— opposite yet balancing forces**

The New Age worldview sees all life as connected to the flow of psychic energy in the universe. Problems arise when the ebb of the natural world is disrupted. The only way to eliminate global injustice is by reestablishing the delicate balance between yin and yang. And the only remedy for social chaos is for everyone to realign themselves with the universal life force.

An implication of this dualistic principle is that, since people are innately divine, they have the psychic ability to harness the healing potential of yin and yang. Physical,

287

psychological, and spiritual ailments are simply the product of improper thinking. This imbalance of energy is corrected by transcending to a level of consciousness where divine awareness can be utilized. Therefore, people should cultivate simplicity and balance so that they might achieve harmony with the ebb and flow of yin and yang, as exemplified in nature. By yielding to the movement of the cosmic life force in their lives, people can experience an inner transformation and eternal peace.

*See also:* BALANCING, CH'I, COSMIC ENERGY, EVIL, PEACE

## YOGA

A Hindu physical and mental discipline. Hinduism teaches that the self is divine and distinct from the activity associated with the body, mind, and will. Through yoga's system of exercises, people can train their consciousness to control the body and mind, thereby attaining a higher state of awareness. Through the regular practice of yoga, people can achieve perfect spiritual insight, tranquillity, and well-being, experiencing freedom from ignorance, suffering, and ultimately achieving rebirth.

The name "yoga" comes from a Sanskrit term that means "to join" or "to unite." This etymology fits with the underlying philosophy of yoga. Hindus claim that God is a vital energy source from which all reality emanates. People are connected to this universal life force and are archetypes of it. According to Hindu teaching, the human predicament is caused by a lack of awareness of this vital link between people and the cosmic consciousness.

The goal of yoga is to help practitioners reexperience their oneness with the universal self. As people practice yoga, a higher level of connection with the infinite Oneness will result. Their view of the world will be radically changed because they will see everything as a particularization of Ultimate Reality.

Several types of yoga exist. *Jnana* yoga refers to the path of discrimination and wisdom, whereas *bhakti* yoga refers to the path of love and devotion to a personal god. *Karma* yoga refers to the path of selfless action, whereas *hatha* yoga, which is popular in the West, stresses physical control over the body by adopting different postures or positions. *Japa* yoga requires the repetition of mantras, or sacred sounds, to enable a person to concentrate without being interrupted by external distractions. *Kriya* yoga enables devotees to channel cosmic energy to their souls in order to establish a harmonious union of the mind, body, and spirit, releasing innate miraculous powers. *Kundalini* yoga emphasizes opening psychic energy centers called *chakras* supposedly located up and down the spinal column. This is thought to animate the Kundalini, a cosmic force coiled at the base of the spine.

Typical exercises, such as those found in *hatha* yoga, are practiced under the tutelage of a guru or yogi, a personal religious guide and spiritual teacher. Gurus teach students to combine a variety of breathing techniques with *asanas,* or relaxation postures. In each of the postures, students must first enter the position, then maintain it for a certain length of time, and finally leave it.

Some in the West incorrectly think of yoga as mere breathing and relaxation exercises to develop, stretch, and strengthen the body's muscles, extend and align the spinal column, and enhance cardiovascular circulation. The practice of yoga serves as a gateway to Eastern mysticism and occult thinking. Certain postures, such as the lotus position, are taken to activate the psychic energy centers. And specific breathing exercises are practiced to infuse the soul with cosmic energy floating in the air. A guru might have students gaze at a single object, such as a candle, to develop and focus concentration. The guru might have them chant a mantra to clear their minds and become one with the object in front of them. The goal is to achieve increasingly higher meditative states until reaching oneness with the cosmic consciousness. This state of being is characterized by a blank stare in which the devotee is receptive to esoteric wisdom from the Universal Mind.

See also: CHAKRA; HINDUISM;
KUNDALINI; LOTUS; MANTRA;
YOGANANDA, PARAMAHANSA

## YOGANANDA, PARAMAHANSA (1893–1952)

One of the earliest teachers of yoga in the West and the founder of the Self-Realization Fellowship (SRF) in 1914. This organization became incorporated in 1935 and established its headquarters in Los Angeles. More than a half million members of SRF practice this Hindu concept. Only those within the group who have taken monastic vows can assume leadership positions in the organization.

Yogananda spoke at the International Congress of Religious Liberals in 1920. He also lectured throughout the United States at churches and college campuses. He achieved significant popularity and fame after publishing a book entitled *Autobiography of a Yogi* (1946). When Yogananda died in 1952, his followers claimed that his corpse did not decay because he had oxygenated his blood through the practice of yoga. He was succeeded by a Kansas millionaire whom he had converted to his teachings.

Yogananda is best-known for developing an Eastern meditative technique called *kriya* yoga. Part of this involves "intelligent self effort," an exercise in which devotees channel cosmic energy to their soul, establish a harmonious union of the mind, body, and spirit, and release innate miraculous powers. By doing this, they can accomplish in thirty seconds what otherwise would have taken them an entire year to achieve. And rather than attain enlightenment through an endless succession of reincarnations, practitioners of *kriya* yoga allegedly can become enlightened in just three years.

See also: YOGA

## YOGI

See: MAHARISHI MAHESH YOGI

# Z

## ZEN BUDDHISM

A Chinese and Japanese sect of Buddhism. The Japanese word *zen* is derived from the Mandarin Chinese *ch'an*. Both words are renderings of *dhyana,* the Sanskrit term for "meditation." This etymology fits the distinctive emphasis of Zen, which is best-known for its assertion that enlightenment can be achieved through meditation, self-contemplation, and intuition. This stands in stark contrast to other religions, which emphasize the study of sacred writings or adhering to particular doctrines.

A Buddhist monk named Tao-Sheng (A.D. 360–434) is thought to have founded Zen. However a Persian, Bodhi-dharma (c. A.D. 534), popularized the sect. Legend holds that he traveled to southern India where he was exposed to Mahayana Buddhism. This liberal form of Buddhism de-emphasizes asceticism, or self-denial, and stresses compassion to others. Bodhi-dharma then traveled to China around A.D. 470 where he became the first Zen master. He is said to have taught "wall-gazing," a contemplative exercise in which devotees sit in front of a wall and meditate for long periods. The *dharma,* or moral law and religious truth of Zen, was passed down to successive masters. Toward the end of the Song (or Sung) Dynasty in China (A.D. 960–1279), Zen was introduced to Japan, where it became a prominent part of art and culture. In the modern era, Zen followers number in the millions, and it is the most popular Buddhism in the West. Many Zen organizations are found throughout the world.

Zen is a mixture of ideas and practices from various Asian religious traditions. Adherents of Zen say a vast emptiness exists within every person. When initiates meditate on their innate divinity and connection with the Universal Mind, they can achieve enlightenment, or *satori,* in this life. This means that people can sidestep endless cycles of reincarnation to attain nirvana, the state of absolute blessedness. Zen focuses on subjective experiences and feelings, not on intellect and knowledge. Devotees will meditate on their union with a particular object, such as a rock, flower petal, wall, or table, as a means of getting in touch with themselves and nature.

For Zen followers, insight is not found in logic and reasoning. They attain insight through the experience of Ultimate Reality. The immediate experience of reality is of supreme importance. Life is an eternal "now," in which the past, present, and future simply do not exist. Enlightenment is characterized by complete harmony with the absolute oneness of the universe and the absence of all individual rationality and awareness. Unlike Christianity, Zen Buddhism has no place for an external authority. Disciples are to look within to find the meaning of life and discover that morals work best for them. All people are inherently divine. Therefore by meditating on their inner self, followers become one in thought with the Universal Mind, with whom they are inseparably united.

The Christian concept of salvation by faith is alien to Zen Buddhism. Every person is responsible for her or his own destiny. Liberation from the endless cycles of death and rebirth allegedly can be achieved by obtaining a clear vision of the divine self and union with the Absolute. This experience is called *bodhi.* Devotees learn that through training and meditation, they can experience a cosmic awakening of themselves to the truth. This is characterized by inner peace and an unconscious awareness of their inseparability from Ultimate Reality.

Zen Buddhism has had a considerable influence on the formation of New Age thought. The divinity of self is a key teaching of occult philosophy. People who acknowledge their inherent godhood allegedly will experience unlimited mental powers.

*See also:* BUDDHISM, HIGHER SELF, ILLUSION, SATORI, TRANSCENDENTAL MEDITATION

## ZENAR CARDS

A deck of twenty-five cards used in extrasensory perception (ESP) experimentation. These cards were first developed by American psychologist Karl E. Zenar for use in his psychic research. One of five symbols appears throughout the deck—a star, circle, square, cross, or waves. Zenar calculated the extrasensory perception of participants by adding the number of correct answers they could get on random tests involving the cards. New Age adherents say the ability to obtain a high score shows evidence of latent psychic powers, such as telepathy, clairvoyance, and psychokinesis. When people display paranormal abilities, they are in contact with spirits from other dimensions. These entities leave the astral plane, enter the material plane, and indwell a human host. The spirit guides are here to assist humanity in evolving to a state of perfection.

*See also:* PARAPSYCHOLOGY, PSYCHIC, TAROT CARDS

## ZIGGURAT

A temple tower used by the ancient Assyrians and Babylonians. The word "ziggurat" comes from the Akkadian term *ziqqurratu,* meaning "summit" or "mountain top." The tower had the form of a pyramid with successively receding outside staircases and a shrine at the top of the structure. The ancient Babylonians developed this huge style of building in the third millennium B.C. Devotees used a ramp or stairway to reach each level of the ziggurat. During certain rituals,

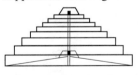

**Ziggurat—meeting place between man and dieties**

the deity of the city was thought to descend from the heavens to copulate with the worshipers in the shrine. Archaeologists generally identify the Tower of Babel described in Genesis 11:1–9 as a ziggurat. Some even speculate that the stairway Jacob saw in his dream reaching from earth to heaven in Genesis 28:12 was a ziggurat.

The ziggurat is often used as an occult symbol of the New Age. Some claim that the object can enable people to perform psychic feats, such as telepathy, clairvoyance, and psychokinesis. Others say the ziggurat is a gateway to the Universal Mind and enables its users to discover the secrets of the past, present, and future of humankind. Some see the ziggurat symbol as a meditative tool, believing that the energy it radiates can heighten their awareness, amplify their thoughts, and raise their vibrational levels.

*See also:* ALTAR, AZTEC CULTURE, BABYLON, MAYANS, PYRAMIDOLOGY

## ZODIAC

A celestial belt of about sixteen degrees marking the path the sun was thought by the ancients to take among the stars. The width of the zodiac was determined originally so as to include the orbits of the Sun and Moon and five planets—Mercury, Venus, Mars, Jupiter, and Saturn. The belt was divided into twelve sections corresponding to the months, each section about thirty degrees long. Each section is dominated by a constellation of stars, which gives the section its name. The zodiac constellations, in order, are (vernal equinox) Aries the Ram, Taurus the Bull, Gemini the Twins, (summer solstice) Cancer the Crab, Leo the Lion, Virgo the Virgin, (autumnal equinox) Libra the Balance, Scorpio the Scorpion, Sagittarius the Archer, (winter solstice) Capricorn the Goat, Aquarius the Water Bearer, and Pisces the Fishes. Some constellations have moved slightly over the centuries from their zodiac placement. The constellations of the modern zodiac date to about the second century B.C. Because of the movement in relation to the vantage point on earth, the zodiac constellations are on about a

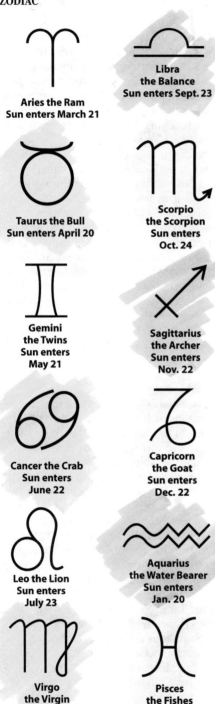

Aries the Ram
Sun enters March 21

Taurus the Bull
Sun enters April 20

Gemini
the Twins
Sun enters
May 21

Cancer the Crab
Sun enters
June 22

Leo the Lion
Sun enters
July 23

Virgo
the Virgin
Sun enters
Aug. 23

Libra
the Balance
Sun enters Sept. 23

Scorpio
the Scorpion
Sun enters
Oct. 24

Sagittarius
the Archer
Sun enters
Nov. 22

Capricorn
the Goat
Sun enters
Dec. 22

Aquarius
the Water Bearer
Sun enters
Jan. 20

Pisces
the Fishes
Sun enters
Feb. 11

**Signs of the Zodiac**

twenty-six-thousand-year cycle. Where they are in that cycle is plotted closely by astrologers as one indication of their influence on people of earth. The placements and their influences, according to astrology, depend greatly on where the constellations were at the time a person was born.

References to the zodiac in text and artwork date at least to the Mesopotamia in which Abraham lived, and it is possibly older. The Chinese zodiac is figured somewhat differently from the Western, and the signs have different names. The twelve signs of the Chinese zodiac are the rat, ox, tiger, hare, dragon, serpent, horse, sheep, monkey, hen, dog, and pig. Independently, the Aztec zodiac was similar to that of the Chinese.

*See also:* ASTROLOGY

## ZONE THERAPY

A method of treatment based on ancient metaphysical and occult beliefs. Practitioners claim that special psychic pathways and connections called zones exist throughout the body, and these correspond to specific systems and organs. They assert that the mind, body, and spirit are an interconnected triad that should be diagnosed and treated as a whole. Illness and pain are results of an accumulation of unbalanced energy that is corrected by realigning the vibrational forces of the mind, body, and spirit. By concentrating on a psychic zone, people supposedly can channel their healing energies to corresponding parts of the body, thereby relieving pain, strain, and stress. Some healers claim these zones can aid in the diagnosis and healing of past, present, and future symptoms.

*See also:* ACUPRESSURE, HOLISM, IRIDOLOGY, MERIDIANS, REFLEXOLOGY

## ZOROASTRIANISM

A dualistic Persian religion that has enjoyed a renaissance with New Age preoccupation in Eastern thought. Zoroastrianism dates to as early as 1200 B.C. Its founder was an Indian or Iranian holy man named Zarathustra (Gk., Zoroaster). The era in which he lived is not known, but he left five poems ("Gathas") that became the primary scriptures for the religion. There are a variety of other holy writings, but none that have the status of divine revelation. In India, Zoroastrians are called Parsis.

Some form of Zoroastrianism had spread through Persia by the time of Israel's Babylonian captivity. It became the official religion under Cyrus the Great (585 B.C. to 529 B.C.). This may explain the close similarity of Zoroastrian beliefs to those of Old Testament Judaism, given the influence of Jewish captives on Persia. It also may explain the tradition that the "wise men" who came from Persia to seek the king of the Jews were Zoroastrian.

Zoroastrianism looks to one God, Ahura Mazda (lit. "Wise Lord"). Ahura Mazda is transcendent, but he is in constant relationship with human beings and the world he created through his attributes. The attributes represent seven sectors of Creation over which God watches: (1) good thought, animals; (2) truth and justice, fire and energy; (3) dominion, metals and minerals; (4) devotion and serenity, the earth and land; (5) wholeness, waters; (6) immortality, plants; and (7) creative energy, human beings.

In the Gathas, Spenta Mainyu, the holy, creative spirit, is opposed to Angra Mainyu, the hostile spirit. Their conflict takes place in the human heart and mind. It rarely affects the material Universe. There are two groups of people on earth, one ruled by good and the other by evil.

Zoroastrian worship involves prayers and symbolic ceremonies before a fire that symbolizes God as light, warmth, and energy.

Zoroastrianism teaches that after life on earth, the human soul is judged by God. Those who chose good over evil go to a sort of heaven, and those who chose evil go to a hell. One knows what is good through the divine help of Vohu Manah (good mind) and Daena (inspired conscience). At the end of time, everything will be purified, including those in hell, who will be renewed and released.

Zoroastrians are mostly of Persian origin, though isolated groups are spread through Central Asia and Armenia and in western India. There are communities in England, Australia, Canada, the United States, and other countries. Most of the spread has been in response to violent persecutions that have broken out at various times where there have been Muslim or Hindu majorities. In the 1990s about ninety thousand Zoroastrians still lived in Iran.

*See also:* AVESTA; BAHA'I; CAYCE, EDGAR; MEHER BA'BA; MYSTERY

# APPENDIX A

# KNOWING THE TRUTH: GOD'S WORD, CULTS, AND THE OCCULT

The Bible has much to say about the component beliefs of occult worship: black and white magic, astrology, precognition by whatever means, autosalvation through secret knowledge and rites, and spiritism. The New Testament church struggled particularly with the Greek search for secret knowledge that blossomed into dualistic religion. Ephesians, Colossians, and Jude are letters that address a church caught in a secular society where mysteries and magic reigned supreme. Pagans looked to a fertility goddess much like the Earth Mother that the Sophia movement would introduce into Christian theology today. The book of 1 John cried out to those for whom Christ was a mere emanation—not part of physical time-space history. And throughout the Old and New Testaments God spoke and still speaks to the underlying idolatry in all non-Christian worldviews. At its base, says Paul in Romans, the problem is rebellion—denial of the self-revealing God, whose demand for submission and holiness does not fit a humanist agenda.

The following Bible texts offer the perspective that nothing is particularly "new" about pagan beliefs in this new age. "For our struggle is not against flesh and blood, but against the rulers, against the powers, against the world forces of this darkness, against the spiritual forces of wickedness in the heavenly places. Therefore, take up the full armor of God" (Eph. 6:12–13).

## SEEKING TRUTH AND AVOIDING FALSEHOOD

### There can be only one ultimate source of truth.

"And Elijah came near to all the people and said, 'How long will you hesitate between two opinions? If the LORD is God, follow Him; but if Baal, follow him.' But the people did not answer him a word" (1 Kings 18:21).

"And the prophets are as wind, and the word is not in them. . . . The prophets prophesy falsely, and the priests rule on their own authority; and My people love it so! But what will you do at the end of it?" (Jer. 5:13a, 31).

"Jesus said to him, 'I am the way, and the truth, and the life; no one comes to the Father, but through Me'" (John 14:6).

"I am amazed that you are so quickly deserting Him who called you by the grace of Christ, for a different gospel; which is really not another. . . . If any man is preaching to you a gospel contrary to that which you received, let him be accursed" (Gal. 1:6–7, 9; cf. Luke 13:24).

"God, after He spoke long ago to the fathers in the prophets in many portions and in many ways, in these last days has spoken to us in His Son, whom He appointed heir of all things, through whom also He made the world" (Heb. 1:1–2).

"But know this first of all, that no prophecy of Scripture is a matter of one's own interpretation, for no prophecy was ever made by an act of human will, but men moved by the Holy Spirit spoke from God" (2 Peter 1:20–21).

"For the testimony of Jesus is the spirit of prophecy" (Rev. 19:10b).

See also Isaiah 44:24–25; Ezekiel 13:3–4; Micah 3:6–7.

### Truth brings clarity and peace, not confusion.

"And the spirits of prophets are subject to prophets; for God is not a God of confusion but of peace. . . . But let all things be done properly and in an orderly manner" (1 Cor. 14:32–33a, 40).

"Now we request you, brethren, with regard to the coming of our Lord Jesus Christ, and our gathering together to Him, that you may not be quickly shaken from your composure or be disturbed either by a spirit or a message or a letter as if from us, to the effect that the day of the Lord has come. Let no one in any way deceive you, for it will not come unless the apostasy comes first, and the man of lawlessness is revealed, the son of destruction" (2 Thess. 2:1–3).

See also Ephesians 4:3–6.

### Truth submits to authority and honors the true God.

"The priests did not say, 'Where is the LORD?' And those who handle the law did not know Me; the rulers also transgressed against Me, and the prophets prophesied by Baal and walked after things that did not profit" (Jer. 2:8).

"Not every one who says to Me, 'Lord, Lord,' will enter the kingdom of heaven; but he who does the will of My Father who is in heaven" (Matt. 7:21).

"And at that time many will fall away and will betray one another and hate one another. And many false prophets will arise, and will mislead many. And because lawlessness is increased, most people's love will grow cold. But the one who endures to the end, it is he who shall be saved" (Matt. 24:10–13).

"But false prophets also arose among the people, just as there will also be false teachers among you, who will secretly introduce destructive heresies, even denying the Master who bought them, bringing swift destruction upon themselves. And many will follow their sensuality, and because of them the way of the truth will be maligned" (2 Peter 2:1–2).

"Yet in the same manner these men, also by dreaming, defile the flesh, and reject authority, and revile angelic majesties. But Michael the archangel, when he disputed with the devil and argued about the body of Moses, did not dare pronounce against him a railing judgment, but said, 'THE LORD REBUKE YOU!'" (Jude 8–9).

See also Isaiah 5:20–21; 9:13–16; Jeremiah 23; 28:15–16.

### Truth accompanies a pure and holy lifestyle.

"For from the least of them even to the greatest of them, every one is greedy for gain, and from the prophet even to the priest every one deals falsely" (Jer. 6:13).

"'For both prophet and priest are polluted; even in My house I have found their wickedness,' declares the LORD. . . . 'Also among the prophets of Jerusalem I have seen a horrible thing: the committing of adultery and walking in falsehood; and they strengthen the hands of evildoers, so that no one has turned back from his wickedness'" (Jer. 23:11, 14a; see also Isa. 28:7; Ezek. 22:26–28; Mic. 3:11).

"Beware of the false prophets, who come to you in sheep's clothing, but inwardly are ravenous wolves. You will know them by their fruits. Grapes are not gathered from thorn bushes, nor figs from thistles, are they? Even so, every good tree bears good fruit; but the rotten tree bears bad fruit. A good tree cannot produce bad fruit, nor can a rotten tree produce good fruit. Every tree that does not bear good fruit is cut down and thrown into the fire. So then, you will know them by their fruits" (Matt. 7:15–20).

"But do not let immorality or any impurity or greed even be named among you, as is proper among saints; and there must be no filthiness and silly talk, or coarse jesting, which are not fitting, but rather giving of thanks. For this you know with certainty, that no immoral or impure person or covetous man, who is an idolater, has an inheritance in the kingdom of Christ and God. Let no one deceive you with empty words, for because of these things the wrath of God comes on the sons of disobedience. Therefore do not be partakers with them" (Eph. 5:3–7).

"But false prophets also arose among the people, just as there will also be false teachers among you . . . and many will follow their sensuality, and because of them the way of the truth will be maligned. . . . For speaking out arrogant words of vanity they entice by fleshly desires, by sensuality, those who barely escape from the ones who live in error (2 Peter 2:1a, 2, 18; see all chap. 2).

"For certain persons have crept in unnoticed, those who were long beforehand marked out for this condemnation, ungodly persons who turn the grace of our God into licentiousness and deny our only Master and Lord, Jesus Christ" (Jude 4).

See also Revelation 2:14, 20.

### Untruth leads toward human degradation.

"O LORD, lead me in Thy righteousness because of my foes; make Thy way straight before me. There is nothing reliable in what they say; their inward part is destruction itself; their throat is an open grave; they flatter with their tongue" (Ps. 5:8–9).

"Because you disheartened the righteous with falsehood when I did not cause him grief, but have encouraged the wicked not to turn from his wicked way and preserve his life, therefore, you women will no longer see false visions or practice divination, and I will deliver My people out of your hand. Thus you will know that I am the LORD" (Ezek. 13:22–23.)

"You are of your father the devil, and you want to do the desires of your father. He was a murderer from the beginning, and does not stand in the truth, because there is no truth in him. Whenever he speaks a lie, he speaks from his own nature; for he is a liar, and the father of lies" (John 8:44).

"And even if our gospel is veiled, it is veiled to those who are perishing, in whose case the god of this world has blinded the minds of the unbelieving, that they might not see the light of the gospel of the glory of Christ, who is the image of God" (2 Cor. 4:3–4).

"But the Spirit explicitly says that in later times some will fall away from the faith, paying attention to deceitful spirits and doctrines of demons, by means of the hypocrisy of liars seared in their own conscience as with a branding iron, men who forbid marriage and advocate abstaining from foods, which God has created to be gratefully shared in by those who believe and know the truth" (1 Tim. 4:1–3).

"Who is the liar but the one who denies that Jesus is the Christ? This is the antichrist, the one who denies the Father and the Son" (1 John 2:22).

See also Jeremiah 14:14–16; 29:8–9.

### Untruth can be attractive and persuasive.

"So Moses and Aaron did even as the LORD had commanded. And he lifted up the staff and struck the water that was in the Nile, in the sight of Pharaoh and in the sight of his servants, and all the water that was in the Nile was turned to blood. . . . But the magicians of Egypt did the same with their secret arts; and Pharaoh's heart was hardened, and he did not listen to them, as the LORD had said" (Exod. 7:20, 22).

"If a prophet or a dreamer of dreams arises among you and gives you a sign or wonder, and the sign or the wonder comes true, concerning which he spoke to you, saying, 'Let us go after other gods (whom you have not known) and let us serve them,' you shall not listen to the words of that prophet or that dreamer of dreams. . . . You shall follow the LORD your God and fear him. . . . But that prophet or that dreamer of dreams shall be put to death, because he has counseled rebellion against the LORD your God. . . . So you shall purge the evil from among you" (Deut. 13:1–3a, 4a, 5).

"Many will say to Me on that day, 'Lord, Lord, did we not prophesy in Your name, and in Your name cast out demons, and in Your name perform many miracles?' And then I will declare to them, 'I never knew you; depart from Me, you who practice lawlessness'" (Matt. 7:22–23).

"For false Christs and false prophets will arise and will show great signs and wonders, so as to mislead, if possible, even the elect. Behold, I have told you in advance" (Matt. 24:24–25; cf. Mark 13:22–23).

"And then that lawless one will be revealed . . . that is, the one whose coming is in accord with the activity of Satan, with all power and signs and false wonders, and with all the deception of wickedness for those who perish, because they did not receive the love of the truth so as to be saved. And for this reason God will send upon them a deluding influence so that they might believe what is false" (2 Thess. 2:8a, 9–11).

"And I saw coming out of the mouth of the dragon and out of the mouth of the beast and out of the mouth of the false prophet, three unclean spirits like frogs; for they are spirits of demons, performing signs, which go out to the kings of the whole world, to gather them together for the war of the great day of God, the Almighty" (Rev. 16:13–14; see also 19:20).

### Mixing truth with untruth is syncretism.

"But they mingled with the nations, and learned their practices, and served their idols, which became a snare to them" (Ps. 106:35–36).

"Come, house of Jacob, and let us walk in the light of the LORD. For Thou hast abandoned Thy people, the house of Jacob, because they are filled with influences from the East, and they are soothsayers like the Philistines, and they strike bargains with the children of foreigners" (Isa. 2:5–6).

"Do not be bound together with unbelievers; for what partnership have righteousness and lawlessness, or what fellowship has light with darkness? . . . Just as God said, 'I will dwell in them and walk among them; and I will be their God, and they shall be My people. Therefore, come out from their midst and be separate,' says the LORD" (2 Cor. 6:14, 16b, 17a).

"We know that we are of God, and the whole world lies in the power of the evil one" (1 John 5:19; see also vv. 18–21).

## EVALUATING CLAIMS OF TRUTH AND KNOWLEDGE

### God gives the tools to understand what is true.

"But the prophet who shall speak a word presumptuously in My name which I have not commanded him to speak, or which he shall speak in the name of other gods, that prophet shall die. And you may say in your heart, 'How shall we know the word which the LORD has not spoken?' When a prophet speaks in the name of the LORD, if the thing does not come about or come true, that is the thing which the LORD has not spoken. That prophet has spoken it presumptuously; you shall not be afraid of him" (Deut. 18:20–22; cf. Jer. 28:8–9; Ezek. 14:7–10).

" 'The prophet who has a dream may relate his dream, but let him who has My word speak My word in truth. What does straw have in common with grain?' declares the Lord" (Jer. 23:28).

"Now these [members of the synagogue at Berea] were more noble-minded than those in Thessalonica, for they received the word with great eagerness, examining the Scriptures daily, to see whether these things were so" (Acts 17:11; cf. Rev. 22:8–9).

"As a result, we are no longer to be children, tossed here and there by waves, and carried about by every wind of doctrine, by the trickery of men, by craftiness in deceitful scheming; but speaking the truth in love, we are to grow up in all aspects into Him, who is the head, even Christ" (Eph. 4:14–15; see also vv. 1–25).

"And do not participate in the unfruitful deeds of darkness, but instead even expose them; for it is disgraceful even to speak of the things which are done by them in secret. But all things become visible when they are exposed by the light, for everything that becomes visible is light" (Eph. 5:11–13).

"See to it that no one takes you captive through philosophy and empty deception, according to the tradition of men, according to the elementary principles of the world, rather than according to Christ" (Col. 2:8; see also vv. 1–4, 16–23).

"Beloved, do not believe every spirit, but test the spirits to see whether they are from God; because many false prophets have gone out into the world. By this you know the Spirit of God: every spirit that confesses that Jesus Christ has come in the flesh is from God; and every spirit that does not confess Jesus is not from God; and this is the spirit of the antichrist, of which you have heard that it is coming, and now it is already in the world" (1 John 4:1–3).

"For many deceivers have gone out into the world, those who do not acknowledge Jesus Christ as coming in the flesh. This is the deceiver and the antichrist. . . . Any one who goes too far and does not abide in the teaching of Christ, does not have God; the one who abides in the teaching, he has both the Father and the Son. If any one comes to you and does not bring this teaching, do not receive him into your house, and do not give him a greeting; for the one who gives him a greeting participates in his evil deeds" (2 John 7, 9–11).

"I know your deeds and your toil and perseverance, and that you cannot endure evil men, and you put to the test those who call themselves apostles, and they are not, and you found them to be false" (Rev. 2:2).

## All divination and astrology are false.

"And when they say to you, 'Consult the mediums and the wizards who whisper and mutter,' should not a people consult their God? Should they consult the dead on behalf of the living?" (Isa. 8:19; cf. 2 Kings 17:15–16; Isa. 19:3–4; Ezek. 13:9; 21:21–23, 29).

"Let now the astrologers, those who prophesy by the stars, those who predict by the new moons, stand up and save you from what will come upon you" (Isa. 47:13).

"And the houses of Jerusalem and the houses of the kings of Judah will be defiled like the place Topheth, because of all the houses on whose rooftops they burned sacrifices to all the heavenly host and poured out libations to other gods" (Jer. 19:13; cf. Isa. 47:13; Jer. 8:1–2; Zeph. 1:4–5).

"Daniel answered before the king and said, 'As for the mystery about which the king has inquired, neither wise men, conjurers, magicians, nor diviners are able to declare it to the king. However, there is a God in heaven who reveals mysteries' " (Dan. 2:27–28a).

" 'You also carried along Sikkuth [Saturn] your king and Kiyyun [star gods], your images, the star of your gods which you made for yourselves. Therefore I will make you go into exile beyond Damascus,' says the LORD, whose name is the God of hosts" (Amos 5:26–27; cf. Acts 7:42–43).

"For the teraphim [household idols or charms] speak iniquity, and the diviners see lying visions, and tell false dreams; they comfort in vain. Therefore the people wander like sheep, they are afflicted, because there is no shepherd" (Zech. 10:2).

"And when they had gone through the whole island as far as Paphos, they found a certain magician, a Jewish false prophet whose name was Bar-Jesus. . . . But Saul, who was also known as Paul, filled with the Holy Spirit, fixed his gaze upon him, and said, 'You who are full of all deceit and fraud, you son of the devil, you enemy of all righteousness, will you not cease to make crooked the straight ways of the Lord? And now, behold, the hand of the Lord is upon you, and you will be blind and not see the sun for a time.' And immediately a mist and a darkness fell upon him, and he went about seeking those who would lead him by the hand" (Acts 13:6, 9–11; see also 16:16–20).

"Many also of those who had believed kept coming, confessing and disclosing their practices. And many of those who practiced magic brought their books together and began burning them in the sight of all; and they counted up the price of them and found it fifty thousand pieces of silver. So the word of the Lord was growing mightily and prevailing" (Acts 19:18–20).

## *Occult beliefs are a rebellion against the true God.*

"Do not turn to mediums or spiritists; do not seek them out to be defiled by them. I am the LORD your God" (Lev. 19:31; cf. 20:6–7; Deut. 18:10–14).

"[King Manasseh] made his son pass through the fire, practiced witchcraft and used divination, and dealt with mediums and spiritists. He did much evil in the sight of the LORD provoking Him to anger" (2 Kings 21:6; cf. 2 Chron. 33:6).

"So Saul died for his trespass which he committed against the LORD, because of the word of the LORD which he did not keep; and also because he asked counsel of a medium, making inquiry of it, and did not inquire of the LORD. Therefore He killed him, and turned the kingdom to David the son of Jesse" (1 Chron. 10:13–14; cf. 1 Sam. 15:23).

"But you who forsake the LORD, who forget My holy mountain, who set a table for Fortune, and who fill cups with mixed wine for Destiny, I will destine you for the sword, and all of you shall bow down to the slaughter. Because I called, but you did not answer; I spoke, but you did not hear. And you did evil in My sight, and chose that in which I did not delight" (Isa. 65:11–12).

"And the rest of mankind, who were not killed by these plagues, did not repent of the works of their hands, so as not to worship demons, and the idols of gold and silver and of brass and of stone and of wood, which can neither see nor hear nor walk; and they did not repent of their murders nor of their sorceries nor of their immorality nor of their thefts" (Rev. 9:20–21).

See also Ezekiel 13:22–23; 21:28–29; Zechariah 10:2–3.

# APPENDIX B

# SCRIPTURE TWISTING

The deliberate misinterpretation and misrepresentation of what individual Bible passages teach in order to uphold New Age doctrines. Scripture twisters commonly wrench verses out of context, read their own ideas into the individual passages, and force meanings that are completely foreign to what God's Word teaches. Scripture twisting bears no resemblance to biblical hermeneutics. This refers to the process of unlocking the meaning of Scripture and explaining it in clear and understandable terms. This extended procedure fully takes into account all the grammatical, contextual, and historical information of the passages under examination. The methods and procedures of proper interpretation are summarized as follows:

- The Bible is viewed as the inspired and inerrant Word of God. What it communicates is straightforward, objective, and absolute. Therefore it sets forth the supreme and final authority in all matters pertaining to God, creation, and humankind.

- The Bible is a harmonious collection of distinctively unique writings that complement and supplement one another. Therefore the message communicated by Scripture is both unified and coherent.

- Even though the Bible is the verbally inspired Word of God, it requires more diligent study and intensive research for proper understanding than any other book known to humankind.

- The interpreter of the Bible must take into account cultural, historical, and geographical considerations surrounding the times during which Scripture was written.

- The interpreter must pay close attention to the language and grammar of the text.

- A word should be understood in terms of its sentence, a sentence in terms of its context, and the context in terms of the original purpose and theme of the author.

- The broader context of all Scripture should be used to unlock the meaning of individual passages that are obscure or difficult to understand.

- The interpreter should demonstrate a keen sensitivity to the various forms and styles of literary expression present in the text.

- A passage should be interpreted in its plain and natural sense, unless the literary form or style dictates otherwise.

- The interpreter should seek to explain the original sense of the writer according to normal, customary, and proper usage of words and language. A particular word or phrase will usually have one appropriate meaning. However the context may suggest multiple meanings or shades of understanding.

- All unfulfilled prophetic passages in the Bible should be interpreted in their literal or normal sense.

- A Bible passage is usually single, fixed, and definite in its original intended meaning, but multifaceted in its ongoing emphasis and application.

- The Bible student should seek to integrate and apply, either directly or indirectly, the universal and timeless principles of Scripture into every segment of life.